A Cultural Geography
of North American Indians

About the Book and Editors

A wide-ranging study, this book focuses on the effects of interaction between Indian and non-Indian peoples and on the complex relationships between Indians and their environments. Contributors confront common misconceptions about Indian groups by reexamining such controversial topics as boundary perceptions, land sharing, causes for migration, and economic conditions on Indian reservations. Issues of land claims, urbanization, patterns of economic development, and forced migration are also discussed. The information presented here is an essential component of an accurate assessment of whether North American Indians can survive as a distinct culture.

Thomas E. Ross is professor and chairman of the Department of Geology and Geography at Pembroke State University. He is coauthor of *Buffer States in World Politics* (Westview, 1986). **Tyrel G. Moore** teaches in the Department of Geography and Earth Sciences at the University of North Carolina, Charlotte.

A Cultural Geography
of North American Indians

edited by
Thomas E. Ross
and Tyrel G. Moore

Westview Press / Boulder and London

A Westview Special Study

Published in 1987 in the United States of America by Westview Press, Inc.; Frederick A. Praeger, Publisher; 5500 Central Avenue, Boulder, Colorado 80301

Library of Congress Catalog Card Number: 87-50529
ISBN: 0-8133-7383-2

Composition for this book was provided by the editors.
This book was produced without formal editing by the publisher.

Printed and bound in the United States of America

6   5   4   3   2

To Professor Edwin H. Hammond
Our mentor, our friend

CONTENTS

List of Figures and Tables.................................... xi
Preface.. xiii

Introduction

1. Indians in North America, *Thomas E. Ross* and
   Tyrel G. Moore... 3

Part One

North American Indians in Historical Perspective

2. Historical Geography and American Indian Development,
   Donald J. Ballas.. 15
3. Two Worlds Collide: The European Advance into North
   America, *David K. Eliades*................................. 33

Part Two

Spatial Awareness and Organization of the Land

4. Sharing the Land: A Study in American Indian Territoriality,
   Patricia Albers and Jeanne Kay........................... 47
5. Indian Delimitations of Primary Biogeographic Regions,
   G. Malcolm Lewis... 93

Part Three

Land Ownership and Economic Development

6. Indian Land in Southern Alberta, *Claudia Notzke*......... 107
7. The Loss of Indian Lands in Wisconsin, Montana
   and Arizona, *Ronald A. Janke*............................ 127
8. The Loss of Lands Inside Indian Reservations, *Richard H.
   Weil*... 149
9. The Choctaw: Self Determination and Socioeconomic
   Development, *Jesse O. McKee*............................. 173

Part Four
Migration, Cultural Change and Fusion

10. The Iroquois Return to their Homeland: Military Retreat or
    Cultural Adjustment, *Victor Konrad* 191
11. Women in Indian Removal, *Joseph T. Manzo* 213
12. Cultural Change and the Houma Indians: A Historical and
    Ecological Examination, *Janel M. Curry-Roper* 227
13. Cultural Fusion in Native-American Architecture:
    The Navajo Hogan, *Stephen C. Jett* 243

Part Five
Population Studies

14. The Urban American Indian, *Terrel Rhodes* 259
15. Early Twentieth Century Hopi Population, *Elliot McIntire* ... 275
16. The Lumbees: Population Growth of a Non-Reservation
    Indian Tribe, *Thomas E. Ross* 297

Conclusions

17. American Indian Problems and Prospects, *Thomas
    E. Ross* 313

Appendix A 319
About the Contributors 321
Index 325

Figures and Tables

Figures

1.1 Distribution of the American Indian, Eskimo, and Aleut Population: 1980......8
1.2 Number of American Indian, Eskimo, and Aleut Persons by State: 1980.......9
2.1 American Indian Culture Areas..19
4.1 Tribal Territoriality: Typical Mapping Procedure Implying
    A Nation-State Model..48
4.2 Overlapping Tribal Ranges on the Northern Perimeter of the Great Plains,
    Ca. 1840..68
5.1 The 'Woods Edge'..97
5.2 Forest-grassland boundary...101
6.1 Regional Setting of the Reserves......................................109
6.2 The Composition of Stoney Land..115
6.3 Peigan Reserve: Areas (recently or presently) Subject to Dispute......118
7.1 Montana Indian Reservations, 1985.....................................129
7.2 Land Ownership Inside Montana Reservations, 1985......................132
7.3 Arizona Indian Reservations, 1985.....................................137
7.4 Land Ownership Inside Arizona Reservations............................138
7.5 Wisconsin Indian Reservations...140
7.6 Land Ownership Inside Wisconsin Reservations..........................143
8.1 Red Lake Band Cessations..154
8.2 Red Lake Reservation Landholdings.....................................156
8.3 The Break-Up of the Great Sioux Nation................................161
8.4 Diminishment of the Rosebud Reservation...............................164
8.5 Cessations of the Sisseton Sioux......................................165
9.1 Choctaw Indian Communities..175
10.1 Hypothetical Iroquois and French Before and After 1660...............194
10.2 Changes in the Iroquois Settlement System, 1664......................196
10.3 Changes in the Iroquois Settlement System, 1670......................197
10.4 Changes in the Iroquois Settlement System, 1673......................198
10.5 Changes in the Iroquois Settlement System, 1680......................199
10.6 "Eleuation des Cabannes Sauvages"....................................203
10.7 "Lac de Frontenac/et Source du Saint Laurent" 205
10.8 Changes in the Iroquois Settlement System............................207
11.1 Factors Affecting Women in Migration.................................223
12.1 The Houma Tribe Migration, 1796-1800.................................229
12.2 Houma Settlements Today..233
16.1 Robeson County in North Carolina.....................................298

Tables

1.1 Distribution of American Indian Population in the United States: 1980 and 1970. 7

4.1 1824: Census of Wisconsin Indians. 62

7.1 Land Ownership Inside Montana Reservations. 132

7.2 Type of Land Owned by the Tribe and by Individual Indians. 133

7.3 Indian and White Allotted Lands Inside Indian Reservations. 134

9.1 Changes in Choctaw Population. 182

9.2 Educational Attainment of the Choctaw. 183

9.3 Changes in Choctaw Employment Patterns. 185

14.1 American Indians in the United States. 262

14.2 Per Capita Median Income for Native Americans. 263

14.3 Native American Median Household Per Capita Income Compared to Majority Income 264

14.4 Poverty Index. 266

14.5 Delayed Education for 15-16-17 Year Old Native Americans. 267

14.6 Incidence of Drinking Among Native Americans (NORC 1980/82). 270

15.1 Examples of Transcriptions of Names. 281

15.2 Married/Widowed/Divorced 1910. 284

15.3 Hopi Census, 1900 & 1910. 286

15.4 Estimated Hopi Population 1900-1910. 292

16.1 Indians in Robeson County and the U.S. Census. 303

16.2 Population by Race and Age, Robeson County, North Carolina: 1980. 304

16.3 Birth and Death and Population Rates in Robeson County, North Carolina 1985. 305

16.4 Family Household Income, by Race, in Robeson County, North Carolina: 1979. 307

16.5 Poverty Status in 1979: Robeson County, North Carolina. 307

Preface

The protest movements of the 1960s were in many respects responsible for the increased academic interest in minority groups. They resulted in the development of courses dealing with blacks, Hispanics and American Indians in many colleges and universities. Instruction in these courses is conducted under many different conditions and in numerous academic disciplines, including geography, anthropology, history, and sociology. It is hoped that this volume, although primarily the work of geographers, would be beneficial to all disciplines dealing with American Indians.

This idea of a book about American Indians was conceived by Thomas Ross in 1983, and in 1984, with funds provided by the Pembroke State University Faculty Research and Development Fund, work began on the project. The objectives of this volume are to provide original works that can complement textbooks of the various disciplines involved in teaching about American Indians, to expose and correct misconceptions about Indians, and to enhance academic interest and understanding of American Indians. The essays in this cultural geography are primarily concerned with the complex relationships between American Indians and the land on which they live and their relationships with Euro-Americans. Although many aspects of culture are discussed in this volume, we make no claim that this collection covers all phases of Indian culture but do believe that it is representative of Indian cultures in the United States and Canada. The omission of a particular cultural trait or Indian group should not be taken to mean that we value any trait or group less than those we have included.

We gratefully acknowledge the cooperation of all authors whose works are included in this book. Thanks must also go to those who initially were involved but were unable to continue to participate. Much appreciation is due colleagues who gave encouragement and suggestions. We are especially indebted to Cheryl Ross, who so conscientiously proofread the entire typeset manuscript and performed innumerable clerical duties without which this volume would still be unpublished. Thanks also to Patricia Moore and the Ross daughters, Candace and Laura, for being so understanding during the development of this volume. We appreciate the work done by Betty Evans, Alice Britt, and Roy Barnhill in the typesetting and layout of this book. We are grateful to Westview Press editors Barbara Ellington and Bruce Kellison for their assistance with this volume. Bruce, thanks for being so kind and for efficiently handling details with which we were unfamiliar.

Thomas E. Ross
Pembroke State University

Tyrel G. Moore
University of North Carolina at Charlotte

Acknowledgements

The editors wish to express their thanks to the following for permission to reproduce illustrations:

The Edward E. Ayer Collection, The Newberry Library, for Figure 10.6 and The National Map Collection, Public Archives of Canada, C16301, for Figure 10.7.

Introduction

Chapter 1
Indians in North America

Thomas E. Ross
and
Tyrel G. Moore

The cultural geography of North America's Indians[1] is, in many respects, a spatial expression of four centuries of cultural and geographic change set in motion by contact between European explorers and immigrants and the native American population. Historical circumstance and geographic reality placed Indians and non-Indians in competition for land within the continent. European aims for a new life in a new land necessarily created a new life for the area's previous inhabitants. Cultural transfers which might have allowed coexistence between Europeans and native Americans were largely pre-empted by dramatically contrasting cultures. Values, economies and technologies of the two groups diverged sharply because of one important commonality in their existence: land, which was an explicit requirement of each culture. Hunting, fishing and gathering, supplemented by shifting cultivation, were forms of extensive land use which comprised the foundation of the Indian economy.[2] In short, Indians were entirely dependent upon the land and were well aware of the land's importance as provider. They understood its productivity, and some Indian groups elevated it to sacred status within their culture.[3] It should be noted, however, that although some Indians revered the land, they were not necessarily kind to it. Recent findings suggest that *some* Indian cultures were not in harmony with nature, but were, in fact, exploitive of their natural surroundings to such a degree that their groups, in some cases, disappeared from the earth because the physical environment became so depleted that it could no longer support life.[4] Thus scholars must be careful with generalizations about how Indians (and other aboriginal groups) prevented environmental damage (i.e., pollution, extinction of game and soil exhaustion). Nevertheless, there is validity in the argument that Indian attitudes toward the land and nature were at variance with Euro-American views and that generally the Indian was less destructive of nature than the Euro-Americans. Perhaps Indian respect for nature may partially be used to explain why vast tracts of land was used only in a semi-permanent manner: the Indians were giving the land time to "recuperate." In the eastern United States, for example, the number of "Indian Old Fields"[5] greatly exceeded the amounts of cleared land needed by the aboriginal population[6] and suggests that the excess was a method by which the land was allowed to "rest." At the time of contact, few Euro-Americans were prepared to follow this practice.

Another difference involved the concept of land ownership. The Indian view of land made individual rights subordinate to those of the group or tribe; individuals should be governed by a sense of compatibility with others in the tribe. Land was cherished by the group, and was not to be divided for the use of only one or a few individuals.[7] The idea of individual land ownership was so alien to the Indians that it placed them at a significant disadvantage in comprehending the culture of their Euro-American counterparts. More important, the aversion to individual ownership weakened the Indian's position in challenges with non-Indians who argued that individual ownership represented a more legitimate claim to contested lands.

Europeans approached North America's lands with a markedly different perspective. Guided in part by Western religious thought which held that man should, among other things, go forth, multiply and subdue the earth, immigrants set out to permanently settle the eastern woodlands of North America. As the Euro-American population grew in numbers and became more detached from western Europe, philosophies shifted toward social and economic change. Access to and ownership of land removed many of the immigrants from the socio-economic stratification of Europe, producing a set of American landscape values which culminated in the establishment of family farms, each much like the other.[8] Dispersed farmsteads, a marked departure from European antecedents, became the dominant rural settlement form. A level of equality, unapproachable in European society and culture became an American ideal — an ideal based on individual ownership of land.

Individualism, so foreign to Indian cultures, therefore lay at the foundation of a set of values carried by Euro-Americans into the contest for land with the Indian. To the Euro-Americans some areas of the eastern United States which were relatively uninhabited by Indians at the time the Colonial era began, were lands which they could claim with impunity. For example, much of the coastal areas from southern Canada to northern Florida may have been occupied by no more than 125,000 Indians and overall densities amounted to perhaps one person per four square miles.[9] Except for some parts of New England, the tendency toward dispersed settlement was strong among the white settlers during the Colonial period; an estimated 90 percent of the pre-Revolutionary War American population lived in rural areas.[10] These new Americans required lots of space and, as a consequence, the Indians suffered great losses of land.

Encroachment into Indian areas continued, spurred on by increasing immigration and by pressures that an expanding agrarian society placed on the land. The contest for control of the land shifted from the eastern seaboard into Indian hunting grounds in the interior. The numerically inferior but tenacious Indian population and its conflicting view of the land became a problem to be faced by the government of the young state. The contrast of cultures was vividly illustrated in arguments posed by American statesmen at the turn of the nineteenth century in which proposals were made to remove the Indians from their lands. Removal was essentially based on the contention that a farming society held superior right to the land over a hunting society.[11] Simply put, the values of the agrarian majority were to be superimposed on the hunting, fishing and gathering minority. Subsequent policy and action pushed the Indian westward, away from the prized frontier (and the Euro-Americans) and into areas of limited or marginal economic potential. Removal of their land base has posed a continuing threat to both the economic and cultural survival of North America's Indians.

This discussion raises several questions. For example, how many Indians are we talking about at the time of European contact? How many at present? And where are they now located if they were pushed away from areas settled by Euro-Americans?

Estimates of the pre-Columbian North American population vary widely, from a few million to a hundred million or more. Many scholars reason that fewer than 10 million "Indians" lived on the continent in the fifteenth century and about one million lived in what now constitutes the United States. At present, the combined Indian and Inuit population in the United States and Canada is approximately 3.0 million, with Canada having about 1.6 million. In both countries the Indian (Native American) population began to grow rapidly in the early to middle nineteenth century and no abatement in the expansion is evident in the near future.

Since 1970, the Indian population of the United States has grown by more than 70 percent, from about 800,000 to approximately 1,400,000 in 1980. This is the first time more than a million Indians have been recorded since the Census Bureau began enumerating them in 1860. Although some of the growth results from natural increase, most is attributed to improved enumeration procedures on reservations and the probability that more individuals of mixed Indian and non-Indian descent reported their race as American Indian in 1980 than in any previous census.

In its report *American Indian Areas and Alaska Native Villages: 1980*, the Census Bureau provided census counts for "indentified American Indian areas which include reservations, tribal trust lands (off reservations) and the historic areas of Oklahoma (excluding urbanized areas.)"[12] *American Indian Areas* are defined by the Census Bureau as reservations, tribal trust lands located outside the reservation boundaries, and the non-urban historic areas of Oklahoma. *Amercian Indian Reservations* are areas with boundaries established by treaty, statute, and/or executive or court order. *Tribal trust lands* are lands in the vicinity of the reservation belonging to or held by the tribes living on reservations. *The Historic Areas of Oklahoma* consist of the former reservations which had legally established boundaries during the 1900-1907 period. These reservations were dissolved during the two to three year period preceding Oklahoma's admission to the Union as a state in 1907. As can be seen in Fig. 1.1, only 24 percent of the Indians live on reservations while 63 percent are scattered throughout the 50 states and District of Columbia.

We can gain a perspective of where the Indians are in the United States by grouping states into regions. The Census Bureau has subdivided the country into four regions, the West, South, Midwest and Northeast. More than 50 percent of the Indians live in the West, 27 percent in the South, 18 percent in the Midwest, and 6 percent in the Northeast (Table 1.1 and Fig. 1.2).

In 1980, almost one-half of the Indian population lived in only four states: California (198,275), Oklahoma (169,292), Arizona (152,498), and New Mexico (107,338). North Carolina, with 64, 536 Indians, most of whom are members of non-federally recognized tribes/bands/groups, had the country's fifth largest Indian population. Other states with more than 30,000 Indians included

Table 1.1

Distribution of American Indian

Population in the United States: 1980 and 1970

Regions	1980	1970	Change, 1970 to 1980 Number	Percent
United States	1,366,676	792,730	573,946	72.4
West[1]	672,683	390,755	281,928	72.2
South[2]	370,198	201,222	168,976	84.0
Midwest[3]	246,365	151,287	95,078	62.8
Northeast[4]	77,430	49,466	27,964	56.4

1. States of Montana, Idaho, Wyoming, Colorado, New Mexico, Arizona, Utah, Nevada, Washington, Oregon, California, Alaska, and Hawaii.
2. States of Delaware, Maryland, Virginia, West Virginia, Georgia, North Carolina, South Carolina, Florida, Kentucky, Alabama, Tennessee, Mississippi, Arkansas, Louisiana, Texas, Oklahoma, and District of Columbia.
3. States of Ohio, Indiana, Illinois, Michigan, Wisconsin, Iowa, Minnesota, Missouri, North Dakota, South Dakota, Nebraska, and Kansas. This was designated as North Central region until June 1984.
4. States of Maine, New Hampshire, Vermont, Massachusetts, Rhode Island, Connecticut, New York, New Jersey, and Pennsylvania.

Source: Compiled from *American Indian Areas and Alaska Native Villages: 1980*. U.S. Census of Population, Supplementary Report, PC80-S1-13. 1984.

New York, Michigan, Minnesota, South Dakota, Texas, and Washington. As shown in Appendix A, Indians are found in all fifty states, though well over 75 percent are living in 14 states. Regardless of where Indians are living today, when the first European settlements were made on North American soil Indians had access to the entire continent. Their lives and cultures were permanently influenced with the advent of European culture — and the attack upon their culture, while not government or public policy, continues.

It is the 350,000 reservation Indians who fare most poorly in contemporary economic settings. High population growth and unemployment rates combine with low per capita incomes as social indicators of the quality of life on the reservations. On Arizona's Navajo Reservation, for example, over 50 percent of the population is age eighteen or younger, only about half of those

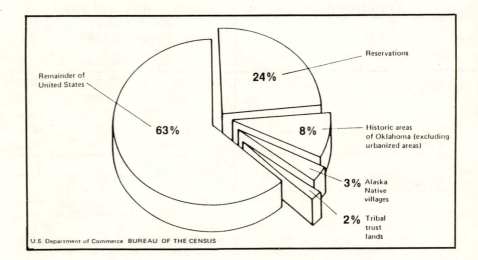

Figure 1.1. Distribution of the American Indian, Eskimo, and Aleut Population: 1980.

Source: Adapted from *American Indian Areas and Alaska Native Villages: 1980.* U.S. Census of Population, Supplementary Report. PC80-S1-13. 1984.

eligible to work have jobs and annual income averages just $2,500 per person. Similar conditions, 50 percent unemployment and per capita incomes of $2,600 exist among the 3,500 Sioux at Fort Totten, North Dakota. Across the country's 278 reservations, unemployment rates average about 60 percent while approaching 85 and 90 percent in more remote, isolated areas. The unemployment problem is exacerbated by the fact that these Indians are unable to qualify for funds contained in a federally designated pool of labor contracts earmarked for Labor Surplus Areas — these Indians have been unemployed too long to be carried on required Labor Department unemployment rolls.[13] That

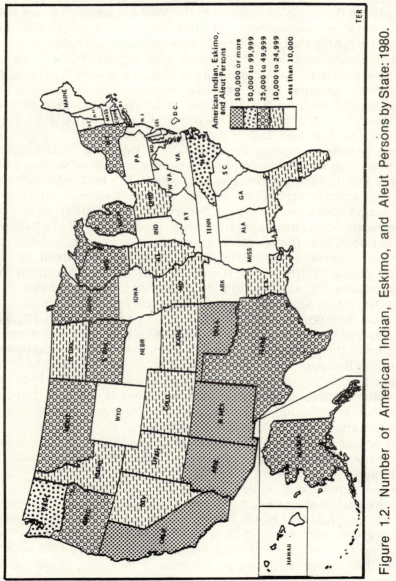

Figure 1.2. Number of American Indian, Eskimo, and Aleut Persons by State: 1980.

Source: Adapted from *American Indian Areas and Alaska Native Villages: 1980.*

the reservations are long standing pockets of poverty is illustrated in the history of multi-state regional planning efforts in America. The Area Redevelopment Act of 1961 and the Public Works and Economic Development Act of 1965 established economic assistance for counties with low incomes and standards of living. Included in the eligibility criteria of the 1965 act were: (1) Areas with substantial unemployment (at that time, rates exceeding six percent), (2) Areas with persistent unemployment, (3) Areas with low median family income, and (4) Indian reservations.[14] Of course, as will be shown in this volume, not all Indians are destitute. Examples of Indian groups with positive experiences in economic development include the Choctaw in Mississippi, Seminole of Florida, Cherokee of North Carolina, Jicarilla Apache of New Mexico, The Colorado River Indian Tribes of Arizona and numerous Native American groups in Alaska. And the Fort Totten Sioux mentioned above are ringing up successes as well with their new factory and its 8 million dollar annual payroll.[15] In fact, Indian groups and reservations across the country are learning that capitalism and Indian initiative have provided much more opportunity and hope for economic development than has government paternalism.

It is hoped that the research articles in this volume will furnish a better understanding of the challenges that still exist to the Indian "way of life" and the extent of change wrought by acculturation and assimilation. It is important, however, to keep in mind that North American Indian groups are numerous, ranging in size from two (2) members (the Cuyapaipi) to more than 100,000 (the Navajo). Not all have or had the same culture, nor have all been affected in the same manner and to the same extent by European cultures. Because of the vast number of Indian groups it is impossible to include chapters devoted to each tribe, but those in this volume reflect a variety of Indian cultures. It is hoped that the tribes/bands selected for discussion in this volume provide a representative view of North American Indians.

In conclusion, fourteen years ago, historian Wilbur Jacobs called for a revision of traditional views of the frontier in American history, particularly those dealing with the relationship and cultural clash between Indians and whites. He argued for an understanding of both cultures, not just one.[16] This book carries a similar intent. The cultural geography of North American Indians is presented in past and present contexts and in a variety of spatial settings. The following chapters consist of previously unpublished works which, rather than being definitive of a theme or inclusive of all Indian groups, opt to provide both reassessments of previous interpretations and a representative view of American Indian life, culture and geography. To better understand Indian cultures, problems and prospects is to better understand cultures of the United States and Canada.

NOTES

1. There is no universally accepted definition of who is an Indian: there are no biological, governmental or legal delimitations. Self-identification   as Indian is probably the most important factor in being identified as Indian.

2. Ralph H. Brown, *Historical Geography of the United States* (New York: Harcourt, Brace and World, Inc., 1948), p. 13.

3. Wilbur R. Jacobs, The Indian and the Frontier in American History — A Need for Revision" in David Ward, ed., *Geographic Perspectives on America's Past* (New York: Oxford University Press, 1979), pp. 72-73.

4. Malcome W. Browne, a *New York Times* writer, reported that more and more scholars are convinced that primitive societies were more destructive to their habitat than had been generally believed. He cited research by Jared M. Diamond (UCLA School of Medicine) and University of Arizona archaeologist Julio L. Betancourt and his colleagues that questions the romanticized concept of aboriginal societies' harmonic relationship with nature and documents primitive human abuse of the land. According to Diamond and Betancourt, examples of primitive man's destruction of plant and animal species abound. Plant species were destroyed in, among other places, Easter Island, southern Greece, and New Mexico. The Maori caused the extinction of the moa bird and early Polynesian settlers in Hawaii wiped out various Hawaiian birds. Diamond believes that many scientists are biased in favor of the harmonic view because "primitive peoples have been so horribly treated by whites over the centuries that many whites today ... feel a sense of guilt. Scientists, among others, sometimes tend to compensate for this in inappropriate ways." Diamond believes that "some societies have directly contributed to their own demise by abusing the lands on which they lived. At the same time, a declining society is likely to abandon sound conservation, making the spiral of decay tighter. *(The Fayetteville Times and Observer,* January 17, 1987, *Saturday Extra,* p. 8E.)   See also "The Trees Fell — and so Did the People," in *US News and World Report, February 9, 1987, pp. 75-76.*

5. Clearings abandoned after being cultivated for ten or so years or until the soil was exhausted.

6. Brown, p. 13.

7. Robert H. Stoddard, David J. Wishart and Brian W. Blouet, *Human Geography: People, Places and Cultures* (Englewood Cliffs: Prentice-Hall, 1986), pp. 116-117.

8. R. Cole Harris, "The Simplification of Europe Overseas," *Annals of the Association of American Geographers* 67 (1977): 470-474.

9. Brown, p. 11.

10. Wilbur Zelinsky, *The Cultural Geography of the United States* (Englewood Cliffs: Prentice-Hall, 1973), p. 47.

11. Stoddard, et. al., pp. 116-117.

12. U.S. Department of Commerce. Bureau of the Census. "American Indian Areas and Alaska Native Villages." Supplementary Report. 1980 *Census of Population.* 1984.

13. Data are from the U.S. Bureau of the Census and the Bureau of Indian Affairs and were covered in a Knight-Ridder Wireservice series appearing in the *Charlotte Observer,* Dec. 28-30, 1986.

14. C.L. Choquill, "Regional Planning in the United States and the United Kingdom: A Comparative Analysis," *Regional Studies* 11 (1977): 139-140.

15. Without this factory, the economic situation on Fort Totten would be even more disastrous and the rate of unemployed would be considerably higher.

16. Jacobs, p. 70.

Part One
North American Indians
in Historical Perspective

Chapter 2

Historical Geography and American Indian Development

Donald J. Ballas

The historical geography of the American Indians and their land is vitally important in thoroughly understanding their present as well as their past. This chapter will present an overview of the subject which may provide background for some of the more specific studies in this volume. It includes discussion of Indian prehistoric geography and cultural diversity, "white" effects on Indian population, voluntary and involuntary movements of American Indians, allotment and alienation of Indian land, and changing economic and social patterns. These themes will be discussed topically in some cases, and partially within a broad framework of the Indian culture areas of the United States.[1]

The author prefers the terms "Indian" or "Amerindians" rather than "Native Americans," since the latter term (as in U.S. Census usage) includes Aleuts and Eskimos as well as Indians. This chapter will emphasize the area which is presently the conterminous United States, although there is of course considerable "overlap" with Canada and Middle America in respect to many historical/cultural features and processes; two of many examples are the diffusion of maize from Mexico to what is now the southwestern United States, and the location of the Northwest Coast culture from northern California through southern Alaska.

THE PREHISTORIC GEOGRAPHY OF NORTH AMERICA

Although the Indians north of Mexico did not have written languages before the coming of Europeans, accounts of Indian life were made by early explorers and settlers before the Amerindians themselves left "written" records. However, other sources of information, such as oral history, legends and archaeological finds, help provide an understanding of the cultural geography of North America before European settlement.

A widely accepted theory "explaining" the arrival of Paleo-Indians in the New World is the "land-bridge" theory. It assumes that the first people in North America were hunters who followed large animals from Asia in the latter stages of the Pleistocene Epoch, "Ice Age," when ocean levels were lower and the now shallow Bering Strait between Alaska and Siberia was dry or relatively dry land. Many Asian migrants came, perhaps over hundreds of years, remained, increased in population, and eventually dispersed over virtually all or most of North and South America.

Most, perhaps all, of the original "Indian" population of the Americas *may* have migrated from Asia by the manner and the route depicted in the land-bridge theory. However, this does not seem to adequately explain how and why so many people moved into North America, how and why they would and could have dispersed across deserts and tropical moist regions, assuming they were of northern Asian ancestry, used to colder climates , and why there is — and apparently for thousands of years *was* — such great diversity among the Indians of the Americas in regard to physical features, languages (with many entirely different linguistic families), and other characteristics.

Until ,rather recently, proponents of the land-bridge theory believed that humans had not been in the Americas for more than 20,000 years, partly because actual human remains were no older than that and partly because it was believed that the last glacial advance in North America (the "end of the Ice Age"?) occurred approximately 20,000 years ago; this would not seem to leave much time for such great dispersals and differentiations among the American Indians.

Now we know that the Wisconsin glaciation ended no more than 10,000 years ago; that would surely not have given "Paleo-Indians" enough time to spread throughout the Americas and to develop such a variety of cultures. We presently also have evidence (specifically from archaeological discoveries on Santa Rosa Island, off the coast of southern California) that humans have been in North America for at least 40,000 years! Carter has suggested that prehistoric peoples, probably *not* "Indians" and perhaps not even "Mongoloids," could have come via open "Land-bridge" routes during several earlier time periods: approximately 55,000 to 65,000, 100,000 to 115,000, and 145,000 to 155,000 years ago.[2]

Historical geographer George F. Carter has long contended that humans have been in the Americas for at least 50,000 years and perhaps for a much longer period of time. He has also been one of the earliest and strongest advocates of the theory that at least some of the early migrants to the "New World" may have come by boat, arriving on the western coasts of Colombia, Panama, or Costa Rica. A great variety of evidence indicated trans-Pacific contacts in prehistoric times: there are Asian plants in the Americas *(Lagenaria siceraria,* the bottle gourd,for one), American plants in Asia, the sweet potato, similarities in names for plants and other things, Japanese pottery of the Jomon period, 5,000 to 6,000 years old, found on the coast of Ecuador, and many other artifacts and traits.

Peoples from southern and eastern Asia or Polynesia could have come via the northern coastal route or in a fairly straight line just north of the Equator by means of the Equatorial Counter Current. Migration by the latter route might help to explain why the early Indian populations in northwestern South America and the southern portions of Middle America were so much larger and more advanced in terms of material culture, etc., than were those farther to the north and south of that area.

Indian movements *within* the Americas present interesting and important topics for research; although much remains to be learned, there have been a number of studies of prehistoric and early historical migrations by geographers. Stephen Jett has contributed much, including a study of "The Origins of Navajo Settlement Patterns," concerning the retention of various features of settlement and economy by Athapaskan-speaking Indians (ancestors of the Navajo and Apache) who moved from the plains of northern United States or southern Canada several hundred years ago.[3]

Other studies are needed on such topics as trading between Indian groups, alterations of the natural environment (the Middle West prairie may have been second-growth vegetation induced by burning of earlier forests), and the diffusion of specific culture traits. Influences from Mexico, the West Indies, and/or Central America (some southeastern tribes had blow guns and darts, which may have diffused from Middle America) also need further attention.[4] Maize and other major crops, perhaps even the idea of agriculture, diffused northward from Mexico. However, few anthropologists or cultural-historical geographers would deny that Indians in what is now the United States independently made significant advances from the initial stimulus.

AMERINDIAN CULTURE AREAS

There were several distinctive American Indian culture areas by the time of permanent European settlement in what is now the United States. An understanding of the great differences between these broad culture regions is important to study of the present as well as the past. Earlier Indian ways of life have often carried over into the modern period, sometimes with good results as with the continued use of fishing skills by the Northwest Coast Indians and sometimes with problems, as in attempts to virtually force most of the nomadic, bison-hunting Plains Indians to become sedentary farmers. In addition, the diversity of languages and culture, compounded by their relatively small total population, has made it very difficult for the American Indians to work together or to develop any real political or economic power.

This discussion of American Indian culture areas will be based on a combination of the classifications by Clark Wissler, who used the term "food areas" and Alfred Kroeber (Fig. 2.1.). Kroeber used "geographical" names such as Plains, Plateau, and Southwest, whereas Wissler denoted culture areas primarily in terms of the major foods or economies of the areas: Salmon, Eastern Maize, Bison, and so forth.[5]

The humid eastern portion of the United States, essentially the areas of Humid Subtropical and Humid Continental climates, was called the Eastern Maize area by Wissler; Kroeber divided it into the Southeastern Woodlands and Northeastern Woodlands, the latter including the southeastern portion of Canada. This large region included a diversity of specific cultures and environments. The native economies were combinations of agriculture and hunting-fishing-gathering, with agriculture generally being more important and better developed in the southern areas. Women did most of the farming (in contrast to the Southwest), raising maize or corn as the major crop. Dwellings, ranging from small "wigwams" to large Iroquois longhouses, were mostly of wooden frames covered with bark or in some cases wood or thatch. Some of the northeastern tribes practiced forms of shifting agriculture, leaving behind "Indian old fields," grassy clearings in the forest once thought to be natural glades.

There were many interesting and quite advanced Indian cultures in the Eastern Woodlands, from the Natchez of the Mississippi Valley region to the Iroquois and their "federation" in the north. The early European settlement of the eastern United States wreaked

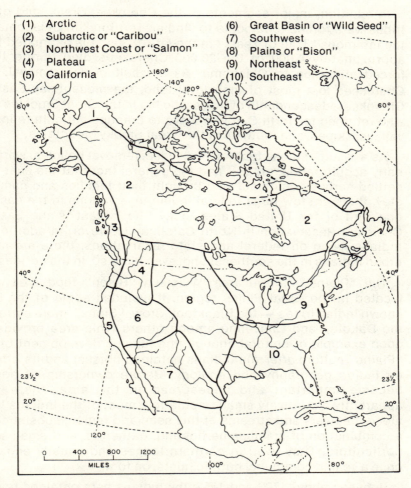

Map designed by Donald J. Ballas and drafted by Daniel J. Beaulieu, Indiana University of Pennsylvania.

Figure 2.1. American Indian Culture Areas.

havoc with Indian populations and cultures. There were great losses through diseases such as measles and smallpox (many northeastern tribes were literally extinct) and warfare when Indians were induced to take sides in "white" wars as well as due to white/Indian conflicts.

In addition, major segments of the Cherokee, Creek, and other tribes were forced to relocate to "Indian Territory" in Oklahoma;on the infamous "Trail of Tears" in the late 1830s, it is estimated that approximately 4,000 of the 20,000 Cherokees died during their forced migration to Oklahoma. As a result of the removal, the Cherokees lost most of their level land; the present-day Eastern Cherokees, descendants of those who hid in the Great Smokies and who returned to North Carolina, have to practice agriculture in the valleys, slopes, and foothills of the Great Smoky Mountains.

As a result of these factors — disease, removal policies, warfare, early acculturation, etc., — and the general fact that the east was settled early by colonists who brought their families and came to stay, there are few large federal Indian reservations in the eastern one-third of the United States today (the largest is the Eastern Cherokee Reservation in North Carolina). However, in addition to Indians living on federal and state reservations, there are many urban Indians in the southeast and, even more so, in the northeast.

The "Plains" culture area, Wissler's "Bison" food area, was located in the Great Plains region; it included some of the best known Indian tribes — the Blackfoot, Crow, "Sioux", more correctly the Dakota, and Cheyenne among others. This area provides a good example of cultural change (the famous development of the "Plains" culture *after* the Indians obtained horses) and its effects on Indian geography and ecology. Before ownership of horses became important and widespread in the area, there was apparently a relatively small population; most of the Indians lived along the rivers and streams of this semi-arid region, subsisting by a combination of small-game hunting, gathering, and small-scale horticulture. They lived in earthern lodges and usually engaged once a year in communal buffalo hunts, on foot.

Between about 1700 and 1750, the Indians here obtained horses and a large proportion of them became full-time nomadic buffalo hunters, inventing the tipi as a portable dwelling and developing their patriarchical "Plains culture." However, some of the tribes did remain sedentary, village-dwelling farmers. Many Indians moved westward *onto* the plains as they got horses and learned of the "affluency" of bison-hunting tribes in the region. Among the tribes which moved to the Great Plains from the upper Great Lakes region, apparently Minnesota, were the famous "Dakota" Indians.[6]

The Indians of the Plains retained their lands longer than did the Eastern Indians. The region was at first considered too dry by early white settlers, and being quite distant from eastern markets was occupied much later by whites. Indian occupance in the Great Plains also endured longer because the nomadic hunters were skilled warriors and quite mobile, with their horses, rather than being "tied" to sedentary villages and fields. Eventually, their primary source of food, the bison, was hunted almost to extinction by whites; this, coupled by the technological superiority of the federal soldiers, proved too much for the Indians. White Americans had begun to settle the region in increasing numbers, needing more land (railroad companies also played a big role in the alienation of Indian lands), and the Plains Indians were forced to settle on reservations in the latter decades of the nineteenth century.

As difficult as it was for the Indians to lose many of their better lands and to be virtually forced to become sedentary farmers on reservations, they might be in fairly good socio-economic condition today if they could have retained all of their reservation land. However, treaties were soon "revised" or simply broken by the federal government as more resources were discovered (as gold in the Black Hills) and as white settlers found that much of the land *was* better suited for agricultural purposes than originally presumed. For example, all of present-day South Dakota west of the Missouri River, plus a small parcel east of the river, was set aside in the Treaty of 1868 as the "Great Sioux Reservation," the Black Hills and other portions of western South Dakota were taken over by the U.S. government in 1876, and during the next two decades much of the remaining was alienated, leaving the Indians with several "fragmented" reservations in place of the one continuous, much larger reservation.[7]

Matters were made even worse by the allotment of Indian lands in the last couple of decades of the nineteenth century and early decades of the twentieth century. The General Allotment Act (or Dawes Act) was passed in 1887; reservation land was alloted to individual Indians, much in the manner in which it was "homesteaded" to white settlers. The idea was to encourage the Indians, as owners of their own land, to more readily become "civilized" farmers, but "surplus lands" on reservations were given to white settlers after the Indians had gotten their allotments, and over the next three decades or so much of the individual Indian land was deeded (sold) to whites. All in all, the result of the Dawes Act was to very significantly diminish the amount of Indian land in many portions of the United States, particularly in the Great Plains. Nevertheless, the relative lateness of white settlement and the original large sizes of reservations help to explain why today the Great Plains, along with the Southwest, has more Indian reservations and people than do most regions of the country.

The Southwest is one of the most interesting and important Indian culture areas. However, its diversity makes even choosing a name for it difficult. Most of the Southwest, and much of Mexico, was designated as the "Area of Intensive Agriculture" by Wissler; the name is not inappropriate, since the bulk of the population, though not all of the tribes *was* supported by quite advanced agriculture, including irrigation. Not all of the Indian peoples in this region lived by intensive agriculture, certainly not the later "immigrants" such as the Navajo and Apache, who were dominantly hunters and gatherers. "Pueblo" is a much more inadequate name for the entire region, since not even all of the sedentary agricultural people lived in pueblos, large two or three storied dwellings of stone or adobe, or were "Pueblo" by culture.

Thus, many simply use the term "Southwest" for this region, as do Kroeber and Garbarino, to include not only the many Pueblo "tribes" and the Athapascans (Apache-Navajo) but other groups, more difficult to classify by culture area, such as the Pima and Papago. There was, of course, never one tribe called the "Pueblo." That name is not equivalent to Mohawk, Cherokee, Crow, etc.; rather, the term refers to the dwellings and settlements in which they lived and, by extension, to their general culture.

Briefly, the Pueblo Indians (tribes such as the Hopi, Zuni, Tewe, Laguna, Acoma, etc.) were sedentary farmers, famous for their pottery, who traced their lineage through the females. In this region, in contrast to the Eastern Woodlands, the men did the farming — but the fields were owned by the women, and young married women and their families lived in their mother's pueblo. Maize (corn) was the most important crop, along with a variety of other vegetables; fruit trees were also important.

Prehistoric Indians in the Southwest were apparently the first to practice agriculture in what is now the United States; corn was grown in New Mexico, as indicated by the Bat Cave find, about 5,000 years ago. This region has a very long and at least partially known history of settlement, from "cliff dwellers" and their predecessors through later pueblo and related cultures. It is not known when the Athapascan migrants, apparently from the Great Plains of Canada, *first* entered the Southwest; some came as late as the sixteenth century, but they moved southward, probably via the Intermontane region as well as the western Great Plains, over a period of centuries, perhaps beginning as early as 1,000 A.D. These people were collectively called "Apachu," a Pueblo Indian (Tewa) word meaning stranger or enemy; one group was later referred to as the "Apachu du Nabahu" ("Enemies of the Cultivated Fields") — the forerunners of the Navajo Indians.

Over the years, the southwestern Indians learned from whites as well as from each other. Slowly, the Navajo adopted some aspects of agriculture and other practices from the Pueblo Indians; the Apache were much more reluctant to take up farming, and many groups did not do so until modern times. The Navajo learned to grow fruit trees, particularly peaches, from the Pueblos (apparently the Hopi), who had in turn gotten the tree from the Spanish in the early seventeenth century.[8] Also, two of the most famous aspects of historic and modern Navajo culture, sheep-raising and silver-working, were learned from the Spanish. Some of the Athapascan-speaking peoples, particularly the eastern Apache, later adopted elements of the Plains Indian culture such as the use of horses in hunting and warfare, and crude "teepees" (tipis) of bark or brush to replace their cone and bee-hive shaped wickiups. Today, the apache and Navajo use their equestrian skills and interests in their pastoral pursuits, the Navajo raising mostly sheep and Angora goats with the Apache more involved in cattle-raising.

Despite their early contact with Spaniards, which included warfare and enslavement, and later encounters with federal U.S. soldiers, the Indians of the Southwest have survived and increased in numbers. This region, combined with the Great Plains, contains a major portion of present-day Indian land and population. Generally speaking, the Indians here have retained more of their Indian culture than elsewhere in the United States. The past is not only present and important in today's culture, but there are many national monuments, such as Navajo National Monument on the Navajo Reservation, and even a national park (Mesa Verde), among other historical and natural attractions, which brings tourists to the area who not only (one hopes) learn of Indian history and culture but help the Indian economy in the process.

The California-Great Basin culture area (the "Wild Seed" food area in Wissler's classification) includes the dry Great Basin region of western Utah and Nevada, plus smaller portions of adjacent states, and most of the present state of California. The northern coastal region of California is normally placed in the Northwest Coast or "Salmon" culture area, while some of the tribes of southeastern California are assigned to the Southwest. The major difference between the classifications by Kroeber and Wissler is that Kroeber places the Indians of the Columbia Plateau in a separate "Plateau" culture area, to be discussed later, briefly, while Wissler considers most of them to be part of the Wild Seed area.

This is generally considered to be the poorest culture area in terms of material culture and food supply, although life was somewhat easier and better in parts of California. The Indians of the Great Basin were often referred to as the "Digger Indians" since their economy included digging for roots, grub worms, and other foods, as well as the gathering of wild plant foods (seeds, nuts, berries, etc.) and the hunting of small game such as rabbits. Their best developed craft was basketry, the baskets being useful in their gathering economy; they practiced no agriculture, and large game was extremely scarce. Acorns were a staple food in a few more "productive" regions, particularly in California. The dominant dwellings were bee-hive or cone-shaped thatched "wickiups."

Most portions of this region, particularly the Great Basin, supported quite low densities of population, which were later decreased further by white diseases and oppression. In California many of the tribes were later collectively known as "Mission Indians," as they were virtually forced to settle in missions started by Spanish priests. Although the intentions may have been good (not necessarily justifiable), living in close quarters facilitated the spread of epidemic diseases. On a more positive vein, the "Mission Indians" learned agriculture and other skills from the Spanish.[9]

The Northwest Coast or Salmon culture area extended along the mild, rainy coasts of North America from northern California to southern Alaska. It was one of the most interesting and advanced Indian culture areas north of Mexico. Oddly, perhaps, most of the tribes — Kwakiutl, Chinook, Makah, Tlingit, Haida, etc. — are virtually unknown to most Americans. Actually, the term "tribe" is even less meaningful here than in many other parts of Indian America; the people were village dwellers, each village being quite distinct, on the order of small "city states," from other villages, even in cases where languages of the same family were spoken.

These Indians certainly prove that highly "civilized" people do not have to be farmers. They practiced no agriculture. They didn't have to raise crops; there was an abundance of wild plants in this moist, predominantly forested climatic region, in addition to much large game such as moose, bear and elk. Fishing was by far the major economy (they even hunted whales in large sea-going canoes and boats), although salmon were the most important fish. There may have been significant cultural influence from the Eskimos to the north, although the extent and details of this are not adequately known.

The Northwest Coast Indians were and are famous for their wood-working skills. They carved totem poles, as well as bowls, masks, etc., and also decorated their large wooden houses, often

50 feet wide by 60 or more feet long, long cedar canoes, and boats with their carvings. The skills of the past are still used by many of the Northwest Coast Indians today, with many employed full-time or part-time in lumbering, fishing, boat-building, and wood-carving.

The "Plateau" culture area is basically a transitional one, with most tribes sharing in varying degrees cultural traits of both the Northwest Coast Indians and the Great Basin ("Wild Seed") Indians. Tribes included the Klamath, Umatilla, Spokan, Nez Perce, and others; some of the eastern tribes, such as the Nez Perce, later adopted traits from the Plains Indians — including tipis and bison-hunting from horseback. Like the Northwest Coast peoples, the Plateau Indians predominantly considered salmon and other fish, such as trout, to be their major food. They tended to live in relatively permanent villages, with homes not usually as large and elaborate as those along the coast, but much larger and more substantial than those typical of the Great Basin. However, they moved to various fishing, hunting, and gathering grounds for parts of the year, and, like the Great Basin Indians, they placed great emphasis on gathering wild plants for food. Most of the remaining Plateau Indians today live on reservations in the Columbia Plateau of Idaho, eastern Oregon, and eastern Washington.

The Arctic culture area includes various Eskimo groups and, according to most authorities, the Aleuts. Eskimos migrated to North America by boat about 5,000 years ago, with Aleuts apparently arriving even more recently. The Aleuts and Eskimos were both highly skilled sea hunters, with some of the "inland" Eskimos also hunting caribous and other land animals ("Eskimo" is an Algonkian Indian word meaning "eaters of raw meat"). Most of the Aleuts still live on the Aleutian and Pribilof Islands; some Eskimo practice the "old lifestyle" on the Arctic tundra coastal plains of northern Alaska and Canada, although many now live in white settlements and have become highly acculturated. The Indians of interior Alaska, as differentiated from the "Salmon" Indians of southern coastal Alaska, and much of adjacent Canada were in the "Caribou" or Subarctic culture area; hunting was the major economy, and many of these Indians today still hunt for at least part of their own livelihood, and/or serve as hunting guides for visiting whites.

ALLOTMENT, TERMINATION, AND DEVELOPMENT

Over the years, federal U.S. policies have varied toward caring for Indian land and attempting to solve or alleviate problems facing the American Indians. Although intentions were often good, most of these policies failed to solve all of the difficult problems on and off reservations, and some have done more harm than good, Indian affairs were first administered within the War Department, but the Bureau of Indian Affairs was transferred to the Department of the Interior in 1849 where it remains today. A brief discussion of a few of the major policies will be presented here, emphasizing their relationships to American Indian developments in general, past and present.

It should be kept in mind that one of the many quite unique aspects of the geography of the American Indians, in contrast to other ethnic/cultural minorities in the United States, is the fact that they, as a group, had *land.* No other large groups have reservations. For some time, early in our history, Indian tribes were treated (for better or worse) as separate "nations," indeed, even today some tribal groups refer to themselves as nations. In a real sense, even though their inhabitants are U.S. citizens with all accompanying rights and obligations, Indian reservations are political enclaves. There IS still great pride and attachment on the part of Indians to their land, and the existence of reservations, with all their problems, permit and even require types of developments (tribal ranches, tribal industrial parks, etc.) quite different from those which may be associated with other socio-cultural groups.

Attempts to deal with Indians fairly as separate nations did not, unfortunately, last long. White settlers continued to increase in population and to encroach on Indian land. Treaties were ignored or changed, and whites eventually called upon the federal government to move the Indians, first farther westward, and later onto reservations. Thus, "removal" became one of the early governmental policies. Andrew Jackson obtained passage from Congress of the Removal Bill on May 28, 1830, giving the president of the United States the power to exchange empty land in the west for Indian lands, coveted by white settlers, in the east. "Indian Territory" was established west of the Mississippi River, being approximately the present state of Oklahoma, and various eastern tribes were forced to move there during the 1830s, particularly the "Five Civilized Tribes" of the southeast — the Choctaws, Creeks, Chickasaws, Cherokees, and Seminoles. Some of the Seminoles refused to be "removed," fought for years against the United States army, and were eventually settled on the Seminole Reservation in Florida.

Eventually, more white Americans settled here, too, and the Indians were forced to give up the western portion of Oklahoma. Land was allotted to the Indians in the 1890s and 1900s, and the

Indians of Oklahoma became part of the general population of the state. Many counties today are primarily Indian; the Osage Indian Reservation is the only large remaining reservation, even though Oklahoma has the second largest Indian population among the states (169,464 in 1980, second only to California with 201,311 Indians — most of whom are also not found on reservations). This and other "removals" obviously caused many problems for the Indians. The hardship of forced migrations and giving up their traditional homelands were accompanied by problems of adjusting to geographical environments quite different from those with which they were familiar.

At least some white persons honestly believed that "removal" was to the advantage of the Indians, who were unable to resist the tide of settlement. Perhaps it did "buy time" for tribes who might otherwise have been devastated by wars fought to obtain their lands. Similarly, the allotment policy was thought by many to be a way to improve the lot of the American Indians. Indeed, that was the intention of Senator Henry Dawes, author of the General Allotment Act. Dawes and many other "friends of the Indian" felt that the Indians would be more independent of federal rule and develop pride in their own land as farmers; they would have the rights of all Americans to use or even to sell their land as they chose. However, the concept of individual ownership of land was basically quite foreign to the Indians, who had usually embraced tribal or communal land tenure. Furthermore, many Indians, particularly nomadic buffalo-hunting males in the Great Plains, had little experience or interest in agriculture; livestock ranching would probably have been a better economy for most of the Plains Indians than crop-farming.

There were other problems with the allotment system. Similar to the early white homesteads in the semi-arid west, the allotments (basically 160 acres for each head of family, plus smaller units for un-married persons and children) proved to be too small to adequately support the occupants. Also, Indian populations had been seriously decimated by the latter decade of the nineteenth century, and no land was saved for any increase in population. "Surplus" lands were homesteaded to whites, who were also later allowed to purchase land, often the best land, from Indians. The Indians of the United States had a total of 138,000,000 acres in 1887; they owned only 52,000,000 acres in 1934, at which time the policy of permitting Indians to sell their land to non-Indians was stopped.[10]

Allotment, fortunately, was not carried out in all parts of the country. Some tribes resisted allotment, as in the Southwest where it was rarely used.[11] This helps to account for the number of large contiguous reservations in the Southwest not fragmented with white land like those in the Great Plains. The Cherokees were also successful in preventing the loss of their lands through allotment. When the government compiled a tribal roll between 1924 to 1927 for the purpose of alloting land to each Eastern Cherokee Indian, the tribal council was appalled to find that persons with as little as 1/128th Indian blood were on the roll. They protested, asking the federal government to not allot their land but instead to hold the land in perpetual trust for the Eastern Cherokee tribe. Congress agreed, and even today no land is owned by individuals on the Eastern Cherokee Reservation; the Tribal Council assigns land to individual Indians.[12]

The Indian Reorganization Act, passed in 1934, was very important to the development of Indian lands and economy. It ended the sale of Indian land to non-Indians and permitted tribes to incorporate, borrow money through government loans, and appoint tribal councils to manage reservation affairs through self-government.

World War II had profound effects on Indian people and their reservations. Many Indians served in the armed forces, learning new skills and trades, and had to learn to live with non-Indians. After the war, these new ideas and skills were often brought back to the reservations, increasing (in some cases, at least) employment opportunities and helping technically to develop the reservations in certain respects. In addition, many Indians used the "G.I. Bill" to attend trade schools and colleges. Many became lawyers, teachers, other professionals and skilled workers.

Two somewhat related policies dominated federal relationships with American Indians in the 1950s and early 1960s: relocation and termination. "Relocation" involved encouraging Indians to relocate from reservations to urban areas, and provided job training to help Indians become part of the "regular" American society and economy. This program played a major role in the movement of more than 100,000 Indians to urban areas.[13] This may also have affected the population structure of many reservations, since for the most part, the more traditional, more "full-blooded" Indians were generally less inclined to relocate to cities.

"Termination" proved to be an ill-conceived policy although its intentions were to help rather than to hurt the Indians. As stated in House Concurrent Resolution 108, passed in 1953, basically the idea was to "get the government out of the Indian business" and give more "freedom" to the American Indians, by letter reservations lose that status and be absorbed into counties and states. Between 1953 and 1962, Congress passed twelve termination acts, affecting approximately a dozen tribes and several hundred small bands and groups in California and Oregon.[14]

Perhaps the best known example of termination was that of the Menominee Reservation in Wisconsin. It was made into a separate county, which meant that the Indians had to pay real estate taxes to fund police, hospital, and other services and facilities. Many of the Indians were pushed further into poverty and welfare rolls grew. Finally, in December 1973, Congress voted to reverse the termination of the Menominee Indian Reservation. From 1973 to 1980, six of the terminated tribes and four of the California bands were restored to federally recognized status by the federal government.

Although it has not been given one generally accepted name ("self-determination" has been one of the most commonly used terms), the basic federal policy toward Indians and their reservations in the 1970s, and 1980s has emphasized Indian self-government and socio-economic development. More educated and skilled Indians are remaining on or returning to the reservations, playing significant roles in the governance and development of their economy and society. Over 80 percent of the Bureau of Indian Affairs work force and almost 90 percent of the agency superintendents are now Indian.[15]

There is still very high unemployment and underemployment on most Indian reservations; the problems to be faced in trying to develop them include lack of resources on some reservations unskilled labor forces, and distances from major markets.[16] Yet, progress has been and is being made. The government is encouraging developments in tourism, light industry, provision of local services (stores, gas stations, restaurants, etc.) as well as in agriculture, mineral exploitation, fishing, and related economies. Irrigation has been developed and extended, afforestation and reforestation have improved environments as well as providing commercial resources and trade schools and community colleges have been established. Some reservations have developed ski resorts, fishing lakes, motels, museums, campgrounds, and similar recreation/tourist facilities.

SOME CONCLUDING THOUGHTS

Developments and conditions on American Indian reservations today, as well as among off-reservation Indians, in many cases reflect aspects of the historical geography of the Amerindians. The very location of reservations and the large number of urban Indians reflect government policies and the general relations between

Indians and "whites." Allotment and alienation of Indian lands, in many parts of the country, have often resulted in the loss of much good land and fragmentation of Indian land. General developments from early pioneer trails to railroads, modern highways, travel and tourism, and industrialization have affected Indians and their land. The present-day geography of Indian tribes and reservations have been affected greatly by "past geographies" and historical-geographical developments in general.

Future development and conditions will be affected directly and indirectly by current and earlier historical geographic processes. As Erhard Rostlund wrote: "The present is the fruit of the past and contains the seeds of the future."[17] The historical geography of the American Indians is a fruitful field of study which historical geographers should continue to cultivate.

NOTES

1. Two very useful, classic volumes on the American Indians in general (both books are available in paperbound form) are *Indians of North America* (Second Edition, Revised) by Harold E. Driver (Chicago: University of Chicago Press, 1969) and *Red Man's America* (Revised Edition) by Ruth M. Underhill (Chicago: University of Chicago Press, 1971).

2. George F. Carter, *Earlier Than You Think: A Personal View of Man in America* (College Station, TX: Texas A&M University Press, 1980) is a scholarly, well-illustrated (54 "figures"!) *readable* book summarizing Carter's views on the antiquity of humans in America. It includes a thirteen-page bibliography.

3. Stephen C. Jett, "The Origins of Navajo Settlement Patterns," *Annals of the Association of American Geographers,* 68 (September 1978):351-362.

4. See for example Janel M. Curry-Roper,"Houma Blowguns and Baskets in the Mississippi River Delta," *Journal of Cultural Geography,* 2 (Spring/Summer 1982): 13-22. This entire issue was devoted to American Indian topics.

5. Merwyn S. Garbarino, *Native American Heritage* (Boston and Toronto: Little, Brown and Company, 1976). This fine textbook contains more "geographical" information than do most anthropological texts on the subject. A revised edition, if forthcoming, would be welcome, but even this first edition is almost a "model" textbook in terms of lucid writing, the mix of facts and theories, illustrations, and an outstanding format in general. Garbarino also wrote the section on "Indian, American" for *The World Book Encyclopedia,* which includes a discussion of culture areas.

6. Donald J. Ballas, "Changing Ecology and Land-Use Among the Teton Dakota Indians, 1680-1900," *Bulletin of the Illinois Geographical Society,* 27 (Fall 1985): 35-47.

7. For a brief account of the reduction of the Great Sioux Reservation (via a set of maps) and the allotment and alienation of Indian lands on the Rosebud and Pine Ridge Reservations in South Dakota, see "Early Agriculture and Livestock Raising Among the Teton Dakota Indians" by Donald J. Ballas, *Bulletin of the Illinois Geographical Society,* 15 (December 1973): 53-62.

8. See Stephen C. Jett's interesting account of "History of Fruit Tree Raising Among the Navajo" in *Agricultural History,* 51 (October 1977):681-701.

9. A fine article surveying the Indians of California, which paints a more realistic and favorable picture of their lifestyles, is "The California Indian Before European Contact" by David Hornbeck, *Journal of Cultural Geography,* 2 (Spring-Summer 1982): 23-39.

10. Bureau of Indian Affairs, *American Indians* (Washington: Government Printing Office, 1984). This well-illustrated booklet presents a good survey of the American Indians, including establishment of reservations, changing government policies, Indian population, economic development on reservations, and related topics. It is available at this writing (stock number 024-002-00083-7) from the GPO at $2.50.

11. Alvin M. Josephy, Jr. *The Indian Heritage of America* (New York: Bantam Books, 1969 plus many subsequent printings). This paperback presents a readable survey of the Indians of North and South America, from prehistoric to modern times.

12. Donald J. Ballas, "Notes on the Population, Settlement, Ecology of the Eastern Cherokee," *Journal of Geography,* 59 (September 1960): 258-267. This article presents an overview of the cultural geography of the Eastern Cherokees.

13. Garbarino (reference 5, p. 484).

14. *American Indians,* 1984.

15. *American Indians,* 1984.

16. Donald J. Ballas, "Cultural Traits Related to Socio-Economic Development on the Rosebud Sioux Indian Reservation," *Geographical Survey,* 2 (January 1973):17-26.

17. Erhard Rostlund, *Outline of Cultural Geography* (Berkeley: California Book Company, 1955), p. 4.

Chapter 3
Two Worlds Collide:
The European Advance
into North America

David K. Eliades

Lacking broad geographical knowledge but rich in imagination, Europeans became imperialistic in the late 1400s. Wherever they went, they invaded, settled, and claimed lands already occupied by indigenous peoples. While their initial interest was the Far East, the Europeans increasingly came to detect the potential of the Americas. In order to develop that potential by Old World standards, the Europeans first had to accommodate, then to eliminate the people Christopher Columbus labeled "Los Indios" — the Indians.

From the beginning of white-Indian contact, the Europeans, with only a few exceptions, refused to see the richness and diversity of Indian cultures. Instead of perceiving and accepting the native cultures as different, the Europeans saw them as inferior, and quickly began to deal with the Indians on the basis of a superior-inferior relationship. In short, the Europeans sought to "civilize" the Indians by conversion and acculturation, to incorporate them into their economic systems as slaves or subordinate trade partners, to use them as military allies in their wars or, if they came to have no function in the European scheme, to eliminate them.

The coming of the Europeans to the New World immediately raised questions concerning the ownership of the land. The colonizing powers argued among themselves about whether visual discovery alone was sufficient to establish a legitimate claim or whether occupation and settlement were also required. In practice, it turned out that occupation decided the issue. The assertion of title against Indian claims was quite another matter; it rested at least in part upon the image of the Indian as deficient. Most of the charters and grants issued for settlement gave permission for the possession of lands uninhabited by a Christian prince or his subjects; if the lands the Europeans claimed were vacant, there was no difficulty. However, differences of opinion arose between the Europeans and the Indians, based on environmental relationships and usage, as to what constituted empty lands. What to the whites appeared vacant or underutilized was seen as owned and fully utilized by the natives, whose lives were largely regulated by the cycles of nature. The problem was further complicated by the differing concepts the two peoples had toward the land — the whites believed in private ownership while the Indians believed in tribally-controlled lands. The European settlers quickly came to argue that they would make "superior use" of the land and that sufficient marginal land existed so that the Native Americans could continue their traditional lifestyle without loss. This argument reflects either a rationalization or ignorance concerning Indian economies and land use. The land issue was a clash of opposing cultures, economies, and ecological values.[1]

Eventually the whites had to abandon the idea that they were claiming vacant lands for it became clear that the lands were occupied, just not in the European fashion. The whites later came to use the concept of the "Right of Discovery" as the basis for their New World claims. According to this doctrine, the government by whose subjects or authority new lands were discovered gained title against the claims of all other civilized governments; this title was then legitimized by some form of actual possession. After reflection and debate over the legal relationship of the Indians to the land, the Europeans concluded that because Indians were able to reason and capable of conversion to Christianity, their rights to the land had to be given proper consideration. Essentially, the whites reasoned that Indian title could be extinguished only by mutual agreement, by some form of exchange or purchase, by lawful wars, or by getting chiefs to acknowledge the supremacy of a European monarch. Land proved to be the most enduring issue in white-Indian relations.[2]

Closely intertwined with the issue of land was the question of Indian sovereignty. This question led the whites to debate the character of the natives, their type of government, and their rights and powers. Did the Indians have supreme authority, jurisdiction and power over their lands and lives? Did native peoples have legitimate rulers and, if so, what was the relationship of their rulers to the monarchs in Europe? What legal and political rights were retained by the Indians after conquest, whether by war or colonization? In response to such questions, the Europeans eventually concluded that tribes had been self-governing and sovereign originally and that they retained that status after colonization. Nevertheless, one of the results of European expansion into America was the steady erosion of Indian sovereignty. This process began with the colonizing powers extending their protection over the tribes within their claimed lands. By taking this action, they established the precedent that the Indians were subjects of the monarch, and consequently the absolute sovereignty of the Indians then became limited sovereignty. Then to protect their Indian subjects, the nations established their jurisdiction over Indian lands which opened the door for the whites to become involved in the internal affairs of the tribe. Often, economic expansion paralleled the extension of political and judicial jurisdiction. While these actions were sometimes taken in good faith, they were also done because it was good business or good politics. White assumption of jurisdiction brought subtle influences to bear on the economies, social values, and ways of life of the Indians, sometimes in positive ways but more often in negative ones.[3]

How extensive the European impact was on Native Americans and their societies continues to be a major topic of scholarly debate. Recent demographic studies indicate that the impact was dramatic and devastating. For decades scholars accepted the Indian population statistics calculated by James Mooney, an ethnologist with the Smithsonian Institute during the early years of the twentieth century. Mooney argued for a total native population of 8 million in the Americas, a figure now seriously challenged. While some of the new population claims seem exaggerated — one scholar has suggested a pre-contact population of 100 million, many scholars are beginning to accept the likelihood of 50 million. While it will always be impossible to obtain precise figures, it is certain that there were substantially more Indians in 1500 than was previously thought, which means the tragedy of Indian destruction was far greater than realized. Indeed, the coming of the Europeans produced for the American Indian death and change on an unprecedented scale.[4]

While Indian slavery and wars, both intertribal and with the whites, took their toll, liquor and epidemic disease were the major decimators of the Indian populations. Liquor quickly became a major trade item, but having no experience with alcohol and dependent on the Europeans for their supplies, the Indians unfortunately never learned to drink in moderation. As a result, drunkenness became a feature of white-Indian relations. Liquor led to exploitation by the traders and to violence on the part of the natives. Recognizing the problems of the trade in liquor, colonial governments tried, usually without success, to prohibit it or to regulate it. Some Indian leaders also realized its destructive effect and pleaded with colonial governments for assistance in controlling its availability, but in most instances the law of supply and demand prevailed.[5]

Although alcohol was certainly a negative factor, far more deadly was the importation into America of virgin-soil epidemics. These are epidemics in which the population at risk have had no prior contact with the diseases that strike them and against which they have no immunity or treatments. It is clear that a number of dangerous diseases — smallpox, malaria, measles, and certainly several others — were unknown in pre-contact America.[6] That they periodically spread among the Indians with devastating effect is clear from the colonial records. In the Carolinas, for example, smallpox destroyed half the Cherokee nation in 1738 and half the Catawba nation in 1759; there were of course numerous other epidemics with similar effect.[7] It is clear that European diseases, more than superior technology or numbers, brought about the eventual destruction of the Native Americans

The Spanish, as the first Europeans in the New World, found the Indians to be, for the most part, a simple, gentle people and America a potential utopia. Before the coming of other Europeans, they had already raised and answered many of the questions prompted by the existence of the Indians in the newly discovered lands. Spanish theologians and scholars had debated such questions as whether the Indians were human or sub-human, whether they had souls and could be converted to Christianity, whether they had to be civilized before they could be saved, and whether conversion had to be achieved peacefully or could be accomplished by force. In 1537 Pope Paul III answered the most fundamental question in his bull *Sublimis Deus* when he declared the Indians to be "truly men" and "capable of receiving the doctrines of the faith."[8] Once the church decreed the legitimacy of the salvation of the Indians, Catholic missionaries undertook a spiritual conquest of America fully as significant as the military conquest.

In addition to the Spanish debates and conclusions, another major influence which shaped the European view of the Indian was the myth of the wild man. Europeans considered everything outside of the established framework of society and Christian norms to be wild. Thus, the wild man was described with such terms as pagan, hairy, mute, irrational, and excessively erotic. Though considered human, it was also believed that because of such factors as poor environment, divine punishment, shock, or insanity, the wild man had reverted to an animal-like condition in a state of nature. However, the wild man could presumably be civilized and even saved.[9]

Although the Spanish were active along the southern frontier and although the French were active in Louisiana and Canada, by the seventeenth century North America had largely become an English preserve. This happened partly because the Spanish were mainly interested in their Latin American lands and partly because the French, though claiming extensive holdings, came in insufficient numbers to control their lands with much effectiveness. The French, less interested in Indian land than in furs and other resources, did generally manage to establish better relations with the natives than the English, but this seems more the result of Indian perceptions of the French as less of a threat than a product of greater French toleration, as often claimed. At any rate, when the English began their colonization of North America in the seventeenth and eighteenth centuries, they were brought into intimate contact with the Indians. They came with the fears of any people advancing into the unknown — were they going to be met by the guileless primitive of utopia, or were they going to be met by savages who were more animal than man? Because of preconceptions derived from the Spanish experience and the wild man myth, and because their only previous experience with an indigenous people had been in Ireland, where they were met with hostility, the English were schizophrenic concerning the natives when they first settled in America. Their image of the Indian would change a number of times during the course of the colonial era.

The English perception of the Indian is important not only for what it reveals about the working of the Anglo-American mind, but also because it influenced English relations with the Indian, helping to shape policies designed to civilize, to control, and ultimately to annihilate him. Images reflected attitudes and attitudes did a great deal to determine policy.

Despite an undercurrent of tension and suspicion, the earliest English settlers in America found the natives more hospitable than antagonistic, and a romanticized view of the Indian prevailed. In those early days commercial interests were more important than agricultural interests, and the settlers were urged to maintain peaceful relations with the Native Americans because trade was possible only with a people who were friendly. Once the issues of trader abuse and land were interjected into white-Indian relations, the situation changed. Misuse and constant territorial expansion by the whites led to several major wars in early colonial history — the attack of the Powhatan Confederation against Virginia in 1622, the Pequot War of 1637, and King Philip's War in 1675. While these wars were of some military importance, their real significance was the impact they had on the image of the Indian in the English mind. They confirmed what the English had always suspected: that the Indians could not be trusted, that they were, in reality, savage beasts. Consequently, the colonists came to believe that they could do anything with the natives that they wished. The settlers then developed a vocabulary of abuse which denied the Indian's humanity — he was described as vicious, lazy, and brutish, to cite a few examples, and this made easier his eventual destruction.[10]

If the Indians were ever considered equals by the English settlers, it was during the formative, uncertain first years of colonization, a period when, of necessity, an interracial democracy of sorts existed among the whites, blacks, and Indians. Once the English created a firm foothold in America, the status of the Indian declined. In the future the Indian's importance would be determined by whether and how he could serve the English and, of course, his image underwent a corresponding change. Indeed, from the outset, the English could never forget that the Indians were different, and as Winthrop Jordan pointed out in *White Over Black,* the English came to America prejudiced against non-whites and feeling superior to all other Europeans. "It seems," Jordan wrote, "as if Englishmen possessed a view of other peoples which placed the English nation at the center of widening concentric circles each of which contained a people more alien than the one inside it."[11] Because Indians were radically different from the English, they could never be truly assimilated into the colonial society and so fell on the losing side of the dividing line.[12]

While outward, often superficial factors played an important part in forming the racial attitudes of the colonials, subtle psychological forces were also shaping their reaction to and image of the Indian. The English who came to America subscribed to a principle of order; they believed that they had a God-ordained mission to bring order out of the chaotic New World. To accomplish this they must civilize the savages who occupied it. This was a two-fold problem, at once practical and theoretical. Practically, they had to make their peace with the Indian and share his environment; theoretically, they had to understand and evaluate the Indian as a type of man. As it turned out, practical considerations outweighed the theoretical, and the Native Americans were not civilized, but destroyed.[13]

The English saw in the Indians what they did not like about themselves and so made them objects of hatred — to destroy the Indian was to destroy savagery, a relic of the past and a latent force in all men, to control the Indian was to prevent the subversion of white culture. In his perceptive *The Savages in America,* Roy Harvey Pearce stated it succinctly when he wrote, "The Indian became important for the English mind, not for what he was in and of himself, but rather for what he showed civilized men they were not and must not be."[14]

The colonials, without knowing it, were practicing the psychological technique of projection: they were seeing in others what they wished to deny in themselves. By creating a negative stereotype of the Indian, they could take action against the natives without sullying their own consciences. Projection is essentially a practice of self-deception, an unconscious mechanism for convincing one's self that evil impulses are found elsewhere, not within one's self. Having been given the image of a savage, the Indian became a victim of this type of psychologically-induced racism.[15]

While prejudice played an important part in the way the English viewed the Indians, there were, nevertheless, factors which differentiated the Indians from the blacks. These factors led the English to try at least to convert and civilize them, if not totally accept them. The individualistic, live-for-the-present culture of the Indians made them difficult to enslave and govern, their numbers and existence as nations gave them identity, and their role as sometime allies gave them importance. Consequently, the English viewed the Indians as superior to the blacks but inferior to themselves.

Nothing is so clear as the fact that the English in their relations with the Indians were increasingly guided by the principle of self-interest. As the Indians became greater obstacles to colonial plans and as the settlers brought more and more land under cultivation, creating a need for cheap labor, they attempted to turn some Indians into slaves. In this effort they experienced limited success, mainly because of governmental opposition and cultural differences. The Indian male, being mainly a hunter and warrior, proved poorly suited to the routine demands of agriculture. Moreover, enslaved Indians, male and female, were difficult to keep from escaping and usually more dangerous to the owner's safety than the black, in both instances because they were in familiar surroundings and knew how to look after themselves in a wilderness environment. Because Indian slavery proved more of a problem than a benefit, most Indian slaves were soon being exported to New England or the West Indies.[16] This business definitely strained relations between the whites and Indians, and became such a source of concern to the colonial officials that they passed laws and issued regulations against "friendly" or "neighboring" Indians being included in this traffic. Yet, despite official objections, the traffic continued. As historian David Ramsay put it, "This traffic was an inhuman method of getting rid of troublesome neighbors . . . "[17] Indian slavery was a major factor in several bloody white-Indian wars, such as the Tuscarora War of 1711.

Paralleling the emergence of Indian slavery and the growth of the colonies was the development of the fur and hide trade. Trading with the Indians actually became an arm of colonial diplomacy and a means for both sides to acquire wanted or needed supplies and goods.[18] Generally coming from the lowest level of society, the traders who moved among the Indians created many problems and contributed heavily to the negative stereotype of the Native Americans. They cheated the Indians when possible, abused them at the slightest provocation and supplied them with liquor, fixing the image of the "drunken savage" permanently on the American mind. The traders were not alone, however, in abusing and misusing the Indians; the problem was almost endemic anywhere and any time the natives were weaker than the settlers. Although colonial governments adopted laws to try to control trader violence and abuses, setting policy was only half the problem; the other half was enforcement of the laws.[19] Given the frontier environment of colonial America, the traders and, to a somewhat lesser degree, the settlers generally continued to follow their own brutally selfish instincts.

Almost paradoxically, because of rivalries with the French and Spanish, the English authorities viewed the Indians as valuable allies. While the British usually managed to maintain strong ties with the more powerful tribes east of the Mississippi, it required all of their diplomatic skill and their superior trade goods to win out over their rivals. This, however, again illustrates the exploitative nature of white-Indian relations. The English care primarily about the Indians as instruments of their imperial policy, though they always professed their undying friendship for their red brothers. Even in the matter of the Indians and war, the settlers were of a divided mind concerning the First Americans. When the Indians were at war with the settlers, their "savagery" and conspiratorial tactics were denounced, but when they were at war with the foreign rivals of England, that same "savagery" became an advantage and a virtue. To illustrate, during the French and Indian War, Captain Raymond Demere, a militia commander, told England's Cherokee allies, "Nothing is more valuable amongst brave Men and Warriors than Trophies of Victory. Nothing is more worthy of Acceptance than the Scalps of our Enemies; I want some and hope that some of you will bring me some French Scalps, or some Indian Scalps that are in Friendship with the French."[20] Tragically, the efforts of the Cherokee to please their white friends only confirmed in the minds of the people that Indians were different and dangerous.

The image of the Indians further suffered because they were "heathens" trying to live in tandem with supposed Christians. While the primary objective of the Society for the Propagation of the Gospel in Foreign Parts was to suppport Anglicanism among white colonists, a secondary objective was the conversion of the Indians and other non-Christians. Dr. Richard Willis, the Dean of Lincoln, delivered the first anniversary sermon celebrating the organization of the S.P.G. and noted, "The design is . . . to be able to converse with the Natives, and to Preach the Gospel to them . . ."[21]

Not unexpectedly, there was considerable oppositon to having missionaries serve the Indians, particularly from the traders who feared that ministers might hinder their efforts to exploit the natives. Though for different reasons, some churchmen shared the traders' view that missionaries had no place among the Indians; those religionists doubted the tribemen's capacity for Christianity and shared the predominant view that they were savage brutes incapable of living a Christian life. Most churchmen, regardless of their attitude toward the Indians felt they should at least be brought into the mainstream of western civilization; a few sought a common base of understanding and were convinced that they were ripe for conversion.

In many ways the religious issue was part of a larger problem. A convincing case can be made for the thesis that the real cause of friction between the whites and Indians was not racism, but the clash of civilization with savagery. In a very real sense, the Indian was a symbol of all that the English were against — they were, by European standards, immoral, pagan, and barbarous, rather than good, Christian, and civilized. So, characteristically, the whites sought to remake the Indian in their own image, using mainly the church and education. Carrying this argument to its logical conclusion, missionaries were engaged in more than soul-winning; they were engaged in a revolutionary enterprise to bring about the radical transformation of Indian culture. The natives were being asked, in effect, to commit cultural suicide.[22] Whether the missionaries understood the possible ramifications of their efforts to assimilate the Indians is exceedingly doubtful; quite simply, most appear to have been decent men seeking to fulfill a divine mission.

There were, in fact, a few observers, such as John Lawson, who saw the Indian in a more balanced light, who saw elements of nobility in the Indian's character. Such observers saw the Indian as a whole man — as a human being with strengths as well as failings. Writing of his backcountry expedition in 1700-1701, Lawson set forth the well-known weaknesses of the Indian — excessive drinking, belief in magic, susceptibility to epidemic diseases, and lack of Christian morals, but he quickly balanced those points by noting their knowledge of natural medicine, their skills as craftsmen, their fighting ability and loyalty, their patience, and their hospitality.[23] Lawson went on to plead for greater understanding of the Indians through increased knowledge of their culture. He felt this could best be achieved by sending missionaries among them, by learning the native languages, and through intermarriage.[24] To say the least, Lawson had better vision than most of his contemporaries, who continued to see the Indian as a malignant force.

Does this mean that the oft-heralded concept of the Noble Savage was a myth? Obviously there were colonials who saw the Indian as nature's nobleman, as did some European intellectuals. The people who subscribed to this idea usually lived far from the dangers or problems of contact with the Indians, or they used the idea as an instrument for attacking the evils of their own society. What the phrase "Noble Savage" means depends on whether you emphasize the idea of nobility or the idea of savagery. It appears that European intellectuals, particularly the philosophers of France, were not as interested in elevating the American Indian as denigrating the European nobility. When viewed from this perspective the concept is no longer especially laudatory, even for the Native Americans. It proves to be just one more example of the ambiguous image of the Indian.[25]

In the final analysis, white-Indian contact was a record of lost opportunities. Instead of mutually beneficial progress, the whites turned the Indian into a negative symbol of their American experience. Conquering the Indian meant surmounting the wilderness and opening a path for European civilization. To do this, the whites created their own version of the American Indian, a convenient version which allowed them to rationalize the policies they adopted and to justify the actions they took, a version which was a refraction of reality and which largely grew from the superior-inferior relationship established by the Europeans and which placed the Indian in the position of victim.

NOTES

1. Robert F. Berkhofer, Jr., *The White Man's Indian: Images of the American Indian from Columbus to the Present* (New York: Alfred A. Knopf, 1978), pp. 120-121, 129-130.

2. Lyman Tyler, *A History of Indian Policy* (Washington: Government Printing Office, 1973), pp. 18-19; Berkhofer, p. 130.

3. Arrell Morgan Gibson, *The American Indian: Prehistory to the Present* (Lexington, Mass.: D.C. Heath and Company, 1980), p. 241; Tyler, pp. 30-31.

4. William M. Denevan, ed., *The Native Population of the Americas in 1492* (Madison: University of Wisconsin Press, 1976), pp. xvii-xix, 1-7; Wilbur R. Jacobs, "The Tip of an Iceberg: Pre-Columbian Indian Demography and Some Implications for Revisionism," *William and Mary Quarterly,* 3rd Ser., 31 (January 1974): 123-132; William H. McNeill, *Plagues and Peoples* (Garden City, N.Y.: Anchor Press/Doubleday, 1976), pp. 1-14, 199-234.

5. The colonial records of South Carolina are filled with references to the evil effects of liquor on the Indians, of its value as a legal and illegal trade item, and of the Indians' demand for it; for selected examples, see William L. McDowell, Jr., ed., *Documents Relating to Indian Affairs, 1754-1965: Colonial Records of South Carolina* (Columbia: South Carolina Department of Archives and History, 1970), pp. 105, 149, 160-161, 296.

6. Alfred W. Crosby, "Virgin Soil Epidemics as a Factor in the Aboriginal Depopulation in America," *William and Mary Quarterly,* 3rd Ser., 33 (April 1976): 289-290.

7. Denevan, pp. 4-5; John Duffy, "Smallpox and the Indians of the American Colonies," *Bulletin of the History of Medicine* 25 (1951): 335, 338.

8. Quoted in Lewis Hanke, "The Theological Significance of the Discovery of America," in *First Images of America,* eds. Fredi Chiapelli, Michael J. B. Allen, and Robert L. Benson, 2 vols. (Berkeley: University of California Press, 1976), I: 368.

9. The best studies of this topic are Edward Dudley and Maximilien Novak, eds., *The Wild Man Within* (Pittsburgh: University of Pittsburgh Press, 1972); and Richard Bernheimer, *Wild Men in the Middle Ages* (Cambridge: Harvard University Press, 1952).

10. Gary B. Nash, *Red, White, and Black: The Peoples of Early America* (Englewood Cliffs: Prentice-Hall, Inc., 1974), pp. xiv-xv, 34-40, 61-63; David Bidney, "The Idea of the Savage in North American Ethnohistory," *Journal of the History of Ideas* 15 (January 1954): 324-325.

11. Winthrop Jordan, *White over Black* (Chapel Hill: University of North Carolina Press, 1968), p. 86.

12. Ibid, p. 89.

13. Roy Harvey Pearce, *The Savages of America* (Baltimore: Johns Hopkins University Press, 1953), pp. 3-4; Bidney, p. 322.

14. Pearce, p. 5.

15. Peter Loewenberg, "The Psychology of Racism," in Gary Nash and Richard Weiss, *The Great Fear* (New York: Holt, Rinehart and Winston, Inc., 1970), pp. 191-193.

16. Almon W. Lauber, *Indian Slavery in Colonial Times within the Present Limits of the United States,* Columbia University Studies in History, Economics and Public Law, vol. 54 (New York: Columbia University Press, 1913; reprint ed., Williamston, Mass.: Corner House Publishers, 1970), pp. 106, 173-178; William H. Snell, "Indian

Slavery in Colonial South Carolina, 1671-1795" (Ph. D. dissertation, University of Alabama, 1972) pp. 34-36.

17. David Ramsay, *The History of South Carolina, from its First Settlement in 1670, to the Year 1808,* 2 vols. (Newberry, S.C.: W.J. Duffie, 1858), I: 86.

18. Verner W. Crane, *The Southern Frontier, 1670-1732* (Ann Arbor: University of Michigan Press, 1929), pp. 22-23.

19. For examples of the kinds of statutes passed, see Thomas Cooper and David J. McCord, eds., *The Statutes at Large of South Carolina,* 10 vols. (Columbia: A.S. Johnston, 1836-1841), 2: 274, 309-316.

20. McDowell, *Indian Documents, 1754-1765,* p. 332.

21. Edgar Legare Pennington, "The S.P.G. Anniversary Sermons, 1702-1783," *Historical Magazine of the Protestant Episcopal Church* 20 (March 1951): 12.

22. For a controversial, polemical, and thoughtful examination of the issue of civilization versus savagery, see Francis Jennings, *The Invasion of America* (Chapel Hill: University of North Carolina Press, 1975), pp. vil-x, 3-14, 43-57.

23. John Lawson, *A New Voyage to Carolina,* ed. Hugh T. Lefler (Chapel Hill: University of North Carolina Press, 1967), pp. 26, 243.

24. Ibid., pp. 244-246.

25. Hayden White, "The Noble Savage," in Chiapelli, *First Images,* I: 124-125, 129-133.

Part Two
Spatial Awareness and Organization of the Land

Chapter 4

Sharing the Land: A Study in American Indian Territoriality

Patricia Albers
and
Jeanne Kay

American Indian territorial systems and use of territory in historic times have been studied from two separate but related perspectives. On the one hand, scholars have examined the meanings which tribes attached to their lands, and the beliefs through which they organized the use of a given territory as an expression of their political and economic systems. On the other hand, they have investigated the spatial patterns of occupance, such as the locations of settlements and sites for hunting, fishing, gathering or farming. Both of these approaches have raised essential geographic questions about relationships between historic Indian populations and the landscapes in which they lived, worked and traveled.

One important question is the extent to which the historical locations of Indian settlements and subsistence sites nest within the boundaries of a group's territory, as defined by group members themselves. In other words, did a group's political and ideological claims to a territory overlap with the geographic distribution of lands actually utilized by that group? Conventionally, at least, the answer given by most scholars has affirmed that a group's own definition of its territorial boundaries neatly corresponded with the locations of its settlements and subsistence sites. With some notable exceptions, most scholars have depicted traditional American Indian territories as discrete segments of the North

American landscape. Maps of pre-reservation Indian lands resemble maps of European nations, where large regions are divided into contiguous pieces of an ethnic jigsaw puzzle, with little overlapping territory (Fig. 4.1). Generally speaking, scholars have treated native territories as attributes of single Indian populations, whether tribe, bands, villages, or family hunting parties. The uncritical portrayal of Indian territories as the exclusive domains of single populations, however, can obscure the cultural diversity of their actual users or occupants, and the conditions which often promoted intergroup access to sites and resources.

When one looks at the historical record from a regional, rather than a group perspective, the picture that emerges is different

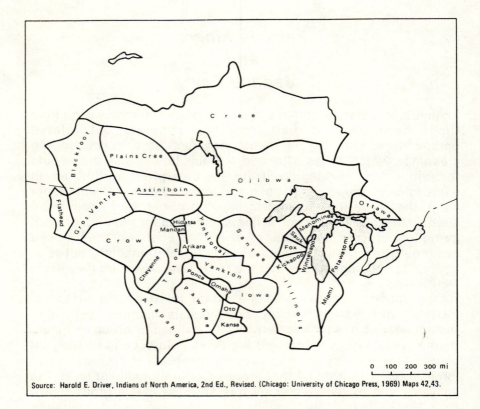

Source: Harold E. Driver, Indians of North America, 2nd Ed., Revised. (Chicago: University of Chicago Press, 1969) Maps 42,43.

Figure 4.1. Tribal Territoriality: Typical Mapping Procedure Implying A Nation-State Model.

from the standard nation-state model of Indian territoriality. Long-term patterns of intergroup "sharing" of lands and resources appear to have been widespread.[1] Although many examples of joint territorial use were of short duration, others were based on stable relationships lasting over a century. And while many areas of the North American landscape were utilized primarily by the people of one group, there were large regions where territorial sharing by members of different groups was the rule, rather than the exception.

Using a regional perspective, this chapter compares the concept of American Indian lands as exclusively claimed and defended territories with historical data on the actual geographic distributions of various Indian populations. In particular, it focuses on empirical examples of territorial sharing by members of different tribes from the western Great Lakes and northern Plains (Fig. 4.1.) before reservations and removals, and examines some of the various factors, such as kinship, which made this sharing possible across large geographic areas.[2] A final discussion concerns theoretical and pragmatic implications of land and resources sharing for conventional understandings of the relationship between tribes and their territories.

TERRITORIALITY AND THE CONCEPT OF TRIBE

The expression "tribe" has appeared widely in journalistic and scholarly writings on the American Indian. From initial European contact through the nineteenth century, the word *tribe* in primary sources was often used synonymously with "nation."[3] Like nation-states, tribes were viewed, at least abstractly, as distinct political entities with separate and clearly-defined territories. In the twentieth century, with the rise of anthropological, historical and geographic research on American Indians, the concept of tribe has been employed in a variety of ways. In most standard interpretations, however, a tribe is an ethnically homogeneous group which corresponds with any one or more of the following: a separate territory, a distinct language, a self-contained breeding pool, a self-sufficient economy, an exclusive sociopolitical body, a unique culture, and even a peculiar personality configuration. Regardless of a tribe's identifying characteristics, it generally has been treated as an independently functioning and evolving system.[4] During the past twenty years, conventional understandings of the tribe have come under attack within the discipline of anthropology because of inconsistencies in its meaning and usage.[5] Yet, in its most basic sense, the term tribe refers to nothing more than an ethnic name.

Over the past twenty years, scholars of the American Indian have given increasing attention to relationships between members of different tribal groups. In addition to a large literature on hostile and competitive relations, there is a growing body of writing on peaceful forms of interaction as well.[6] Much has focused on native trading systems and military alliances.[7] However, there has also been an interest in intertribal relations based on kinship and co-residency.[8] The evidence from these studies suggests that although American Indian populations maintained distinct ethnic identities, unique culture patterns, and even differentiated sociopolitical structures, they did so while embedded in geographically far-ranging and ethnically-mixed systems.[9] These systems are regional in character, and as William Elmendorf put it, "relations between different ethnic groups and those internal to each group are mutually interdependent."[10]

The growing recognition that American Indian populations were nested in regional systems raises some important issues about the relationship between tribal identities and territoriality. Did tribal allegiances assume primary importance in monitoring relationships to lands and resources? Or did other allegiances, such as kinship, assume equal significance in defining these relationships, such that rights to occupy and use a given area of land were extended to members of different tribes?

In prevailing views, scholars have assumed that the people who identified with the same tribe, and who were so identified by others, maintained exclusive territorial rights. There is, then, an implicit assumption that a shared tribal identity is also associated with a shared and clearly-bounded territory. This assumption, however, is open to debate. It is not — in any inevitable sense — an empirical fact, but a testable proposition that must be examined against the ethnohistoric record for specific geographic regions. If it cannot be assumed, *a priori,* that tribal names are associated with sociopolitical groups that determine territorial boundaries, then we must ask who are the people, or who are the groups, that manage and negotiate land-use rights?

There is widespread agreement that the primary territorial allegiances of American Indian populations were localized in pre-reservation times, and that rights to use and manage a given territory were vested primarily in the band or village population who habitually lived in that area. There is less consensus, however, in the extent to which sociopolitical institutions beyond bands and villages monitored land-use. Much of this lack of consensus relates to variations in native sociopolitical organizations. Whereas band-type societies, such as the Comanche or Ojibway, lacked highly developed sociopolitical structures beyond the band level, tribal-type societies had superordinate institutions which organized relationships between members of localized, band or village groupings.

Among many of the nomadic populations on the Plains, for example, there were tribal councils made up of leaders from different bands. The councils met in association with specific activities, such as the Sun Dance and the summer buffalo hunt. During these gatherings, the bands in attendance reached mutual decisions on a variety of matters including war, trade, and territorial movements, and all of those present were bound, at least theoretically, to the interests of the collectivity.[11] The composition of the bands who were represented at a particular council varied from one situation to another and over time. Among many of the larger populations on the Plains, such as the Cree, Assiniboin, Dakota, Crow, and Blackfeet, the entire body of a tribe rarely, if ever, came together to make joint decisions in council. It is important to note as well that members of one tribe could join in the council of another and become party to the decisions reached by members of a different ethnic group. Thus, people who had the same tribal identity did not always share the same political, economic, or territorial interests. Indeed, in some cases, they had more in common with neighbors from other tribal groups than with the members of their own tribe. Thus, while many American Indian populations in the northern Plains, and western Great Lakes as well, had superordinate, centralizing institutions characteristic of tribal-type social organizations, the workings of these institutions did not necessarily have to be structured along single tribal (ethnic) lines.

It is important to emphasize here that sociopolitical and economic institutions can have an existence that is independent of the tribal identities of the people who participate in them. To be sure, all institutions take on unique expressions among particular tribal groups. Even so, these institutions can still derive much of their meaning and support from a field of relationship that is regionally integrated and tribally mixed.[12] In this context, we postulate institutions governing land-use, including kinship, that have properties extending beyond the boundaries of single tribes. That this may be the case is revealed by two separate but related kinds of data.

On the one hand, a rich body of data reveals that certain areas of the northern Plains and western Great Lakes were jointly occupied and used by members of more than one tribe for long periods of time. While some of this "sharing" took place by invitation in a context where the boundaries of tribal territories were clearly established, other cases indicate that such boundaries were either ambiguous or non-existent. In either situation, the evidence from these regions indicates that when lands were jointly utilized in a peaceful fashion, there were extensive kinship ties connecting the involved groups.

On the other hand, there is the information based on the ideological claims that different tribes have asserted over specific geographic areas. In the western Great Lakes and northern Plains, there are many geographic areas where more than one tribe has had an historic claim during the same period of time. A comparison of maps of historic tribal lands as identified in the ethnohistories and ethnographies of peaceful neighboring groups reveals contemporaneous areas of overlap, and a review of historical as well as ethnographic descriptions of tribal boundaries often yields the same conclusion. Most ethnohistorians are well aware of the problem of overlapping tribal claims to specific regions but have usually viewed its resolution in terms of advancing the legitimacy of one tribe's claims over those of another. While it has been acknowledged by some scholars that more than one tribe can have a rightful claim to a region through a history of joint use and occupancy, the theoretical and methodological implications of this have not been fully explored.

Since the social systems of American Indians have been studied primarily from the perspective of single tribes, it is not surprising that scholars have often assumed that the ethnic allegiances of a people overlap the "societies" or "communities" they live under. Nor is it fortuitous that they have also presumed that these allegiances correspond in a one-to-one fashion with the "ownership" and use of discrete areas of geographic space. Whether or not tribal separateness has been viewed as a *prima facie* reality, it has established, nonetheless, the boundaries of much scholarly inquiry on American Indian territoriality. Through a tribal lens, problems have focused, data have filtered, and results have been framed. Thus, in the fashion of a self-fulfilling prophecy, scholars have seen native land-rights and patterns of land-use primarily in tribal terms. By taking what Carol Smith has aptly called "a worm's-eye rather than a bird's-eye view" of their subject, scholars have been unable to determine whether or not institutions exist beyond tribal boundaries that also manage land-use and occupancy.[13]

In order to understand American Indian territoriality it is

necessary to look at land-use from a regional rather than tribally-biased perspective, and to distinguish between ideological claim to and the actual use of a specific territory. In such an approach, the focus of research becomes a geographic region within which the actual locations and uses of the area by various groups are documented and compared against the territorial claims of these groups. In areas which have a history of multiple tribal use, the conditions of "sharing" must be analyzed to determine what kinds of land-claims members of different tribes hold and on what basis these rights are being asserted. What are the sociopolitical bodies which hold land in common and are these groups always organized along single tribal lines? Can relationships, then, such as those based on kinship, manage land-rights independent of tribal allegiances?

The ways in which American Indian populations conceptualized their territorial claims is not fully understood. Aside from variations in territorial concepts and their application over time and across geographic areas, there are disagreements among scholars on how to interpret these ideas. Among publications on historical Indian territorial systems, Wallace's remains a classic summary for tribes of the northeastern United States.[14] Through an examination of historical records, he argued that Indians recognized unambiguous boundaries to their tribal lands. Right of conquest or legendary affiliations legitimized a tribe's claim to a particular territory. Tribal lands were held in common by members of a tribe, rather than in severalty, but their concepts of ownership most closely resembled the European idea of usufruct. Members of another tribe could use a given tribe's land through invitation, however. Wallace provided examples of some longstanding invitations, where members of one tribe occupied a portion of another's land over a period of several decades. Without invitation, intrusion of members of one tribe onto lands claimed by another was regarded as aggression, and warfare often followed. He essentially described a nation-state model of tribal territoriality, modified by the concept of "sharing by invitation" of land between different tribes.

In much of the northern Plains, by contrast, territorial boundaries were less rigidly fixed. Daniel Harmon, a resident in the prairies and parklands of Canada, argued:[15]

> Every tribe has its particular tract of country; and this is divided again, among the several families which compose the tribe. Rivers, lakes and mountains, serve them as boundaries; and the limits of the territory which belongs to each family are well known by the

tribe, as the lines which separate farms are, by the
farmers in the civilized world. The Indians who reside
in the large plains, make no sub-divisions of their
territory, for the wealth of their country consists of
buffaloes and wolves, which exist in plenty everywhere
among them. But the case is otherwise with the
inhabitants of the woody countries.

The lack of fixed and rigid territorial boundaries was also noted
by Joshua Pilcher, an early trader and government agent on the
upper Missouri.[16] In one of his many comments on the subject,
Pilcher described the territorial ranges of various tribes along the
Upper Missouri and wrote: "But it is difficult to point out the exact
limits of any of these wandering tribes, because they observe none
themselves."[17] A similar position is echoed in the words of John
Ewers who remarked:[18]

Whether a tribe was at war or peace with its neighbor
certainly was reflected in the territorial spacing of
tribes. There was little need for tribal boundaries
between allied tribes, but it was common for an area
of marginal or debatable land to separate hostile tribes
— lands in which they passed en route to make raids
on enemy camps.

In the northern Plains, an aboriginal territory included the entire
expanse of land and waterways that a given population utilized.
Access to territory was not conceptualized as a property
relationship to which individuals or groups had inalienable and
private rights. No one "owned" the territorial range they covered
nor the natural resources that this area contained. Although the
notion of possession in relation to land and water was an alien
idea, groups did have a concept of usufruct. Local populations who
customarily occupied and traveled a given area became identified
with that region and its use. The persistent utilization of an area
by one population, however, did not exclude outsiders from coming
into the region to use it temporarily or on a more permanent basis.[19]
When groups were military allies and related to each other through
extensive kinship ties, they shared access to the use of a
commonly-held territorial range. As Father Belcourt wrote during
the 1830s, "The Crees and Assiniboins regard themselves as
equally masters of these lands with the Chippewas, having
acquired them jointly with the latter, at the expense of their
blood."[20] In the northern Plains territorial associations were not
concretized and marked in a clear-cut way until tribes entered into
treaty relationships with the United States and Canadian
governments.[21] There were no lines drawn across the prairies which

delineated where one area of aboriginal occupation began and another ended. However, there were social relationships which stipulated how groups would separately or jointly occupy a given landscape.

In the western Great Lakes, the conceptualization of territorial boundaries and claims appears to have been variable. Whereas some sources report territorial associations of the kind described by Wallace for the Northeast, others like an Indian factor from eastern Wisconsin reported:[22]

> It is difficult to ascertain the definite boundaries of different Indian tribes, living within a few miles of each other. The Indians themselves give vague and unsatisfactory accounts of their own boundaries, and so do some intelligent traders; who have been, from twenty to thirty years, trading with them.

To what extent the differences in interpretation of the rigidness of territorial boundaries and claims are the result of observer bias, cultural variations, or changing historical conditions is difficult to determine. However, in a discussion of Santee Dakota, Claude Stipe noted that notions of territorial exclusiveness became more pronounced over time, first in terms of trapping areas (a pattern following the impact of the fur-trade elsewhere) and second in relation to lands claimed in treaty negotiations with the United States government.[23]

Recently, Hardesty and Gold have pointed out severe limitations of our knowledge of territorial beliefs among American Indians.[24] The European-American notion of territoriality as "any form of behavior displayed by individuals and groups seeking to establish, maintain or defend specific bounded portions of space . . . as a fundamental expression of social organization," may not apply to systems developed by quite different cultures to conceptualize and occupy the landscape.[25] Hardesty probed the issue further:[26]

> Even if a habitat or resource is 'owned,' boundaries are sometimes crossed with ease by other groups. Social relationships between groups are such that some groups interact more frequently and more intensely than others. Such groups are separated by 'loose' social boundaries and members may be frequently exchanged, either for purposes of marriage, visits, cooperation in subsistence activities or for a variety of other reasons. As long as the social boundaries between groups are loose, 'owned' physical space becomes more a theoretical concept than an expression of actual behavior. Consequently,

resources or land belonging to one group can be used
by others if the social relationships are sufficiently
close to make the outsiders practicing, if not actual,
members of the group. Of course, social boundaries
may change and groups that are the same physical
distance apart may feel that they belong to the same
group at one time and very different groups at other
times.

Hardesty's point is well-taken, for what distinguished and
separated the *actual* land-use of various groups was not some
abstract territorial claim or boundary across the landscape, but
rather the relationships among groups who lived in proximity to
each other.

The character of these relationships ranged from hostility and
war, to trade and symbiosis, and to sharing and merger.[27] As these
relationships changed, so did the character of the territorial
boundaries separating neighboring groups. During the 1680s, when
portions of the southwestern Chippewa and Santee Dakota were
trade partners, some Chippewa were given permission to hunt
and settle on Dakota lands. In later years, however, competition
between these Chippewa and Dakota resulted in prolonged warfare
along a bitterly contested border.[28] The buffer zone that developed
along this border, while off-limits to the hostile Dakota and
Chippewa, became a hunting area for the politically neutral
Menominee who traveled long distances from their own customary
territories to utilize this area.[29] In general, territorial boundaries
became much more heightened and clearly delineated when groups
were at war. However, when groups stood in a peaceful, symbiotic
relationship with each other, they often recognized the existence of
tribally distinct territories, but utilized each others lands
through invitation or other mechanisms. Yet, in another kind
of peaceful situation, members of distinct tribes could utilize a
specific geographic area jointly without a sense of exclusive
"ownership" by any one group. Thus, when segments of the Cree
and Assiniboin, described by Sharrock, became amalgamated into
a single sociopolitical body, members of the two groups hunted
and lived together with little conflict and in areas where territorial
boundaries (if these existed at all) were highly permeable.[30]

Although most scholars recognize that territorial associations
among American Indians were complex and variable, there is still
a need for more studies which analyze the extent to which, and the
conditions under which, Indians of different tribal affiliations
shared each other's land and resources: their villages, hunting
grounds, fishing spots, mineral diggings, and trade entrepots.

There is also a need to examine more carefully the social relationships under which this sharing took place, and particularly the role that kinship played in organizing land-use. In the remaining portions of this chapter, we examine some of the factors, particularly kinship, that influenced the joint use of lands by different tribal groups.

The following discussion, based on evidence drawn for the western Great Lakes and northern Plains, is programmatic. It draws attention to examples of territorial "sharing" which are suggestive of wider trends in these two regions. The ethnohistoric information that is presented is not exhaustive of the available sources on this subject, nor is the analysis of the data fully developed theoretically. The need for a broad and unified theoretical framework in which varied relations between members of different tribal groups are understood as interdependent facets of geographically far-ranging and ethnically-mixed systems still awaits further development.

THE WESTERN GREAT LAKES

The years 1620-1830 roughly and generously span the period before Indians were alienated by the American government from their tribal domains in the region west of Lake Michigan. Historical documents of that period, summarized below, contain numerous references to individuals of more than one tribe inhabiting the same village and peaceably hunting long distances from their generally acknowledged tribal lands. During the nineteenth century, the frequency of observations of jointly occupied villages along the west coast of Lake Michigan and the current Wisconsin-Illinois border suggest that sharing of villages was the norm in those areas. Some of the examples of shared villages and hunting grounds support Wallace's model of "sharing by invitation" by tribes with a generally acknowledged claim to the territory jointly occupied.[31] Other examples do not fit this model as well; as, for example, when land vacated by an emigrant or depopulated tribe was re-occupied by mixed villages or when small tribes actually merged with larger ones.

Joint residency and use of particular places relate to a variety of factors, further suggesting that cooperative territorial occupancy cut across ethnic, social, and environmental boundaries. One of the most important factors triggering co-residency appeared to be self-defense in time of warfare, particularly following the devastating Iroquois Wars of the seventeenth century. However, members of different tribes also shared sites in peace time throughout the study period, for reasons of trade, ceremonial participation, and subsistence. This section reviews the kinds of territorial sharing which occurred west of Lake Michigan, organized according to their apparent explanations.

Much of the sharing of land, resources, and settlements in the western Great Lakes area related to populations which were disadvantaged militarily. Before 1700, many tribes of the eastern Great Lakes left their homelands because of Iroquois attacks. Examples of the migrant tribes include the Miami, Kickapoo, and Mascouten, who shared a large village west of Green Bay by 1668; and the Fox, who lived among Sauk, Potawatomi, Winnebago, Mascouten, and Kickapoo in settlements at Green Bay and Milwaukee.[32]

The region's resident tribes were similarly affected by warfare with new and old neighbors. The Illinois confederation and the Winnebago were reported devastated by warfare, and subsequently shared villages with neighboring tribes.[33] When the French destroyed the Winnebago's village in 1721, the tribe temporarily migrated to the Mississippi River, where they hunted with the Sioux.[34] The firm alliance of the Sauk and Fox began in the 1730s in response to the latter's defeat in the Fox Wars. Black Hawk explained:[35]

> ... they held a council and a national treaty of
> friendship and alliance was concluded upon ... The
> Foxes abandoned their village and joined the Sacs.
> This arrangement being mutually obligatory upon both
> parties, as neither were sufficiently strong to meet
> their enemies with any hope of success, they soon
> became as one band or nation of people.

The two tribes subsequently established separate villages and retained their identity, but their close cooperation and sharing of land and resources continued for over a century.[36]

Small-sized populations or population declines clearly influenced mergers and joint use of territory in the Lake Superior region. The Noquets were a small "nation" of Michigan's upper peninsula who were almost destroyed by the Iroquois in 1668 and who disappeared from the published records after 1721. Hickerson's argument that they and other tribelets of Lake Superior were proto-Chippewa clans is compelling on linguistic grounds.[37] However, contemporary writers described the Noquets as a small tribe, degraded and incorporated with several others, such as the

Menominee.[38] Hickerson identified the Amikwa of Lake Superior as the Beaver clan of Chippewa, but concluded that some Amikwa also incorporated with the Missisauga, Nipissing, and perhaps Ottawa.[39] Similar examples are the reduction and amalgamation of the Kaskaskia-Tamaroa-Michigamea and of the Cahokia-Peoria, into the Illinois tribe. The Mascouten incorporated into the Kickapoo tribe in Indiana by the late eighteenth century.[40]

The impacts of the Iroquois Wars and European disease-related depopulation were important causes of mixed villages in the seventeenth century. The subsequent Fox Wars produced some of the same effects. It would be a mistake, however, to view co-residency by members of different tribes as only a temporary defense against a few devastating historical events. Sharing of villages and resources occurred during peaceful times, as well, and over more years than the duration of intense conflicts. Even during stressful war times, members of various tribes shared villages and resources for reasons having more to do with ceremonial, subsistence, or trading activities than for mutual self defense. Moreover, Kay recently showed that tribes who remained in the western Great Lakes area after 1700 actually increased in population and vigor.[41] Therefore, additional explanations of shared territory must be examined.

One reason for Indians of the western Great Lakes interacting across tribal boundaries was to participate in important ceremonies. The Feast of the Dead, described in considerable detail by Hickerson was a major triennial event in which members of various tribes came together to celebrate and establish alliances for trade and military purposes.[42] One Feast of the Dead, for example, held at Chequamegon Point on Lake Superior and reported on by Radisson and des Grosseillers, brought members of a variety of tribes together, including the Chippewa, Sioux, Ottawa, and Huron.[43] While the Feast of the Dead could be termed an infrequent and temporary event, intertribal adoptions were a typical feature of the ceremony, suggesting one vehicle whereby members of one tribe could appear as essentially permanent residents of another tribe's territory. Subsequently, the Medicine Dance was performed and spread in intertribal settings.[44]

Before European fur traders penetrated the interior, a few large, accessible villages became fur trade entrepots, such as Mackinac, Sault Sainte Marie, Chequamegon Point, and Green Bay. Delegations from different tribes would temporarily reside in these villages to conduct their trade. For example, Chequamegon was a site that drew Indians as far distant as the Illinois.[45] The Illinois traded in slaves, indicating another means by which members of one tribe might be found living far distant from their tribal lands. Green Bay was a fur-trade center for temporary as well as permanent multi-ethnic settlements, which included varying combinations of Menominee, Miami, Sauk, Potawatomi, Winnebago, Mascouten, Kickapoo, and Fox.[46] Generally the same groups who traded with each other, and who co-occupied villages on a seasonal as well as more enduring basis, also formed ties for the defense of jointly used sites in the production and exchange of major resources.

The joint use of lands and sites for subsistence, and the presence of tribally-mixed foraging groups, is documented in many primary sources from the seventeenth to nineteenth centuries. For example, when Radisson and des Grosseilliers wintered near Sault Sainte Marie with the Saulters (Chippewa/Ojibwa) in 1660, a Cree hunting party joined them.[47] In the same area, pre-Chippewa peoples joined Ottawa and Huron to fish for whitefish. At Chequamegon Point, and along the Rainy River, Chippewa and Ottawa jointly hunted and fished.[48] According to Hickerson, Chippewa also hunted on Sioux lands at the turn-of-the-eighteenth century.[49] In northern Minnesota and adjoining areas of Ontario, Cree and Assiniboin joined together to hunt, fish and collect wild rice.[50] In the eighteenth century before Sioux-Chippewa hostilities solidified, a variety of Indian groups from Green Bay and Chequamegon travelled long distances to hunt on Sioux lands. The Rock Island Indian Agent, Thomas Forsyth reported the Sauk inviting Kansas Indians to hunt with them north of the Missouri; and the Sauk accepting an invitation from Winnebago of Lake Koshkonong to work their lead mines.[51]

The Menominee shared lands claimed or occupied by other tribes to such an extent that sharing would have to be considered one of their principal economic strategies. During the late seventeenth century, Menominee occupied a mixed village at Green Bay with Potowatomi and Sauk (Sac), and together these groups fished at the mouth of the Fox River.[52] During the eighteenth century, Menominee were reported hunting as far distant from their northeastern Wisconsin homeland as the upper Mississippi. They eventually expanded their hunting grounds into central Minnesota.[53] The politically neutral Menominee were permitted to use Dakota territory and lands contested between ·Dakota and southwestern Chippewa through the 1830s.[54] Some Menominee joined a hunting party of Sauk in 1815; an event which the Sauk chief Black Hawk regarded as so commonplace that he was at a loss to respond when an American questioned his reasons for inviting the Menominee.[55] Mixed villages of Menominee and Chippewa fished through the ice of northern Green Bay for subsistence during the 1820s and 1830s.[56]

Whether different tribes came together for subsistence, ceremony, trade, or defense, there is ample evidence that they lived together for brief or extended periods in common settlements. In 1660, Radisson and des Groseilliers shared the lodge of an "ancient and witty man" of the Menominee who was living at an Ottawa village on a northern Wisconsin Lake.[57] By 1666, these Ottawa had allied with some refugee Petun (Huron) and formed a substantial village on Chequamegon Point. In the same period, Miami, Kickapoo, and Mascouten shared a large village west of Green Bay, and the Fox lived in villages at Green Bay and Milwaukee among the Sauk, Potowatomi, Winnebago, Mascouten, and Kickapoo.[58]

While some early mixed villages may have been temporary arrangements for mutual defense, the same cannot be argued for settlements considered in censuses during the early nineteenth century. For example, the Green Bay Indian Agent in 1817 reported:[59]

> The Chippewas are intermixed with Minominies and Ottawas, it is at present impossible to make a probable estimate of their numbers. They occupy the whole Country from Michillimackinac to the head Waters of the Mississippi River. Numbers visit this Agency in the Spring and fall.
>
> The Indians in the vicinity of Millwakee are composed of Renigadoes from all the tribes around them (viz) The Sacques, Foxes, Chippewas, Minominies, Oattawas, Winabagoes and Potawatamies. Estimated at Three hundred Warriors.

The warrior census conducted for the Green Bay Indian Agency district in 1824 listed 22 settlements, divided among Menominee, Chippewa, and Winnebago, with a few Ottawa and Potawatomi (Table 4.1).[60] Nine of these villages were peopled by members of more than one tribe. Almost half the Indian populations reported for the Green Bay Agency that year lived in mixed villages. A geologist traveling overland from Chicago to Prairie du Chien in 1823 encountered five native settlements of which four had mixed populations.[61] Jonathan Carver reported Cree, Assiniboin, and Chippewa in 1767 living in mixed bands along the Rainy River between Minnesota and Ontario.[62]

Table 4.1

1824: Census Of Wisconsin Indians

INDIAN AGENCY OFFICE GREEN BAY 1st. September 1824
Thomas L. McKenney, Esqur.

SIR-1st. This Agency is located three miles Above Fort Howard on the Fox, and on the opposite shore.

2d. [Adjacent to] Munnoaminees, Winnebagos, Chippewas, Ottawans, and some Putawatimies.

3d. Names of tribes

Courses		distance miles	Indians in Numbr
From Green Bay to Bay de Noque.........................	N.N.W.	120.	
From Green Bay to Little Bay de Noque-Chippeways.......	N.N.W.	100.	50.
From Green Bay to Munnoaminee River Munno and Chippe	North	80.	90.
From Green Bay to Pishetagon River Munno and Chippe	North	45.	50.
From Green Bay to Caunton River Munnoaminees	North	30.	30.
From Green Bay to Goose River Munno and Chippe	N.E.	20.	12.
From Green Bay to Tail point Munno and Chippewa	N.E.	45.	20.
From Green Bay to Sandy point in the Bay Munnoaminees	N.E.	9.	20.
The little Kakalin and No. of Indians in its vicinty Munnoaminees......................................	S.W.	9.	30.
from Green Bay to big Kakalin Munnoaminees	S.W.	18.	30.
from Green bay to the first rappids at the entrance of Winnebago Lake Winneboagos	S.W.	36.	50.
from Green Bay to Garlic Island Winneboagos	S.W.	45.	20.
from Green Bay to Wolf village, and this side of the Butte de Mort Winneboages	S.W.	57.	50.
from Green Bay to Font de Lake Munno and Winneb	S.W.	66.	40.
from Green Bay to Village de Calumet Munnoaminees	South	57.	30.
to Green Bay to Wilf River Mun and Chip	West	100.	100.
from Green Bay to Lake Shawoinon Mun and Chipp	West	75.	60.
from Green Bay to Butte de Mort in Fox River to the Ouisconsin and the Indians in its vicinity Winneboagos	S.W.	114.	120.
from the portage of the Ouisconsin to the upper Ouisconsin Winne and Munno North................		120.	120.
from the portage of the Ouisconsin to Rock River Winneboagos....................................	South	60.	150.
from the portage of Ouisconsin to the Kuskawoinanque great village Winneboagos	South	100.	200.
from Green Bay to Munnetoowock River Ottawaus	South	45.	25.
from Green Bay to Millwackey-North side River Ottaw. Chipp. and the Indians in its vicinity Putawatimies South...		130.	300.
Hunters and Warriours, not including old men............			1627.

Women and children, which may be put down at three times that number, as many of them have two wives.

Source: Reuben Thwaites, ed. "The Fur Trade in Wisconsin, 1812-1825," *Wisconsin Historical Collections,* Vol. 20 (1911), pp. 349-350.

First-hand observers described a few ethnically mixed bands or villages in the western Great Lakes as composed of outcasts from different tribes. Jonathan Carver, in describing his narrow escape from a robbery on the upper Mississippi, wrote that: "The party of Indians who thus intended to plunder me, I afterwards found to be some of those straggling bands, that having been driven from among the different tribes to which they belonged for various crimes, now associated themselves together ... "[63] Milwaukee, in Potawatomi territory, was from its inception a village of many tribes. Its reputation as a village of "renegadoes" suggests that it developed according to Carver's explanation.[64] Whatever the merit of these allegations, the idea of individuals driven from their tribes by social conflict and banding together fits the pattern of mergers caused by warfare and depopulation. In such cases, amalgamation of members of different tribes would be advantageous at the band or village level for defense, cooperative subsistence activities, and social interaction.

Sharing of villages and resources was more common along tribal boundaries than in the heart of tribal lands. For example, Chippewa frequently lived among their Algonquian neighbors in eastern Wisconsin and with their Cree neighbors in western Minnesota, but there are few records of individuals from other tribes residing in Chippewa villages within remote areas of northern Wisconsin. Along territorial boundaries — such as the west shore of Lake Michigan and northern Illinois — jointly occupied villages were the rule, and ethnically separate villages, the exception.[65]

The preceding examples are a small sample of what could be marshalled to support the contention that the geographical boundaries of tribal territories west of Lake Michigan were extremely "loose," and that Indians often resided in or used resources in lands far distant from their tribal homelands. And yet one could also assemble evidence from the region to support the more traditional interpretations of tribes as inhospitable nation-states, jealously maintaining their territorial prerogatives. The Fox Wars, Miami-Potawatomi hostilities, Sioux-Chippewa buffer zone are examples. Ecological, political, and cultural explanations of intertribal partitioning of land and resources are only partly satisfactory, however. Some tribes shared productive game habitats peacefully and other tribes went to war over them. Some intertribal political alliances were of short duration, while others resulted in tribal mergers. By the 1830s, the Siouian Winnebago were generally wary of their former hunting partners, the Siouian Dakota, but the Algonquian Menominee hunted with impunity on the Santee Dakota's choicest wildlife habitat, while maintaining good relationships with the Dakotas' enemies, the Chippewa. The Potawatomi had ousted other tribes as they expanded their territory east and south of Lake Michigan; yet they were peacefully infiltrated by Menominee, Chippewa, Ottawa, Sauk, Fox, and Winnebago people on their northwestern margins.[66]

We argue that the most compelling explanation of intertribal sharing of land and resources is that intertribal kinship ties, through intermarriage and adoptions, were common in the Great Lakes region. The logical corollary would be that lack of extensive kinship networks discouraged, though did not necessarily preclude, intertribal sharing.

In the western Great Lakes, intermarriage was a common occurrence. A fur trader in 1795 described Milwaukee's population as: "a large number of Pottawattomies, but mingling freely with them were Sacs and Foxes, and a few Winnebagoes who had married into the other three tribes."[67] Another trader noted: "The Menomonees had continually many Chippewas mixed up with them, and frequent intermarriages occurred; the Winnebagoes, in the earlier days, were tabooed from select Menomonee society."[68] A geologist in 1823 noted Menominees living in territory claimed by the Potawatomi, but explained, "The Menomonees are allowed to remain there, on account for their being connected by intermarriages."[69]

Intermarriages also took place between tribes who were not previously on friendly footing, and they were used to promote trade and military alliance. A seventeenth century French writer, before Sioux-Chippewa enmity, stated that the two tribes formed an economic alliance. The Chippewa requested permission to hunt on Sioux lands, and the Sioux desired trade goods from Chippewa middlemen. To seal this relationship, they agreed to exchange young women for marriage partners. The Winnebago with the Potawatomi, Sauk, and Fox subsequently acknowledged the cession of their hostilities with an exchange of brides.[70]

Adoption of prisoners of war was commonly practiced.[71] Not only did it serve as a means to augment tribal strength, but it created kinship connections between enemy tribes. Such links were used to facilitate moves to peaceful relationships. Raudot, a French observer of western Great Lakes tribes in 1709, commented: "When they adopt the slaves that they have taken, which they do not fail to do when they have lost many people, they make them come into their cabins, regard them as being one of their nation."[72] Raudot also wrote that in addition to adoptees used to replace the dead,

prisoners of war were sometimes exchanged with yet other tribes
in order to forge new political alliances.

Adoptions also occurred between friendly groups and often took
place at the Feasts of the Dead. Indeed, intertribal adoptions were
so common that one observer of the Sauk and Fox in the 1820s
estimated the number of Sauk warriors at 1,000, but thought that
only 200 were of pure Sauk ancestry. The others were products of
adoptions into the tribe.[73]

The connection between intertribal kinship ties and access to
resources is clear. Individuals who married or were adopted into
another tribe had access to their families' villages and hunting
grounds. Jedediah Morse, in concluding an interview with
Chippewa men from northeastern Wisconsin, commented (1822):[74]

> The Chippawas and Oattawas, who possess and
> inhabit the country we have been describing, in many
> parts of it, hold their lands in common, hunt together,
> intermarry, understand each the language of the other,
> there being but little difference between their
> languages, and may be considered, as to all purposes
> and measures relating to their civilization, as one
> people.

Marston, commanding officer of a fort near the Sauk and Fox
villages, stated :[75]

> The Sauk and Fox nations ... are so much mixed
> by intermarriage, and living at each others villages, it
> would be difficult to ascertain the proportion of each
> with any great precision.

Finally, intermarriage explains the Menominees' distant hunting
trips and residences:[76]

> Judge Reaume, an Indian Trader, who has resided at
> Green Bay thirty years, said to me — "The
> Menominees, in great part, are of mixed blood,
> Ottawas, Chippawas, Pottawattamies, Sacs, and
> Foxes, with whom they intermarry. There is an intimate
> intercourse between all these tribes, who have a
> common language (the Chippawa) which they all
> understand, and many of them hunt together in the
> interior of the N.W. Territory, on the head waters of the
> Fox and Ouisconsin rivers."

Intermarriage and intertribal adoptions probably most commonly
affected only the kinfolk of an intermarried couple. They would have
had access to resources of their relations living across tribal
boundaries. Access to agricultural fields, fishing sites and hunting

grounds were allocated at the village level, so intertribal sharing probably operated most often at the level of extended families, rather than bands or entire tribes. For example, the Winnebago village of Koshkonong had many inter-married Sauk among its population.[77] It was this village which issued an invitation to the Sauk to work their lead mine. Probably this invitation extended not to the entire Sauk tribe, but to the kinfolk of the mixed families. (A general invitation would only further suggest the efficacy intertribal kinship networks in facilitating resource sharing and amicable intertribal relationships.)

Instances of inter-familial sharing across tribal boundaries should not be regarded as isolated cases, however, because of the frequency of mixed villages west of Lake Michigan. For example, if the Menominee "tribe," although primarily full-blooded Indians, were not full-blooded Menominee, the extent of their intertribal kinship ties and access to resources must have been extensive, indeed. Records of their hunting destinations throughout the region support this conclusion. In contrast, the Winnebago were considered by their neighbors to be an aloof, even untrustworthy tribe, who did not intermarry with the Menominee in early years. There are correspondingly few records of territorial sharing among these two tribes, although seventeenth century Winnebago were reported as hunting with the Sioux (with whom they intermarried) and as sharing their lead mines in the nineteenth century with the Sauk (with whom they also intermarried). Paradoxically, the Menominee and Winnebago considered their tribes as *political* bodies to have friendly relations. By the nineteenth century, Wisconsin's Chippewa were considered to be at war with the eastern Dakota, and as having uneasy political relationships with the Winnebago. However, Chippewa shared villages, hunting grounds, and fishing sites with Menominee and Ottawa; with corresponding contemporaneous descriptions of extensive intermarriage between Chippewa and members of the latter two tribes.

Beyond established kinship networks, western Great Lakes tribes were generally in communication with one another. Chippewa was a widely used second language throughout the region in the nineteenth century.[78] Indians appeared to have traveled long distances to meet with members of other tribes. Schoolcraft summarized the conditions which made extensive kinship ties and joint occupancy of territory a logical corollary:[79]

> The several tribes within the region of the upper lakes
> have a free and ready communication with each other.

Affiliated by the ties of the common original language [Algonkian], throwing out the Wyandots [Huron] and Winnebagoes [Siouian] by long established customs, and the facilities of a wide reaching intercourse by water, they are well advised to each others affairs, and keep up a verbal correspondence by persons passing to and fro. The circle of this correspondence is irrespective of political boundaries, and extends wherever the tribes are actually located. Their sympathies and feelings are united on all general questions.

THE NORTHERN PLAINS

The kinds of territorial sharing and intertribal relations described for the western Great Lakes were also reported in the northern Plains from the seventeenth through nineteenth centuries. In this region, members of different tribal groups lived together, shared the use of common territories, and participated in joint subsistence, ceremonial, trading, and raiding activities. The character of alliances between segments of different tribes, and the conditions under which they emerged, were highly variable. And while some examples of shared settlements and subsistence areas were clearly a response to the displacements and migrations of tribes resulting from war, especially the prolonged expansionary thrust of the Dakota into a wide area of the Plains, others took place in a general climate of peace where there was little threat to the territorial integrity of local groups.[80]

The best reported example of joint territorial occupancy among Plains Indian populations involves the Cree, Assiniboin, Chippewa, Saulteux, and Metis. The pioneering works of Arthur Ray and Susan Sharrock have made available a well-documented record of multi-tribal land-use over a vast territorial range which extended from the Red River west to the South Branch of the Saskatchewan River and from the Missouri River north to the aspen-parkland belt of Manitoba and Saskatchewan.[81]

In the eastern portions of this territorial range, which includes southern Manitoba and adjoining areas of North Dakota, there is an uninterrupted history of joint land-use and occupancy from prehistoric times to the beginnings of the reservation era. According to Leigh Syms, archaeological evidence suggests that southwestern Manitoba was occupied co-terminously by a number of different cultural groups, some of whom appear to have intermarried and even lived together.[82] During the first century of European contact there are numerous references to resident Cree and Assiniboin living in the same camps, hunting together, and covering the same territorial range (Fig. 4.2).[83] In addition, the two groups formed joint war parties and traveled together on trading expeditions to the horticultural villages on the Missouri River as well as to European posts on the Red, Pembina and Assiniboin Rivers.[84]

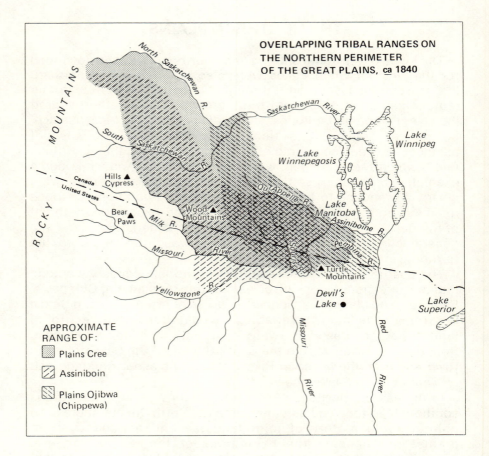

Figure 4.2. Overlapping Tribal Ranges on the Northern Perimeter of the Great Plains, ca. 1840.

By the turn of the nineteenth century, migrating bands of Chippewa, Saulteux, and Ottawa added to the ethnic complexity of the region. Not only did these newly arrived groups intermarry and live together, but they also formed close alliances with the region's indigenous Assiniboin and Cree.[85] The narrative of John Tanner, a white captive among an Ottawa band who migrated into the area, frequently mentioned the intermingling of ethnically diverse Indian groups:[86]

> The people that remained to spend the winter with us were two lodges, our own making three; but we were at length joined by four lodges of Crees. These people are relations of the Ojibbeways and Ottawwaws ... (sic) Their country borders upon that of the Assiniboins, or Stone Roasters; and though they are not relations, nor natural allies, they are sometimes at peace, and more or less intermixed with each other.

In the decades after 1830 most of the Assiniboin and Cree in the United States were concentrated in areas west of the Turtle Mountains.[87] Nonetheless, as late as 1849, buffalo hunting parties consisting of Chippewa, Metis, Assiniboin, and Cree continued to be reported on the eastern prairies of North Dakota.[88] These ethnically-mixed hunting groups emerged not only for defensive reasons (i.e., because the hunts sometimes brought them in contact with their Dakota enemies), but also for ecological ones. The distribution and changing patterns of buffalo migrations in the region created situations where ethnically diverse groups had to join together in hunting certain herds, or forego their dependence on the animal. Of course, these groups could have competed with each other over access to the dwindling buffalo population, but the historical record indicates that they did not.

Moving further west to an area which stretched from the Souris River west to the Wood Mountains, and from the Missouri to the Qu'Apelle River, the pattern of ethnic diversity in land-use and social organization was repeated. During the first half of the nineteenth century, the ethnohistoric record is filled with references to Assiniboin, Cree, and Chippewa covering the same territory, hunting buffalo together, allying in war, living in the same encampments, and traveling in joint trading parties to posts on the Missouri, Assiniboin, Qu'Apelle and Saskatchewan Rivers.[89]

The Wood Mountain region, along the Montana-Saskatchewan border, represented a classic example of an area with multi-ethnic occupancy. From 1820-1840, it was repeatedly referred to as a winter campsite for bands of Cree, Assiniboin, and Chippewa.[90]

Mixed parties of Cree and Assiniboin, who wintered at Wood Mountain regularly traveled to Fort Union to trade.[91] In subsequent decades, as the herds of buffalo retreated west, the Cypress Hills became another favorite wintering spot for Metis, Cree, Chippewa, and Assiniboin, and it was also an area where joint raiding and buffalo hunting parties were formed in the summer.[92]

As in the western Great Lakes, the joint use of lands took place most visibly along the territorial borders of single ethnic groups. Thus, in the extreme north where the prairie met the aspen-parkland belt, the Cree were the largest population with small bands of Assiniboin and Saulteux scattered in their midst. Conversely, along the Missouri and in areas to the south, the Assiniboin were dominant although Cree and Chippewa were present in smaller numbers as well. Nevertheless, there was a vast territory, which followed the 49th parallel from the Turtle Mountains to the Cypress Hills, that was used by all three populations as well as by growing concentrations of Metis. Including areas within the United States as well as Canada, this was the region where frequent references to ethnically-mixed residence groups appear. It was also this region that gave rise to the formation of a new ethnic group, the Cree-Assiniboin. First reported by Alexander Henry in 1811, this ethnically mixed population was described in the literature as a population distinct from either the Cree or the Assiniboin.[93] Among the Assiniboin, these amalgamated bands were known as the *sahiyaiyeskabi* or Cree-Talkers, and among the Cree, they were called *Niopwatuk,* or Young Dogs.[94]

The fusion of segments of the Cree and Assiniboin into a mixed ethnic population, and the regular interactions between other branches of these two populations created a people who were conversant in two distinct languages and culturally identical in many respects. Daniel Harmon, a Northwest Company trader, describes these populations as". . .Crees and Assiniboins: or as some call them, Kinistinoes and Stone Indians. Both of them are numerous tribes; and as they often meet and intermarry, their manners and customs are similar; but there is no resemblance in their languages."[95] Similarly, three decades later, Maximillian, Prince of Wied-Neuwid wrote:[96]

> The Crees live in the same territory as the Assiniboin
> . . .They live like the Assiniboins, in leather tents, and
> follow the herds of buffalo. . .Their customs, games,
> and religious opinions are said to agree with those
> of the Assiniboin. Their language has an affinity with that
> of the Ojibways, but entirely different from that of the

Assiniboins or Sioux, though many of the Cree learn the latter.

The case of the Assiniboin and Cree as well as the allied Saulteux and Chippewa was not unique in the northern Plains, however. Further west along the North Branch of the Saskatchewan River in Alberta, there was another region where ethnically-diverse groups intermarried, lived together, and shared access to common hunting areas. At the turn-of-the nineteenth century, the Sarcee, a small Athapaskan-speaking population were reported to be allied with and living amongst Cree, Blood, and Blackfoot.[97] There are also references to friendly visits and rivalries between these groups as well.[98] During the same period, the Western Cree and Northern Blackfeet were close allies — fighting together, intermarrying, trading, and living together.[99] By 1815, however, the peaceful encounters among these populations ended. The Sarcee were aligned with the Blackfeet and Gros Ventres and opposed to the Cree and Assiniboin for reasons described elsewhere.[100] In the years after 1830, the Sarcee were reported almost exclusively with the Blackfeet and were described as virtually indistinguishable, except in language, from these allies.[101] Interestingly, only twenty years before Henry had described them as identical to the Cree in their culture and appearance.[102]

The degree of enmity between Sarcee and Blackfoot, on the one side, and Cree and Assiniboin on the other was not uniform, however. The most enduring and bitter enmities took place among local groups in the vicinity of the Red Deer and South Saskatchewan Rivers.[103] Along the north branch of the Saskatchewan, resident bands were not unaffected by the deepening hostilities to the south. Nevertheless, many attempts at peace were made among the northerly groups. During peaceful interludes the Sarcee as well as Blackfoot were reported living among Cree, and vice versa.[104]

The ethnic complexity of the region is further substantiated when one examines the actual membership of bands associated with particular tribes, and the actual ethnic ancestry of the individual band members. For example, Diamond Jenness found in 1921 that there were five bands among the Sarcee, two of which were predominately Sarcee in membership.[105] The others included Sarcee mixed with Blackfoot, Cree, and Blood respectively.

Also reported in secondary sources was the close relationship between the Flatheads and the Short Robes band of Piegan, the presence of Gros Ventres in Arapaho camps, the long-standing association of the Kiowa and Kiowa Apache, and the incorporation of two bands, the Watapio and Mazikota, with Dakota origins into the body of the Cheyenne tribe.[106] Beyond these and many other less documented examples of co-residency between members of different tribes, there are numerous references to joint hunting, trading, and war parties among the allied tribes of the northern Plains.[107] In general, when one begins to examine the ethnohistoric record from a regional rather than a tribally-biased perspective, it becomes apparent that joint cooperation and sharing of land among ethnically-diverse groups was not exceptional.

The other major groups in the northern Plains were the horticultural villagers located along the upper reaches of the Missouri. In the historic and ethnographic literature on the Arikara, Hidatsa, and Mandan, there is ample evidence of collaboration and sharing across ethic boundaries. Until the early decades of the nineteenth century, these three populations were embedded in competitive trade networks that connected gun-suppliers from the northeast with horse-suppliers from the southwest.[108] In one trade-chain, for example, the gun-supplying Assiniboin and Cree were tied to the Mandan who in turn were connected to Cheyenne horse suppliers.[109] The villages were centers of trade which revolved not only around the exchange of European commodities but native products like corn and hides as well.[110] Nomads who traded often lived among their horticultural village neighbors for brief and extended periods of time, and conversely, the horticultural villagers often joined nomads on hunting and military expeditions.[111] Individuals and groups from nomadic tribes lived in the horticultural villages as friends and relatives, and some even became fully assimilated to a horticultural way of life.[112]

The northern Plains tribes who formed strong sociopolitical alliances exhibited little sense of territorial exclusiveness.[113] These tribes freely traveled, hunted, and lived within each others' recognized territories. While some of this sharing may have been negotiated by formal "invitation" within clearly recognized territorial limits, it is also clear that much of the joint use of land took place in areas where exclusive claims were either ambiguous or non-existent. In fact, when alliances involved extensive co-residency and reached a stage that Sharrock calls "hybridization," access and claims to territory were not divided along single tribal lines.[114] This was especially true in the case of the Cree-Assiniboin. Indeed, it is largely in reference to declines in natural resouces (e.g., buffalo and beaver) and to land cessions that native ideas of territorial exclusivity are expressed in the ethno-historic record of the northern Plains.[115]

As in the Great Lakes, a variety of factors influenced joint territorial usage and mergers. One of the more important was the distribution of divergent ecotones on the northern Plains and the migratory habits of large game like the buffalo. The aspen-parkland belt of Manitoba was a joint use area from prehistoric times to the beginning of the reservation era for a variety of ecological reasons which are amply enumerated elsewhere.[116]Contrary to Hickerson's idea that buffer zones were largely contested, northern plains populations adapted to these kinds of areas in mutually beneficial ways as well. In some instances groups joined together and utilized buffer zones cooperatively, but in others they remained separate and used these areas in specialized fashions.[117]

The character and locations of the fur-trade were also important in defining the dominant nature of relationships between groups. In circumstances where groups' geographical locations provided them with complementary goods to trade, they usually stood together as allies against competing trade networks. However, when traders bypassed native middlemen and destroyed the basis of their symbiosis, the involved groups either merged or went to war.[118] The case of the Cree and Assiniboin is clearly an example of the former, whereas the nineteenth century relations of the Cree and Blackfeet represent the latter.

The dictum of strength and safety in numbers also influenced several instances of intertribal mergers. Taylor, for example, demonstrated that population losses through epidemics fostered alliances and mergers.[119] In the case of the Cree and Assiniboin, merger tendencies had already appeared well before the 1837-38 smallpox epidemic wiped out large numbers of people from both groups.

Nonetheless, this devastating epidemic probably accelerated further mergers as suggested by the trader, Edwin Denig. He wrote that: "The nation (Assiniboin) being small and continually losing men at war, with others from disease, and the old in the course of nature, it is not likely they will be able to hold out much longer as a distinct people, but may exist some length of time if united with the Crees."[120] In the example of the Arikara, by contrast, they did not merge with their erstwhile enemies, the Mandan, until their numbers had so dwindled that they could no longer fight off the growing encroachments of neighboring Dakota.

What enabled tribes to amalgamate and rework alliances across ethnic boundaries was kinship. As in the western Great Lakes, peaceful encounters did not take place on a random basis among anonymous social parties; they were always embedded in some kind of kinship nexus, whether real or fictive. Kinship ties across ethnic boundaries were initiated and maintained either through marriage, adoption, or capture.

Interethnic marriages commonly sealed alliances in trading networks.[121] They were an institutionalized feature of tribal mergers, establishing the necessary connections which made the joint-use of territories possible.[122] Finally, they were initiated to bring about a peace between groups formally at war.[123]

In conjunction with marriage, adoption was another means of creating kinship ties between two populations. Alfred Bowers offers an elaborate description of the character of these adoptions among the Hidatsa.[124] His data suggest two things. On the one hand, when two parties wished to be placed in a relationship involving continual, reciprocal obligations and sharing, the adoption was structured in the manner of a sibling relationship. This was the most common form of adoption when people of the same or different ethnic backgrounds joined military societies. On the other hand, when the relationship entailed a complete alienation and transfer of some form of property from one person to another, it was usually organized along the lines of a parent-child relationship. This form was especially common in trading partnerships.[125]

Even under a state of war, tribes maintained relations of kinship with each other. In his narrative based on experiences among the Crow, Thomas LeForge mentions an instance when Teton rivals were hosted in a temporary visiting and gift-giving encounter.[126] Such peaceful interludes were conducted along kinship channels, established through the widespread practice of abducting women and children. Besides opening avenues for temporary encounters, these relationships were used to negotiate a more enduring peace as well.[127] As a matter of fact, the Hidatsa were reported to have kept enemy peoples in their midst as kin in order to open avenues for trade.[128]

The evidence from the northern Plains clearly suggests that the conventional model of tribal organization and territoriality does not adequately account for the complexity of relationships that cut across ethnic boundaries. Indeed, it seems to indicate that ties of kinship as much as a common ethnic ancestry may have organized the distribution of people and resources across geographic space.

THEORETICAL IMPLICATIONS

The preceding data are but a sample of what could be marshalled to support the view that Indian sharing of territory was a widespread feature of Indian life in the western Great Lakes and northern Plains before reservations and removals. The question remains, however, given long standing notions of tribal autonomy: What factors made the sharing of lands and resource sites so common? This section attempts to answer this question in two ways: (1) a review of some of the ecological, demographic, political, and economic factors which contributed to joint territorial use; and (2) a discussion of the importance of kinship in formulating such relationships.

First of all, the environment of a region plays a very critical role in determining whether particular geographic areas will be utilized by more than one group.[129] But while ecological factors may establish constraints and incentives for the use of an area by multiple tribal parties, these do not "cause" a singular set of responses. Even under similar environmental conditions, different ethnic groups historically adapted themselves to each others' presence in varying ways. The literature from the western Great Lakes and northern Plains suggests at least three types of adaptive strategies, including: (1) war — where groups divide and fight over land-use; (2) merger — where they join together and share in the utilization of a common territory; and (3) symbiosis — where groups remain separate and either specialize or cooperate in the exploitation of resources in the same region.[130]

If multiple ethnic groups accommodated their use of a single geographic region in more than one way, then what influenced the particular adaptive strategy that was finally selected? In historic times, at least, the character of the fur trade and the location of its entrepots were critical factors in defining the kinds of relationships that prevailed among the members of diverse tribal groups. Groups who, because of their strategic locations, were able to exchange complementary goods (e.g., guns against horses) did so, and they formed allied, trade chains which often stood in competition with those of neighboring tribes.[131] The ethnohistorical record testifies to the importance of formalized trade relationships between tribes that were underwritten by kinship and involved the joint use of territory. In the absence of symbiotic relations, the ethnohistorical sources suggest that groups either fought or merged with each other. In the western Great Lakes and in the northern Plains as well, one of the inevitable consequences of Euro-American traders bypassing native middlemen was the destruction of symbiotic relations. It is not fortuitous, for example, that when Euro-American trading posts were established within direct reach of both the Mandan as well as the Blackfeet, the symbiotic alliances with their former Cree and Assiniboin trading partners fell apart. In both instances, the outcome of the break-up was war. Yet, there is also evidence in the ethnohistorical literature that when symbiotic relations were undermined, merger took place as well (e.g., Sac-Fox, Cree-Assiniboin).

Whether groups shifted to relations of merger or war in the absence of trade appears to have been linked, at least in some instances, to demographic factors. Tribes decimated by war or epidemics often attached themselves to larger populations. Fragments of tribal groupings that were once much larger amalgamated and took on a common ethnic identity. Such a process clearly occurred with the formation of the Peoria, and it may also have been the basis of the formation of the Ojibway in southwestern Ontario.[132] Again, while demographic conditions were important in influencing whether war or merger would dominate relationships between the members of any two tribes, in the absence of trade, these factors alone cannot explain the final outcome. This can be illustrated by the example of the Sarcee, who fit the pattern of a small group aligning itself with a larger population. During the early contact period, however, they were aligned simultaneously with two large neighbors, the Cree and Blackfeet. Then, why in the years after 1815 did they become associated almost exclusively with the Blackfeet? The probable answer is because the Blackfeet had come to occupy a more strategic position in the circulation of trade commodities and in their access to buffalo hunting grounds than the Cree. Thus, just as reductionist forms of ecological causation alone are inadequate to understanding the character of intertribal adapations, demographic explantions are equally problematic when they are divorced from the wider historic context in which shifts in relationships took place.

Even though specific kinds of ecological as well as demographic factors provide necessary conditions for joint land-use, neither is sufficient, in and of itself, to explain either the frequency or directions of territorial sharing. This chapter argues that the determinant effects of ecology and demography cannot be understood apart from the social and historical circumstances in which native peoples jointly or separately utilized a given geographic space.

Historic American Indian populations of the Western Great Lakes and northern Plains were under the influences of two distinct but interdependent social systems. One system, the fur-trade, was organized largely by a mode of production that rested on mercantilism. Among other things, Euro-American markets created a set of requirements that had to be met in order for Indian populations to acquire and replenish their supplies of European trade items. Whether markets operated under the French, British, or Americans, they had two immediate sorts of consequences: (1) native economies were channeled in the direction of products (e.g., furs, hides, food provisions) demanded by the market; and (2) these products had to be produced in excess of what native populations would have needed for their own use or for simple exchanges with their neighbors. In order to maintain their relationships with Euro-American markets, American Indian populations were forced to involve their neighbors, either directly or indirectly, in the appropriation and circulation of fur-trade commodities. Market conditions influenced not only where groups would be located to secure strategic advantages in the trade, but they also played an important role in defining how groups in a given region would relate to one another.[133]

The incorporation of American Indians into the fur-trade, as producers and consumers, was informed by the character of indigenous social systems as well. These systems were organized, in the main, by varying principles of kinship that had evolved within economies oriented around the production of subsistence needs and secondarily around the production of simple trade commodities. Through their bonds of common descent and their ties in marriage and adoption, the Indians of the Western Great Lakes and northern Plains were embedded in far-reaching and ramifying social networks. These networks provided the channels in which reliable links of reciprocity in trade were maintained, in which avenues to peace were opened among enemies, and in which the joint sharing of land was facilitated.

How these networks were organized at particular points in history must have influenced relations across ethnic boundaries and the concomitant management of geographic space. Differences between tribes in the elementary characteristics of their kinship systems and other social institutions probably had an impact not only on the terms of their relationships as ethnically distinct and separate groups in allied hunting, trading, and warfare expeditions, but also on the ways in which some of their members lived together in the same bands, tribes and villages for brief as well as extended periods of time. The evidence from the northern Plains suggests that while the sedentary village tribes of the upper Missouri regularly assimilated individuals, either through marriage or adoption, in their midst, they did not readily incorporate large population aggregates.[134] Thus, when the Arikara joined the Mandan in the mid-nineteenth century, the involved populations collaborated with each other and utilized much of the same territory but maintained separate settlements. A parallel situation occurred in the western Great Lakes, when the Sac and Fox were closely allied for a period lasting nearly a century. Similarly, the once sedentary, village-based Cheyenne incorporated Dakota bands into their ranks, but these bands maintained a clearly differentiated position within the context of multi-band councils and encampments.[135] These cases contrast with the situation of the nomadic, band-type organization of the Cree and Assiniboin where sizable segments of their respective populations formed "hybridized" settlements in which differences in ethnic origins did not organize or serve as a marker of social differentiation.

Whatever impact different kinds of indigenous social organizations may have had on the character of intertribal relationships, one thing is clear, and that is, all relationships between various tribes, including war, were embedded in some kind of kinship nexus. The importance of kinship as a medium of integration were its underlying moral imperatives. These imperatives established customary guides for interaction, most of which obligated kin to share and cooperate with each other.[136] Food provisioning, territorial defense, and ceremonial activity were major areas in which kin were expected to collaborate. The ideological imperatives of kinship were not ironclad, however: considerable room was allowed to adjust relations to the demands of the moment. Thus, where ties of kinship existed, they offered an opportunity, not a necessity for alliance. On one level, kinship ties represented a series of cross-cutting genealogical links, which created the structural matrix from which concrete alliances were built. These links, however, could lay dormant until activated in some appropriate situation (e.g., kin ties between enemy tribes always existed but were not utilized until a temporary or enduring peace was established). On the other level of alliance, kinship organized the actual working relations among people. Thus, when members of two different tribes traded with each other, the circulation of commodities was ordered according to pre-existing or newly created kinship links.[137] In short, kinship was the language of relationship through which American Indians defined and established structural connections not only among themselves but with incoming Whites as well.[138]

Since the total range of any tribe's kinship links was never activated at the same moment in time, a gap always existed between the genealogical and alliance level of relationship. The networks of acknowledged genealogical linkage were always much larger and more stable than the ties of alliance. At any given point in time, only a portion of a group's genealogical ties were activated in the alliances that organized concrete forms of collaboration. Yet, it was precisely this sort of discrepancy that allowed American Indian populations to flexibly rework their relations as situations demanded.[139]

In this light, the density of kinship networks between groups was probably important in determining the future of their relationships. In situations where the number of kin connections between two tribes were small and restricted in their geographic distribution (as was the case between Chippewa and Dakota), the destruction of a symbiotic alliance and a move towards war would not have been impeded by kinship. In contrast, generations of intermarriage between Cree and Assiniboin over a wide geographic area created kinship networks of high density. Thus, when factional conflicts did emerge between various segments of these two groups, the overlapping and ramifying character of their kinship ties probably served as a buffer, preventing intermittent hostilities from breaking into a full-scale conflict.

It must also be noted, however, that even when two groups were closely related to each other, as was the case with the northern and southern branches of the Cheyenne before they separated, other conditions could override the effects of kinship. Before the 1850s, the Cheyenne had multiple links to outside groups, European as well as indigenous, that covered the entire expanse of their territorial holdings. With the separation of buffalo into northern and southern herds, and the emergence of trade entrepots in the far reaches of their territory, the Cheyenne split into two divisions. One group established itself in a southern regional system, which included Kiowa and Comanche, and the other became embedded in a northern network, where they became closely tied to the Teton (Lakota). Here the changing conditions of trade and the habits of the buffalo combined to alter the Cheyenne's patterns of alliance and ultimately the composition of their genealogical networks as well.[140]

A strong case could be made for the western Great Lakes as well as the northern Plains that kinship was as important as ethnicity in defining alliances and that the strong sense of tribalism ascribed to many of the Indian populations in these areas developed in relation to the historical circumstances they faced in the post-contact period. Larger populations, such as the Chippewa, Dakota, and Blackfeet, seldom if ever met together for any purpose. Although segments of these populations came together under the presence of centralizing political structures, the impact these structures had on monitoring the external relationships of participating groups was limited to the duration of their joint political and/or economic efforts. Intertribal relationships were often forged through local channels, and individual groups frequently established relations with members of other tribes that were independent of their larger ethnic body.[141] Thus, it is clear that in the case of the Cree, some members had closer ties to neighboring Assiniboin than they had to distant people from their own ethnic group. Similarly, certain bands of the Menominee appear to have been more closely tied to other tribes than to the members of their own tribal body. However, since kinship ties generally coincide with tribal ascriptions, it is often difficult to separate the effects of ethnicity from those of kinship.

Ultimately what this means is that the appropriate focus for studying certain aspects of American Indian social organization and territoriality may not be the tribe.[142] Rather, what may be required are regional units of analysis that are not prejudiced by the ethnic identities of the Indian populations who interacted with each other and utilized a common geographic area. By extension, then, the significant questions we ask, and the concepts we use, will necessarily change to reflect more faithfully the multi-ethnic character of many indigenous social systems and land-use patterns from prehistoric times to the formation of reservations.

PRAGMATIC IMPLICATIONS

A historical examination of American Indian social organization and territoriality has important practical applications. Scholarly notions about American Indian tribes and their relationships to specified areas of land have had an important impact on modern Indian claim cases and other legal-political decisions.

In this light, the whole notion of tribal territory needs to be intensively re-examined. The concept of tribal lands as sovereign domains with discrete and bounded borders analogous to nation-states, may have been acceptable historically for formulating tribal jurisdictional rights when treaties were negotiated. Today, it certainly has currency in relation to the legal-political and economic status of modern tribes and their reservation trust lands.[143] The problem, however, is that historically many treaties did not recognize the jurisdictional rights of all the native peoples who may have occupied a specified territory. Treaties often established jurisdictional boundaries based on incomplete or inaccurate information, and they were negotiated sometimes without full representation or consent of the populations who lived on the lands being ceded. In short, they did not faithfully denote actual occupance patterns, since members of one tribe may have lived amongst neighboring tribes or may have shared their lands with their neighbors.

During the years when the Indian Court of Claims heard cases, many decisions rested on evidence for or against a tribe's exclusive occupancy of a specific territory. One such territory included a large tract of land in northeastern Montana, claimed by Cree and Chippewa. Neither of these tribes were awarded claims for this land on the grounds that it had not been exclusively occupied by either of them. The Court of Claims response to the petition of one group, the Rocky Boy Chippewa-Cree, read as follows:[144]

> We have carefully reviewed the evidence in this case, and, as summarized herein, we have concluded that it fails to indicate any area within the claimed territory which was used and occupied by Cree or Chippewa Indians. . .Such title must be based on *evidence of actual exclusive use and occupancy of a defined area for a long time. Such evidence is totally lacking in this case. The facts to be drawn from the record in this case are that the claimed area was used as a common hunting ground by many tribes and neither the Cree nor the Chippewa can validly claim it as their aboriginal habitat. . .We conclude that the plaintiffs have failed to prove that either the Cree or the Chippewa, or any combination of Cree and Chippewa Indians, ever exclusively used and occupied any part of the claimed area* (emphasis ours).

It is clear that this judgement was correct when defined by a model which presumes that native land-use was organized by exclusive tribal groups. Yet, its is equally obvious that the standard tribal model, against which the historical evidence has been judged, is problematic.

Although some of the more recent decisions of the Claims Court acknowledge the joint use and occupation of specific territories by different tribes in historic times, this recognition has not generally led to compensation for the parties making claim on the land. Here, once again, the notion of "exclusive tribal occupancy" comes to the fore as a precedent in scholarly as well as legal interpretation. The problem, however, is that the interpretation has rested on a model which was presumed, *a priori,* to be true. The fact of the matter is that the model is not applicable in all cases. Like any other theory, the idea of tribal exclusivity must be tested against the empirical record. When it fails, as it has in many recent tests, new theories and concepts must be developed that more adequately describe and explain the actual relations of different ethnic groups to a specified territory. By extension, then, new kinds of legal decisions will have to be formulated that reflect in a more just and accurate way the variable ways in which American Indians utilized and made claim to the lands they historically occupied.

CONCLUSION

Horsman has argued recently that book-length tribal histories were generally competent but unimaginative, following established formulae which analyze political and economic relations within narrow ethnic confines.[145] Other recent reviewers of American Indian historiography have noted that geographers had contributed some of the most valuable ethnohistorical work in recent years.[146] The discipline's emphasis on regional and environmental perspectives appear to be what these reviewers valued. American Indian ethnohistory is apparently ready for more studies incorporating spatial topics.

At the very least, ethno-historians need to re-evaluate the meaning of tribal territories. Clearly, the boundaries of lands claimed by a given tribe did not encompass all of its members, nor did these boundaries necessarily identify the ethnic background of all the people who lived within them. Locations of tribal lands changed over time, as tribes migrated, expanded, or contracted their occupied places. The kinship explanation developed in this paper suggests a means whereby peaceful changes in the location and extent of tribal lands could take place.

A regional perspective which considers kinship relations opens up new possibilities for ethnohistory. It should have important implications for preparing and studying maps of indigenous territories. It should make significant contributions to understanding the diffusion and distribution of cultural institutions across ethnic boundaries. Finally, it should bring new interpretations to tribally-focused histories.

Regional, interethnic studies of American Indians, which incorporate the full range of social and economic activities shared between tribes, could be benefited by scholarly research in all the disciplines which contribute to American Indian ethnohistory. Anthropology's long-standing concern with culture and social relationships, geography's emphasis on environmental and regional systems, as well as history's expertise in archival research provide a solid foundation for achieving a more vigorous and accurate ethnohistory, and ultimately, more just solutions to Native land claims cases.

NOTES

1. By the expression, "sharing," we refer to situations where lands were jointly used and occupied, whether exclusive territorial claims were acknowledged or not.

2. The time period covered in this manuscript extends roughly from the mid-seventeenth to the mid-eighteenth century.

3. Some important works on defining American Indian tribes of especial relevance to this study are: Patricia C. Albers and William R. James, "To Be or Not To Be Santee: On the Dialectics of Ethnicity," *Journal of Ethnic Studies* 14 (1986): 1-27; Fredrick Barth, *Ethnic Groups and Boundaries: The Social Organization of Cultural Differences* (Boston: Little, Brown and Company, 1969); Ronald Cohen, "Ethnicity: Problem and Focus in Anthropology," *Annual Review in Anthropology* 7 (1978): 379-403; Leo Despres, ed., *Ethnicity and Resource Competition in Plural Scoieities* (The Hague: Mouton Publishers, 1975); Morton Fried, *The Tribe* (Menlo Park, California: Cummings Press, 1975); John Moore, "The Cheyenne Nation: A Social and Demographic History" (Unpublished manuscript), p. 37; Susan Sharrock, "Crees, Cree-Assiniboin, and Assiniboines: Interethnic Social Organization on the Far Northern Plains," *Ethnohistory* 2 (1974): 95-122.

4. Sharrock, 'Crees, Cree-Assiniboin, and Assiniboines," pp. 95-99.

5. Albers and James, "To Be or Not To Be Santee"; Fried, *The Tribe;* Sharrock, ibid.

6. In the ethnographic literature on historic Plains Indians, at least, the primary focus of research in the area of intertribal relations was warfare. This was true until the 1960s when increasing numbers of studies focused on peaceful forms of interaction between different tribes.

7. Angelo Anastasio, "The Southern Plateau: An Ecological Analysis of Intergroup Relations," *Northwestern Anthropological Research Notes 6* (1972): 109-229; Hugh Dempsey, *Crowfeet: Chief of the Blackfeet* (Norman: University of Oklahoma Press, 1972); John Ewers, *The Blackfeet: Raiders on the Northwestern Plains* (Norman: University of Oklahoma Press, 1958); John Ewers, "Intertribal Warfare as the Precursor of Indian-White Warfare on the Great Northern Plains," *The Western Historical Quarterly* 5 (1975): 397-410; Susan Giannettino, "The Middleman Role in the Fur Trade: Its Influence on Interethnic Relations in the Saskatchewan-Missouri Plains," *The Western Canadian Journal of Anthropology* 4 (1977): 22-33; Harold Hickerson, "The Genesis of a Trading Post Band: The Pembina Chippewa," *Ethnohistory* 3 (1956); Harold Hickerson, "The Feast of the Dead among the Seventeenth Century Algonkian of the Upper Great Lakes," *American Anthropologist* 62 (1960): 81-107; Harold Hickerson, *The Chippewa and their Neighbors: A Study in Ethnohistory* (New York: Holt, Rinehart and Winston, 1970); Joseph Jablow, *The Cheyenne in Plains Indian Trade Relations, 1775-1840,* Monographs of the American Ethnological Society 19 (Seattle: University of Washington Press, 1950); Charles Kenner, *A History of New Mexican-Plains Indian Relations* (Norman: University of Oklahoma Press, 1969); Alan Klein, "Adaptive Strategies and Process on the Plains: The Nineteenth Century Cultural

Sink" (Ph.D. dissertation, State University of New York at Buffalo, 1977); John S. Milloy, "The Plains Cree: A Preliminary Trade and Military Chronology 1670-1870" (Master's thesis, Carlton University, Ottawa, 1972); Polly Pope, "Trade in the Plains: Affluence and Its Affects," *Kroeber Anthropological Papers* 34 (1966): 53-61; Arthur J. Ray, *Indians in the Fur Trade: Their Role as Hunters, Trappers and Middlemen in the Lands Southwest of Hudson Bay, 1660-1870* (Toronto: University of Toronto Press, 1974); Katherine Weist, "An Ethnohistorical Analysis of Crow Political Alliances," *The Western Canadian Journal of Anthropology* 7 (1977): 34-54; Raymond W. Wood, "Plains Trade in Prehistoric and Protohistoric Intertribal Relations," in *Anthropology on the Great Plains,* eds. W. Raymond Wood and Margot Liberty (Lincoln: University of Nebraska Press, 1980), pp. 98-109.

    8. Patricia C. Albers, "The Regional System of the Devil's Lake Sioux" (Ph.D. dissertation, University of Wisconsin-Madison, 1974); William W. Elmendorf, "Coast Salish Status Ranking and Intergroup Ties," *Southwestern Journal of Anthropology* 27 (1971): 353-380; Robert Owen, "The Patrilocal Band: a Linguistically and Culturally Hybrid Social Unit," *American Anthropologist* 67 (1965): 675-690; "Variety and Constraint in Cultural Adaptation," in *Modern Systems Research for the Behavioral Scientist,* ed. Buckley (Chicago: Aldine, 1968); Sharrock, "Crees, Cree-Assiniboin, and Assiniboines"; Wayne Shuttles, "Affinal Ties, Subsistence and Prestige Among the Coast Salish," *American Anthropologist* 62 (1960): 296-305; Wayne Shuttles, "The Persistence of Intervillage Ties Among the Coast Salish," *Ethnology* 2 (1963): 512-525.

    9. In our perspective, ethnic groups are not, as some scholars claim, the exclusive properties of advanced nation-states. Although they take on distinct attributes under pre-state conditions, ethnicity and ethnic differentiation are universal phenomena. To assert that ethnicity is only a feature of certain kinds of social structures is like saying there is no religion without a church, no economy without a market, and no polity without a state. This kind of reasoning is specious because it gives the impression that a substantive gap exists between state and pre-state conditions when, in fact, the separation is structural. Obviously, the manner in which ethnic groups are formed and articulate with each other differs from one level of social organization to another. Nevertheless, even under pre-state conditions, ethnic groups are incorporated in wider systems with identifiable patterns and dynamics (Carol Smith, *Regional Analysis: Social Systems, Volume II* (New York: Academic Press, 1976).

    10. Elmendorf, "Coast Salish Status Ranking and Intergroup Ties," p. 354.

    11. Albers, "Pluralism in the Native Plains" (Unpublished manuscript in possession of author); Moore, *The Cheyenne Nation;* Symmes Oliver, "Ecology and Cultural Continuity as Contributing Factors in the Social Organization of Plains Indians," *University of California Publications in American Archaeology and Ethnology* 48 (1962): 1-90.

    12. Albers and James, "To Be or Not to Be Santee"; Elmendorf, "Coast Salish Status Ranking and Integroup Ties."

    13. Smith, *Regional Analysis,* p. 3.

    14. A.F.C. Wallace, "Political Organization and Land Tenure Among the Northeastern Indians, 1600-1830," *Southwestern Journal of Anthropology* 13 (1957): 301-321.

    15. Jedediah Morse, *A Report to the Secretary of War of the United States on Indian Affairs* (New Haven: S. Converse, 1822 [reprinted by: New York: August M. Kelley Publishers, 1970]); Appendix, pp. 352-353.

16. Andrew Jackson, "Message From the President of the United States in Compliance with a Resolution of the Senate Concerning the Fur Trade and Inland Trade to Mexico," 22nd Congress, 1st Session, Vol. 2, *Senate Document* 90 (1832): 90.

17. Ibid.

18. John Ewers, "Ethnological Report on the Chippewa Cree Tribe of the Rocky Boy Reservation and the Little Shell Band of Indians," *Chippewa Indians,* Vol 6 (New York: Garland Press, 1974), p. 11.

19. Irene Spry, "The Great Transformation: The Disappearance of the Commons in Western Canada History," in *Canadian Plains Studies: Man and Nature on the Prairies,* ed. R. Ailen, Vol. 6, pp. 22-24.

20. Quoted in Ermine Vogelin and Harold Hickerson, "The Red Lake and Pembina Chippewa," *Chippewa Indians,* Vol. 1 (New York: Garland Press, 1974), p. 117.

21. Spry, "The Great Transformation," p. 23.

22. Morse, *A Report to the Secretary of War of the United States on Indian Affairs;* Appendix, pp. 48-49.

23. Claude Stipe, "Eastern Dakota Acculturation: The Role of Agents of Culture Change" (Ph.D. dissertation, University of Minnesota, 1970), pp. 120-123, 180-181.

24. Donald L. Hardesty, *Ecological Anthropology* (New York: John Wiley and Sons, 1977); John R. Gold, "Territoriality and Human Spatial Behavior," *Progress in Geography,* 6 (1982): 44-67.

25. Ibid.

26. Hardesty, *Ecological Anthropology,* p. 186.

27. An extended discussion of the varying kinds of intertribal relationships found among American Indians is found in Albers, "Pluralism in the Native Plains," and also in Anastasio, "The Southern Plateau."

28. Harold Hickerson, "The Sociocultural Significance of Two Chippewa Ceremonials," *American Anthropologist* 65 (1963): 67-85; Harold Hickerson, "The Virginia Deer and Intertribal Buffer Zones in the Upper Mississippi Valley," in *Man, Culture and Animals: The Role of Animals in Human Adjustments,* eds. A. Leeds and A.P. Vayda (Washington, D.C.: American Association for the Advancement of Science, 1965), Publication No. 78, pp. 43-66; Hickerson, *The Chippewa and Their Neighbors.*

29. Jeanne Kay, "Wisconsin Indian Hunting Patterns, 1634-1836," *Annals of the Association of American Geographers* 69 (1979): 402-418.

30. Sharrock, "Crees, Cree-Assiniboin, and Assiniboines"; Susan Sharrock, "Cross-Tribal, Ecological Categorization of Far Northern Plains Cree and Assiniboine by Late Eighteenth and Early Nineteenth Century Fur Traders," *The Western Canadian Journal of Antrhroplogy* 4 (1977): 1-7.

31. Wallace, "Political Organization and Land Tenure Among the Northeastern Indians."

32. Emma H. Blair, ed., *Indian Tribes of the Upper Mississippi and Great Lakes Region* (Cleveland: The Arthur Clark Co., 1911), Vol. 1, p. 321; Louis R.G. Hennepin; *A New Discovery of a Vast Country in North America (1698),* ed. Reuben Gold Thwaites (Chicago: McLurg and Co., 1903), pp. 130, 166, 307; Reuben Thwaites, ed., *The Jesuit Relations and Allied Documents* (Cleveland: The Burrows Brothers Co., 1899), Vol. 54, pp. 197-207.

33. Thwaites, ibid., Vol. 54, pp. 197-207; Vol. 58, pp. 21-23, 39, 41, 97, 265.

34. Lyman C. Draper, ed., "Canadian Documents," *Wisconsin Historical*

Collections 5 (1868): 89-104; E.B. O'Callaghan, ed., *Document Relative to the Colonial History of the State of New York* (Albany, 1851), 9: 1052-1058.

35. Donald Jackson, ed., *Black Hawk: An Autobiography* (Urbana: University of Illinois Press, 1964), p. 46.

36. William T. Hogan, *The Sac and Fox Indians* (Norman: University of Oklahoma Press, 1958).

37. Hickerson, *The Chippewa and Their Neighbors,* p. 44.

38. Thwaites, *Jesuit Relations,* Vol. 54, pp. 132-133; Blair, *Indian Tribes of the Upper Mississippi,* Vol 1, p. 292-93; Pierre Margry, ed., *Decouvertes et Etablissement des Francais dans le Sud de l'Amerique Septentrionale 1614-1734: Memoirs et Documents Originaux* (Paris: D. Jouast, 1886), Vol. 5, p. 120; P.F.X. Charlevoix, *Journal of a Voyage to North America,* ed. L. P. Kellogg (Chicago: The Caxton Club, 1923), p. 55; Augustin Grignon, "Seventy-Two Years' Recollections of Wisconsin," *Wisconsin Historical Collections* 3 (1957), p. 265.

39. Hickerson, *the Chippewa and Their Neighbors,* p. 79.

40. Ives Goddard, "Historical and Philological Evidence Regarding the Identification of the Mascouten," *Ethnohistory* 19 (1972): 123-134.

41. Jeanne Kay, "The Fur Trade and Indian Population Growth," *Ethnohistory* 31 (1984): 265-287.

42. Hickerson, "The Feast of the Dead."

43. Ibid.

44. Hickerson, "The Sociocultural Significance of Two Chippewa Ceremonials."

45. Thwaites, *Jesuit Relations,* Vol. 54, p. 167. For a recent review of Indians in the fur trade, see Jacqueline Peterson and John Anfinson, "The Indian and the Fur Trade: A Review of Recent Literature," in *Scholars and the Indian Experience: Critical Reviews of Recent Writing in the Social Sciences,* ed. W.R. Swagerty (Bloomington: Indiana University Press, 1984), pp. 223-256.

46. Thwaites, *Jesuit Relations,* Vol 54, pp. 197-207; Hennepin, *A New Discovery,* pp. 130, 166, 307.

47. A. T. Adams, ed., *The Explorations of Pierre Esprit Radisson* (Minneapolis: Ross and Haines, Inc., 1961), p. 95.

48. Margry, *Decouvertes et Etablissements des Francais,* Vol. 5, pp. 81-83; Thwaites, *Jesuit Relations,* Vol. 54, pp. 151, 167; Edwin James, ed., *A Narrative of Captivity and Adventure of John Tanner During Thirty Years Residence Among the Indians of the Interior of North America* (Minneapolis: Ross and Haines, 1956, reprint of 1830), pp. 61-62.

49. Harold Hickerson, *Sioux Indians I: Mdewakanton Band of the Sioux Indians* (New York: Garland Publishing, 1974), pp. 13-47.

50. J.L. Burpee, ed., *Journals and Letters of Pierre Gaultier de Varennes de la Verendrye and His Sons* (Toronto: The Champlain Society, 1927), pp. 240-243; John Parker, ed., *The Journal of Jonathan Carver and Related Documents, 1766-1770* (St Pauls: Minnesota Historical Society Press, 1976), pp. 100, 130-132.

51. Thomas Forsyth, Letters to William Clark, 10/4/1823, 5/29/1826, and 6/25/1828, in *Letter Books* (State Historical Society of Wisconsin), Vol. 8, pp. 37, 31, 121.

52. Thwaites, *Jesuit Relations,* Vol. 54, pp. 197-207.

53. Jeanne Kay, "Wisconsin Indian Hunting Patterns, 1634-1836," *Annals of the Association of American Geographers* 69 (1979): 402-418.

54. Harold A. Innis, *The Fur Trade in Canada,* revised edition (Toronto: University of Toronto Press, 1956), p. 102; *Taliaferro Papers, 1813-1868* (St. Paul: Minnesota Historical Society, letter of Sept. 26, 1823).

55. Jackson, *Black Hawk: An Autobiography,* p. 84.

56. Albert G. Ellis, "Fifty-Four Years' Recollections of Men and Events in Wisconsin," *Wisconsin Historical Collections* 7 (1876), pp. 223, 241.

57. Adams, *The Explorations of Radisson,* p. 130.

58. Blair, *Indian Tribes of the Upper Mississippi,* Vol. 1, p. 321; Hennepin, *A New Discovery,* pp. 130, 166, 307; Thwaites, *Jesuit Relations,* Vol 54, pp. 197-207.

59. Reuben Gold Thwaites, ed. "Letter of John Bowyer to Lewis Cass, 8/12/1817," in "The Fur Trade on the Upper Lakes," *Wisconsin Historical Collections,* 19 (1910), p. 471.

60. Reuben Thwaites, ed., "The Fur Trade in Wisconsin, 1812-25," *Wisconsin Historical Collections 20 (1911): 349-350.*

61. William H. Keating, *Narrative of an Expedition to the Source of St. Peters River, Lake Winnepeek, Lake of the Woods, etc.* (1824), pp. 172-192, 225.

62. Parker, *The Journal of Jonathan Carver,* pp. 130-131.

63. Jonathan Carver, *Travels Through the Interior Parts of North America* (Minneapolis: Ross and Haines, Inc., 1956, reprint of 1781 edition), pp. 53-54.

64. Louis B. Porlier, "Narrative by Louis B. Porlier," *Wisconsin Historical Collections* 15 (1900): 226-227; Reuben Thwaites, ed., "Narrative of Peter J. Vieau," *Wisconsin Historical Collections* 15 (1888): 221-226.

65. Jeanne Kay, "The Land of La Baye: The Ecological Impact of the Green Bay Fur Trade, 1634-1836" (Ph.D. dissertation, University of Wisconsin-Madison, 1977), Appendices A,B, and C.

66. James A. Clifton, *The Prairie People: Continuity and Change in Potawatomi Indian Culture, 1665-1965* (Lawrence: The Regents Press of Kansas, 1977).

67. Thwaites, "Narrative of Peter J. Vieau," p. 22.

68. Porlier, "Narrative by Louis B. Porlier," p. 445.

69. Keating, *Narrative of an Expedition,* pp. 178-179.

70. Blair, *Indian Tribes of the Upper Mississippi,* pp. 277, 301.

71. E.A. Cruikshank, ed., *Simcoe Correspondence,* Vol. 1 (Toronto, 1923), p. 390.

72. Antoine Denise Raudot, "Memoir Concerning the Different Indian Nations of North America, in *The Indians of the Western Great Lakes 1615-1760,* ed. W. Vernon Kinietz (Ann Arbor: University of Michigan Press, 1940), p. 356.

73. Keating, *Narrative of an Expedition,* p. 225.

74. Morse, *A Report to the Secretary of War,* p. 46.

75. Ibid., Appendix, p. 125.

76. Ibid., Appendix, p. 58.

77. Ibid., Appendix, p. 59; Forsyth, "Letters to William Clark."

78. Caleb Atwater, *Remarks Made on a Tour to Prairie du Chien ... in 1829* (Columbus, Ohio, 1850), p. 81; Grignon, "Seventy-Two Years" Recollections of Wisconsin," p. 229.

79. In T.H. Crawford, "Annual Report of the Commissioner of Indian Affairs," 25th Congress 3rd Session, Vol. 5, *Senate Document* 9, p. 485.

80. Cf. Richard White, "The Winning of the West: The Expansion of the Western Sioux in the Eighteenth and Nineteenth Centuries," *The Journal of American History* 65 (1968): 319-343.

81. Ray, *Indians in the Fur Trade;* Sharrock, "Crees, Cree-Assiniboin, and Assiniboines."

82. Leigh E. Syms, "Cultural Ecology and Ecological Dynamics of the Ceramic period in Southwestern Manitoba," *Plains Anthropologist,* Memoir 12 (1977).

83. Burpee, *Journals and Letters of Pierre Gaultier de Varennes de La Verendrye,* pp. 243-244; Daniel W. Harmon, *A Journal of Voyages and Travels*

in the Interior of North America (New York: Allerton Book Company, 1911), p. 72; Alexander Henry and David Thompson, *New Light on the History of the Great Northwest,* ed. Elliot Coues (Minneapolis: Ross and Haines, Inc., 1965, reprint of 1898), Vol. 1, pp. 152, 166, 191, 199, 204, 228, 314, 408, 413, 419, 516; James, *A Narrative of Captivity,* pp. 37, 71, 77, 137, 142; Ray, *Indians in the Fur Trade,* pp. 27-31; Sharrock, 'Crees, Cree-Assiniboin, and Assiniboines," pp. 109-110; Susan Sharrock and Floyd Sharrock, "History of the Cree Indian Territorial Expansion From the Hudson Bay Area to the Interior Saskatchewan and Missouri Plains,"*Chippewa Indians,* Vol 6 (New York: Garland Press, 1977), pp. 35-38.

84. Hickerson, "The Genesis of a Trading Post Band"; James, *A Narrative of Captivity and Adventure of John Tanner,* pp. 44-45; Milloy, "The Plains Cree," pp. 94-107, 123-124, 142-148, 152-153; Reuben Thwaites, ed., *Original Journal of the Lewis and Clark Expedition, 1804-1806* (New York: Dodd and Mead Co., 1904-1905), p. 222.

85. Henry and Thompson, *New Light,* Vol. 1, pp. 191, 196, 204, 257, 269, 429; Hickerson, ibid.; James, *A Narrative of Captivity,* pp. 44-45, 70, 78, 137, 142.

86. James, ibid., p. 132.

87. Ray, *Indians in the Fur Trade,* pp. 207, 212; Sharrock, "Crees, Cree-Assiniboin, and Assiniboines"; Sharrock and Sharrock, "History of the Cree Indian Territorial Expansion."

88. Vogelin and Hickerson,"The Red Lake and Pembina Chippewa," p. 123.

89. Harmon, *A Journal of Voyages,* pp. 42-44, 78, 81, 85, 103-104, 120; Milloy, "The Plains Cree," pp. 94-107; Sharrock, 'Crees, Cree-Assiniboin, and Assiniboines," pp. 106-111; Sharrock and Sharrock, "History of the Cree Indian Territorial Expansion," pp. 23-33.

90. Edwin Denig, *Indian Tribes of the Upper Missouri,* ed. John Ewers (Norman: University of Oklahoma Press, 1961), pp. xxvi-xxxvii, 80-81, 101, 110-111; *Fort Union Letterbook* (Chouteau File, Missouri Historical Society Archives, St. Louis, 1833-1835); Charles Larpenteur, *Forty Years a Fur Trader on the Upper Missouri: The Personal Narrative of Charles Larpenteur,* ed. Milo M. Quaife (Chicago, 1933), p. 92.

91. Robert Campbell, The Private Journal of Robert Campbell, ed. George R. Brooks (Missouri Historical Society Bulletin 20, 1963), pp. 23, 108; *Fort Union Letterbook,* 1834, 1835.

92. Denig, *Indian Tribes of the Upper Missouri,* pp. 82, 110-111; Sharrock, "Crees, Cree-Assiniboin, and Assiniboines," pp. 112-113.

93. Henry and Thompson, *New Light,* Vol. 2, p. 120; Sharrock, ibid., p. 111; Sharrock and Sharrock, "History of the Cree Indian Territorial Expansion," pp. 90-91.

94. Sharrock, ibid., p. 10.

95. Harmon,*A Journal of Voyages,* pp. 14-15.

96. Alexander Maximillian, Prince of Wied-Neuwied, *Travels in the Interior of North America,* ed. R. Thwaites (Cleveland: Arthur M. Clark Co., 1906), Vol. 23, p. 13.

97. Henry and Thompson,*New Light,* pp. 110, 200.

98. Ibid., pp. 720, 737, 756.

99. Victor G. Hopwood, ed., *David Thompson Travels in Western America, 1784-1812* (Toronto: Macmillan of Canada, 1971), pp. 192-197; Milloy, "The Plains Cree," pp. 49-50, 59-60, 64-76; Ray,*Indians in the Fur Trade,* pp. 19-23.

100. Ray, ibid., pp. 98-99, 104-105.

101. Hugh Dempsey, *Crowfeet: Chief of the Blackfeet* (Norman: University of Oklahoma Press, 1972) p. 111; John Palliser, *Papers Relative to and Further Papers Relative to the Explorations of Captain Palliser of that Portion of British North America Which Lies Between the North Branch of the River Saskatchewan*

and the Frontier of the United States; and Between the Red River and Rocky Mountains (London, 1859), pp. 76, 203-204; Sir George Simpson, *Overland Journey Around the World,* Vol. 1 (Toronto, 1875), pp. 101-104.

102. Henry and Thompson, *New Light,* pp. 531-532.

103. Milloy, "The Plains Cree," pp. 208-209, 225-227.

104. Diamond Jenness, *The Sarcee Indians of Alberta* (Bulletin No. 90 of the Publications of the National Museum of Canada, Anthropological Series 23, 1932), p. 8; Milloy, ibid., pp. 210-211, 213, 216, 226-227.

105. Ibid., p. 15.

106. Ewers, *The Blackfeet,* pp. 185-189, 217; Regina Flannery, *The Gros Ventres of Montana: Social Life,* Vol. I (Washington, D.C.: Catholic University of America, Anthropological Series, 1953), pp. 89, 97-98; William Bittle, "A Brief History of the Kiowa Apache," *Papers in Anthropology* 12 (1971): 1-34; Charles Brant, "Kiowa Apache Culture History," *Southwestern Journal of Anthropology* 9 (1949): 195-202; Moore, *The Cheyenne Nation.*

107. Ewers, "Indian Trade of the Upper Missouri"; Ewers, "Intertribal Warfare," Jablow, *The Cheyenne;* Weist, "An Ethnohistorical Analysis"; Raymond W. Wood, "Northern Plains Village Cultures: Internal Stability and External Relationships," *Journal of Anthropological Research* 30 (1973): 1-16; Wood, "Plains Trade."

108. Jablow, *The Cheyenne,* pp. 42-43; Milloy, "The Plains Cree," pp. 64-76, 151-172; Frank R. Secoy, *Changing Military Patterns on the Great Plains* (Monographs of the American Ethnological Society 21, 1953).

109. Jablow, ibid.; Milloy, ibid.

110. Ewers, "Indian Trade of the Upper Missouri," p. 27; Wood, "Northern Plains Village Cultures"; Wood, "Plains Trade."

111. Alfred Bowers, *Hidatsa Social and Ceremonial Organization* (Washington, D.C.: Smithsonian Institution, Bureau of American Ethnology Bulletin, Vol. 194, 1965), pp. 216-219; Milloy, "The Plains Cree," pp. 142-248.

112. Henry A. Boller, *Among the Indians: Four Years on the Upper Missouri 1858-1862,* ed. M. Quaife (Lincoln: University of Nebraska Press, 1959); Bowers, *Hidatsa Social and Ceremonial Organization,* pp. 216-219; Edward Bruner, "Mandan," in *Perspectives in American Indian Culture Change,* ed. Edward Spicer (Chicago: University of Chicago Press, 1961), pp. 187-278; Ewers, "Indian Trade of the Upper Missouri"; James Howard, "The Cultural Position of the Dakota: A Reassessment," in *Essays in the Science of Culture,* eds. Gertrude Dole and Robert Carneiro (Ann Arbor: University of Michigan Press, 1960), p. 257.

113. Ray, *Indians in the Fur Trade,* pp. 166-181; Sharrock, "Cree, Cree-Assiniboin, and Assiniboines," pp. 107-111.

114. Sharrock, ibid., pp. 111-115.

115. Spry, "The Great Transformation"; Vogelin and Hickerson, "The Red Lake and Pembina Chippewa," pp. 111-115.

116. Ray, *Indians in the Fur Trade,* pp. 27-50; Syms, "Cultural Ecology."

117. Ray, ibid., pp. 27-40.

118. Albers, "Pluralism in the Native Plains," pp. 21-39.

119. John F. Taylor, "Sociocultural Effects of Epidemics on the Northern Plains: 1734-1850," *The Western Canadian Journal of Anthropology* 7 (1977): 55-72.

120. Denig, *Indian Tribes of the Upper Missouri,* p. 293.

121. Albers, "Pluralism in the Native Plains"; Sharrock, "Crees, Cree-Assiniboin, and Assiniboines"; Weist, "An Ethnohistorical Analysis."

122. Sharrock, ibid.

123. Weist, ibid.

124. Bowers, *Hidatsa Social and Ceremonial Organization,* pp. 213-216.

125. The use of different forms of adoption in intertribal relations is clearly more widespread. It is illustrated in the various forms of kinship address used in many of the treaty negotiation speeches from the Great Lakes.

126. Thomas B. Marquis, *Memoirs of a White Crow Indian* (Lincoln: University of Oklahoma Press, 1974, reprint of 1928), pp. 99-101.

127. Weist, "An Ethnohistorical Analysis," pp. 41-47.

128. Jablow, *The Cheyenne,* p. 46.

129. For a review of Indian environmental relations, see Richard White, "Native Americans in the Environment," in *Scholars and the Indian Experience,* pp. 179-204. Regarding environments of the study area, see Kay, "The Land of La Baye"; Kay, "Wisconsin Indian Hunting Patterns"; Ray, *Indians in the Fur Trade,* pp. 27-50; Syms, "Cultural Ecology."

130. Patricia Albers, "Towards a Model of Plains Intergroup Relations," Paper presented at the Plains Anthropology Conference, Calgary, Alberta (1982).

131. Patricia Albers and William R. James, "Historical Materialism Vs. Evolutionary Ecology: A Methodological Note on Horse Distribution and American Plains Indians," *Critique in Anthropology* (1986): 92-93.

132. Adolph Greenberg and James Morrison, "Group Identities in the Boreal Forest: The Origin of the Northern Ojibwa," *Ethnohistory* 29 (1981): 75-102.

133. Albers and James, "Historical Materialism and Neoclassical Ecology," p. 93; Jablow, *The Cheyenne,* pp. 21-26; Klein, "Adaptive Strategies," pp. 116-274.

134. Bowers, *Hidatsa Social and Cermonial Organization,* pp. 217-219; Wood, "Northern Plains Village Cultures."

135. Moore, *The Cheyenne Nation.*

136. More detailed information on those aspects of American Indian kinship which obligated kin to share and collaborate can be found in a wide range of ethnographic sources, including: Albers, "The Regional System of the Devil's Lake Sioux"; Anastasio, "The Southern Plateau"; Bowers, *Hidatsa Social and Ceremonial Organization;* Bruner, "Mandan"; Clifton, *The Prairie People;* William W. Elmendorf, *The Structure of Twana Culture* (Pullman: Washington State University Press, 1960); Flannery, *The Gros Ventres of Montana;* William T. Hagan, *The Sac and Fox Indians* (Norman: University of Oklahoma Press, 1958); Jenness, *The Sarcee Indians of Alberta;* David Mandelbaum, *The Plains Cree: An Ethnographic, Historical, and Comparative Study,* Canadian Plains Studies No. 9 (Regina: Canadian Plains Research Center, University of Regina, 1979); Suttles, "Affinal Ties";; James Teit, "The Salishan Tribes of the Western Plateau," *Annual Reports of the Bureau of American Ethnology,* Vol. 45 (Washington, D.C.: U.S. Government Printing Office, 1930).

137. Extended discussions of this issue are found in: Albers, ibid.; Anastasio, ibid.

138. Cf. Peterson and Anfinson, "The Indian and the Fur Trade."

139. Albers, "The Regional System of the Devil's Lake Sioux."

140. Jablow, *The Cheyenne;* John Moore, "Cheyenne Political History, 1829-1894," *Ethnohistory* 2 (1974): 329-359.

141. Albers, ibid., Sharrock, "Crees, Cree-Assiniboin, and Assiniboines"; Weist, "An Ethnohistorical Analysis."

142. For an independent critique of the conventional tribal history, see James A. Clifton, "The Tribal History: An Obsolete Paradigm," *American Indian Culture and Research Journal* 3 (1979): 81-100.

143. Vine Deloria, Jr., and Clifford Lytle, *The Nations Within: The Past and Future of American Indian Sovereignty* (New York: Pantheon Books, 1984).

144. Indians Claims Commission, " Chippewa Cree Tribe of the Rocky Boy's Reservation, Montana, Joe Corcoran, on behalf of the Chippewa Cree Tribe, Blanche Patenaude, Joseph Richard, Joseph Gooselain, John B. Slayter, Wm. John Delorme, William Trottier, on behalf of the Little Shell Band of Indians and the Chippewa Cree Tribe," Docket No. 221-B, *Chippewa Indians,* Vol. 1 (New York: Garland Press, 1974), pp. 524-528.

145. Reginald Horsman, "Well Trodden Paths and Fresh Byways: Recent Writing on Native American History," *Reviews in American History* 10 (1982): 234-244; Clifton, "The Tribal History: An Obsolete Paradigm."

146. Peterson and Anfinson, "The Indian and the Fur Trade"; Richard White, "Native Americans and the Environment," in *Scholars and the Indian Experience.*

ACKNOWLEDGEMENTS

We wish to thank William James, Richard White, James Clifton, John Moore, and Alan Klein for their helpful comments and suggestions on earlier versions of this manuscript.

Chapter 5
Indian Delimitations of Primary Biogeographic Regions

G. Malcolm Lewis

Scientific delimitation of biogeographic regions on small-scale maps of North America may be said to have begun in 1830 with the publication of a strange untitled map accompanying a paper "On the geographical distribution of plants."[1] During the next hundred years, at least sixteen different biologists published original maps showing the major floral and/or faunal regions.[2] These had several common characteristics: each was compiled and published by a relatively eminent biologist and represented a significant contribution to biogeography; all were intended to further the understanding of the principles governing the distribution of life forms; and each used boundary lines to indicate what in reality were transition zones between regions characterized by different associations of life forms. They were not, however, the earliest examples of maps delimiting the primary biogeographic regions of North America. For these one must look to the maps of eighteenth century Indians and fur traders and to two published maps that were in part derived from them.

INDIAN MAPS

From at least protohistoric times onwards, Indians and Inuits throughout the continent are known to have made what from contact times onwards Euro-Americans called maps. Indigenously, they were used in instructing others, conveying messages, planning spatial strategies and preserving information about the past. Made on a variety of materials, they involved a range of technical skills and employed a number of representational techniques. Representational style differed from culture to culture and was closely related to pictography. Indeed, from the Indians' point of view mapping would appear to have been an undifferentiated part of their pictographic mode of communication. Except for those made to preserve information for posterity, such maps tended to be treated as ephemera.[3]

Indian maps differed from post-Renaissance European maps in two fundamental respects: geometrical structure and the selection and ordering of information content. Whereas by the sixteenth century most European maps were structured according to combinations of Euclidean and projective geometries, involving some kind of co-ordinate systems, Indian maps were always topologically structured. Their geometry was akin to an iconic representation of a familiar object done on an elastic surface and then differentially stretched, but not ruptured, thereby conserving connectivity between the parts but distorting distance, angles and, hence, shape. Modern maps are sometimes classified according to their information content: general maps representing a mix of several diverse phenomena and thematic maps representing one phenomenon or a limited number of closely related phenomena. In both, however, representation is standardized and systematic, i.e., *all* settlements above a stated size threshold classified according to predetermined and mutually exclusive categories. In contrast, almost all Indian maps were made to serve specific functions in particular contexts. As such, they were usually parsimonious in content and never attempted to adopt or adhere to thresholds of representation or to utilize systematically ordering categories based on magnitude. Thus, for example, on the same map, one lake might be represented large and approximately according to plan and a larger lake by a small symbol, whereas an even larger one might be omitted. Cultural importance and the purpose for which a map was made determined both what was represented and the relative emphasis given to its several components.

Maps made by Indians were usually treated as maps by Euro-Americans. Though inferior in quality they were apparently similar in structure to their European equivalents. Especially in the immediate post-contact period of exploration, they were used throughout the continent in communicating to Euro-Americans spatially arranged information about the environment. From the Euro-Americans' perspective the most important information related to their *terrae incognitae* and *terrae semicognitae:* lands on or beyond the frontiers of exploration, about which they knew nothing or little but wished to find out.[4] Because the maps were treated as ephemera by Indians and most Euro-Americans alike, remarkably few originals have survived. Indeed, those made in sand, snow and the ashes of campfires were unpreservable, except in transcript form. In the relatively rare cases in which a transcribed map has survived in conjunction with other documents it is, however, sometimes possible to infer and even to demonstrate the way in which its information content was absorbed into the geographical lore of the frontiersmen and how, in turn, that lore became incorporated into the Euro-Americans' formal geography of the continent.[5]

Content analysis of all extant Indian maps would probably reveal that for the continent as a whole hydrology was represented most frequently and vegetation least frequently. Likewise, an analysis by size of area covered would certainly reveal that maps of small to intermediate areas far exceeded in number those of larger areas. It is fortuitous, therefore, that transcripts of a number of disparate maps have survived that together represent aspects of the vegetation of extensive areas of the northern interior, that it is possible to infer their influence on maps made by fur-trader frontiersmen and in turn to demonstrate the influence of frontiersmen's maps on the formal geographies of the period.

THE TUNDRA/FOREST AND FOREST/GRASSLAND TRANSITIONS

The transition between the tundra to the west of Hudson Bay and the boreal forest beyond occupies a 150 to 600 kilometer (93 to 372 miles) wide zone. Even prior to clearance of parts of it for agriculture, that between the forest and interior grasslands was somewhat narrower, rarely exceeding 300 kilometers, except to the south of 43°N, where the prairie openings in the Ohio valley increased its maximum width to almost 900 kilometers (558 miles). These are two of the zones which Indians, eighteenth-century fur traders and nineteenth-century biologists mapped as boundaries.

In the 1760s Hudson's Bay Company officials at Churchill and York Factories intensified their efforts both to find a Northwest Passage and to locate copper mines that had been reported far to the north. During the same period the northwestward expansion of the sphere of activity of Canadian fur traders forced the Company's traders to go inland from the Bay in order to seek contacts with the Indians on whom they had begun to depend for their supplies of best quality furs. Explorations both inland and up the coast from Churchill led to the realization that, in contrast with conditions around the southern end of Hudson Bay, there was a treeless coastal zone of undetermined width. This was known as "the barren grounds." Three consequences of its treelessness soon became apparent: it contained few natives; supported few commercial fur-bearing animals; and was both difficult and hazardous to traverse during much of the year. It was therefore essential to establish its inland limit. The first indications of it are on three contemporary transcripts of Indian maps.[6] Viewed separately, none of these clearly delineates the transition between the barren grounds and woods but seen as a set they do reveal that the Indian map makers were attempting to represent it (Fig. 5.1). Matonabbee, one of the two Chipewyan Indians responsible for the last of the three maps, later led Samuel Hearne on his third and successful attempt to reach the copper mines. It is significant that Hearne reported the strategic significance which Matonabbee consciously gave to the 'woods edge' in planning the route to be followed and in scheduling the various stages of the journey in relation to seasonal conditions.[7] Hearne's manuscript map of 1772, which had been compiled in part on the basis of a strict enquiry of the natives; clearly depicted the 'woods edge' for a distance of more than one thousand miles between Churchill Factory and a point well to the west of the lower Coppermine River.[8]

   That the 'woods edge' continued to be of significance to the native peoples and to alien explorers alike is revealed by its representation as a boundary line on two sketch maps collected in 1894 by the geologist Joseph B. Tyrell: one from the Chipewyans Jimmy Anderson and Curleyhead and the other from Powon, an Inuit.[9] The Chipewyans' map is particularly interesting in that it implies the existence of the transition zone between the continuous forest and the unbroken barren grounds by delimiting one extensive exclave of 'large timber' in the widest part of what is now generally designated the 'tundra-open woodland region of lichen, birch and shrubs with patches of needleleaf trees: There are no other known examples of Indian delimitations of macro biogeographic regions but the ability of Indians to comprehend and represent macro spatial patterns was quite widespread. Indeed, Indians would seem to have been conceptually capable of operating at all but the first of the six hierarchical levels recognized by Ackerman as having characterized Euro-American geographical methodology prior to the 1960s.[10] Their recognition and delimitation of macro biogeographic regions certainly involved "the identification of generic relations: categorization, classification, differention" and had the "objective of ... reducing to

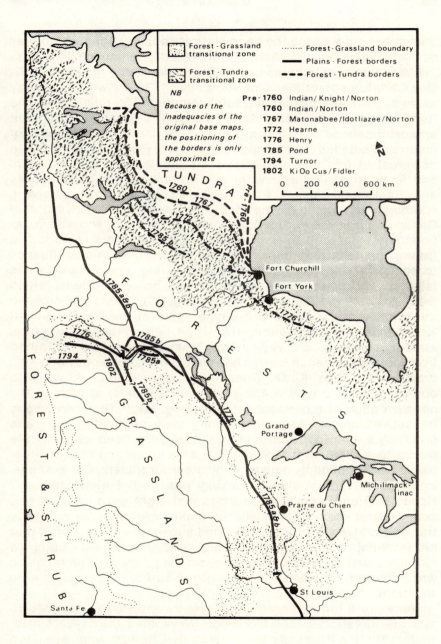

Forest - Grassland transitional zone

Forest - Tundra transitional zone

Forest - Grassland boundary

Plains - Forest borders

Forest - Tundra borders

NB

Because of the inadequacies of the original base maps, the positioning of the borders is only approximate

Pre - 1760 Indian / Knight / Norton
1760 Indian / Norton
1767 Matonabbee / Idotliazee / Norton
1772 Hearne
1776 Henry
1785 Pond
1794 Turnor
1802 Ki Oo Cus / Fidler

0   200   400   600 km

TUNDRA

1760

1767

1772

1785b

Pre - 1760

Fort Churchill

Fort York

1776

FOREST

1785 a & b

1776

1785b

1794

1785a

1802

1785b

1776

FOREST

Grand Portage

Michilimack-inac

FOREST & SHRUB

GRASSLANDS

1785 a & b

Prairie du Chien

1785 a & b

St Louis

Santa Fe

Figure 5.1. The 'Woods Edge.'

comprehensible scope the nearly infinite observations which may be made concerning the distribution of earth phenomena."[11]

A manuscript map presented by Alexander Henry the Elder to Sir Guy Carleton sometime in or soon after 1776 shows a boundary extending for approximately 1500 kilometers (930 miles) from the Red River in approximately 49°N towards the Rocky Mountains in approximately 53°N.[12] (See Fig. 5.1). This line is colored blue or green and labelled 'The Course of the Great Plaines.' To the south and west of this line bold captions indicate 'Great South Plain' and 'Great North Plaine' in what are now respectively North Dakota and Saskatchewan — Alberta. Three of the four surviving contemporary copies of the map first drawn in 1784 by another Canadian fur trader of American origin, Peter Pond, show a similar boundary extending for more than 4,000 kilometers (2480 miles) from a point a little to the west of the Mississippi-Ohio confluence to somewhere in the Peace River valley. On one version this is labelled 'ye Eastern Boundares of those immense Pleins which reaches to the great Mountains' (See Fig. 5.1).[13] Pond had crossed the forest/grassland during his nine years in the Northwest but Henry had crossed it once only. Their delimitations, therefore, almost certainly derived much from information obtained from Indians. Evidence for this has not survived but a copy of a map drawn in 1802 by Ki Oo Cus, a Blackfoot Chief, shows with considerable accuracy a 450 kilometer (279 mile) stretch of the northern edge of the grasslands (See Fig. 5.1).[14] There are vague indications on another contemporary copy of Pond's map[15] and on Henry's map that both men may have also been aware of the tundra/forest transition (See Fig. 5.1). This information could either have been supplied by natives or by other fur traders. For example, in October, 1775 Matthew Cocking was visited at Cumberland House by Henry and perhaps Pond just eight days after he had taken charge from Hearne and he must have been aware of the transition.[16] On the other hand, Pond subsequently indicated that his information about "Mr. Herring" (i.e. Hearne) was obtained "from the natives," according to whom the country to the far north was "destitute of wood" lacking "firing sufficient to pass a long winter on."[17]

There are a few clues as to why Henry and Pond attempted to plot the forest/grassland transition. More than thirty years after visiting the Plains, Henry recollected that he had seen live oxen (bison), red deer and wolves and the skins of foxes, bears and cougars but made no mention of beaver.[18] There is circumstantial evidence that Pond also recognized that the grasslands were not a significant source of beaver. Whilst "the country east of the great plains (boundary) under (this presumably should have been 'over') latitude 45 . . . are the chief Beaver Grounds . . ., the country to the west as far as '54⁰ North is well stocked with a good breed of horses, some mules and asses and herds of Buffaloes . . . "[19] As in Henry's recollections, there was no reference to beaver in this area. At a slightly later date Hudson's Bay Company officials must also have realized that beaver became scarcer as one passed from the forest to the grasslands. Thus, in 1794, Philip Turnor incorporated observations made by Peter Fidler in 1792/3 in delimiting with considerable accuracy a 200 kilometer (124 mile) stretch of the northern edge of the grasslands.[20]

THE ACCURACY OF THE DELIMITATIONS

Eighteenth-century attempts to represent transitions by means of boundary lines were perforce crude approximations and relating the boundaries to modern maps is exceedingly difficult. The only step in the hierarchy of Euro-American geographical methodology for which the Indians had no equivalent was what Ackerman called the "accurate determination of the shape and extent of the physical matrix."[21] Nevertheless, with a few exceptions the Indians and fur traders would seem to have been reasonably successful in representing the main outlines (See Fig. 5.1.).

In depicting the tundra/forest transition there was a tendency to locate the boundary nearer the outer limit of the wood exclaves than the inner limit of the openings. This is understandable in that, in contrast with the open tundra, even small woods provided shelter, fuel and a reasonable chance of finding game.

Pond's delimitation of the forest/grassland transition was false to the north of the Saskatchewan and progressively erroneous to the south of Prairie du Chien. Between these, both Henry's and Pond's delimitations tended to fall nearer the inner limit of the grassland openings than the outer edge of the woods. To fur traders approaching from the forest these openings were the first signs of a significant change in the environment. Conversely, in marking the outer limit of the woody exclaves, Ki Oo Cus, was doubtless reflecting the strategic significance for Indians of the absolute limit of trees in relation to the availability of fuel, tepee poles and certain types of game, concealment from enemies and protection from blizzards and fires. In several of these respects the factors that determined the location of the boundary were those that had influenced Matonabbee and others some thirty to forty years before in delimiting the tundra/forest boundary.

DISSEMINATION OF IDEAS ABOUT THE TRANSITIONS

Knowledge of the existence and position of these biogeographic transitions was vital to the wellbeing of Indians and the success of the fur traders. However, in the late eighteenth century their existence was apparently but little known among geographers or, if known, their significance was not apparent to them.

In the course of compiling his little-known 'Map of the Lands around the North Pole, Alexander Dalrymple had access to manuscript maps of both the Hudson's Bay Company and Peter Pond.[22] He portrayed the boundary by means of which Hearne had represented the tundra/forest transition as a line of tree symbols but there is no indication on the map as to which side of the line was tundra and which forest. Furthermore, whereas on his manuscript map Hearne had used what are now accepted as conventional coniferous-tree symbols, Dalrymple adopted the rounded deciduous form, thereby doubtless misleading the observant but uninformed.[23] Dalrymple's map also depicts by means of a fine line part of what is indisputably Pond's boundary between the forest and grassland as represented on the Public Record Office version of his map. However, this is unexplained on the map and referred to in the accompanying memoir as "a tract."[24] The error can easily be explained. Whereas the Crevecoer version of Pond's 1784 map clearly indicated the nature of the boundary, the Public Record Office version (which Henry Hamilton had forwarded to England and manuscript copies of which would seem to have been in circulation in London) showed the boundary without indicating its nature.[25] It links a series of eleven points labelled A1 to A11 but the key to these and several other sets of points on the map was either never sent to London or became lost soon after it arrived. Dalrymple's maps of 1790 depicted the tundra/forest transition in the same misleading way but omitted the Pond boundary.[26]

Aaron Arrowsmith also had access to the maps of both the Hudson's Bay Company and Peter Pond. The 1796 revision of his 'Map Exhibiting all the New Discoveries in the Interior Parts of North America . . . ' depicted the 'Woods Edge' to the east and west of the Red Deer River according to Turnor.[27] This had not been shown on the original edition of the previous year and was omitted from the 1819 and subsequent revisions. Nevertheless, it is of of interest as the only printed map known to have depicted

Figure 5.2. Forest-grasslands boundary.

unambiguously any of the boundaries discussed in this chapter (Fig. 5.2).

Europeans and residents on the Atlantic seaboard failed to recognize the existence of these two biogeographic transitions because the original documents on which they were depicted and in which they were alluded to were almost without exception unpublished and unknown. The Hudson's Bay Company did not in general allow outsiders to examine its records. Nothing is known for certain concerning the whereabouts of Henry's maps after it was presented to Sir Guy Carleton in 1776 until it was purchased by the Library of Congress in 1906. Henry's own account of his travels of 1775-76 in the Saskatchewan Country was not published until more than thirty years after. Likewise, Hearne's *Journey* ... was not published until almost a quarter of a century after he reached the copper mines and even then the published map did not depict the tundra/forest transition. Three versions of Pond's 1784 map were sent to Paris and at least one copy of the accompanying memoir. However, this was at a time when French interest in North America was in decline and the map would not appear to have had any influence. The version of Pond's 1784 map which Henry Hamilton sent to England would appear to have been known to several people in London in the years just before and immediately after 1790 but in the absence of either the memoir or a key the critical boundary was meaningless. Finally, in the spring of 1785 Pond failed in an attempt to interest the United States Congress in his map. Consequently, Americans, who might have been quicker than Europeans to recognize the significance of the forest/grassland transition, knew nothing of it. Like the forest/grassland transition it awaited rediscovery by scientists in the nineteenth century: scientists who were unaware that they were beginning to do what some Indians had attempted long before.

NOTES

1. Charles Pickering, "On the geographical distribution of plants", *Transactions of the American Philosophical Society: New Series,* 3 (1830): 274-284.

2. G. Malcolm Lewis, "Regional ideas and reality in the cis-Rocky Mountain west", *Transactions and Papers of the Institute of British Geographers,* 30 (1966): footnote 29, p. 149.

3. The characteristics and roles of Indian 'maps' are reviewed by G. Malcolm Lewis in "Pre-literate cartography of North America" to be published in J. Brian Harley and D. Woodward, eds., *History of Cartography,* vol 3 (Chicago: University of Chicago Press, forthcoming). For a much shorter account

see G. Malcolm Lewis, "The indigenous maps and mapping of North American Indians," *The Map Collector,* 9 (December 1979): 25-32.

4. G. Malcolm Lewis, "Indian maps," in Carol M. Judd and Arthur J. Ray, ed., *Old Trails and New Directions: Papers of The Third North American Fur Trade Conference* (Toronto: University of Toronto Press, 1980): 9-23.

5. For a case study of this process see G. Malcolm Lewis, "Indicators of unacknowledged assimilations from Amerindian *maps* on Euro-American maps of North America: some general principles arising from a study of La Verendrye's composite map (1728-29)",*Imago Mundi,* 38 (1986): 9-34.

6. Post 1719 (Sketch of rivers between Prince of Wales' Fort and the 'Northernmost Coper Mine' — giving Indian names), manuscript on paper, 67x52 cm, G.1/19; 1760 *Moses Norton's drt. of the northern parts of Hudsons Bay laid down on Indian information and brot. home by him anno 1760, manuscript* on parchment, 87x65 cm, G. 2/8; 1767 *A draught by two northern Indian leaders call'd Meatonabee and Idotly-azee of ye country to yet northward of Churchill River viz Hudson's Bay,* manuscript on paper, 145x72 cm. G.2/27: Hudson's Bay Company Archives, Winnipeg.

7. Samuel Hearne, *A Journey from Prince of Wales's Fort, in Hudson's Bay, to the Northern Ocean* ... (London: Strahan and Cadell, 1795); edition edited by Richard Glover (Toronto: Macmillan, 1958), pp. 47, 49, 59 and 65.

8. Samuel Hearne 1772 *A Map of part of the inland country to the Nth. Wt. of Prince of Wales Fort ... Saml. Hearne,* manuscript on linen-mounted paper, 83x76 cm, G.2/10, Hudson's Bay Company Archives, Winnipeg; and Samuel Hearne, 1795 (Glover, 1958, edn.): 1xxii.

9. Joseph B. Tyrell, 1894, (Map of the west shore of Hudson Bay and vicinity by the Inuit Powon), manuscript map on brown paper, 91x61 cm.; and *Map of the country west of Hudson Bay by Jimmy Anderson and Curleyhead,* manuscript map on linen, 39x30 cm, compiled from an untitled map on four sheets measuring 68x45 cm. All three maps in the Tyrrell Papers, Thomas Fisher Rare Book Library, University of Toronto, Toronto.

10. G. Malcolm Lewis, "Amerindian antecedents of American academic geography", in Brian W. Blouet ed., *The Origins of Academic Geography in the United States* (Hamden, Connecticut: Archon Books, 1981): 19-35.

11. Edward A. Ackerman, *Geography as a Fundamental Research Discipline,* University of Chicago Department of Geography Research Paper no. 53 (Chicago: Department of Geography, the University of Chicago, 1958): 4.

12. Alexander Henry, 1776. *A map of the north west parts of America. With the utmost respect. Inscrib'd to His Excellency Sir Guy Carleton ... By his most obedient servt. Alexr. Henry,* manuscript on linen-mounted paper, 213x101 cm. Geography and Map Division, Library of Congress, Washington, D.C.

13. Peter Pond/J. Hector St John de Crevecoeur, 1785. *Copy of a map presented to the Congress by Peter Pond ... copied by St. John de Crevecoeur for hi Grace of la Rochefoucault,* manuscript map on linen-mounted tracing paper, 71x53 cm. Add. Ms. 15,332-C, British Museum, London.

14. Ki Oo Cus/Peter Fidler, 1802. (Untitled map of the upper Missouri and upper South Saskatchewan basins drawn by Peter Fidler from a draft by Ki Oo Cus, a Blackfoot Chief), 48x37 cm, in Fidler's journals of exploration and survey, 1789-1804, vol 2., E.3/2, ff. 104 v. and 105 r., Hudson's Bay Company Archives, Winnipeg.

15. Peter Pond, 1785. (Map without title of the region from Hudson Bay to the Pacific Ocean and from Lake Michigan to the Arctic Ocean), manuscript

map on linen-mounted paper, 72x49 cm, MPG 425, Public Record Office, Kew, London.

16. Edwin E. Rich, "The history of the Hudson's Bay Company 1670-1870", vol. 2 *Hudson's Bay Record Society,* vol. 22 (London: Hudson's Bay Record Society, 1959): 13-16; and Arthur S. Morton ed., *The Journal of Duncan M'Gillivray of the Northwest Company* (Toronto:MacMillan, 1929): xxix.

17. Peter Pond, *Amerique Septentrionale. Remarques sur la carte presentee au Congres le ler Mars 1785,* note 7, fol.2, Add. Ms. 15, 332-E, British Museum, London; reproduced in Gordon C. Davison, *The North West Company* (Berkeley: University of California Pres, 1918): 260.

18. Alexander Henry, *Travels and Adventures in Canada and the Indian Territories between 1760 and 1776* (New York: I Riley, 1809): 299.

19. Peter Pond, *Amerique Septentrionale. Remarques ... ,* notes 1 and 16, fols. 1 and 3.

20. Philip Turnor, 1794. *The the Honorable the Governor, Deputy Governor and Committee of the Hudson's Bay Company this map of Hudson's Bay and the rivers and lakes between the Atlantick and Pacifick Oceans is most humbly inscribed ... ,* rolled manuscript on linen-mounted paper, 259x193 cm, G.2/32, Hudson's Bay Company, Winnipeg.

21. Edward A. Ackerman, *Geography as a Fundamental Research Discipline:* 4; and G. Malcolm Lewis, "Amerinidan antecedents of American academic geography": 20-21.

22. Alexander Dalrymple, *Memoir of a Map of the Lands around the North Pole* (London: George Bigg, 1789):1 and 4.

23. Alexander Dalrymple, *Map of the Lands around the North Pole by A. Dalrymple 1789* (London: A Dalrymple, May 4th 1789); and *Memoir . . .: 11.*

25. Peter Pond/J. Hector St. John de Crevecoeur, 1785; and Peter Pond, 1785.

26. Alexander Dalrymple, 1790. *A map of Hudson's Bay and the various lakes and rivers adjecent as far as known,* manuscript map on transparent paper, 71x33 cm, Greater London Record Office (Middlesex Division), London; and *A map of Hudson's Bay and of the rivers and lakes between the Atlantick and Pacifick Oceans,* manuscript map on paper, C.O. 700 (Canada) no. 42, Public Record Office, Kew, London.

27. Aaron Arrowsmith. *A Map Exhibiting all the New Discoveries in the Interior Parts of North America . . . additions to 1796* (London: Aaron Arrowsmith, 1796).

ACKNOWLEDGEMENTS

The author gratefully acknowledges financial support from the University of Sheffield Research Fund in connection with parts of the research on which this chapter was based.

Part Three
Land Ownership and Economic Development

Chapter 6
Indian Land in Southern Alberta

Claudia Notzke

Land may be viewed as the cornerstone of Indian people's ethnic and cultural identity. Western Canadian Treaty Indians consider the development of their reserves as ethnic homelands to be one of their paramount goals. Ethnic homelands are closely linked to the Indian people's desire to survive not only as individuals, but as a people. Retention of group identity really means that Indian people gain control of the economic and social development of their communities, within a framework of legal and constitutional guarantees for their land and their institutions.[1] The evolution of Canadian Indian policy shows quite clearly that Indians as a collectivity as well as their reserves were (and are) regarded as a transitory feature of Canadian society. Reserves were not considered lands reserved for Indian people's homelands but as government-granted lands to be used as schools for civilization. Once this purpose had been fulfilled the reserved lands were to be abolished. On the other hand, Indians still promote the idea of the reserve as an ethnic homeland. Although the majority of western Indians reside on their reserves, most of the urban migrants retain close ties to their home community and Indian politicians endeavor to maintain the homeland ideology. Thus the purpose of this chapter is to explore the unique problems encountered by Indians in southern Alberta in their attempts to regain lost land and to retain and manage their remaining landbase.

The Stoney and the Peigan Reserves, located in southern Alberta in an area encompassing the largest Indian reserves in Canada, are examined here. The Stoney Indians have a landbase of approximately 195 square miles at their disposal. The Morley Reserve comprises 178 square miles and is the main reserve and includes the uninhabited Rabbit Lake Reserve. It centers around the township of Morley, roughly 35 miles west of Calgary. The Morley Reserve as well as the smaller Bighorn and Eden Valley

Reserves to the north and south are all in the foothills of the Rocky Mountains. The Stoney population totals 2,296 and 1,812 Peigan Indians inhabit approximately 175 square miles in the southwestern corner of the province. The main reserve is centered around Brocket which is 50 miles southwest of Lethbridge (Fig. 6.1).

Historically, the reserves in southern Alberta are Treaty Seven Reserves. The so-called Blackfoot Treaty was the seventh in a series of eleven post-confederation treaties, and was signed in 1877 between the Crown and the native tribes occupying the area that today is southern Alberta. While sharing a common origin, the resultant reserves have developed quite differently, due to differences in culture, natural resources, political leadership and dealings with provincial and federal governments. The discovery of natural gas on their land has made the Stoneys a relatively wealthy tribe, whereas the Peigan depend on a very narrow resource base, namely land and water.

LAND: THE OPEN QUESTION

A discussion of Indian lands would be incomplete without some elaboration on the topic of Indian land claims which have been a feature of almost all periods of Canada's history. Legal and political factors prohibited Indians from bringing claims forward before the 1970s and 1980s. Native land claims have affected such different issues as the controversies over the patriation of the Canadian Constitution and northern development projects.

There are various types of claims. So-called specific claims are based on lawful obligations and include those for lands due to native people as part of a treaty agreement with the Crown, or may involve lost land, surrendered under often dubious circumstances since the creation of the reserves.

The vital importance Indian people ascribe to their landbase cannot be overemphasized. Marie Marule[2] speaks for most Treaty Indians when she states that "The elimination of reserve lands inevitably means the termination of status and rights for Indian people. The easiest way to destroy the distinctiveness of Indian people and their cultural heritage is to eliminate the landbase."

Today strong economic interests are at stake especially, in Alberta; but most Indians still view their land as much more than a piece of real estate. Constant assaults on this landbase have been made by the government through repeated amendments of the Indian Act and, more recently, through the White Paper.[3] These actions have bred an attitude of distrust among Indians where their land is

109

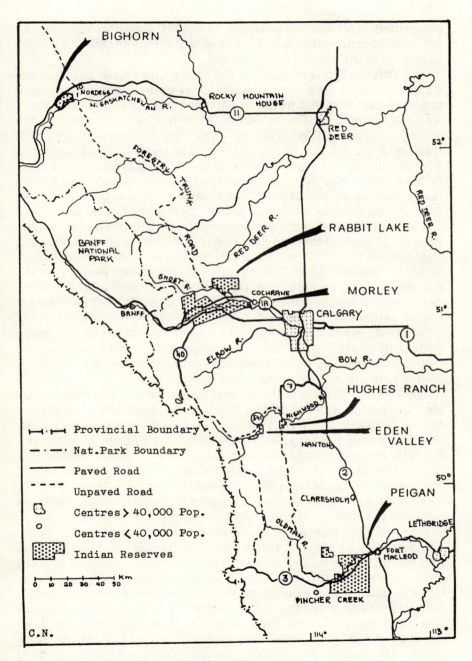

Figure 6.1. Regional Setting of the Reserves.

concerned, and not surprisingly the land question remains an unresolved issue with both the Stoneys and Peigan. Some of these date back to the days of Treaty Seven.

The Wesley Stoneys' (one of the three Stoney bands) Bighorn-Kootenay Plains land claim is a typical example. Through oversight and manipulation this northern Stoney band's traditional territory was not covered by Treaty Seven. After the establishment of the Morley Reserve (intended for all three Stoney bands) one-third of this band moved out of the reserve and back to their ancestral hunting grounds along the banks of the North Saskatchewan River in 1894. When they first petitioned the Department of Indian Affairs for a reserve in the North Saskatchewan headwaters, in 1909, Alberta had already provincial status. Control of Crown lands was still retained by the federal government. In 1910 the Indian Affairs Branch actually accepted the Indians' claim, and consequently approached the Minister of the Interior requesting that the Crown release land for an Indian reserve at Kootenay Plains. In the following year, though, the Department suddenly reversed its decision and rejected the request on the grounds that permament Indian settlement in the upper North Saskatchewan Valley would exterminate wildlife. According to Larner[4] the true reason rested with anticipated economic development, suggested by the Geological Survey's involvement with commercial interests seeking mineral concessions in the Bighorn Valley.

The Forestry Branch of the federal Department of the Interior was also instrumental in opposing Indian establishment at Kootenay Plains. In 1910 the Rocky Mountain Forest Reserve had been created, encompassing the entire eastern slope of Alberta. The Forestry Branch, charged with its management, sought to position its rangers in the centrally located Kootenay Plains. As a result, there were two branches within the Ministry of the Interior vying for the Kootenay Plains: Indian Affairs and Forestry. No agreement between the conflicting interests was reached.

Most of the Kootenay Stoneys pursued a traditional semi-nomadic way of life, but some had built houses, planted gardens and owned numerous horses and cattle. Over one hundred head of cattle were moved from Morley to the Plains because of the deteriorated grazing conditions on the reserve. Forestry officials permitted the Stoneys the use of forestry ranches upon payment of fees, and the provincial Department of Agriculture issued them licenses to hunt. They were still regarded as squatters and in 1915, Indian Affairs and the Forestry Branch jointly embarked upon a program of forcible removal and subsequent compensation of the

Kootenay Plains Indians. Action was proposed in 1918, but objected to by Indian Commissioner Graham on the basis that the reserve was unable to sustain 200 head of cattle. The plan was postponed and finally abandoned. Thus the Stoneys were again encouraged, albeit obliquely, to remain on their ancestral lands.

When the 1930 Natural Resources Act transferred natural resources or more specifically, the Crown lands, from the federal to the provincial government, the chances of a reserve being granted within the Clearwater Forest Reserve were further reduced. Ottawa was in a position to conveniently rid itself of any responsibility. However, there was no attempt to remove the people to Morley. Eventually, the initiative of John Laurie, the Secretary of the Indian Association of Alberta, led the Province of Alberta to agree to cooperate with the federal government in making a 5,000 acre tract available to the Stoneys in 1947. The reserve was not part of the Stoneys' native land on the Kootenay Plains but at the confluence of the Bighorn and North Saskatchewan Rivers. By the Treaty Seven land/people ratio of one square mile or 640 acres per five persons, the reserve land should have been in the neighborhood of 12,800 rather than 5,000 acres. The allocated acreage was neither capable of accommodating the extant number of horses and cattle nor of developing a ranching or farming economy with the production of winter feed. Indians attending the 1947 meetings apparently believed all the time (and were given the impression) that additional land was forthcoming, and that the Bighorn Reserve was just "a waiting place."[5] In the summer of 1948 an Order-in-Council established the special Bighorn Reserve 144A. The official document emphasized two points: 1) The Stoney band had no claim to the land in question, having already received land grants consistent with the terms of Treaty Seven, and 2) The mineral rights would be withheld from them.

After the Natural Resources Act the federal government had given up any effective enforcement of the treaty Indians' right to hunt and fish in unoccupied Crown land. By and large the Albertan government kept the agreement and allowed Stoneys to hunt in the Rocky Mountain Forest Reserve, but it introduced an increasing number of restrictions. The transfer agreement in 1947 for example, stipulated that the number of Indian horses be reduced to a minimum to rid provincial lands of the wild or semi-wild horses and reduce pressure on valuable hay. In the 1950s, Dominion and provincial forestry officials systematically rounded up and killed horses at Bighorn-Kootenay Plains. Many of them were Stoney horses. This was a considerable economic loss for the Indians. At the same time the upper North Saskatchewan valley was thrown open to the major North American oil corporations for seismographic surveys. Hundreds of miles of seismic cuts crisscrossed the region. Service access roads were cut through the valley. Large and small game were driven from the district by these activities, and the Bighorn Stoneys, as well as those residing at Morley, suffered extreme loss of food and fur trapping income.

The fatal blow to the Bighorn Stoneys' remaining self-sufficiency was dealt by the provincial government and Calgary Power Limited in the early 1970s. The construction of the Bighorn Dam on the North Saskatchewan River inundated virtually the entire claim area of Kootenay Plains, flooding cabins, graves, campgrounds and pastures. Moreover, it eliminated the Stoneys' livelihood derived from hunting, guiding hunters and fur-trapping. About 95 percent of the Bighorn Stoneys, formerly the most self-reliant section of the tribe, have been on welfare since the dam was completed in 1972.

The Stoneys and the Indian Association of Alberta had tried in vain to prevent the implementation of this hydro-electric project. When the tribe realized in 1969 that further attempts to prevent the construction of the dam would be futile, it decided, instead, to get the government to acknowledge and guarantee the rights of the Bighorn Indians. They requested that the provincial government compensate them for any losses due to the effects of the dam. This compensation included financial assistance to help establish economic projects and job training programs, but the main thrust aimed to establish a reserve in the Kootenay Plains area. The provincial government felt, that if there was to be any meaningful settlement, particularly if it involved land, the Stoneys would have to prove legal entitlement to the land. The federal government also saw itself in a position to respond only to a legal claim since all complaints and problems relating to the dam were a matter of provincial jurisdiction. This ruling gave rise to the report by Getty and Larner.[6] The Indian Affairs department provided the Stoneys $30,000 (Canadian) to conduct this oral and documentary study for their entitlement to land in the Kootenay Plains.[7] Even while the research was being conducted, the provincial government indicated that, if the federal government acknowledged that there was an outstanding treaty claim of land, it would not hesitate to provide land as obliged by terms of the 1930 Natural Resources Act.[8] The federal government was presented the Kootenay Plains land research report in April 1972 and both the Stoneys and the federal government asked Dr. Barber, Indian Claims Commissioner, to evaluate the findings. He recommended to the Department of

Indian Affairs that the report confirmed the Bighorn Wesley Band's unfulfilled claim to treaty land in the Bighorn district, and that the federal government should settle the claim as soon as possible. For fear of establishing a precedent that could lead to claims from other bands across Canada, there was considerable stalling on the part of the government, but finally, in January 1974, the Department of Indian Affairs officially acknowledged that the Bighorn Stoneys should be given reserve land.

Treaty Seven provided one square mile of land for each family of five persons. Problems arose as to the date that should be selected for determining the population figure. Should it be based on the population of 1877 when the treaty was signed, the early 1900s when the federal government first promised to establish a reserve in that area, 1948 when the existing small reserve was set aside, or the present-day census figure, when the terms of the treaty were to be honored? After lengthy negotiations, a figure of 144 persons residing on the reserve as of December 31, 1972, was finally agreed upon. This translated into a reserve of approximately 18,000 acres.

Apparently all that remained to be done was the provincial government's provision of the land requested, as spelled out by the laws of the province. Instead, after further delays, the Government of Alberta rejected the federal government's request to provide the land to meet the outstanding treaty obligation. They opted to challenge in court the legality of the Stoney claim in spite of the fact that the Indian Claims Commissioner and the federal government had already acknowledged its validity. On December 2, 1977, the Wesley Band formally filed a claim with the federal government. To date, the question is still before the courts.

It can be speculated that things might have taken a different turn if environmental and social impact assessment legislation of the 1960s had been similar to that of today. As Howard[9] points out, planning of the dam involved no assessment of the social and environmental costs. Certain economic costs were also excluded from the assessment, such as those for road construction, bridge and campground redevelopment, and land clearing. Had these been included, as today's more intensive economic analysis would have required, it is possible that the dam would never have been built. The fact that there were no public hearings prior to construction further removed public objections and political processes of review. Public expectation of participating in the development and conservation of the environment has risen since the 1960s. Although it is questionable whether the issue of native land claims would have been addressed in the context of social impacts, a somewhat more humane treatment of the Stoneys could likely have occurred.

Another observation, made also by using the knowledge and vision of hindsight, is that the Stoneys' unwillingness to use pressure tactics considerably weakened their bargaining position[10] because the government knew that they could delay and procrastinate without having to worry about any negative repercussions. The Bighorn people could have organized boycotts, demonstrations, sit-ins, picket lines, or even tried to obtain a court injunction to stop construction. All these kinds of tactics would have focused public attention upon the problem and, to whatever degree they were successful, it would have increased pressure on the government. Instead, the Stoneys chose to trust the government without having the means to make them live up to their promises.

The Bighorn-Kootenay Plains land claim may be the most serious grievance the Stoneys have, but it is not the only one. Still in the courts is the problem of mineral rights in the highway exchange land. When the Transcanada Highway was constructed in 1961 and widened in 1968, using reserve lands, the Stoneys received surface rights to land adjacent to the northern and southern boundary of the main reserve plus a small addition to the Rabbit Lake Reserve in exchange for the highway right-of-way (Fig. 6.2). The Stoneys feel that building a major highway across their land amounts to the same as giving up the mineral rights and insist on compensation. This is more than a political quibble, for this ruling prevents the Indians from participating in the exploitation of the Ghost natural gas field.

A contentious issue with the Peigan Tribe which was settled only recently stemmed from the question of who owns the Oldman River waterbed. In contrast to the United States, Canadian Indian reserves have no generally applicable water right. Thus, water-related questions are particularly complicated. In 1979, the Peigan became involved in a dispute with the Province of Alberta, and by implication with the Lethbridge Northern Irrigation District (L.N.I.D.) regarding that part of the L.N.I.D. system which runs through the reserve and includes a diversion weir, a canal and a flume. The Peigan contended that these facilities were located on unexpropriated land and therefore were in place illegally. They asked the Province of Alberta to pay them compensation retroactively for the presence of these facilities on what they perceived as Band lands and also that a yearly fee system be inaugurated for each acre of land irrigated by the L.N.I.D. system.

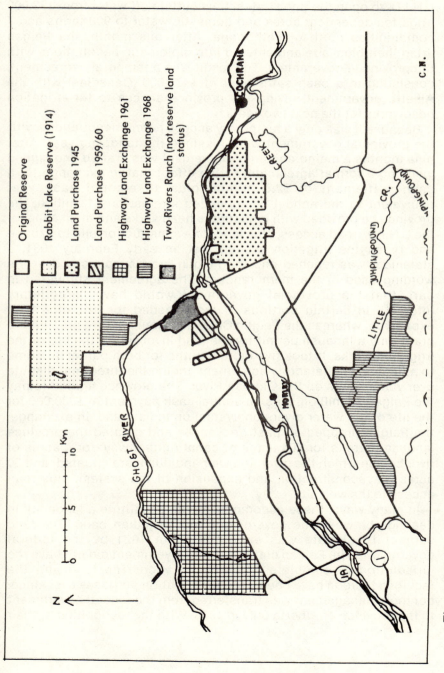

Figure 6.2. The Composition of Stoney Land.

When these demands were not met, in April 1979 the Peigan set up a blockade on the Oldman River and refused to allow officials of the L.N.I.D. to open the flood gates, thus cutting off water from 133,000 irrigation-dependent acres and domestic water to 900 farms and 7 communities north of Lethbridge. After one month, the Peigan lifted their blockade and entered into diplomatic negotiations with the provincial government. The result was a temporary agreement, consisting in a cash settlement of $435,000 (Canadian) with the Alberta government, giving the province access to the irrigation headworks for the next two years.

Because it was only a temporary access permit negotiations with the provincial government were resumed the following year. After nine months a memorandum of agreement was drafted and signed (pending a formal agreement) to the effect that in exchange for a cash settlement of $2.5 million plus an amount each year equivalent to the annual compounded interest on $1 million, the province be provided with land for the headworks and main canal of the L.N.I.D., road access, plus land for a construction site to expand and repair the irrigation system. Yet, in early February 1981, a stalemate was reached and the Peigan grew suspicious over the wording used in the memorandum. The agreement stipulated in part, that the provincial government would have "proprietary interest" in certain portions of land needed for irrigation weir expansion, whereas the Peigan Chief and Council were prepared to grant only a landuse permit for the land involved for the life of the irrigation works. It took five more months for both parties to come to a final and satisfactory agreement ending the three year dispute over water rights on the Oldman River. The province agreed to pay the Peigan $4 million, plus an annual cash payment of $300,000 for the life of the water diversion system on Indian land. In exchange, the Peigan dropped all past grievances and granted the province landuse permits for 204 acres of canal right-of-way, for 4 acres of river bed on which the diversion weir and flume are situated, and 50 acres for reconstruction and expansion of the system, plus road access to the weir site.

In many ways, these accomplishments constitute a landmark in dealings between the government and an Indian band. The land subject to dispute was expropriated in 1921 by the federal government. The Peigan claim that the government did not have the jurisdiction to complete this expropriation. The land and the facilities thereon have been used for irrigation purposes ever since, but their management was transferred from the federal government to the Province of Alberta only in 1976. With the recognition of their rights to the Oldman River waterbed the Peigan won the first major land claims settlement in western Canada. Another breakthrough was their successful resistance to an expropriation by means of a land surrender and subsequent lease in favor of a permit system, where the band retains ownership of the land in question and regains control when/if the L.N.I.D. works are no longer needed.

The allegation of improper surrender of the northwest corner of their reserve forms the basis for another land claim of the Peigan. This claim dates back to the early twentieth century, when the reserve system was being questioned as a means of assimilation. In 1907 the Indian Act was revised accordingly, making it simpler and more attractive for bands to surrender their reserves. Whereas today surrenders are made only for the purpose of leasing land, then surrendered reserve lands were to be sold to white farmers and ranchers. The topic of a land surrender on the Peigan Reserve was first brought up by the Indian agent in May 1909. Though the band told him in June that they did not want to surrender land, he went ahead with plans for a surrender of three to five sections with access to the Canadian Pacific Railway tracks and the Brocket townsite.[11] The chiefs objected, and sought the services of a Fort Mcleod lawyer. Still determined to obtain a surrender, the agent decided that the band might be more inclined to give up some other portion of its reserve, and so selected 45 sections in the northeast corner. He forced a vote in July. With their lawyer present, the band members defeated the surrender 46 to 39.[12] The Indian agent pressed a second vote at the end of July. This time it was defeated 60 to 42. Twice defeated in the northeast, the agent then selected a new surrender site in the northwest (Fig. 6.3). He succeeded in having the band's lawyer barred from observing the vote, received instructions as to price per acre from the Department of the Interior, and had the land surveyed on August 10, 1909. This time he won and the surrender was carried on August 17. Even though the vote was not in accordance with Indian Act stipulations concerning surrenders, even though the agent had obviously brought pressure to bear on the Indians, and despite all protest representations made to Ottawa by the tribe's chief and its lawyer, the federal government did not intervene.

The government's neglect did not stop with the surrender. By law, the surrendered lands were to be sold at competitive auctions. Though auctions were held in 1909, 1910, and 1913, Land Titles Records indicate that lands were sold in other ways as well.[13] Moreover, rather than being paid directly by the government for their land, the tribe was forced to accept time payments from

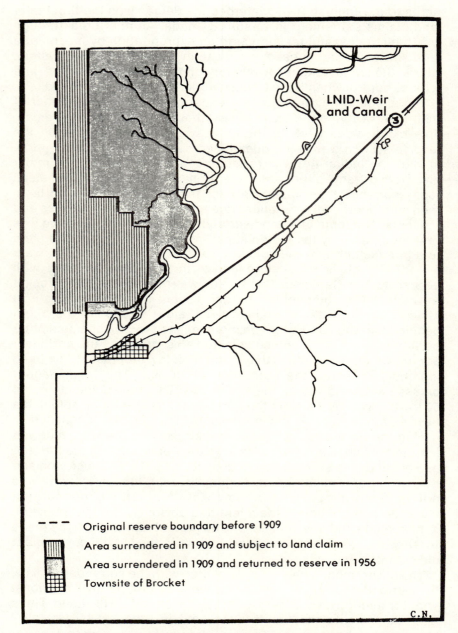

LNID-Weir
and Canal

C.N.

- - - Original reserve boundary before 1909

Area surrendered in 1909 and subject to land claim

Area surrendered in 1909 and returned to reserve in 1956

Townsite of Brocket

Figure 6.3. Peigan Reserve: Areas (recently or presently) Subject to Dispute.

purchasers, many of whom defaulted. This limited the tribe's access to funds for agricultural development. While the Peigan were paid interest on these accounts (with the department taking an administrative fee, of course), the actual sale value was reduced since only 10,300 acres of 22,338 acres were actually ever sold. The remaining 12,038 acres were retained by the government from 1909 to 1956 when, at last they were returned. In the interim, Ottawa had leased those lands to non-Indians. After seventy-one years of frustration, the Peigan finally hired a Calgary law firm to take the case to court. The lawyers did not simply put together an oral testimony of band elders but, instead collected every detail of the history of the surrender and prepared a complete economic assessment of earning capacity lost to the Peigan tribe. This multi-million-dollar case was just about to go to trial when the federal government opted for an out-of-court settlement in 1984 and decided to pay the Peigan Tribe for its loss. The actual settlement though, is still pending.

All this "unfinished business" has far-reaching consequences for the development of the reserves. Not only does it directly affect the resource base and financial situation of the bands, but it also has an impact on their general relationship to government departments and thereby may influence decisions concerning not only the reserve communities, but also the larger society. Examples are the controversy over the eventual construction of a natural gas processing plant on the Morley Reserve and the recent discussion of where to locate a major on-steam storage facility on the Oldman River.

LAND: QUANTITY AND TENURE SYSTEM

The Treaty Seven Reserves were originally allocated on the basis of one square mile per family of five. Due to the transient character of the population an exact enumeration was a well-nigh impossible task, and population figures in government documents vary considerably. When their reserve was surveyed in 1879, the Stoneys were given 109 square miles; the number of families was given as seventy-one according to Indian Affairs.[14] The first Indian Affairs Annual Report (1881) enumerated a population of 610. The Peigan Reserve, surveyed in 1882, encompassed 183.4 square miles for 193 families, a population of 849. Since then there have been some changes with regard to both reserves.

In 1914 the Rabbit Lake Reserve was transferred to the Stoneys, adding 20 square miles. In 1945 the Stoneys purchased two ranches adjoining the eastern extremity of the Morley Reserve, comprising 23 square miles. The Eden Valley Reserve (7 square miles) was established in 1946, and Bighorn (8 square miles) two years later. Some parcels of land located north of the Ghost Reservoir were purchased 1959-60. In the land exchange for the Transcanada Highway right-of-way 29 square miles of reserve land were added adjacent to the northern boundary of the Morley Reserve in 1961. Seven years later the widening of the highway resulted in the addition of 17 square miles to the south side of the Morley Reserve plus 4 square miles to Rabbit Lake. Finally, in the late 1970s, the Stoneys bought the Two Rivers Ranch north of the Ghost Reservoir (See Fig. 6.2). This adds up to about 224 square miles, without deducting the land lost to reservoir, powerlines and highways, where there are no data available. It means an increase in the Stoney landbase of roughly 100 percent. At the same time — based on the available statistics — the Stoney population increased by 244 percent. Due to the possibly illegal surrender the Peigan even experienced a reduction of their reserve lands, while their population grew by 113 percent. A likely explanation for the striking difference between the Peigan and Stoney population is an inadequate enumeration of the latter due to their continued nomadic lifestyle in the early reserve days. In both cases there now is an obvious discrepancy between a stationary landbase and a rapidly growing population. It is not surprising, therefore, that the population density of both reserves is somewhat higher than that of the provincial census divisions the reserves are part of.

Land-tenure systems can have far-reaching effects on the landuse pattern. As the Red Paper points out, "In the culture of Western Canadian Indians, the land is the gift of the Great Spirit, the common legacy of all. The true owners are the children yet unborn. The Indians naturally view their land as a trust with a permanent sign on the corner-post, 'Not for Sale!'"[15]

The Indian Act describes reserves as lands "set apart for the use and benefit of a band." Some judicial decisions have held that the band has a real property right in the reserve, a personal and usufractuary right to the use and benefit of the land. Another method of describing the band's position is to speak of the Crown holding reserve lands in trust for the band, the band being the beneficiary. Indians are opposed to any system of allotment that would give individuals ownership with rights to sell, but rather want the Indian Act changed to give Indians control of lands without changing the fact that the title is now held in trust. Presently the land holding system on reserve and surrendered lands is characterized by a continuing discretionary power of the Minister of Indian Affairs. In the past the Department of Indian Affairs made all the decisions as to what land would be used for certain purposes, who used it, how long it was used, and, where applicable, what payment was made for the use of land. Nowadays on most reserves, including the Peigan and Stoneys, these powers have been transferred to Chief and Council. The band manages its own lands, and negotiations with outside parties are carried out directly by the Band Council. The Indian Act still demands the final approval by the department, but in practice this is a mere formality, and Indian Affairs does not interfere with the substance of agreements.

When the reserves were first established, the plains tribes had no concept of individual use and ownership of land.[16] Initial sedentary settlement tended to be in "villages," often corresponding to the traditional bands within the tribes,[17] where farming was attempted on a communal basis. But the government's goal was for Indian society to be "atomized." Thus, the government would deal with individuals rather than with tribes. Their desire for individualization extended to breaking up the villages in the reserves, and to put an end to communal farming and ranching. The Indian was to be taught to be an individual farmer or cattle raiser on his own piece of land. Consequently, reserves were increasingly subdivided into small plots and individuals were given their own parcel of land to work.

Many bands, particularly on the prairies, and including the Peigan and Stoneys, choose not to use "Certificates of Possession" or any of the Indian Act provisions for internal Indian land holding on reserves. They adhere to what may be called "customary" or "traditional" land allotment patterns, in contrast with those found in the Indian Act. These bands allot land to individual band members, but do so at the discretion of the band council. They avoid any Ministerial validation of the allotment. The allottee, on the other hand, has no more legal security of tenure than the band council is prepared to permit. The practice of this land policy and the problems encountered slightly vary from reserve to reserve.

On the Peigan Reserve 94 square miles, or 57 percent of the reserve's landbase, have been individually allotted. Much of today's distribution pattern goes back to the 1920s, when the Peigan population numbered around 500. The educational policy of this period (industrial schools) placed particular emphasis on manual training and agricultural instruction, and band members interested in agriculture were allocated a parcel of land by the Indian agent.

Yet, the relapse small-scale agriculture experienced after World War One was to repeat itself in the 1950s, when mechanization and related changes intensified, and farming in the old way become just too uneconomical. Many of the older individuals on the reserve interviewed during a sample survey recalled working their land with a horse-drawn plow until the late 1950s. Then they resorted to leasing their plots to non-Indian farmers and ranchers because they saw no other way of making a living. While reserve land had been leased before, it was only at this point that band members turned to leasing out their small individual plots to off-reserve enterprises. With the onset of self-government in the 1960s, political factors gained importance in the process of land allocation.

Today there are about 170 landholders on the Peigan Reserve. Around 60 percent of them occupy arable land as well as grazing land. The average size of a large holding is 960 acres, while small holdings average 160 acres. Small plots account for 75 percent of all individual land holdings. Sixty percent of the individually allocated grazing land is leased out, and 90 percent of the arable land. This becomes understandable after another look at the land-people ratio. An economic unit for an Indian farmer would require 1,200 acres. This would enable the individual to pay one-quarter share of return to the tribe for the use of the resource, to pay for the required machinery, and would guarantee a reasonable standard of living for the operator and his family. With regard to ranching it is assumed that a satisfactory living could be made on a pasture capacity of 115 animal units. Based on a general carrying capacity of 25 acres per animal unit per year this translates into 2,875 acres per ranch. Even if this acreage were reduced by the use of a six months grazing system, supplementary feed and use of the community pasture, the discrepancy between the actual holdings and economic units is still evident.

Not even the large holdings on the reserve, which constitute only a small percentage of the individual plots, reach minimum economic unit size. The resultant pattern is the exorbitant leasing out of valuable land with two-thirds of the revenue leaving the reserve and only one-third being paid to the "owner." Almost all of the reserve's arable land is farmed by non-band members on a share-cropping basis, and a sizeable portion of the reserve's pasture is being grazed by off-reserve cattle. A survey indicates that 66 percent of the landowners interviewed (21 out of 32) leased their land; of these only two leased it to fellow band members. All economic strata are represented among these "armchair farmers. " While a few individuals argue that they are just not interested in either farming or ranching, the majority expresses considerable inclination to go into full-time ranching if more land and capital were available. As things are, the leasing of land seems to be a legal and socially acceptable way of contributing to one's living on the Peigan Reserve. If there is a degree of resentment among the landless (which is likely), it does not manifest itself in the same way as it did a few years ago on the neighboring Blood Reserve, where a landless band member demonstratively erected his tipi beside the band's administration building, and where political pressure groups tried to force the tribal council to set up a workable land policy. The land question was for a long time the most controversial and emotional subject on that reserve.

There is no definite land policy on the Peigan Reserve; the council handles disputes over land individually. The main source of contention apparently is the question of inheritance. Normally this matter is decided within the family, and the parcel of land is transferred to the surviving spouse or handed down to one child. But increasingly people appeal to council to settle arising disputes; and in some cases the land returns to the band to be transferred to a new applicant.

Individual land tenure on the Stoney Reserve is subject to the same customary system. Here, however, it is even more flexible and informal. The division between "landowners" and landless band members is less pronounced than on the Blackfoot Reserves, as every family by custom has the right to fence off or use a parcel of land to graze some livestock. There are "acceptable" limits as to the size of holdings an individual may fence off for himself, the majority measuring under 160 acres. Sixty-nine percent of a Stoney sample claimed a parcel of land, with the majority being uncertain about its exact size. Only two out of twenty-two landholders utilized larger areas, in the neighborhood of 640 acres. There is no land registry, and as a result there are no data regarding the number of landholders or size of holdings. At the same time no land has been formally designated as bandland (except a band ranch); although some unsettled areas have a tradition of communal use, theoretically individuals are allowed to take their share of this land. About 60 percent of the main Morley Reserve have been taken up individually. Naturally certain holdings came to be associated with certain families, and the land distribution pattern goes back a long time in history. With over 400 households on the Morley Reserve and its physical features imposing limitations on settlement and utilization of some parts, there is a pronounced land shortage. The individual holdings are uneconomically small, especially in view of the fact that the wooded character of a major part of the reserve necessitates even larger ranch units to make a living than the Peigan Reserve. Nevertheless all the individually used land is utilized for grazing livestock, and none is leased to non-band members. Although leasing was practiced before self-government, it was discontinued more than a decade ago as a matter of policy, and thanks to their gas royalties (regular per capita distribution) band members do not depend on this source of income. Use of reserve land is free for the Stoneys. There is no defined land policy; disputes arising over questions of inheritance or transactions are handled by council individually.

Thus the land situation on the reserves is characterized by a peculiar tension caused by the combination of hard economic facts, perceived and/or real political favoritism and the enduring Indian wholistic concept of land ownership. Pointing towards supposed communal ownership of the landbase, the landless feel justified to ask where their profit from this resource is likely to occur. Due to population increase and historically established distribution patterns only a limited number of families can reap the major benefits. Sober economics — as they govern Western society — would even call for a complete re-allotment process in order to create economic ranching and farming units. It is obvious that this is totally unrealistic. An editorial in *Kainai News* [18] tackling this problem, suggests that if all band members could reach consensus that all landholders must work their own land, then an acreage payment could be poured into the band capital account and benefit all band members. The farmers/ranchers would get a percentage, and the landless would receive a percentage. The acreage payment could be invested in a high interest account which in the future could enable the tribe to buy more land off the reserve. But whatever solution will eventually be attempted, the implementation of any land policy will infringe upon long established individual rights, and many problems will have to be overcome.

CONCLUSION

This chapter has illustrated a number of circumstances concerning Indian lands, which have no counterpart in the adjoining "white" areas: efforts to regain lost land and problems connected with the retention, control and management of the existent landbase. There is much indication that Indian people's collective survival hinges on the retention of this landbase. This is true ideally in terms of a conceptualization of the reserve as an ethnic homeland, providing a special social security, freedom from competition with non-Indians and a chance to realize one's own brand of progress and socio-economic development, while at the same time constituting a patrimony to be held by Indians for their descendants. It is also true economically, as any degree of self-determination is only meaningful with a sound economic base, i.e. the opportunity for Indian people to gain the advantage from their own natural resources. It goes without saying that these aspects are inseparably intertwined.

The land as provider is a familiar concept to the Indian of old and new times alike. Therefore, activities evolving from the landbased economy — be it agriculture, forestry, outdoor recreation or mineral extraction — can be interpreted as having some degree of continuity from the Indians' traditional mode of economy. John Snow, chief of the Wesley Band of Stoneys, points out a striking analogy when he says: "We do not see a difference between the gas and the buffalo. It is all part of our world. As we once were helped by the buffalo and used them wisely, so we can now be helped by the gas, if we use it wisely."[19] Just as the buffalo was the staff of life in their traditional subsistence, the gas has eased their transition into modern times. Both are considered gifts of the land they are living on.

1. G. Manuel and M. Posluns, *The Fourth World* (Don Mills: Collier-Macmillan Canada, 1974), pp. 221-222.

2. M. Smallface Marule, "The Canadian Government's Termination Policy: From 1969 to the Present Day" in *One Century Later. Western Canadian Reserve Indians since Treaty 7,* eds. I.A.L. Getty and D.B. Smith (Vancouver: University of British Columbia Press, 1978): 111.

3. Government of Canada, *Statement of the Government of Canada on Indian Policy 1969,* presented to the First Session of the 28th Parliament by the Honourable Jean Chretien, Minister of Indian Affairs and Northern Development. The *White Paper,* as this document came to be called, advocated an undisguised assimilation policy and proposed among other things the removal of trust status from Indian lands. Due to nationwide Indian resistance this policy was (at least officially) not put into practice.

4. J.W. Larner, "The Kootenay Plains Land Question and Canadian Indian Policy, 1799-1949: A Synopsis," *The Western Canadian Journal of Anthropology* 4, (1976): 83-92.

5. J. Snow, *These Mountains are our Sacred Places* (Toronto: Samuel-Stevens Publishers, 1977), p. 89; Larner, p. 89.

6. I.A.L. Getty and J.W. Larner, *The Kootenay Plains and the Big Horn Wesley Stoney Band — An Oral and Documentary Historical Study, 1800-1970,* Unpublished Research Report (Morley: Stoney Tribal Council, 1972). This report explores in detail the events during the treaty-signing period, and shows beyond doubt, that

the northern Stoney band's territory was not covered by Treaty 7, and that as a result, the tribe did not receive its fair share of treaty land.

7. This was the first time the Department of Indian Affairs had provided any kind of a grant to an Indian band to help them carry out research on treaty rights. Since that time, the department has provided some research funds to other Indian bands and organizations.

8. The Natural Resources Act provided for the ownership of all Crown land (except National Parks and Indian Reserves) to be transferred to the provincial government. One of the provisions of the Act though, stipulates that if at any time in the future the federal government was obliged to provide reserve land for an Indian band to fulfill a treaty commitment, the province would provide unoccupied Crown land for this purpose. However, this provision does not indicate what the federal government would have to give in return for new reserve land, nor does it stipulate that the province has to provide the specific land requested.

9. L. Howard, *Social Impact Assessment — The Bighorn and High Arrow Dams in Retrospect,* Unpublished M.E.D. Thesis (Faculty of Environmental Design, University of Calgary, 1979), p. 131.

10. This point is raised by W.E.A. Getty,*A Case History and Analysis of Stoney Indian-Governmental Interaction with Regard to the Bighorn Dam: The Effects of Citizen Participation — A Lesson on Government Perfidy and Indian Frustration,* Unpublished M.S.W. Thesis (Faculty of Social Welfare, University of Calgary, 1975).

11. J. Rieber, "Historical Time Bombs,"*Calgary,* (April 1981):111.

12. For a surrender to be legal, a band meeting or referendum must be held. A majority of the electors must approve the surrender. If a majority of all eligible electors do not vote at the band meeting, then a second meeting can be held provided a majority of those voting at the first meeting approved the surrender. In the second meeting a majority of the participants voting is sufficient to approve the surrender. The Indian Act makes no provisions for reversing a surrender and restoring land to reserve status.

13. Rieber, p. 112.

14. Indian Affairs, *Description and Plans of certain Indian Reserves in the Province of Manitoba and the Northwest Territories 1889,* (Ottawa: Indian Reserve Plans).

15. Indian Chiefs of Alberta, *Citizen Plus,* A Presentation by the Indian Chiefs of Alberta to Right Honourable P.E. Trudeau, Prime Minister and the Government of Canada. June 1970. The *Red Paper* was the Alberta Indians' response to and violent rebuttal of the "White Paper."

16. For an interesting comparison of property concepts in European and Indian society see Leroy Little Bear's testimony at a hearing of the Berger Commission in Toronto in M. O'Malley, *The Past and Future Land. An Account of the Berger Inquiry into the Mackenzie Valley Pipeline,* (Toronto: Peter Martin Associates Limited. 1976): 238-243.

17. The Canadian usage of the terms "tribe" and "band" is interchangeable. More correctly, however, we would have to say, that the Stoney Tribe consists of three bands — Chiniki, Wesley and Bearspaw — who have a limited degree of political autonomy and their own chiefs and councillors, while the Peigan Tribe comprises six recognized bands who have mainly cultural significance (for example in the transfer of ceremonial bundles).

18. *Kanai News,* February 1982, No. 2.

19. Snow, p. 141.

Chapter 7

The Loss of Indian Lands
in Wisconsin, Montana and Arizona

Ronald A. Janke

To one who has even a cursory knowledge of Indian affairs in the United States, the story of Indian confinement to reservations due to government "treaties" is both familiar and tragic. Not only have such treaties resulted in the loss of Indian lands, but through subsequent laws, much of the land contained inside the reservations is owned today by non-Indians.

This chapter examines the process whereby this land was lost to the Indian, presents the magnitude of the lands involved, and comments on the problems that result from this tragic series of events. The problem is discussed as it has developed in three states: Arizona, Montana, and Wisconsin. All three contain sizable tracts of Indian land but possesses distinctive environmental areas. Moreover, each represents the different classes of land tenure now present on Indian reservations.

MONTANA

Indian tribal areas in Montana were in a constant state of flux long before contact with whites. Most of the tribes had settled there during the seventeenth century, yet did not occupy a particular area or hunting territory at the time of the Lewis and Clark expedition of 1805-1806. Fighting for new hunting territories was further complicated by the arrival of the horse as tribes from other Indian culture regions moved and tried to establish their own hunting territories. Conflicts over tribal areas continued into the nineteenth century even as the United States was trying to force these Indians onto reservations.

Divided by the Bitterroot range of the Rockies, the Indians of Montana represented two culture groups: the Eastern Plains Indians and the Western Plateau Indians. Predominant among the Eastern Plains tribes were the Blackfoot and Crow. Bands of Sioux, northern Cheyenne, the Gros Ventre, and the Assiniboine were scattered among the other Eastern Plains tribes in Montana. Until about 1730, the Blackfoot Confederacy, consisting of Algonquian stock, lived in the present Province of Saskatchewan. They drifted southwest where buffalo and other game were more abundant and engaged in considerable warfare over buffalo ranges with other tribes.[1] The Crow, of Sioux origin, had been an agricultural people, but with the arrival of the horse changed to a buffalo economy. They broke away from their ancestral group and settled along the valleys of the Yellowstone and Bighorn in northern Wyoming and northeast Montana.[2] As late as 1860, when the United State Army was attempting to settle a number of tribes on reservations, the Crow were still at war with other Indian tribes, competing for hunting territory. Enemies of the Crow were the northern Cheyenne who moved into southeastern Montana, and small bands of Dakota Sioux, which occupied northeastern Montana.

The Western Plateau tribes included the Salish (Flathead) and the Kootenai. The Salish moved into the Bitterroot Valley before 1800, forced westward by the marauding Shoshoni and Blackfoot. Their traditional home had been on the eastern slopes of the Rocky Mountains in present Montana and Alberta, Canada, but they were pushed westward by the Blackfoot with whom they were almost constantly at war until they were confined to Indian reservations.[3]

Treaty Restrictions

Among the early treaties of particular importance in placing the Montana Indians on reservations was The Fort Laramie Treaty of 1851. It set aside a vast area for the Blackfoot tribes and also established the Crow reservation[4] which consisted of approximately thirty-eight million acres, roughly one-fourth of the entire state. In 1885 a government treaty with the Blackfoot and several neighboring tribes provided for the use of a large portion of the original reservation as a common hunting territory.[5] The Blackfoot hunting territory, however, was considered too large for their effective use and was subsequently reduced. By a legislative act of 1888,[6] the area was broken up to form three separate reservations: the Blackfoot Reservation in Glacier and Pondera Counties; the Flathead Reservation in Lake, Sanders, Missoula, and

Flathead Counties; and Fort Belknap Reservation of the Gros Ventre and Assiniboine tribes, located in Blaine and Phillips Counties (Fig. 7.1).

In 1889 the Fort Peck Reservation was established for the Assiniboine and Sioux tribes located in Roosevelt, Valley, Sheridan, and Daniels Counties.[7] The Rocky Boys Reservation was established in 1916 to provide a land base for the homeless Chippewa and Cree Indians who had moved back and forth across the International Boundary Line. The treaty unfortunately did little to help the Chippewas and Crees economically because the reservation was located in the center of the Little Rocky Mountain area, a domal uplift of rocky terrain unfit for most kinds of agriculture.

A number of government actions reduced the size of these reservations soon after they were established. The huge Crow Reservation lost thirty-million acres by treaty in 1868, and in 1882, an act of Congress further reduced their land.[8] More land was ceded to the government in 1890 for a cash settlement, and after

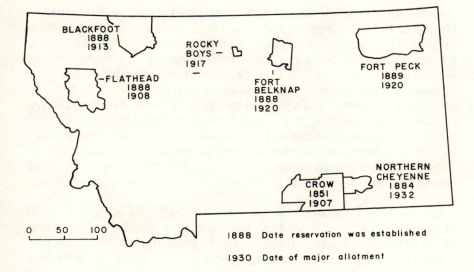

Figure 7.1. Montana Indian Reservations, 1985.

the last large land cession in 1905, only about three million acres remained.[9] The Crow Indians had lost a total of thirty-five million acres of land and received an average of five cents per acre compensation.

Allotment Restrictions

Land cession by treaty, however, was only one way the Crow lost land. Additional acreage passed from Indian ownership after the passage of the General Allotment Act (Dawes Act) in 1887. To discourage further inroads on Indian land and release supposedly "unused" areas for white settlement, the government eliminated tribal land by settling each Indian or family on his own land. Though ostensibly a means of helping to bring about an economic use of the land, it further reduced the reservations and became one of the most effective ways of taking Indian land.[10]

The Indians also suffered tremendous losses through government sales of surplus lands following allotment of reservation lands. One and half million acres of Crow reservation land was lost in this way, as were 1,500,000 of the 3,017,934 acres on the Blackfoot Reservation, and 598,741 of 2,094,144 acres on the Fort Peck Reservation.

Once the reservations were allotted, further reductions of Montana Indian lands continued. Through various means, non-Indians were permitted to buy Indian allotments. In the beginning, Indian land was under a 25-year Federal trust period although some reservations had a ten-year trust period. After that period, the Indian landowner was granted a fee patent and was allowed to sell his allotment. Pressure was asserted by white farmers to reduce delays of the trust periods and speed the process of Indian land alienations. Congress passed legislation in 1902 that allowed adult heirs of any deceased Indian to immediately sell inherited land.[11] In 1907 Montana Indian agencies were authorized to sell unused allotted Indian land. Under these provisions, over two and one-half million acres were alienated.

On the Crow Reservation, which had 2,400,174 acres in 1891, about 2.2 million acres of land were allotted leaving only 200,000 acres of rough mountain areas in tribal ownership. Much of this has since been alienated and today over a million acres is owned by whites.[12] Thus, in addition to the loss of land, the reservation is fragmented in ownership.

A large portion of the four largest remaining reservations also was allotted and lost to white owners. The Fort Peck Reservation, consisting of 622,000 acres has 470,000 allotted acres, 100,000 of which are white-owned. The Blackfoot Reservation, containing 1,520,000 acres, has 721,000 allotted acres, 600,000 of which are white-owned. Finally, the 1,248,000 acre Flathead Reservation has 720,000 allotted acres, 640,000 of which have been passed to non-Indian owners.[13]

Typically, little was done with the proceeds of the sale. The government distributed it to individual members of the tribe on a per capita basis. No systematic programs were using funds from the sale of Indian surplus or allotted land. If widespread programs existed, such as a loan program to all Indians to buy farming equipment, such money would be useful. The small per capita payments were often either wasted or too small to aid Indian farmers or ranchers.

After the Allotment Act, Montana Indians lost 5,332,317 of their original 11,631,407 acres. The United States government realized problems were associated with allotments and tried to stop the process in 1934 by passing the Indian Reorganization Act to reverse the trend of the Allotment Act and eventually return land to tribal use. It forbade the allotting and selling of Indian lands and authorized annual appropriations for the purchase of new tribal lands.[14] In Montana, landless Cree and Chippewa were helped with acquiring small, individual allotments in already existing Montana Reservations. Approximately 60 Cree and Chippewa were located next to the Blackfoot Reservation, 50 Cree inside the Flathead Reservation, and 625 Chippewa and Cree were given 6,000 acres of submarginal land inside the Fort Belknap Reservation. An additional 124 landless Chippewa, Cree, Sioux, and Cherokee were given scattered tracts inside the Crow Reservation, 99 Chippewa were scattered inside the Fort Peck Reservation, and finally 2,000 landless Cree and Chippewa were permitted to live on and used the tribally-owned land inside the Rocky Boy Reservation.[15]

The 1985 land-ownership statistics, shown in Table 7.1, clearly illustrate the Indian Reorganization Act's failure to change land patterns inside Montana Indian Reservations.[16]

Despite the purchase of additional land for the homeless Cree and Chippewa Indian tribes, total Indian acreage actually decreased during the 40 years period. Over one million acres were lost. Most of the land losses are in the relatively dry reservations, located in the eastern half of the state, and their losses coincide with a renewed interest in dry farming, particularly by non-Indians.[17] Although the Indian Reorganization Act was supposed to make it extremely difficult for individual Indian allotments to be sold, land

Table 7.1

Land Ownership Inside Montana Reservations

	Alienated White Land (Acres)	Indian Allotted Land (Acres)	Indian Tribal Land (Acres)
1934	5,332,317	5,065,628	1,233,462
1985	6,386,479	3,617,089	1,627,839

Source: *United States Indian Population and Land, 1934-1985.*

sales continued. Total tribal acreage increased, chiefly by transfer of allotted Indian lands. Thus, the main accomplishment of the Indian Reorganization Act was to buy allotted land and return it to the reservations for tribal use, never resolving the Montana Indian's basic problem of too little land.

Except for the small Rocky Boys Reservation, which was never allotted, and the Cheyenne River Reservation, which most of the land inside was allotted in 1932, most of the land inside the Montana Reservations has passed into white hands (Fig. 7.2). Much of the allotted land is in fairly small size plots and is frequently intermingled with white-owned plots.

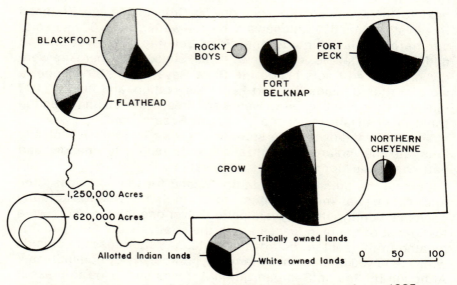

Figure 7.2. Land Ownership Inside Montana Reservations, 1985.

The land ownership problem becomes even more acute when one considers suitability of this land for agriculture. A major feature of the Allotment Act was to allot only land potentially suitable for agriculture, therefore the best lands on the Montana Reservations were allotted. Table 7.2 shows that most of the farming land and land suitable for irrigation is owned by non-Indians.[18]

Table 7.2

Type of Land Owned by The Tribe and by Individual Indians

Land Classification	Tribal	Individual	Total
Grazing	177,147	1,069,266	1,246,413
Commercial Timberland	12,800	18,185	30,985
Non-commercial Timberland	72,000	6,000	78,000
Other Wild Lands	9,732	---	9,732
Dry Farm	660	180,915	181,575
Irrigated	160	25,425	25,589
Miscellaneous	---	2,100	2,100
TOTALS	272,499	1,301,895	1,574,394

Source: Compiled by author from: J.M. Crow, "The Crow Indians."

Not only was most of the best Indian land allotted, but over 80 percent of the best allotted land was alienated to non-Indians (Table 7.3). This fact can be seen by comparing classes of land owned by Indians with that owned by the whites. In the Crow Reservation, 44 percent of the two million acres of allotted land is owned by non-Indians.[19]

Most of the remaining Indian land is leased to whites and not used by Indians. In the Crow Reservation, sixty-six percent is being leased to whites. In the Blackfoot Reservation, fifty-three percent is leased; Fort Peck Reservation, thirty-six percent is leased; and in the Fort Belknap Reservation, forty-eight percent is leased.[20]

A major reason for this high proportion of leased land is the large number of land plots which have been shared by interest owners. Shared interest developed from the federal Indian inheritance laws which forced heirs of an estate to have a divided interest in any land that was a part of the estate. A study of leased land on the Crow Reservation revealed that in 1954, 92.1 percent of all land leased

Table 7.3

Indian and White Allotted Lands Inside
Indian Reservations

Land Classification	Indian Allotted Land (Acres)	White Allotted Land (Acres)
Agriculture	26,059 . . . 11%	208,033 . . . 89%
Irrigable	25,429 . . 14%	155,240 . . . 86%
Grazing	1,169,266 . . . 66%	607,625 . . . 34%
TOTAL	1,220,754 . . . 56%	970,898 . . . 44%

Source: *United States Indian Population and Land, 1934-1985.*

was in the form of heirship status.[21] Heirship status so subdivides Indian lands into multiple owners that the only possible way to get any return from the land is to lease it.

In situations where a white owns land along a stream, and a Crow owns adjacent land without water, the Indian's holdings are of little value because there is no access to water. However, for the white with water, leasing Indian land at a very low rate can be very profitable.

Because Indian-owned land consists of small, scattered parcels, its potential is greatly limited and often more limited by complex tenure. An extreme case illustrates the problem. One 160 acre allotment made in 1887 had passed to 312 heirs by 1985. Of these, the largest holding was about four acres, and the smallest was 0.0009 acre. The land was not physically divided, but all of the heirs held an interest in it and shared any income derived from it. Almost all land with many owners is leased by the B.I.A., and annual payments are made to the heirs. The yearly income for the person owning the 0.0009 acre tract was less than a cent. The leasing problem in the Montana Reservation has thus reached extremely uneconomic proportions.[22]

Montana Reservations present serious land problems for the Indians, who originally had title to the entire eighty-five million acres of the state. Treaties, allotment, and sale of surplus land has reduced Indian holdings to only five million acres. Because so much of the Montana Indian Reservation land is owned by whites, there is a high degree of fragmentation among white and Indian lands. This problem is even more severe because most of the Indian lands are in the form of allotments; the best Indian land is allotted and best allotted land is owned by non-Indians. This not only leaves the Indian with the poorest land, but also leaves him with his best land in the form of fragmented allotments. Tribally owned land, the land which the Indians could most effectively use, is the poorest and occurs in the smallest tracts found on the reservations. While three and one-half million acres of Indian land is in the form of allotments, only one and one-half million acres are tribally owned. Furthermore, whites lease three million acres of the Indian allotted land. Indian land that is used, or could be used by the Indians, is limited to 100,000 acres of alloted land and approximately 1,600,000 acres of tribal land. Indian farmers and ranchers before allotment had somewhat workable systems of land tenure. After allotment, Indian farming and ranching shows a marked decline inside Montana reservations, a decline that is tied to the lease and sale of allotted land. In Montana, fewer Indians were farming and fewer livestock were grazing fewer acres after allotment than before. A marked decline occurred in the value of livestock and in farming products. The conclusion is that Indian farmers and ranchers are further behind white farmers and ranchers in 1980 than they had been in 1900.

ARIZONA

In contrast to Montana, where all the Plains tribes were recent arrivals, most Arizona Indians have lived in that area for many years. The Hopis in the northeast, Pimas and Papagos in the south, and the Yuncan groups in the west are all descendants of peoples who occupied what is now Arizona for at least 10,000 years. Only the Navajos and Apaches are relative newcomers.[23]

Treaty Restrictions

The Navajos, members of the large family of Athabascan Indians, moved into the Arizona area from Alaska and Canada in the early part of the fifteenth century, and had become an aggressive and powerful tribe by the end of the seventeenth century. The first United States Military expedition into Arizona territory was made in the winter of 1846 when a treaty was signed creating the Navajo Reservation.[24] The Navajos had no single governing leader, so the treaty was entered into with a minor leader of the tribe. The treaty was misunderstood by the American Army leaders who held all Navajos subject to the treaty, and subsequently resulted in twenty years of increased fighting. After the establishment of a number of other treaties, the decision was made to send all the Navajos to Fort Sumner, New Mexico, where they could be put on separate plots of land and taught agricultural life. Most of them fled into the far western and northern parts of the state and remained undisturbed for many years.[25]

Recognizing the failure of the Fort Sumner Experiment and acceding to Navajo appeals, a Government treaty in 1868 established a reservation of three and one-half million acres.[26] This land extended north from Fort Defiance to the Utah-Colorado border, and ran westward from Shiprock to Chinle. Unlike the Crow Reservation in Montana, which was reduced in size by subsequent treaties, the Navajo Reservation actually increased; from 1878 to 1934, the reservation area rose to approximately fifteen million acres.[27] Most of the treaties involved exchanges through which the Indians received more acreage, but relinquished land more useful for agricultural purposes. For example, when lands were exchanged for the construction of the Southern Pacific Railroad, the Navajos were given an additional 900,000 acres of land which was in no way comparable to the agricultural quality of lands lost.[28]

Another recent arrival to the Arizona area was the Apache, also of the Athabascan family. They came to the southwest from northern Colorado in the tenth century and effectively controlled their land for a number of years.[29] As white immigrants moved into the southwest, many years of warfare began. Defeated in 1873, the remnant hostile Apache bands were settled on the San Carlos Reservation. This reservation was later divided into two reservations: the San Carlos and Fort Apache, containing 853,000 and 1,660,000 acres respectively (Fig. 7.3).

The Hopis, the only descendants of the Pueblo Indian culture in Arizona, lived in the northeast on three high mesas which served as natural fortifications against hostile tribes.[30] Their ownership was recognized when the 2,470,000 acre Hopi Reservation was established in 1878. The Paiutes also lived in this northern area of Arizona and were confined to the 120,000 acre Kaibab Reservation on the northern rim of Grand Canyon in 1917.

South of the Kaibab Reservation is the Hualapai Reservation, organized in 1883. The reservation consists of 990,000 acres of gorges, cliffs, and inaccessible mesas which are a continuation of the Grand Canyon. Temperatures there vary from 18°F. below zero to 110°F. or above and elevations range from 2,000 feet at the river to nearly 7,000 feet at nearby peaks. Life for the 410 Hualapai Indians

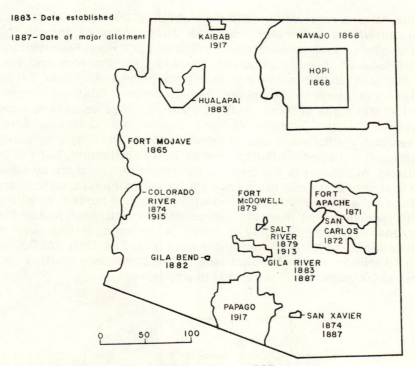

Figure 7.3. Arizona Indian Reservations, 1985.

is a struggle.[31.]

   In 1865 a small Indian Reservation of 23,700 acres was established along the Colorado River for the Mohave Indians who had inhabited this area, living on wild food, game, and fish, since prehistoric times. The Colorado River Reservation, which consisted of 225,000 acres, was later created for the Mohave Indians.

   Far to the south of the Mohave, the Papagos occupy three reservations: the Papago (2,700,000 acres), the Gila Bend (22,000 acres), and the San Xavier (70,000 acres). Finally the Gila and Salt River Reservations, both occupied by the Pima Indians, were established in 1879 and 1883, respectively.[32]

Allotment Restrictions

   Almost all of the area inside Arizona Indian reservations is classified as desert land unfit for agriculture and therefore was little affected by the General Allotment Act of 1887. The Gila Bend Reservation, located in a more productive agricultural area than other Arizona reservations, did have about 12,000 acres of its land sold to whites as surplus land after allotment, even though the reservation was never allotted. The Gila and Salt River Reservations were located in early irrigation districts near Phoenix and had 97,600 and 25,000 acres allotted, respectively. The San Xavier Reservation, next to the present-day agricultural fields of Tuscon, had 41,600 acres allotted. In 1915, about 8,000 acres of land were allotted for the Mohave Indians inside the Colorado River reservation. Allotment and related policies were spectacularly successful in opening Indian land to white settlement, but not in Arizona. According to the General Allotment Act, land not suitable for agriculture or grazing was not allotted. Arizona reservations are located in arid or semi-arid areas with ninety-five percent of all the land receiving less than ten inches of rain in a year. Inside the Arizona Reservations, only a small percentage of the land is classified in white or Indian allotments (Fig. 7.4). Only 185,000 of the 18 million acres of Indian land in the state were allotted and only 12,000 acres are in the hands of whites.

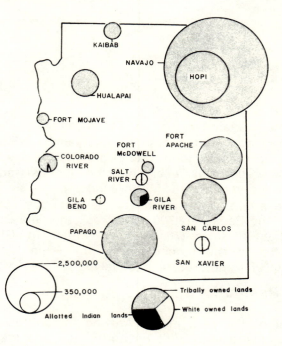

Figure 7.4. Land Ownership Inside Arizona Reservations, 1985.

The majority of the Arizona Reservations are under tribal ownership, thus, most of the economic development is a tribal enterprise. For example, timber land in most reservations is selectively cut by the tribe and the profits divided among them. The Navajo Reservation is capable of producing an estimated fifty-three million board feet of timber each year for the next century.[33] The Navajo sawmill, also a tribal enterprise, has cut approximately seventeen million board feet of timber annually. Profits are divided among the tribes and the mill provides considerable employment for their members.

Farm land in many of the reservations is under a community farm system with tribal guidance. Crops such as cotton, are communally produced. Over eighty-six percent of the Indian land in Arizona is classified and used as range for Indian-owned livestock. Tribal range land generally is used freely by members, and in the Navajo Reservation a large number of small herds seasonally graze parts of the reservation, generating profits shared among the Navajos.[34]

Some of the tribal lands are leased. Oil, gas and coal are produced on the Navajo and Hopi Reservations and asbestos on the San Carlos Reservation. Returns from these mineral leases improve the welfare of the Indians.

In summation, the Arizona Indians originally held title to the entire state's sixty-six million acres, but by treaties, have been confined to eighteen million acres of reservation lands. Problems of fragmentation do not exist since 99 percent of the land is Indian-owned and used by members of the tribe. Likewise, inheritance problems never arose because individual Indians did not own small plots of land. The land was almost all tribally-owned with profits divided among the tribe. This appears to be the most feasible use of the land especially since environmental conditions preclude small plot farming. Some tribes leased parts of the reservation for mining purposes, but little of the reservation has been leased to whites for farming. Therefore, in the tribal reservations of Arizona the usual problems associated with land losses have not occurred.

WISCONSIN

Like the Indians of Montana, the Indians of Wisconsin were in constant movement throughout the state during the Pre-Columbian period.[35] The most populous tribes were the Menominee, Potawatomie, and Chippewa, who arrived in the state approximately 4,000 years ago.[36] The Menominee Indians came from the Indiana area, moved along the shores of Lake Michigan and settled around Green Bay. The Potawatomie also came from the south and settled around the unpopulated area of northeastern Wisconsin. The Chippewa came from the Sault Ste. Marie area, moved across the northern part of the state and settled in northwestern Wisconsin. Most numerous in Wisconsin were the Chippewas.

Treaty and Allotment Restrictions

Early government negotiations with the Chippewas aimed toward moving them westward across the Mississippi, completely out of Wisconsin. To hasten their departure, President Zachary Taylor issued an executive order revoking their privileges of hunting, fishing, and gathering wild rice on Wisconsin lands. After three years only one-third of the Indians had moved, and weighing public opinion, the Board of Indian Commissioners met with representatives of the Chippewa in the fall of 1854 and established the principal Chippewa Reservations in Wisconsin.[37] The reservations provided were Bad River, Red Cliff, Lac du Flambeau, and Lac Courte Oreilles (Fig. 7.5).

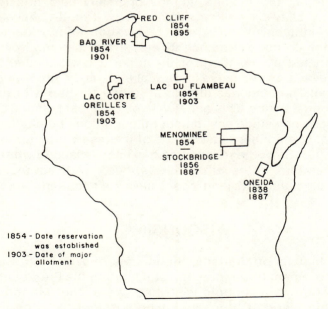

Figure 7.5. Wisconsin Indian Reservations, 1985.

The Bad River Reservation is the largest in Wisconsin, containing 120,000 acres of land. Most of this land had been allotted in eighty-acre plots to individual Indians and only 7,000 acres are tribally owned. Of the 113,000 acres of allotted land, 66,000 acres are white-owned.[38]

The Lac Courte Oreilles Indian Reservation once consisted of over 70,000 acres. Now reduced by allotment, little more than half remains in Indian hands and only 3,000 acres are tribally owned.[39] A similar situation exists on the Lac du Flambeau Reservation where barely half of the original 70,000 acres of land given the Lac du Flambeau band remains in Indian hands. The most valuable land within the reservation, especially that with lake frontage, has long since been alienated to non-Indian owners.[40]

The small Red Cliff Reservation, (total area of 14,000 acres), is divided into approximately 6,000 acres of allotted lands and 1,000 acres of tribal lands, 7,000 acres being lost to whites.[41]

Other tribes were forced into the state from the east. The Stockbridge Indians, originally from western Massachusetts, were forced to move five times before they settled permanently on land in Shawano County.[42] They moved first in 1815 to New York, in 1818 they went to White River, Indiana to find no land when they arrived. Forced to move again, they were joined by the Munsees, a Delaware tribe, and in 1822 moved to the Green Bay, Wisconsin area. Twelve years later, when white settlers wanted their land, the Indians moved to the east side of Lake Winnebago, at the site of the present town of Stockbridge-Munsee Indians.[43] The Allotment Act of 1887 resulted in the sale of almost all of the Stockbridge lands, but under the Indian Reorganization Act, the government purchased some 2,000 acres for them, and today they have 2,000 acres of tribal lands and 15,000 acres of Indian allotted lands.[44]

Another eastern tribe, the Oneidas, moved to Wisconsin from New York in 1823. Associated with Europeans longer than other Indians, their culture had been altered greatly by contact with white men.[45] As early as 1794, the Oneidas obtained legal title to western New York land grants when the government signed a treaty honoring them for their help in the Revolutionary War. However, as white settlers expanded westward, the Oneidas were forced to sign a new treaty moving them to Wisconsin. In 1838, after several negotiations, they were given a reservation of about 65,000 acres in the east central portion of the state, west of Green Bay in Brown and Outagamie Counties.[46]

Though they had experienced the white man's way of life for over a hundred years, with the passage of the General Allotment Act, the

Oneidas lost more of the land to white speculators. By 1930 only a little over 1,000 acres remained in Oneida hands. In 1933, the Indian Reorganization Act helped reorganize the Oneidas into a tribe which purchased some 3,000 acres of land. Today, the original 70,000 acre Oneida Reservation has been reduced to 2,000 acres, only 500 of which are tribally owned.[47]

The Menominee live in approximately the same area today as they did in the mid-seventeenth century.[48] With the westward migration of American colonists, Menominee lands began to be ceded in a series of treaties wherein the Menominee were asked to move to Minnesota. Strongly united under their chief, Oshkosh, they refused to move. After ten years of negotiating, they signed a treaty in 1854 which gave them 276,000 acres of forested land, reduced later by the formation of the Stockbridge-Munsee Indians Reservation.[49]

With the passage of the General Allotment Act, the Menominees were to have had their reservation allotted; however, they again refused to cooperate with the government. For years they resisted all the federal government's plans to divide their reservation and with the passage of the Indian Reorganization Act, it remained intact.[50]

In the mid-1950s, the federal government singled out the Menominees as one of the tribes ready for termination of all special relationships and treaty guarantees with the United States government. In 1961, their reservation passed from federal to state jurisdiction and became the seventy-second county of Wisconsin. Termination was nearly disastrous until, on December 22, 1973, a hard-fought campaign restored their tribal status.[51] Today the Menominee Reservation contains 230,000 acres, the same amount it contained in 1856.

The tribal ownership of the Menominee lands is very prominent among Wisconsin's Indian lands (Fig. 7.6). Most of the land inside the other reservations is white-owned land and the majority of the Indian-owned land is in the form of allotments. This Wisconsin map, like that of Montana, illustrates a dismal picture of Indian land ownership. A high percentage of these lands intermingled with white and Indian plots produces inefficient land use.

The fact that the Menominee Reservation was never allotted is extremely important to the economic use of its land because timber is the major resource of the reservation. Sustained-yield forestry can be practiced best on large contiguous areas under one operation, thereby permitting logging and reforestation to progress

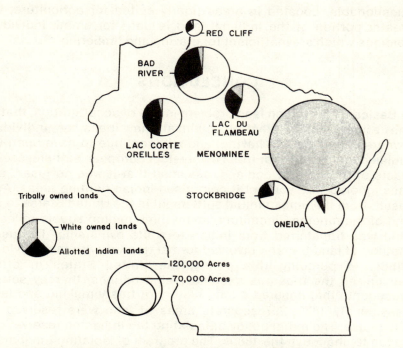

Figure 7.6. Land Ownership Inside Wisconsin Reservations.

systematically over logging units related to topography and transport lines.

With the exception of the Menominee, the basic lost land problems appear on Wisconsin Reservations. Indians originally had title to the entire state's thirty-two million acres, but by treaties were confined to 613,000 acres of reservation lands. The passage of the General Allotment Act took some 228,000 acres through the selling of allotted lands. Because of the small size of the reservation when the Allotment Act was passed, no surplus land losses resulted. This leaves the Indians with some 398,000 acres of land. The land losses become even more obvious when the Menominee Reservation is excluded from the figures. In the six allotted reservations of Wisconsin, 228,000 acres are white-owned, 165,000 acres are in the form of Indian allotments, and only 23,500 acres are tribally owned.

In Wisconsin, allotted reservations suffer from lack of usable land. Nearly half of their land is alienated by whites. Furthermore, the feasibility of allotting much of this land is somewhat questionable. Located in areas poorly suited for agriculture, the greater portion of the Indians' land is unfit for small, individual holdings which are inefficient for grazing and timbering.

CONCLUSIONS

Basically, the Indian land problem is one of acculturation, that is, the effect which Western civilizations' ideas of individual ownership has had, is having, and will continue to have upon the Indian peoples' ideas of tribal ownership. European settlers, seeing tracts of uncleared woodland, assumed that it was not used, and thus ignored the fact that it comprised Indian hunting areas. As a result, from the time of initial settlement in the United States to the end of the nineteenth century, some three million square miles of land was transferred from Indian to white ownership. The usual method of land transfer involved formal treaties with the individual tribes. In pursuing this policy, the United States in effect recognized the tribes as quasisovereign nations, thereby setting precedents that ensured a long history of treaty making and land cession. By 1870, 297 separate areas of land were reserved for Indian use. The initial policy of isolating the Indian on reservations began to change in the 1880s. The program of isolating the Indians had proven to be shortsighted. No spot in the United States could any longer be thought of as a permanently isolated area. Isolation being patently impossible, there was nothing to do but consider ways and means of integration. During the 1880s citizens and officials steadily evolved a program of "civilization" which crystallized in the passing of the General Allotment Act in 1887.

The central idea of this Act was the assimilation of the Indian culture into the white culture by means of individualization. The primary method of individualizing the Indian was the allotting of land in individual assignments to Indian families. It was thought that the basis of civilization consisted in knowing how to handle individual property. From this experience would come responsibility and awareness of the obligation of citizenship. Hence, if tribal lands were now reassigned on an individual basis, there would appear stimulus for economic improvement. The tribal ties, which were believed to be conducive to lack of industry and lack of individual responsibility, would melt away and the Indians would become industrious participants in the American nation.

The major result of the General Allotment Act of 1887 was the loss of eighty-six million acres of Indian land. In Montana and

Wisconsin almost all the reservations were allotted and land losses were extreme. The concentration of allotted Indian reservations is in the grazing areas of the Great Plains and the forests of the northern Great Lakes. In these areas, maps which show Indian reservation boundaries present a false picture of Indian ownership. The size of the reservations are shown as they were originally established. For example, the Crow Indian Reservation, in southeastern Montana, is shown as its boundaries were in 1905. In reality, the Crow own only about one-half of the three million acres shown on the map. On an average, over 70 percent of land inside allotted Indian reservations is owned by whites.

Not only is a large percentage of the best land inside the reservation white-owned, but the allotted land is also intermingled and fragmented. Both Indian and non-Indian lands are located in close proximity, creating a checkerboard land pattern. This makes it difficult or impossible for Indian owners to use their land for grazing or lumbering. Practical utilization of these grazing and timber regions by whites requires large tracts for efficient operation. The allotment of timber lands discourage the practice of scientific forestry and a sustained-yield cutting, while the allotment of grazing lands encouraged the idle, non-use of huge acreages because a herd of cattle could not be sustained on such small land plots. This land problem of having small, fragmented land plots is severe in allotted Indian reservations. In its present geography, the resource of allotted Indian reservations can never be fully realized by Indian peoples.

In Arizona, almost all of the reservations are tribally owned and land losses have not occurred. According to the General Allotment Act, land not suitable for agriculture or grazing was not allotted; therefore the tribally owned reservations are located in desert areas. The concentration of tribal Indian reservations is in the hot deserts of the Southwest (Arizona and New Mexico) and the colder deserts of the Basin and Range region (eastern California, Nevada, western Utah and southwestern Idaho). In the United States over 70 percent of all tribally owned Indian land is found in the state of Arizona.

The reservations in Arizona are very "closed" in comparison to the "open" reservations in Wisconsin and Montana. Much of the desert and steppe environment remains in its original tribal state and all settlements and economic activities throughout the entire reservation are Indian. This is in sharp contrast to the allotted reservations in Wisconsin and Montana, where much of the original prairie and forests are removed and replaced by white farming, grazing, forestry, and recreational activities. In Arizona, tribal resource programs have brought a dynamic change in the agricultural and commercial development of Indian lands. Lumbering and livestock raising are becoming increasingly important to the economy of the Indians of Arizona, and even mixed farming is taking hold where irrigation permits. Since 1900, the number of Indian farms has increased in Arizona, while in Montana and Wisconsin the number of farms has declined.

Arizona has thirty-three tribal businesses. The industries range from the manufacture of timber products, tribal sawmills, tribal grazing operations, commercial tribal farming, to a number of highly successful tourist facilities. Tribal income from any of the Arizona reservations is higher than income from any of the reservations in Montana and Wisconsin.

Furthermore, unemployment rates are twice as high in the allotted reservations of Montana and Wisconsin as unemployment rates inside Arizona's tribal reservations.

There is real hope and expectation that resource problems on the Arizona reservations can and will be solved, whereas there is no such optimism in the Wisconsin or Montana reservations that the tenure problems can or will be solved in time to rescue the land base for these Indians. Certainly satisfactory solutions on a large scale have not yet been worked out and applied.

This chapter has portrayed the basic types of land ownership on a number of reservations. A number of problems inherent to the present land system invites further study. Among them are the Indian land inheritance system, the problem of plot fragmentation, and the effectiveness of present leasing arrangements. These and other elements of the reservation land system must be analyzed before our understanding of reservation land tenure is anywhere near complete.

NOTES

1. J. Fahey, *The Flathead Indians* (Norman: University of Oklahoma Press, 1958).

2. E. Denig, *Of the Crow Nation* (Washington, D.C.: Government Printing Office, 1953).

3. Fahey, *The Flathead Indians.*

4. C.C. Royce, "Indian Land Cessions in the United States," *Eighteenth Annual Report of the Bureau of American Ethnology* (Washington, D.C.: Government Printing Office, 1899, pp. 812-815.

5. Ibid., pp. 864-865.

6. Ibid., pp. 864-865.

7. Ibid., pp. 786-787.

8. Ibid., pp. 909-919.

9. Ibid., pp. 924-925.

10. S.L. Tyler, *A History of Indian Policy* (Washington, D.C.: Government Printing Office, 1973), pp. 5-7.

11. Felix Cohen, *Handbook of Federal Indian Law* (Washington, D.C.: Department of the Interior, 1941), pp. 411-412.

12. U.S. Department of the Interior, Office of Indian Affairs, *Annual Report of the Commissioner of Indian Affairs to the Secretary of the Interior, 1875-1985.*

13. U.S. Department of the Interior, Office of Indian Affairs, United States Indian Population and Land, 1934-1985.

14. Tyler, *A History of Indian Policy,* pp. 123-125.

15. U.S. National Resources Board, Land Planning Committee, *Indian Land Tenure, Economic Status, and Population Trends* (Washington, D.C.: Government Printing Office, 1935), pp. 10-15.

16. U.S. Department of the Interior, Office of Indian Affairs, *United States Indian Population and Land, 1934-1985.*

17. M.W.H. Hargreaves, *Dry Farming in the Northern Great Plains* (Cambridge: Harvard University Press, 1957).

18. J.M. Crow, "The Crow Indians," MSS.

19. U.S. Department of the Interior, Office of Indian Affairs, *United States Indian Population and Land, 1934-1985.*

20. W.H. Ketcham, *Conditions of the Flathead and Fort Peak Indian Reservations* (Washington, D.C.: Government Printing Office, 1915); Missouri River Basin Investigation Project Report, No. 139, *Leasing of Indian Trust Land on the Crow Reservation* (Washington, D.C.: Government Printing Office, 1954); D. Rodnick, *The Fort Belknap Assiniboine of Montana* (New Haven: Yale University Press, 1938); R.L. Trosper, "The Economic Impact of the Allotment Policy on the Flathead Indian Reservation" (Ph.D. Dissertation, Harvard University, 1974).

21. Missouri River Basin Investigation Project Report No. 139, *Leasing of Indian Trust Land on the Crow Reservation,* pp. 5-7.

22. Tyler, *A History of Indian Policy,* pp. 25-34.

23. W.H. Kelly, *Indians of the Southwest* (Tucson: University of Arizona, 1954) and D. Smith, *Indian Tribes of the Southwest* (Stanford: Stanford University Press, 1933).

24. Royce, "Indian Land Cessions in the United States," pp. 850-885.

25. O.O. Howard, *Account of General Howard's Mission to the Apache and Navajo* (Washington, D.C.: Government Printing Office, 1892), pp. 75-79.

26. Royce, "Indian Land Cessions in the United States," pp. 850-851.

27. Ibid.

28. R.W. Young, ed., *The Navajo Yearbook* (Window Rock: Navajo Agency, 1981), pp. 253-255.

29. Smith, *Indian Tribes of the Southwest,* pp. 91-105.

30. W. Hough, *The Hopi Indians* (Cedar Rapids: University of Iowa Press, 1915), pp. 25-125.

31. J.F. Martin, "A Reconsideration of Havasupa: Land Tenure," *Ethnology 17 (1968):450-460.*

32. R.A. Hackenberg, "Economic Alternatives in Arid Lands: A Case of the Pima and Papago Indians," *Ethnology* 1 (1962):186-196.

33. Young, *The Navajo Yearbook,* pp. 57-59.

34. Ibid.

35. J.M. Erdman, *Handbook on Wisconsin Indians* (Madison: Governor's

Commission on Human Rights, State of Wisconsin, 1966); W.U. Kinietz, *The Indians of The Western Great Lakes, 1615-1760* (Ann Arbor: University of Michigan Press, 1965); R.E. Ritzenthaler, *The Woodland Indians of the Western Great Lakes* (New York: Natural History Press, 1970).

36. G.I. Quimby, *Indian Life in the Upper Great Lakes, 11,000 B.C. to A.D. 1800* (Chicago: University of Chicago Press, 1960), pp. 80-84.

37. C.J. Kappler, ed., *Indian Affairs: Laws and Treaties* (Washington, D.C.: Government Printing Office, 1904), pp. 264-366.

38. R. Janke, "Chippewa Land Losses," *Journal of Cultural Geography* 2 (1982):84-100.

39. Ibid.

40. Ibid.

41. Ibid.

42. O. Kownlke, "The Settlement of the Stockbridge Indians and the Survey of Land in Outagamie County, Wisconsin," *Wisconsin Magazine of History* 40 (1956):31-35.

43. Royce, "Indian Land Cessions in the United States," pp. 700-702.

44. U.S. Department of the Interior, Office of Indian Affairs, *United States Indian Population and Land, 1934-1985.*

45. J. Backman, *The Cultural Background of the Oneida Indians* (Washington, D.C.: Government Printing Office 1953) and R.E. Ritzenhaler, "The Oneida Indians of Wisconsin," *Bulletin of the Public Museum of the City of Milwaukee 19:1-52.*

46. Royce, "Indian Land Cessions in the United States," pp. 700-702.

47. U.S. Department of the Interior, Office of Indian Affairs, *United States Indian Population and Land, 1934-1985.*

48. *P.K. Onrada,* The Menominee Indians: A History (Norman: University of Oklahoma Press, 1979).

49. Royce, "Indian Cessions in the United States," pp. 700-702.

50. Onrada, *The Menominee Indians: A History.*

51. National Committee to Save the Menominee People and Forests, *Freedom with Reservation: The Menominee Struggle to Save Their Land and People* (Madison: Impressions, Inc., 1972).

Chapter 8
The Loss of Lands
Inside Indian Reservations

Richard H. Weil

When considering reservations as sovereign entities, their geographical components must be taken into account. Two centuries of often contradictory governmental policies towards American Indian lands has shattered the territorial bases of many reservations. This has hindered tribal sovereignty and made the delivery of some reservation services both more costly and less uniform than they would otherwise be.

Law enforcement is a service with strict geographical constraints, and has been particularly affected by fragmentation of the reservations. This chapter examines several services. Law enforcement, because of its geographical constraints, is the focus of study. In this context three reservations in the Upper Midwest are examined. The first, Red Lake in northern Minnesota, is a tribally-owned area with little land held by people outside of the band. Most of the jurisdictional questions here are between the reservation government and the state. The second, Rosebud, has a fragmented land base, which has led to jurisdictional questions among the tribe, the State of South Dakota, the local governments, federal authorities, and private citizens. In the final case, Sisseton-Wahpeton, disintegration of the reservation's boundaries has created a chaotic land ownership pattern across parts of both North and South Dakota.

LAND AND LEGAL STATUS OF AMERICAN INDIANS

Since the 1778 treaty between the Confederation and the Delaware Indians,[1] both the federal government and Indian groups have attempted to define their respective rights within the national territory. A considerable body of law has grown out of this effort, some of it is contradictory, and all of it is subject to substantial and occasionally unpredicatable revisions by both Congress and the courts.[2]

The history and problems of mixed jurisdictions on Indian lands have been discussed in detail, particularly in the series begun by Cohen.[3] From a geographical standpoint, many of the jurisdictional difficulties associated with the relationships between reservations and federal and state governments are related to the varying legal status of lands in or near reservations. With occasional minor exceptions such as forts and churches, initially all of the lands in these territories were considered to be owned by the tribes. Nationally, much tribal land remains, although on different reservations policies concerning its actual use varies. On some of them much of the land is leased, sometimes to non-tribal members. On others this is not the case. Red Lake is a rare example of a reservation in which almost all of the land is held, or leased between, tribal members.

Closely related to tribal land is that which is held in trust. The existence of this category of land ownership is a historical outgrowth of nineteenth century attempts to "civilize" Indians by turning them into individual farmers. Trust land was restrictively deeded to tribal members for a set period of time. At the end of this period the Indians were expected to have reached a stage of independence where they could own their lands outright. Allotments were made from the mid-nineteenth century on, but the major drive occurred after 1887 when the Dawes (General Allotment) Act was passed.[4] In effect until 1934, this legislation resulted in the loss of much tribal land. Although allotments are no longer made, on some reservations most of the land remains in this category.

Tribal and trust land constitute what is legally called "Indian Country." Paradoxically, this may not constitute all of the land within the boundaries of reservations, but it may include territory outside of them. The reason for this geographically confusing situation can be traced back to the initial sizes of the allotments granted under the Dawes Act. Basically, most were too small to allow for profitable farming. The exact size varied depending upon such factors as whether the petitioner was a minor or a head of a household, but many were 160 acres. Often the land was too poor to support a farm of this relatively small size. The result was that many former allotments were eventually sold to non-Indians. In cases where the lands were retained by the allottees, the terminations of their trust periods legally made their real estate private properties, after which they were sometimes forfeited for back taxes. Thus, considerable amounts of real estate, outside jurisdictions of the reservations, but within their boundaries, were titled as non-Indian lands.

As noted above, the theory behind the Dawes Act was that Indians would become independent farmers. With their allotments granted, the next logical step was to throw open the remaining tribal lands for public sale. This further confused the land ownership patterns within reservations. In some cases it also led to the redrawing of reservation boundaries with much of the "surplus" land now outside of them. In this chapter this is discussed in the case of Rosebud, where parcels of trust and tribal land lie scattered far beyond the boundaries of the reservation.

As United States citizens, Indians have the same rights to use general government services as do other residents of the country. However, in many cases neither government services, nor the payments to be made for them, are equal for tribal and other citizens living in close proximity to one another. Those tribal members who are living on tribal or trust lands are not subject to real estate taxes, or to income taxes for work done on them, and this has occasionally created bitterness among their neighbors.[5] Also, not all Indians in an area may be equally eligible for the available government services. The reservation governments are primarily concerned with members enrolled in their particular groups, a determination individually made on the basis of ancestry (normally, the "quantum blood" of a prospective enrollee must be at least twenty-five percent). Offspring with an insufficent number of ancestors in a reservation's particular band, and spouses of tribal members, may, however, be eligible for some services from both the Bureau of Indian Affairs (BIA) and the Indian Health Service (IHS). They also may be eligible for such services if they are living off the reservations — but only up to those distances which are officially proclaimed by the Department of the Interior in *The Federal Register.*

The foregoing problems clearly compound the service delivery difficulties associated with the geographically confused land ownership patterns existing on many reservations. Particularly difficult problems are associated with law enforcement.

LAW ENFORCEMENT ON THE RESERVATIONS

Until the late nineteenth century, the federal government did not explicitly assume authority for crimes committed on reservations. An 1883 case changed this situation.[6] Crow Dog, a Sioux leader on the Rosebud Reservation, shot Spotted Tail during a dispute over who would head the agency's police force.[7] Tried by the Dakota Territory, he was convicted of murder. On appeal, the United States Supreme Court released him on the grounds that the federal government lacked jurisdiction. Following tribal custom, Crow Dog made restitution by giving goods to Spotted Tail's family and by losing status with his peers.

Public incomprehension of this form of justice led to an 1885 law which gave the federal government authority over certain crimes committed on reservations.[8] Still known after their original number, these so-called "Ten Major Crimes" include murder, manslaughter and arson.[9] If committed off reservations, most acts in this category would be under state jurisdiction.

The federal government has additional powers on reservations, such as the right to protect its property, and it is usually understood that Indian Country is subject to all national laws. Since the 1970s Washington has also taken the position that lesser crimes committed during the course of "major" ones may be tried in federal courts.

When an offense is committed which the reservation authorities deem to be serious, the Federal Bureau of Investigation (FBI) is usually called in. If the FBI finds sufficient evidence, it can then petition the local United States Attorney for an arraignment. One difficulty with this arrangement is that the "major" crimes may have varying interpretations.[10] This, as well as budgetary constraints, may explain why U.S. Attorneys have been estimated to reject about eighty percent of the reservation cases brought before them.[11]

Another problem with the existing law enforcement system is that a person may occasionally plea bargain a federal offense into a tribal one. Since reservation courts are limited by law to imposing fines of no more than five hundred dollars, and prison sentences no greater than six months, local whites have occasionally been angered when serious offenders received comparatively light sentences.

Many reservations also have their own law enforcement services. Frequently these are tribal police units, products of a system that developed in the nineteenth century.[12] On some reservations these departments are enhanced or supplemented by BIA police forces, professional organizations which can trace their roots back to 1906 when the Liquor Suppression Force was created.

Investigations by tribal or BIA police may later be duplicated by the FBI. In addition another federal agency, the U.S. Marshals Service, may become involved on reservations if prisoners are to be transported or federal property protected.

To further complicate the law enforcement picture, a 1977 U.S. Supreme Court decision held that reservations have no jurisdictional rights over non-tribal members who commit crimes within their territories.[13] Local non-reservation police may be extremely reluctant to attempt to assert jurisdiction over persons on tribal or trust lands. Thus, this decision undercuts a major segment of reservation law enforcement. With private lands, which are subject to state and county jurisdiction, often intermixed with reservation ones, determining who has authority in a particular case can be confusing. Police working around Indian Country sometimes carry tape measures and plat books.[14]

Many attempts have been made to overcome the problems associated with reservation jurisdictions. The major efforts have gone towards terminating reservations. The first major attempt was the Dawes Act. As noted above, the allotments resulting from this law severely fragmented, but did not eliminate, reservations.

During the 1950s, a new termination effort occurred. One result was Public Law 83-280,[15] which is commonly known as "P.L. 280." This 1953 statue transferred the civil and criminal jurisdictions for a number of reservations from federal to state authorities. It did not, however, affect all states. For example, disclaimers in the constitutions of North and South Dakota, coupled with a refusal by the federal government to share the costs of these programs, resulted in those two states being excluded.[16] Also, within the affected states some tribes were exempted. In Minnesota, Red Lake was excluded and the state later retroceded criminal jurisdiction over the Bois Forte-Nett Lake Reservation. These circumstances explain why the three reservations considered in this paper are not subject to state or county jurisdiction. Expansion of P.L. 280 to these, or to other, reservations appears unlikely because the law has been amended to require Indians to request such action, something which no tribe has ever done.

In his study of exclaves, Robinson suggested that such territories are subject to unusual constraints due to the laws of the countries which surround them.[17] Although his work dealt with bits of territory which one nation held inside another, on a domestic level tribal and trust lands are in a very similar status so far as most state jurisdictions are concerned. The following cases examine some of the difficultires associated with this situation, and how the participants have tried to solve them.

RED LAKE

The connected Upper and Lower Red Lakes form the fifth largest freshwater body in the United States. Well stocked with fish, having fertile soil to the south and surrounded on the other sides by thick forests, these waters are the focus of the reservation which is home to a band of Chippewa (Ojibwe) Indians.

The Arikara, the Mandan and the Hidatsa (Gros Ventres) once lived at Red Lake. By 1634 the Sioux (Lakota) had pushed them west. During the eighteenth century this group in turn migrated towards the open prairie. The Chippewa, using guns obtained from the French, fought the weakening Minnesota Sioux and by 1770 had gained control of the region. Around 1792 a permanent settlement was made at Red Lake and by 1830 white fur traders were living there. In 1839 a federal agent's census recorded a village of 230 Pembina Chippewa. During the 1850s missionaries arrived, augmenting with winter wheat the rich fish and wild rice resources there.[18]

Since the Red Lake Indians were both remote and peaceful, the government made no attempt to move them. However, they were forced to cede land. By treaties in 1863 and 1864 about eight million acres in northern Minnesota and North Dakota were lost (Fig. 8.1). In

Figure 8.1. Red Lake Band Cessions.

1871, 1,049 tribal members were counted in the reduced domain. During the following two decades whites began to press Congress to open their fertile and well-forested area. In 1889 an act was passed whose stated purpose was the "relief and civilization of the Chippewa Indians."[19] Working on the same logic as fueled the Dawes Act, a commission was then appointed to negotiate the ceding of "surplus" Indian land in Minnesota.

Since the commission's mandate extended to all Chippewa groups in the state, their time at Red Lake was limited. After a week of discussion, agreement was reached under which the band yielded 2,905,000 acres. Although this understanding also specified that the remaining tribal lands were to be kept solely for allotments in trust, the Indians may have expected to keep a coherent reservation.[20] If so, they were correct as Red Lake is one of the very few reservations never to have been allotted.

Why almost all of Red Lake's land remained in tribal hands is not entirely clear. It seems that a combination of foresight and luck was involved. Like the leaders of many other tribes, the band's elders opposed the entire allotment system. That would not have stopped the process except that the government commission did not have time to argue the point. Minutes of the negotiations reveal that the whites expected a new team to arrive once proper surveys were made. This did not occur. Another unusual outcome of the 1889 negotiations was the commission's failure to have the band formally cede its remaining lands to the federal government for a reservation. This gave Red Lake's government a greater degree of aboriginal sovereignty over its territory than most reservations are able to enjoy today.

The commission drew the shrunken boundaries of the reservation with some long-term concern for the welfare of the band. Much pine forest land remained in tribal hands. Stream mouths were sometimes placed outside of the reservation so that logging would not conflict with Indian lifestyles. The boundaries of the reservation were proclaimed in 1889,[21] and the ceded townships opened to settlement in 1896.

Privately held real estate finally appeared on Red Lake in 1905 when a rail line was built from Bemidji to the reservation (Fig. 8.2).[22] Only 320 acres, most of it in the town of Redby, were taken.[23] Although a convenience for the reservation, the line did not carry enough timber to be profitable and it was abandoned in 1937.[24] The Redby lands largely remain in the hands of one family who maintains good relations with the tribe. Later offers to expand privately held land by selling lakeshore properties to willing resort

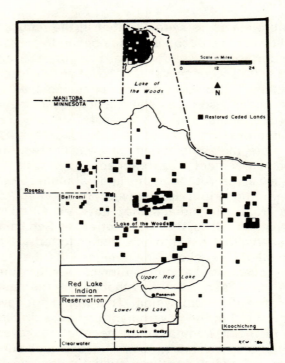

Figure 8.2. Red Lake Reservation Landholdings.

owners, although considered by some tribal members, were always rejected by the band's elders.

Although escaping allotment, Red Lake was forced to sell land deemed "surplus." Under pressure from white settlers, Congress in 1904 appropriated 136,288 acres.[25] This was taken as a unit from the western end of the reservation, so a block of 407,240 acres of solidly held tribal land (less that taken for the railroad) remained. The law which took this land also recognized the legal uniqueness of Red Lake's territory by separating it from all claims and agreements relating to other Minnesota Chippewa.

Since the 1920s the reservation has made efforts to increase its territorial holdings. The tribal government apparently believes that the 1889 commissioners meant to include all of Upper Red Lake within the then-unsurveyed boundaries of the reservation. This territory is claimed by the reservation, as is the 81,700 acre Red Lake Wildlife Management Area.[26] Neither demand appears likely to be accepted by state or federal authorities. An earlier attempt to obtain a drained lake bed which was lost in 1889 also failed.[27]

Other attempts to regain land were more successful. The band never accepted the Indian Reorganization Act, but it did receive the law's benefits in the retrocession of abandoned public lands which had originally been taken from them.[28] During the 1940s many small parcels which had been used for ill-conceived drainage ditch schemes in the swamplands north of the reservation were retroceded.[29] Also regained was most of the "Northwest Angle," Minnesota's enclave on the Canadian side of the Lake of the Woods. Given to the United States in 1783 because it was thought that the Mississippi began further north,[30] the interior of the territory was used after World War I as an area for veterans to homestead in.[31] That project failed, and while the shoreline remains a white-owned summer resort area, the remainder of the area has been returned to the tribe.

In all, about 157,000 acres were added to the reservation through retrocession. Red Lake thus exists as a coherent block of territory with numerous exclaves across northern Minnesota. Almost all of the band's approximately 4800 people live around the southern shores of Lower Red Lake in Clearwater and Beltrami Counties. The rest of the reservation is used by them primarily for logging and hunting.

In some respects Red Lake presents a distinct geographical identity in its service delivery systems, which in other ways it is indistinguishable from nearby rural territories. The entire reservation is outside the zoning ordinances of the counties it is located in and has both its own school district and IHS hospital. Aside from the Menominee tribe of Wisconsin, it is also the only reservation to issue its own license plates ("Famous Red Lake Walleye"), and vehicles so licensed are exempt from state insurance laws.

In contrast to these differences, residents within each county's part of the reservation can use their appropriate jurisdiction's library, obtain advice from its agricultural extension agent, and join its credit union in those where one exists.

Welfare is a service only partially integrated into the surrounding jurisdictions. On a case basis, each county treats Indians the same as other clients. However, because much of Beltrami County's caseload is in the reservation area, a branch office has been established there. Redby is another instance in which this county recognizes the unusual jurisdictional conditions on the reservation. As noted earlier, some of this community's land is privately held. Apparently Beltrami County never planned to collect property taxes on this real estate, but the residents agreed to be taxed so that street lights could be installed and maintained there.

Law enforcement differences between the reservation and the surrounding jurisdictions are very sharp. For example, extradition from Red Lake to other reservations or to Minnesota have to be approved by a majority vote of the tribal council.[32] This is usually not given for misdemeanors.

Cross-deputization, in which police officers from one jurisdiction hold privileges usually given to those of another, has occurred at Red Lake. For several years Clearwater County has had such an agreement with the tribal government. In Beltrami County the agreements have historically been informal. This generally worked well, but there were some problems. For example, in one case a traffic violation in Redby was allegedly mishandled by the tribal court, which did not have jurisdiction on the privately held land there, while the state declined to intervene.[33] Since 1986 the county has cross-deputized those BIA officers at Red Lake who have had professional training equivalent to that required of Minnesota's non-reservation police. In turn, Beltrami County's sheriff and his deputies have been empowered by the BIA. Since Red Lake's government is considering the removal of all BIA officers from its police department and then expanding the force of tribal officers, the future of these agreements remains in doubt. However, if their BIA authorizations are revoked, appropriate personnel in the sheriff's office may continue to have authority on the reservation. Because Bemidji, the seat of Beltrami County, has a federal magistrate, the sheriff and his sworn staff have been appointed deputy U.S. marshals. Whether they would attempt to exercise jurisdiction on this basis would probably depend upon the circumstances.

The scattering of tribal lands outside the main body of the reservation has led to a number of administrative problems. In the numerous parcels across northern Minnesota, differences between tribal and state game hunting regulations have made uniform enforcement difficult. A frequent problem has been hunters accidentally crossing over the jurisdictional boundaries. To handle this problem and to aid in enforcement of the law, local officers in Minnesota's Department of Natural Resources have been cross-deputized by Red Lake's game wardens, who are themselves considered to be tribal police. Another complexity is that Red Lake's hunting seasons are not exactly the same as Minnesota's. During the periods when the seasons are not overlapping, the state allows tribal members returning from the scattered reservation properties to transit its territory with their game.

Despite such agreements, other matters remain unresolved. Minnesota claims jurisdiction over all public roads and driveways in the state, but as a practical matter exercises such control in Red Lake only with the cooperation of the tribal council. The state's Department of Transportation negotiates each right-of-way, taking care to meet both tribal and BIA engineering requirements. The State Patrol, which theoretically has jurisdiction over all roads, remains outside of the reservation unless specifically requested to enter. To retain its sovereign intergrity, the Patrol has not accepted BIA offers of cross deputization. Patrol officers are occasionally invited to the reservation to share their expertise in reconstructing accident scenes, teaching defensive driving, and inspecting school buses.

The assertion of law enforcement powers by the reservation is closely bound to deeper questions of sovereignty and who governs the reservation. In 1958 the old system of government by a group of tribal elders ended and an eleven member elected council was formed. In 1986 Roger Jourdain, the chairman initially installed, was serving his eighth successive term. In 1979 allegations over mismanagement of tribal funds led to three days of rioting, two deaths, and the burning of seven buildings, including Jourdain's home. In support of Red Lake's elected government, the reservation's police force was temporarily increased from twelve to forty-two, with the BIA bringing officers in from Wisconsin and the Dakotas.[34] About forty U.S. marshals were also sent there and two FBI agents were permanently stationed in Bemidiji to handle reservation cases. The situation did not reach the extremes of Pine Ridge, South Dakota, where the tribal government, FBI, and the marshals engaged in a long and violent siege with a group who rejected the chairman's authority.[35] However, strong feelings were raised on all sides.

For the counties, a hesitancy to be closely involved with the law enforcement problems of the reservations seems to have arisen from the 1979 troubles. For the tribal government, stronger assertions of its sovereignty was one result. These claims became particularly evident in 1985 when serious questions were raised over the procedures of Red Lake's tribal court. Two men, one of whom had been involved in the 1979 disturbance, were arrested for allegedly selling drugs. The court records involved were seized by the tribe when a newspaper asked to review them, but in 1986 the case was dismissed by U.S. District Court on the grounds of violation of due process.[36] (However, because of its federal status Minnesota attorneys remain unable to practice at Red Lake without rarely-given permission.) Shortly after the federal court's ruling the tribal council promulgated the requirement of a passport-license for any non-tribal person who wishes to do business on the reservation. This regulation generally does not interfere with private travelers to Red Lake, or with anyone who accepts the tribe's open invitation to play in its bingo parlor, but does provide some control over all other "foreign" visitors.

In summary, Red Lake has retained its geographical coherence. Its government can enforce within a contiguous territory what jurisdictional rights Congress and the federal courts have never taken away. While problems in administering the outlying parcels do occur, and not all of the issues have been resolved within the main body of the reservation, a substantial degree of tribal sovereignty does exist. If the original white idea of reservations was to create geographically and administratively cohesive units, then Red Lake comes close to this model.

ROSEBUD

The Rosebud Reservation is located in the rugged and generally dry country of south central South Dakota. Farming prevails in the eastern part of the area, while ranching dominates in the west. About 9700 tribal members live here.

In the eighteenth century Teton Sioux (Lakota) displaced earlier groups such as the Ponca and Pawnee. Adapting their culture to the prairie, they became the classic Plains Indians of American lore. Eventually contained within "The Great Sioux Nation," a reservation comprising western South Dakota (Fig. 8.3), their territory was gradually dismembered.[37] One group, led by the Spotted Tail later famous in the *Crow Dog* case, came, to the area around the Rosebud River. When the great reservation was finally broken up in 1889, this became the nucleus for a separate jurisdiction.

The Rosebud Reservation originally consisted of most of the territory between Pine Ridge and the Missouri River, and ran from the White River to Nebraska. However, over time most of this land was lost.[38]

The first stage in extinguishing tribal title to much of the reservation's land involved issuing allotments. Because the Dawes Act did not have any geographically-related provisions, Rosebud soon became a crazy-quilt of tribal and allotted trust lands.[39] Half

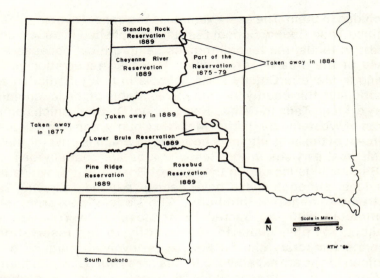

Figure 8.3. The Break-up of The Great Sioux Nation.

the reservation's land, in particular the more fertile eastern part of the territory, was declared "surplus" and opened to white homesteading.[40] Thus, the reservation was impoverished as much of its best land was lost. Although allotments were supposed to have stopped in 1934, for many more years it appears that the federal government allowed land to be sold to non-tribal members. During the 1950s, when termination of the reservation was a distinct possibility, 104,775 acres of trust land were turned over to private ownership.[41]

The last reduction of the Rosebud Reservation involved the loss of the Missouri River bottomlands. Although relatively few tribal landholdings existed in the area, the reservation government claimed the territory under the 1889 agreement setting its boundaries. This did not stop the Corps of Engineers from condemning this fertile area in 1954. The land was subsequently flooded as part of a massive damming of the Missouri River.[42]

The remaining Rosebud Reservation is a fragmented land base, with a core area in Todd and southern Mellette Counties, plus numerous parcels scattered across the South Dakota counties to the east. However, as is discussed below, even within the core not all lands are held in trust or tribal status.

Within Rosebud's core area there are some spatially coherent reservation service systems, although not all tribespeople are included in them. The best example is the school system. There is a unified Todd County School District, established in 1964 with local and BIA funds, the federal monies being critical because the tax base of the area is very limited. However, reservation residents living in Mellette County go to schools in that jurisdiction's three districts. In this county the intermixed status of the landholdings is very evident. Thus the White River School District, which comprises most of Western and Central Mellette County, can only tax the sixty percent of the land within its boundaries which is privately held.

Medical services in the Rosebud area are spatially divided. An IHS hospital is located in the town of Rosebud. It provides limited services, although these have been expanded following recent extremely negative publicity. The federal government has contracted with the Sacred Heart Hospital in Yankton, South Dakota, for physicians to regularly fly to the reservation and operate temporary clinics. For cases involving surgery, or when difficult births are expected, patients are flown back with them.

Confusion in the services delivery system is particularly prevalent in the scattered parcels of land forming jurisdictional exclaves in predominantly white-owned areas. Within six miles of Tripp County's seat of Winner there are at least forty-two pieces of the reservation.[43] Completely outside of the county's zoning and law enforcement systems (one includes a housing development), they are too distant from the main body of the reservation to be easily administered. In this general area, with a sixty mile zone of such enclaves, Rosebud employs only one police officer.

A similarly complex situation exists within the Todd County core of Rosebud. This area was not politically organized until 1979 when it was detached from the administration of Tripp County.[44] Todd (and the Pine Ridge Reservation's core area of Shannon County, which was simultaneously detached from Fall River County's control) are allowed to contract for governmental services from their adjoining counties. From an economic standpoint this is probably necessary since there are very limited tax bases on the reservations. In Todd County this has resulted in officials such as the auditor and the state's attorney remaining in the Tripp County city of Winner. Although the jail for non-Indian prisoners who are arrested on the reservation is also in this community, there is a Todd County sheriff (and, after considerable delay, a jail was built in the town of Rosebud for tribal prisoners). The sheriff was appointed in 1983 by the elected Todd County Commissioners, and has the aid of a part-time deputy. However, these officers only have authority over people who are not members of the Rosebud Sioux

Tribe. The local BIA police force handles the reservation's citizens, who comprise seventy-eight percent of Todd and thirty-nine percent of Mellette Counties' inhabitants.

The situation in the town of Mission is more complicated than that facing other police in the Rosebud area. An incorporated community with a 1980 population of 748, of whom only sixteen percent were Indians, almost all of the town's land is privately owned. The state has long maintained that this area, although within Todd County, is not part of the reservation. The tribe appears to have accepted this interpretation, even entering into a cross-deputization agreement with the local police force. However, when Mission attempted to license a liquor store and a golf course, the tribe opposed these moves because the reservation prohibits the sale of alcohol. In response to the resulting suit, a federal court ruled in 1982 that the town was part of the reservation.[45] Because Mission obtained most of its revenue from liquor sales, the closure of the disputed facilities severely damaged the town's budget. The loss of revenue resulted in the discharge of five of the government's nine employees, including the entire police force.

Since its beginnings the landholding situation at Rosebud has not been static. Besides the allotments, Congressional legislation detached from the reservation and "opened" to settlement some of the most fertile lands. Gregory County was taken in 1904, Tripp and southern Lyman Counties in 1907 and Mellette County in 1910 (Fig. 8.4). In 1977, following a suit by the tribal government to regain sovereignty in these areas, the legality of the legislation "diminishing" the reservation was upheld by the United States Supreme Court.[46] This decision has been the subject of later analysis,[47] and has never been accepted by the tribe.

On a smaller scale, the tribe has also attempted to reconstruct its land base. Instrumental in this is the Tribal Land Enterprise operation, founded in 1942. Between 1971 and 1980 this unit was able to obtain loans totalling 8.502 million dollars from the Farmers Home Administration, which made possible the purchase of 514,363 acres by the reservation. Apparently the tribe's initial strategy was to buy as much land as possible within the 1889 boundaries of the reservation. Complaints by whites about the loss of taxable lands in their counties seems to have led to a shift of focus so that tax-exempt trust allotments are now being bought by the tribe. Also, there was a change in the geography of land purchases over time, from buying any available land to consolidating the core area of Todd and southern Mellette Counties. In a program with which some tribal members disagree,

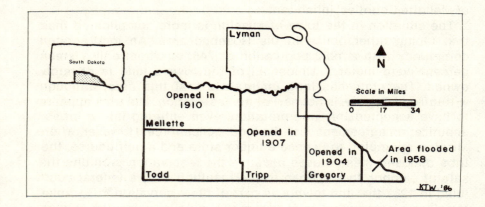

Figure 8.4. Diminishment of the Rosebud Reservation.

the tribe began in 1984 to sell off its more isolated tracts, using the funds to purchase lands nearer to the reservation core. The previous year a change in federal law made it easier for the tribe to consolidate small trust landholdings divided among the heirs of an original allottee.[48] However, later legislation tightened the requirements allowing such action, thus dampening the tribal government's pursuit of a consolidated land base.[49]

Rosebud is thus struggling to regain its original land base. At the same time, it is offering some services which are difficult to adequately provide away from its core area. Perhaps in time a coherent system of land use, with an accompanying rational service delivery system, will emerge.

SISSETON

The Sisseton-Wahpeton Reservation, usually referred to by only the first half of its name, but formally known as Lake Traverse, extends across parts of eastern North and South Dakota (See Fig.

8.5). In a broad and fertile valley, the best croplands lie to the east along the Big Stone River, with wooded areas to the west across a dry strip. In 1983 the BIA estimated that about 3000 reservation members lived here, ninety-two percent of them in South Dakota.

The tribespeople are Santee Sioux (Lakota), traditionally woodland dwellers who were more sedentary than the nomadic Plains-oriented Teton Sioux of the Rosebud. After white attempts to establish a "Northern Indian Territory" in the region failed, the federal government in 1851 forced the Santee to cede their southern lands and then in 1874 their western lands (Fig. 8.5). The resulting reservation's odd triangular shape, with a range-and-township system unrelated to any other in the United States, was apparently dictated by both the shape of the valley and the distribution of various tribal bands within it.

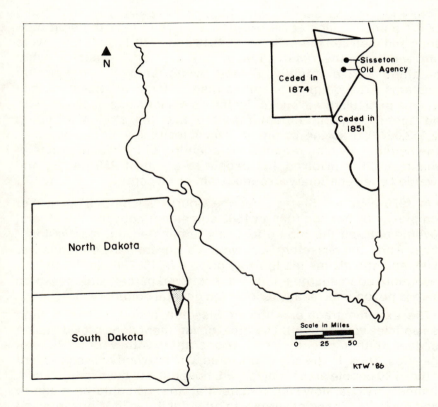

Figure 8.5. Cessions of the Sisseton Sioux.

Sisseton is one of the most severely allotted reservations in the United States. The process began in 1875, twelve years before the Dawes Act was passed, and accelerated after 1888. More than 310,000 acres had been allotted by 1892, when almost 574,000 acres more were declared "surplus" and opened to homesteading.[50] The geographical problem with allotments at Sisseton stemmed from the tendency of the tribal members to take up lands which supported their traditional forest culture. Since the allotment system was designed for farmers, people often took two separate parcels; one in the wooded area on the western side of the reservation, and another in the fertile eastern bottomland. After an 1891 law allowed allottees to lease their lands,[51] the Sisseton tribespeople tended to live in the woods and rent their farms to homesteaders. By 1900 at least half the tribe was living on these rents.[52]

New legislation dealing with allotments, passed in 1902[53] and 1906,[54] made it much easier for trustholders to take titles on their lands and then sell them. Between 1910 and 1930, 60,000 acres were removed from the reservation in this fashion.[55] Much of what remained was extremely divided by heirship. While heirship problems are common on other reservations, at Sisseton they became particularly vexatious. By the time allotments ended in 1934 the agency superintendent reported that his clerk was using 56,582,064,000 as the common divisor for reservation properties. One heirship division required the counting of individual grains of wheat. Another involved 150 people in a will of 250 pages, and awarded one beneficiary an annual rent of 1.6 cents.

In 1975 a United States Supreme Court decision added further complexity by holding that an 1889 agreement between the federal government and the tribe effectively terminated the reservation.[56] Thus, while the Sisseton Reservation's government continues to exist, and still claims the territory given it in 1867, its authority has been reduced to a large number of scattered parcels around which there is no longer a legally recognized general boundary.

The extreme fragmentation of Sisseton makes coherent land use policies very difficult. The tribal government does provide some services, either directly or in cooperation with various federal agencies. Thus, in the city of Sisseton, where twenty-seven percent of the 2789 people are Indian, an IHS hospital has been established. Limited services, however, require that arrangements be made to send patients in need of surgery to other facilities in Minnesota and the Dakotas.

Around the reservation settlement of Old Agency, where about half of the population (1066 out of 1976) in this and the surrounding townships are Indian, the Economic Development Administration funded an industrial park for the tribe. The Department of Housing and Urban Development also constructed neighborhood facilities there.

As is often the case in reservation areas, law enforcement is the major jurisdictional problem. One effect of the Supreme Court's ruling that the reservation no longer had an established border was that non-tribal police and sheriffs could continue operating within the original boundaries of the reservation, something which had been in doubt under a 1974 court ruling. But the difficulty of providing uniform police services between reservation and non-reservation lands remains. This has been a particularly serious matter regarding both traffic violations and policing of the various tribal housing developments, one of which is within Sisseton City's municipal limits. Cross-deputization between the tribe and various other jurisdictions has been erratic. The agreements with both Roberts County and Sisseton City ended after the 1975 ruling, when the county commissioners decided that they did not need to empower tribal officers. Marshall County's agreement ended in 1982. Although some South Dakota Highway Patrol officers have maintained cross-deputization arrangements, there is no guarantee that these will continue. When William Janklow, a man widely perceived as being "anti-Indian," was elected Governor of the state in 1977, the BIA withdrew all of its cross-deputization agreements, and returned only some a year later.

In 1983, the tribal police force was reduced to seven officers, after losing five positions because the Comprehensive Employment Training Act (CETA) program ended. Although this is a small force for a reservation with such widely scattered landholdings, the tendency of the tribe from the early 1970s on has been to increasingly assert its sovereignty, thus reducing the likelihood of agreements to share law enforcement powers with other jurisdictions.

Like all of South Dakota's other large reservations, Sisseton has actively attempted to consolidate its land base. From 1971 to 1983 the Farmers Home Administration loaned the tribe's Land Acquisition Account 5.6 million dollars. This, and some small amounts from other federal programs, allowed the Sisseton Reservation to acquire title to 16,384 acres in South Dakota and 480 more in North Dakota. Such activity, plus the recent changes in heirship laws discussed in the Rosebud section, may allow further consolidation. Whether a coherent territory is ever regained within a predominantly white-owned area remains an open question. Time, money, patience and — for coordinated service delivery systems — cooperation with surrounding jurisdictions will be needed. The likelihood of such a combination is uncertain.

CONCLUSION

The three reservations examined in this work exhibit widely varying percentages of privately held lands within their claimed boundaries. In a sense, the lands not in private ownership, that is, those held by the tribes and those in trust (which effectively cannot be alienated from tribal members) are historical relics. Real estate holdings which the Dawes Act and subsequent legislation intended to eliminate from the face of America, have survived and, under various tribal programs, have grown in size. This retention and expansion of a territorial base has allowed the tribal governments to offer their members some services and thus to exercise a certain degree of sovereignty.

If there is at least a vestigal sovereignty inherent in reservation governments, it is hampered by the chaotic geography of the lands they control. At Red Lake this is not a serious problem on much of the reservation, although administration of outlying fragments is subject to some problems. Perhaps a large and intact land base, along with the long occupancy by the band of one location, has helped to make this reservation agressive in asserting its sovereignty. Compared to Rosebud, where a much larger intermixing of tribal and private lands occurs, it certainly has made it easier to provide coherent services. At Sisseton, the situation is even more difficult as the reservation's territory is so diffuse that coherent boundarylines around it can no longer be discerned.

The fragmentation of a reservation's land base, and its intermixing with properties under the jurisdictions of other governments, can have many negative effects. Among the services which the reservations provide, law enforcement is one of the most geographically sensitive, since jurisdictional lines are sharp and laws can be very different on either side of a boundary. The more intermixed reservations are with other governments, the harder it is to coordinate this particular and vital service.

One often finds maps produced at the state or federal level which show Indian reservations as solid blocks of land. Similarly, during the last few years the opening clauses of federal legislation which, for purposes of their scope, have defined the "United States" have on occasion referred to Indian reservations as territories separate from the fifty states. Although such attention is laudable in recognizing the unique and continuing relationship which inhabitants of these territories have with the national government, such a point of view ignores the geographic reality existing today. The problems resulting from the difference between theoretically coherent units of government and territory and fragmented pieces of land are comparable to those which might be found at the international level enclaves and their surrounding alien states.

There appears to be no easy solution to the problems raised by the fragmented natures of most reservations. Economically, reconstitution of their territories would be prohibitively expensive, even if it were politically feasible. Perhaps the best that can be hoped for is that, when services must be delivered, there will be trust and cooperation between all of the parties involved. As this chapter has also shown, reservations do not operate in a vacuum, nor are the non-Indians who live nearby unaffected by what occurs on them. Much cooperation does occur between citizens on each side of the cultural and political borders. Thus, joint problems are often dealt with by the people who must directly face them. Whether this is enough to overcome the legacy of social, economic and geographical divisions which have arisen from a mutually difficult history remains to be seen.

NOTES

1. *Treaty with the Delawares* (Art. 6, 7 Stat. 13, 14).

2. American Indian Lawyer Training Program, Inc., *Manual of Indian Law* (No City: No publisher, 1976).

3. Felix S. Cohen, *Handbook of Indian Law* (1982 edition), (Charlottesville: Michie Bobbs-Merrill, 1982).

4. General Allotment (Dawes) Act (24 Stat. 388).

5. Carol Cranford, "A Position Paper on the Perspective of County Government with Regard to the Problems of Counties Vis-A-Vis Indian Tribes in South Dakota, and a Request for Action," Corson County Board of Commissioners, 1977. (Mimeographed.)

6. *Ex Parte Crow Dog,* 109 U.S. 556 (1883).

7. Jan. M. Dykshorn, *Leaders of the Sioux Nation* (Pierre, SD: State Historical Society, 1975.)

8. Ten Major Crimes Act (23 Stat. 362, 385).

9. 18 U.S.C. 1153.

10. Institute of Indian Studies, *Indian Problems of Law and Order* (Vermillion: State University of South Dakota, 1957).

11. American Indian Policy Review Commission, *Report on Federal, State and Tribal Jurisdiction. Task Force Four: Federal, State, and Tribal Jurisdiction. Final Report to the American Indian Policy Review Commission* (Washington: Government Printing Office, 1976).

12. William T. Hagan, *Indian Police and Judges* (New Haven: Yale University Press, 1966).

13. *Oliphant v. Susquamish Indian Tribe.* 435 U.S. 199 (1977).

14. J. White, *Examination of the Basis of Tribal Law and Order Authority.* National American Indian Court Judges Association, vol. 4 (Washington: Government Printing Office, 1974).

15. 18 U.S.C. 1162, 28 U.S.C. 1360.

16. James J. Abourezk, "South Dakota Indians," *South Dakota Law Review 11* (1966):101-118.

17. G.W.S. Robinson, "Exclaves," *Annals of the Association of American Geographers* 49 (1959):283-295.

18. Erwin F. Mittelholtz, ed., *Historical Review of the Red Lake Indian Reservation* (Clearbrook, MN: Leader-Record Press, 1957).

19. Act of January 14, 1889 (25 Stat. 642).

20. Ronald A. Janke, "Chippewa Land Losses,"*Journal of Cultural Geography* 2 (1982):84-100.

21. Executive Document Number 247.

22. United States Government, Bureau of Indian Affairs, *The Red Lake Indian Reservation: Its Resources and Development Potential,* Planning Support Group Report No. 253 (Billings: Bureau of Indian Affairs, 1979).

23. Act of February 8, 1905 (33 Stat. 556).

24. Harold T. Hagg, "Logging Line: History of the Minneapolis, Red Lake and Manitoba," *Minnesota History* 43 (1972):123-135.

25. Act of February 20, 1904 (33 Stat. 46).

26. *Red Lake Neighborhood Centers Newsletter,* v. 1, n. 117, (August 13, 1971), 1.

27. *United States v. Holt State Bank,* 270 U.S. 49 (1926).

28. United States Government. Department of the Interior, Solicitor's Opinion M-29616.

29. R.W. Murchie and C.R. Wasson, "Beltrami Island, Minn. Resettlement Project,"*Bulletin* Minnesota Agricultural Extension Service, 334 (1937).

30. William E. Lass,*Minnesota's Boundary with Canada* (St. Pauls: Minnesota Historical Society Press, 1980).

31. Thomas J. Wilsh, "Logging on the Northwest Angle," *Minnesota History* 25 (1954), 1-8.

32. *Redlake Neighborhood Centers Newsletter* v.1, n.61 (June 19, 1970), 1.

33. J.W. Lawrence, "Tribal Injustice: The Red Lake Court of Indian Offenses," *North Dakota Law Review* 48 (1972):639-659.

34. *Redlake Newsletter,* v. 1, n. 12 (September 14, 1979), 7.

35. Richard H. Weil, "The Distribution of Police Services in North and South Dakota," (Ph.D. dissertation, Rutgers University, 1983).

36. United States District Court of Minnesota, 6-85-508.

37. Leonard J. Jannewein and Jane Borman, eds., *Dakota Panorama,* 3rd ed. (Freeman, SD: Pine Hill Press, 1973).

38. Robert M. Utley, *The Last Days of the Sioux Nation* (New Haven: Yale University Press, 1963).

39. Richard H. Weil, *Loss and Reconstitution of Sioux Tribal Lands in South Dakota* (Las Cruces: ERIC/CRESS, 1979).

40. Leonard A. Carlson, *indians, Bureaucrats, and Land* (Westport, CT: Greenwood Press Press, 1981).

41. United Sioux Tribe,*Presenting the Rosebud Sioux Tribe* (n.p., n.d.).

42. Michael L. Lawson,*Dammed Indians: The Pick-Sloan Plan and the Missiouri River Sioux, 1944-1980* (Norman: University of Oklahoma Press, 1982).

43. Richard Lashua and Jerry Bergum, *Tripp County Lane Use Study* (Pierre, SD: Fifth Planning and Development District, 1975).

44. South Dakota Codified Laws, 7-44-33.

45. *United States v. Mission Golf Course, Inc., and City of Mission, South Dakota,* 548 F. Supp. 1177 (1982).

46. *Rosebud Sioux Tribe v. Kneip,* 430 U.S. 548 (1977).

47. Lee Philip Petzer, "Jurisdictional Decisions in Indian Law: The Response of Extra Legal Factors in Judicial Decision Making," *American Indian Law Review* IX (1981): 253-272.

48. Act of January 2, 1983 (96 Stat. 2515).

49. Joint Resolution of Congress, October 30, 1984 (98 Stat. 3171).

50. D.S. Otis, *The Dawes Act and the Allotment of Indian Lands* (Norman: University of Oklahoma Press, 1973).

51. Act of February 28, 1891 (26 Stat. 749).

52. Roy W. Meyer, *History of the Santee Sioux* (Lincoln: University of Nebraska Press, 1967).

53. Indian Appropriations Act of 1902 (32 Stat. 888).

54. Burke Act (34 Stat. 182).

55. United Sioux Tribe, *Presenting the Sisseton-Wahpeton Sioux Tribe of the Lake Traverse Reservation* (n.p., n.d.,).

56. *DeCoteau v. District County Court,* 420 U.S. 425 (1975).

The author wishes to thank Kristine Wharton Cannon, J.D., for her helpful comments during the preparation of this paper.

Chapter 9

The Choctaw: Self Determination and Socioeconomic Development

Jesse O. McKee

Socioeconomic indicators which measure quality of life and economic development show that the American Indian is frequently below the national norm in most evaluative categories. Because of this disparity, various U.S. governmental policies have been implemented during this century to assist the Indian. Some have retarded while others have accelerated Indian development. This chapter focuses on important U.S. Indian policies that have been implemented during the past 50 years. Particular emphasis is placed upon the early policy of termination and its succeeding policy of self-determination. The Mississippi Band of Choctaw Indians is examined as a case study to illustrate and better understand the effects of these policies on tribal government, economic development on the reservation and changes in the socioeconomic well-being of the tribal members.

The Choctaw, one of the "Five Civilized Tribes" in the southeastern portion of the United States, have resided predominantly in Mississippi for more than 500 years. After their initial contact with the explorer Hernando DeSoto, the Choctaw subsequently came in contact with the French, English and American settlers. The first Choctaw treaty with the U.S. government was the Treaty of Hopewell in 1786. After more treaties and several land cessions and acquisitions, most of the Choctaw were removed from Mississippi during the falls of 1831, 1832 and 1833 to the Indian Territory (Oklahoma). However, many Choctaw remained in Mississippi after removal, living as squatters on the land and later as sharecroppers.[1]

After finding extreme poverty among the Choctaw in the early twentieth century, the U.S. Government established the Choctaw Indian Agency of the Bureau of Indian Affairs at Philadelphia,

Mississippi, in 1918. The government authorized $75,000 to assist the Choctaw in economic development, education and health. These funds were directed toward the purchase of farmland, farm supplies and education. A day school program was initiated in 1920, a land-purchase program began in 1921, and in 1926 a 35-bed Indian hospital was established in Philadelphia. By 1930, elementary schools had been established in all seven communities (Fig. 9.1). In December of 1944, a reservation was established, and in 1945 the Choctaw reformed its tribal council and adopted a constitution and bylaws. Thus, between 1918 and 1945 much progress was made in the areas of education, health, land acquisition and the creation of a tribal government. But throughout these early years, the Choctaw remained impoverished, living as subsistence farmers in isolated rural Choctaw communities in east-central Mississippi.

During the period between 1933 and 1945, when John Collier was Commissioner of Indian Affairs, much of the focus of the Bureau of Indian Affairs (BIA) was to enact reforms advocated in the Indian Reorganization Act of 1934, also known as the Wheeler-Howard Act of 1934. This period is generally viewed as the era of growth for the American Indian nationally, and as a result, most Indian tribes in the U.S. were better prepared to manage their own affairs and reestablish Indian community life. The Indian Reorganization Act of 1934 attempted to reverse the trend of having the BIA reservation superintendent serve as the center of government on the various reservations — a system which existed in the latter part of the nineteenth and early part of the twentieth centuries.

The traditional Choctaw system of government ceased to exist in Mississippi following the Treaty of Dancing Rabbit Creek in 1830. After the removal of the Choctaw to the Indian Territory, there was no functioning Choctaw tribal government in Mississippi that was recognized by the United States government between 1830 and 1945. Thus the Choctaw had virtually no control over the programs and services rendered at the Choctaw Agency after 1918. Too, the Choctaw were ill-prepared to exercise much power or influence over their communities prior to 1945. Even after 1945 the Choctaw Tribal Council had little power, controlled no resources and was ill-equipped to influence community development. So despite the intentions of the Indian Reorganization Act of 1934, the BIA exercised a very powerful influence on the reservation and little change was witnessed in this pattern until the late 1960s.

By 1946, Collier's successor, William Brophy, was advocating that the Bureau's main objective was to organize the tribes so they could manage their own affairs and adapt their native institutions

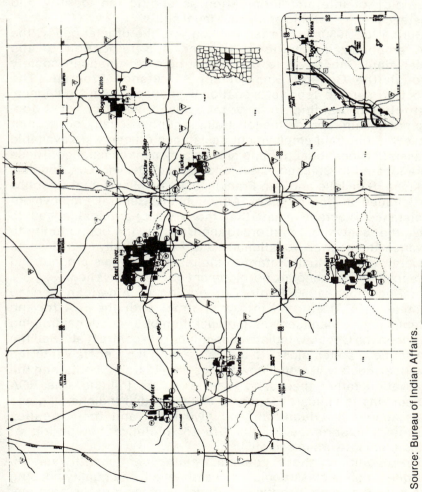

Source: Bureau of Indian Affairs.

Figure 9.1. Choctaw Indian Communities.

and culture to modern society — a policy called "termination." It was felt that the BIA should be abolished and federal supervision and control over the Indian should be terminated. On August 1, 1953, the Termination Act (House Concurrent Resolution 108) was adopted by the U.S. Congress. The intent of the resolution was to acculturate the Indians into American society and to allow them to become "full-fledged" American citizens, free from federal supervision. Although most Indian groups liked the idea of self-rule, they did not interpret termination as ending the identity and existence of their ethnic group as a legal entity.

During the 1950s, while termination was the official policy, the BIA emphasized vocational training and relocation of the Mississippi Choctaw into the mainstream of American society through the General Employment Assistance Program. The Choctaw were to receive "vocational counseling and guidance, institutional training in any recognized vocation or trade, apprenticeship, and on-the-job training, either locally or in other areas."[2] Eight field employment assistance offices were available to assist in vocational training and employment assistance. These were located in Chicago, Cleveland, Dallas, Denver, Los Angeles, Oakland, San Jose and San Francisco. Many Mississippi Choctaw participated in this program. Although the General Employment Assistance Program meant that those who participated had to leave the reservation, it afforded the Choctaw the oppportunity to advance themselves vocationally and economically. While some Choctaw did eventually return to the reservation, this program did little to improve economic development on the reservation.

In December, 1966 Radio Corporation of American Service Company (RCA) entered into a contract with the BIA for the establishment, management and operation of a vocational training center on the Choctaw Indian reservation. This contract allowed the BIA to move a step closer to mainstreaming the Choctaw into the American society. It would now be possible to train Choctaw on the reservation rather than send them away for training. The RCA project was to "impart vocational skills to adult Indians, upgrade their academic education, and give them and their families sufficient experience in city life to minimize the period of adjustment into urban society."[3]

To accomplish these goals a training center with custom-designed mobile classrooms was established, and quality housing was provided as an incentive to attract families into the program. The program was intended to enable Choctaw to become self-supporting and productive individuals, although the program made it necessary for most trainees to leave the reservation after graduation.

The vocational training program was "designed to equip the trainee with the skills and work habits necessary to secure employment in assembly line types of occupation at unskilled and semi-skilled levels."[4] Teaching good work habits and adjustment to an urban social environment were included as part of the training. The program lasted about two years. Several graduates later found work in such cities as Jackson, Mississippi and Memphis, Tennessee. Present evaluation of the RCA program shows that it had at least a modest amount of success.

President John Kennedy's administration placed less emphasis on termination, and in the early 1960s concluded that the federal policy towards the native American was better fostered by "development rather than termination." During the 1960s, therefore, different acts and programs (i.e., Area Development Act of 1961, Civil Rights Act of 1964 and the Economic Opportunity Act of 1964) were passed by Congress to aid the economic and social development of the Indian. The Choctaw were able to benefit from these programs, but termination remained the official policy until the late 1960s.

President Johnson, in an address to the Senate on March 6, 1968, called for an end of termination and the implementation of a new policy stressing self-determination which would provide freedom of choice for the American Indians. Indians could remain in their homelands if they choose, or move to the towns and cities of America. Thus, the President was proposing "a policy expressed in programs of self-help, self-development and self-determination." On September 11, 1968, Congress passed Senate Concurrent Resolution 11 which was an effort to replace House Concurrent Resolution 108 (termination) which had been adopted in 1953. Then in that same year Congress passed the Indian Civil Rights Act (Public Law 90-284) which was designed for the reservation Indian. New goals were established in 1968 which included raising the standard of living of the Indian, providing an option of remaining on a reservation or moving to a city, and increasing the opportunity to share in the benefits of modern America.

Richard Nixon's presidency continued the new official attitude towards Indian policy. His administration supported "self-determination without termination," and stated that the Indians' future should be "determined by Indian acts and Indian decisions."

Early in 1970, changes were occurring in the policies of the BIA. Emphasis was being placed on transforming the Bureau from a management to a service organization, area offices were beginning to place greater emphasis on technical services, tribes were given the option to take over many or all of the BIA program functions whenever they felt prepared to take control, and the BIA reaffirmed

the trust status of Indian land. Even though self-determination was
accepted as official policy in 1970, Congress did not enact the
Indian Self-Determination and Education Assistance Act (Public
Law 93-638) until 1975.

The Self-Determination Act of 1975 was:[5]

> To provide maximum Indian participation in the
> Government and education of the Indian people; to
> provide for the full participation of Indian tribes in
> programs and services conducted by the Federal
> Government for Indians and to encourage the
> development of human resources of the Indian people;
> to establish a program of assistance to upgrade Indian
> education; to support the right of Indian citizens to
> control their own educational activities; and for other
> purposes.

This act permitted Indian tribes to participate in all social programs
and services conducted by the federal government, and tribal
leaders could formulate plans and establish priorities and goals
free of federal intervention. The tribal governing body became the
major authority in influencing the manner in which programs would
function. Title II of the Act, the Indian Education Assistant Act, was
to make public schools attended by Indian children more
responsive to their needs.

Although the major objective of self-determination is to develop
tribal independence, political independence must also be
accompanied by economic viability. Should federal funds to
sponsor many social, economic, health and educational programs
be extensively reduced, there will be an increased demand on the
non-Indian society and the Indians themselves to fund these
programs. Therefore, economic viability of the reservations is a
goal worthy of pursuit. For some reservations this may be difficult
to obtain.

In 1966 funding of the Choctaw Community Action Agency, under
the Office of Economic Opportunity, allowed the Choctaw
government to begin experiencing self-government.[6] Continued
assistance from the Office of Economic Opportunity helped the
Choctaw to establish its own philosophy of self-determination in
conjunction with President Nixon's 1970 Policy Statement of Indian
Self-Determination. Published in 1972, some of the basic premises
established by the Choctaw on self-determination included: 1) the
substitution of "tribal control for federal management of Indian
Reservations," 2) "lasting change on an Indian reservation must
derive from action by the Indian people," and 3) changes on an
Indian reservation "can only be achieved by a strong

democratically elected Tribal Government."[7] Of course, one of the long range goals of the Choctaw leaders was to reduce the physical and psychological conditions of poverty. The report also tried to establish the manner in which the tribe could be politically reorganized to adequately administer federal programs and manage key improvements in health, education and economic development.

The Health Care Improvement Act of 1976 (Public Law 94-437) delineated several programs that Indians could contract to manage. Then in 1978, Congress passed the Indian Child Welfare Act (Public Law 95-608) which provided funds to Indian tribes to assist in the development of their child welfare programs. President Reagan has continued the policy of self-determination and has stated that his policy is to "get the BIA off the reservations."

CHOCTAW ECONOMIC DEVELOPMENT

During the 1950s and early 1960s, when termination was the official policy, many Choctaw received vocational training on and off the reservation and several were relocated. However, the quality of life for persons living on the reservation was low and most of the Choctaw were living in poverty. Unemployment was high, housing was inadequate and the majority had a low level of education. Most of the Choctaw were farm laborers, or worked in the pulpwood and lumber industries. For most of the 1950s and early 1960s, the Choctaw leaders struggled to improve the quality in their health, education and housing needs, and to provide employment and economic opportunity for their people.

During the middle 1960s, as the policy of termination began to soften, the Choctaw began to take steps toward improving the quality of life on their reservation. A high school was established at Pearl River in 1963, and the tribe began receiving benefits from the Economic Development Administration, the Manpower Development and Training Act, the Economic Opportunity Act and from other federal programs.

Choctaw leaders recognized that they had to exert more influence in the planning and development of their reservation. "Self-help" and "self-determination" were critical to meeting the future needs of the Choctaw people. Besides having a hand in implementing and directing tribal policy, economic development and industrialization on the reservation were needed ingredients if the Choctaw were to become self-sufficient. Obviously changes in federal policy toward the American Indian in the 1960s enabled the

Choctaw to take advantage of these policies and to begin to determine their own destiny.

As early as 1964, the Choctaw received a seed grant of $15,000 to plan the construction of houses, offices and utilities on the reservation. Then in 1968 the BIA and HUD entered into an agreement to jointly provide a program (Mutual Help Housing Program) whereby Indians could acquire a home. This agreement can be considered as a major impetus in getting the Choctaw into the construction business, which subsequently led to the building of an industrial park and the attraction of industrial firms to locate in the park.

The Chata Development Company was created in 1969, and since its establishment numerous homes have been built or repaired and several community centers and important tribal buildings have been constructed. With assistance of a $564,000 grant from the Economic Development Administration, the Choctaw began to develop an industrial park. The 30 acre park was completed in 1973, but it was not until 1977 that an industrial firm agreed to locate in the park. Chief Phillip Martin contacted the Packard Electric Division of the General Motors Corporation, and after much negotiation and careful planning, Packard, which makes electrical wire harnesses for automobiles, built a plant on the reservation. In February of 1979 the first wire harness came off the assembly line at the Chata Wire Harness Enterprise plant. The plant employs about 160 persons. By 1982 the business had become so successful that an expansion of the plant was undertaken.

After the Chata Wire Harness plant had been operating for about a year, Chief Martin invited officials from American Greeting Corporation to visit the reservation and to consider locating a plant in the industrial park. Discussions went well and the Choctaw Greeting Enterprise plant opened in 1981. Workers at the plant glue and paste ornaments on greeting cards and make complicated folds. Because the greeting card business is seasonal, employment ranges from about 150 to 300 employees.

In 1985 the Choctaw enticed the Oxford Investment Company of Chicago, which manufactures automobile radio speakers, to establish a plant on the reservation. This plant, known as Choctaw Electronics Enterprise, employs about 60 persons.

In a desire to expand economic opportunities for the Choctaw beyond the industrial park at Pearl River, new industries are being created in the outlying Choctaw communities. A new 22,000 square foot facility, which will serve as a satellite to the Choctaw Enterprise Plant 2, was established in 1986 in Kemper County at

DeKalb's John C. Stennis Industrial Park. The new plant will manufacture automotive and non-automotive wiring harnesses. It is expected to eventually employ 150 to 200 persons. In addition, the Choctaw Manufacturing Enterprise plant was opened in Carthage in 1986. This plant produces wiring assemblies for various electrical systems in automobiles such as dash gauges for Ford, tailgate assemblies for Chrysler, and sunroof harnesses for General Motors. The plant also builds parts for Westinghouse's "people movers." People movers are the moving walkways often utilized at airports.

Not counting the employees working at the new plants established in 1986, approximately 850 Choctaws are employed on the reservation and more than 300 Choctaw hold full time jobs off the reservation. Economic progress during the past several years has not been easy, but through self-determination, job training programs and aggressive tribal leadership, progress is being made.

SOCIOECONOMIC MEASURES OF ECONOMIC DEVELOPMENT

Despite early attempts at relocation, the population of the Mississippi Choctaw has been growing steadily during the past three decades. In 1950 Mississippi had a total of 2,502 Choctaw living in the state with approximately 2,000 of that number living on or near the reservation within the Choctaw Agency Service Area in east central Mississippi (Table 9.1). The state's Choctaw population increased to 3,119 in 1960 and to 4,133 and to 6,313 in 1970 and 1980, respectively. Independent population surveys conducted during the last several years show that the number of Choctaw living in the Choctaw Agency Service Areas was 2,594, 3,127, 3,783, and 4,393 in 1960, 1968, 1974 and 1982, respectively.

In 1982, approximately 60 percent of the Choctaw in the Choctaw Agency Service Area were under 25 years of age, and the sex ratio was approximately 100 (i.e., 100 males per 100 females).[8] Although there were some sex ratio differences according to age structure, it is not significant.

Ninety-two percent of the Choctaw currently residing in the Agency Service Area were born in Mississippi[9] and 52.8 percent of the heads of households have not moved during the past seven years, while only 32.9 percent have moved once.[10] Most Choctaw (85%) desire to remain in their present community.[11] Thus the mobility of the Choctaw is quite low, but about 175 Choctaw during the period 1975 through 1982 returned to the Agency Service Area.[12]

Table 9.1

Changes in Choctaw Population

Year	1950	1960	1970	1980	
Total in Mississippi[1]	2502	3119	4133	6131	
Year	1950[2]	1960[3]	1968[4]	1974[5]	1982[6]
On or Near Reservation	2000	2594	3127	3783	4398

1. Figures from U.S. Bureau of Census.
2. Estimated.
3. Wilbur Smith & Associates, *Comprehensive Plan, Mississippi Band of Choctaw Indians,* (Columbia, S.C.: Wilbur Smith & Associates, 1974), 10.
4. John H. Peterson, Jr., *Socio-economic Characteristics of the Mississippi Choctaw Indians.* Report 34, (Starkville: Mississippi State University Social Science Research Center, 1970), 9.
5. Barbara G. Spencer, John H. Peterson, Jr., and Choong S. Kim, *Choctaw Manpower and Demographic Survey,* (Philadelphia: Mississippi Band of Choctaw Indians, 1975), 5.
6. Mississippi Band of Choctaw Indians, *Demographic Survey,* (Philadelphia: Mississippi Band of Choctaw Indians, 1982), 2.

Source: Compiled by author from publications cited above.

The maor reasons given for returning were available work (35.4%) and housing (24.6%).[13] The reasons given for returning in 1982 were much different from an earlier survey taken in 1968 when homesickness or sickness in the family was the leading response.[14] Also in 1968, respondents indicated that they returned to the reservation to be closer to friends and relatives and to enable their children to attend an Indian school.[15] It appears that increased job oppportunity and available housing through policies of self-determination on the reservation since 1968 have been leading migratory "pull" factors for many Choctaw who responded to the 1982 survey.

Closely associated with economic development and the attraction of industrial firms and increased job opportunity is the educational training and skill level of a population. During the 1960s and 1970s the Choctaw worked hard through various federal programs to train and educate their populace to the needs of a modern day work force.

As early as 1962, only 14.5 percent of the heads of household had 8 years or more education.[16] By 1968, this figure had increased to 19.6 percent.[17] For persons 16 years of age or older, 32 percent had 8 or more years of education, but 38.2 percent had 3 years or less[18] (Table 9.2). By 1974, 26.7 percent had 3 years or less, but 50.8 percent had 8 years or more with 6.9 percent of this figure achieving more than 12 years of education and 13.6 percent having completed 12 years.[19] The median grade completed in 1968 was 6, but increased to 8 in 1974.[20] By 1982 15.6 percent had completed 12 years, and 7.7 percent had more than 12 years of education.[21] These data show continued and rapid improvement in the educational attainment of the Choctaw people, and certainly the establishment of a high school on the reservation in 1963 together with federal financial assistance and local tribal leadership have all contributed in some way to the betterment of Choctaw education.

Table 9.2

Educational Attainment of the Choctaw

Year	1968[1]	1974[a] [2]	1982[b] [3]
Highest grade Completed		(Percentage of Population)	
0-3 yrs.	38.2	26.7	36.0
4-7 yrs.	29.8	20.9	18.9
8-12 yrs.	28.9	43.9	36.3
12 yrs.	3.1	6.9	7.7

a. Column does not amount to 100 because 1.7 percent was not reported.
b. Column does not amount to 100 due to rounding.

1. John H. Peterson, Jr., *Socio-economic Characteristics of the Mississippi Choctaw Indians,* Report 34, (Starkville: Mississippi State University Social Science Research Center, 1970), 21.
2. Barbara G. Spencer, John Peterson, Jr., and Choong S. Kim. *Choctaw Manpower and Demographic Survey,* (Philadelphia: Mississippi Band of Choctaw Indians, 1975), 27.
3. Mississippi Band of Choctaw Indians, *Demographic Survey,* (Philadelphia: Mississippi Band of Choctaw Indians, 1982), 17.
Source: Compiled by author from publications cited above.

Prior to the early 1960s many Choctaw were subsistence farmers and there was little unemployment as we think of it today since almost everyone farmed. Average household income in 1962 was $1,214, and increased to $3,456 in 1967 and to $9,680 in 1982, while per capita income increased from $220 to $628, and to $2,080 for the corresponding years.[22] In 1970 the median family income for the Choctaw was $3,120, compared to $6,068 for the state of Mississippi and $9,590 for the nation.[23] By 1980 the median family income for the Choctaw had increased to $8,676,[24] while the state's median family income in 1979 was $14,603 and the national was $19,908. Choctaw median family income in 1970 was just 51 percent of the state's average and only 33 percent of nation's average. By 1980, Choctaw median income was 59 percent of the state's average and 43 percent of the national average. Between 1970 and 1980 the median family income for Choctaw increased 178.1 percent, while the state increased 140.7 percent and the nation 107.6 percent.

As the Choctaw began to implement the provisions of self-determination employment in the government sector began to swell, particularly between 1968 and 1983 (Table 9.3). The largest employer on the reservation is the tribal government with 337 employees. Off-reservation employment among the Choctaw more than doubled (143 to 300 persons) between 1968 and 1983, and non-government employment on the reservation increased from 2 to 328 between 1968 and 1983 as industrial firms were attracted to the reservation to provide employment opportunities. Employment in agriculture decreased from 177 to 5 between 1968 and 1983, and the total labor force increased from 932 to 1462 (Table 9.3). Despite this increase in jobs, unemployment in 1983 was 22.2 percent.[25] However, unemployment is on the decline.

CONCLUSION

The continuation of certain federal programs and financial support are critical to continued improvements in education, health, housing and job opportunity for the Choctaw people. Self-determination has enabled the Choctaw to consolidate their political power and decision making and to expand their economic base. More reduction in poverty and unemployment, and increased job opportunity and income, together with overall improvements in the socioeconomic well-being of the Choctaw, are still needed in order to get the standard of living closer to the Southeastern region and national averages.

Table 9.3

Changes in Choctaw Employment Patterns

Year	Labor Force	Agricultural Employment	On-Reservation Non-Agricultural Employment		Off-Reservation Employment	Unemployed
			Government	Non-Government		
1961[1]	900	500	150	2	25	223
1966[2]	1065	372	196	2	150	345
1968[3]	932	177	234	2	143	376
1983[4]	1462	5	505	328	300	324

1. Survey made by the Choctaw Agency with assistance of Wilfred C. Bailey.

2. Mississippi Band of Choctaw Indians, *Comprehensive Overall Economic Development Program*, (Philadelphia: Mississippi Band of Choctaw Indians, 1966).

3. John H. Peterson, Jr., *Socio-economic Characteristics of the Mississippi Choctaw Indians*, Report 34, (Starkville: Mississippi State University Social Science Research Center, 1970).

4. Steve Murray, "Analysis of the Labor Market on the Mississippi Choctaw Indian Reservation," mimeographed (Starkville: Mississippi State University, 1983).

Source: Compiled by author from publications cited above.

To be sure, the past 20 years has to be considered a major era in the history of the Choctaw people in Mississippi during this century. And from all indications, progress in economic development will continue. Certainly when progress under the policy of termination is compared to progress under the policy of self-determination it becomes quite evident that the Choctaw have benefitted under self-determination and are an excellent example to what Indians can do to help themselves when given the opportunity.[26]

NOTES

1. For more discussion on the historical development of the Choctaw see Jesse O. McKee, and Jon A. Schlenker. *The Choctaw: Cultural Evolution of the Native American Tribe.* (Jackson: University Press of Mississippi, 1980).

2. U.S., Department of the Interior, Bureau of Indian Affairs, Choctaw Agency. *The Mississippi Band of Choctaw Indians.* mimeographed (Philadephia: Choctaw Agency, Circa, 1972), p.7.

3. RCA Service Company. "Training Program for Choctaw Indians." (Camden, N.J.: RCA Service Company, Circa, 1967), p.1.

4. *Ibid.*

5. Indian Self-Determination and Education Assistance Act. January 4, 1975, Public Law 93-638, 88 Stat. 2203, 25 USC 450.

6. Reginald Gardner, "Choctaw Self-Determination: An Overview." in *A Choctaw Anthology*, (Philadelphia: Choctaw Heritage Press, 1983), p. 56.

7. Mississippi Band of Choctaw Indians. *Accelerated Progress Through Self-Determination.* (Philadelphia: Mississippi Band of Choctaw Indians, 1972), pp. 14-16.

8. Mississippi Band of Choctaw Indians. *Demographic Survey.* (Philadelphia: Mississippi Band of Choctaw Indians, 1982), pp. 2-3.

9. *Ibid,* p. 3.

10. *Ibid,* p. 8.

11. *Ibid.*

12. *Ibid.*

13. *Ibid.*

14. John H. Peterson., Jr., *Socioeconomic Characteristics of the Mississippi Choctaw Indians,* Report 34. (Starkville: Mississippi State University Social Science Research Center, 1970), p. 27.

15. *Ibid.*

16. *Ibid,* p. 15.

17. *Ibid.*

18. *Ibid,* p. 21.

19. Barbara G. Spencer, John H. Peterson, Jr., and Choong S. Kim. *Choctaw Manpower and Demographic Survey.* (Philadelphia: Mississippi Band of Choctaw Indians, 1975), p. 27.

20. *Ibid.*

21. *Demographic Survey,* op. cit., footnote 7, p. 17.

22. Steve Murray, "Analysis of the Labor Market on the Choctaw Indian Reservation." mimeographed (Starkville: Mississippi State University, 1983, p. 16; *Demographic Survey,* op. cit., footnote 7, pg. 16.

23. Wilbur Smith & Associates, *Comprehensive Plan, Mississippi Band of Choctaw Indians.* (Columbia, S.C.: Wilbur Smith & Associates, 1974), p. 23.

24. Murray, op. cit., footnote 21, p. 18.

25. *Ibid,* p. 20.

26. Some of the information for this chapter has been modified from Jesse O. McKee and Steve Murray, "Economics Progress and Development of the Choctaw Since 1945." in *After Removal: The Choctaw in Mississippi,* Edited by Samuel J. Wells and Roseanna Tubby. (Jackson: University Press of Mississippi. 1986), pp. 122-136.

Part Four
Migration, Cultural Change and Fusion

Chapter 10

The Iroquois
Return to their Homeland:
Military Retreat
or Cultural Adjustment

Victor Konrad

In the mid 1660s, abatement of hostilities with New France and her native allies gave the Iroquois an opportunity to expand tribal territories and establish settlements on the north shore of Lake Ontario. By 1673 seven villages occupied strategic locations in extended territories of the Seneca, Cayuga and Oneida. In 1688 all the settlements lay abandoned after the Iroquois returned to their traditional homeland south of the lake. Explanation of settlement expansion and then later retrenchment helps to answer the broader question of why the Iroquois drew back and consolidated in their original territories at the end of the seventeenth century.

For some ethnohistorians the answer is simple: the Iroquois were defeated soundly by the French, and to a lesser degree their Algonquian allies, then forced to retreat to the enclave of Confederacy villages.[1] Others suggest that the Ojibwa, a coalition of Algonquian-speakers, were responsible for destruction and rout of Iroquois warriors in a series of battles in the lower Great Lakes area.[2] Many ethnohistorians of the period consider the question unresolved and, due to a marked lack of recorded evidence, are content to accept the Iroquois as proud survivors of the conflict based on their record of conquest earlier in the seventeenth century.[3] All of these alternatives are based on selectively biased evidence: the "French and Indian allies thesis" primarily draws on Jesuit and French colonial documents;[4] the "Ojibwa thesis" depends on oral tradition;[5] and the "Iroquois perspective" finds support in Dutch and English colonial documents and oral tradition of the Iroquois.[6] Each maintains an ethnocentric bias, emphasizing one perspective while discounting other points of view.

In this chapter these views are scrutinized and re-evaluated by examining closely the range of written records, maps and oral traditions describing the Iroquois return from the north shore of Lake Ontario. The initial objective is a balanced interpretation of Iroquois-Algonquian-French relations in the critical process of Iroquois retrenchment. Was the return from the north shore a retreat or a calculated adjustment of a highly structured settlement system? Resolution of this question promises greater understanding of Iroquois consolidation on other fronts during the final years of the seventeenth century. The approach in this chapter is to examine and mitigate earlier interpretations; the return to the Iroquois homeland is not treated as an event in a military campaign, nor is it evaluated as a step in cultural displacement. Iroquois removal from southern Ontario involved several native cultures in a complex of massive resettlement, considerable subsistence shifts, expanded trade, extensive migration and strained political realignment. Conflict, both ritual and outright warfare, was but one dimension of frustrated interaction on a frontier as alien to the native tribes as it was to the Europeans.[7] Viewed together, the elements of culture in change on this frontier illuminate substantial cultural alteration among native groups and suggest adjustments to a new order. Cultural change and adjustment overshadow warfare, make the cross-cultural skirmishes pale by comparison, and yield a more accurate interpretation of Iroquois-Algonquian-French relations.

THE AMERINDIAN NEW WORLD OF THE LOWER GREAT LAKES IN THE SEVENTEENTH CENTURY

In the seventeen century, Amerindians living in the lower Great Lakes region experienced greater culture change than in centuries before or after. The removal of the St. Lawrence Iroquois, the virtual extermination of the Huron and Petun, the dispersal of the Neutral, Wenro and Erie are all well documented as are substantial relocations of Algonquian-speakers in the region.[8] Most of this massive dislocation, a combination of decimation from disease, attrition from Iroquois raids, and a migration from southern Ontario, took place in a few decades at mid-century.[9]

Before 1660, the Iroquois extended their territorial control beyond the Huron country centered on the former Jesuit mission at Saint-

Marie and raided as far east as the French settlement at Montreal (Fig. 10.1). Maps of the period[10] and Jesuit accounts[11] record the presence of Iroquois camps located at strategic points to maintain supply lines to the homeland and establish Iroquois control north of Lake Ontario. After 1660, five large and two small villages, all of them permanent, appear on the historical maps[12] and are mentioned by the Sulpician missionaries who lived in them.[13] Settlement at these locations was designed to control northern fur trade routes and to parallel the tribal alignment of villages in the Iroquois homeland. Previously occupied camps became permanent settlements in extended tribal territories: the Seneca, on the western flank of the Confederacy, settled on the western end of Lake Ontario; the Cayuga, next to the Seneca south of the lake, moved beside the Seneca north of the lake.[14] In 1673, Count Frontenac travelled to the region and established a fort at Cataraqui, now Kingston.[15] The objective, to control Iroquois traffic and thus the fur trade, was not realized for the Indians merely travelled to the north shore by the longer route around the western end of Lake Ontario.[16] The French presence in the lake basin expanded with the seigneurial grant to LaSalle at Cataraqui.[17] With French exploration in the lower Great Lakes,[18] increased missionary activity,[19] and a growing military posture,[20] the Iroquois began to pull back from the north shore and return to villages in their home territories.[21] Skirmishes with the Ottawa, Mississauga and other Ojibwa accelerated Iroquois retrenchment.[22] Construction of Fort Denonville at the mouth of the Niagara River contained Iroquois permanent settlement south of Lake Ontario,[23] although Iroquois tribes, and particularly the Mohawk, continued to hunt and trap north of the Lake.[24]

The decades between 1660 and 1690 saw Iroquois migration and resettlement, subsistence pattern and trade linkage changes, and political alliance shifts. All of these realignments challenged the highly structured tenets of Iroquois culture and life.[25] When posture and bravado no longer served to forestall French designs in the lower Great Lakes,[26] and when defeats at the hands of enemies around them diminished their military prowess as well as their numbers,[27] the Iroquois pulled back and embraced the culture and land they knew. Orderly return to the homeland, replaced territorial extension. Otherwise their system hardly changed in spite of the vortex of change around them. The Iroquois remained principal actors in the new world they helped create and managed to keep, at least temporarily, the integrity of their culture and their homeland

194

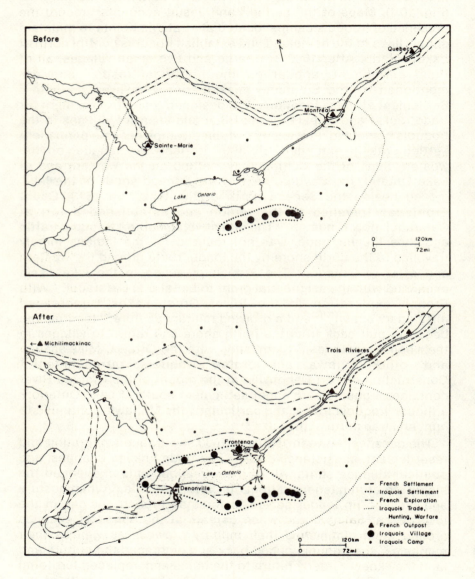

Figure 10.1 Hypothetical Iroquois and French Before and After 1660.

whereas virtually every other native tribe in the Great Lakes region suffered dislocation and cultural disintegration.[28]

CONFLICT AND THE SIMPLIFICATION
OF CULTURAL BREAKDOWN

Viewing the Iroquois retrenchment as a retreat in military terms immediately colors interpretation of the process and focuses attention on the details of conflict rather than the complex of activity surrounding it. A focus on conflict among Iroquois, Algonquian, French and Dutch is over-emphasized in the literature and tends to simplify explanation. The Iroquois win or they lose; the Ojibwa gain victory or suffer defeat. Early studies, such as George T. Hunt's *The Wars of the Iroquois* [29] unfortunately set the tone for singular perspectives and simplified explanations of inter-tribal relations, building on a fascination with native warfare initially documented by Champlain and French missionaries.[30] More recent studies, Otterbein's insistence on Iroquois victory,[31] and Eid's demand for recognition of Ojibwa victory,[32] continue to seek more evidence to support one view or the other rather than applying new or neglected information to the resolution of broader problems of culture change.

Iroquois aggression, and the rapid expansion of territorial control at mid-century, invite a countervailing argument for their defeat in the late seventeenth century. Adventures in the Canadian Shield, the Ohio valley, the Appalachians, the lower St. Lawrence and east of Lake Champlain are attributable to the exuberance of young warriors as much as to the ambitions of the Confederacy. Indeed, a constant struggle is in evidence between the policy set by the Council of the Old Men and the glory-seeking ambition of the young men and boys.[33] Unbridled during the mid-seventeenth century, aggression was subdued when over-extension became evident in later years. Safeguards for overextension were built into their society. Tribal and League control was asserted when a threat was imminent to village, tribe and consequently League safety.[34] Iroquois adjustment to external threat was rapid and ultimately insured a strong hold on their traditional territory as well as control of access to adjacent lands. This outcome, and not the victory or defeat in any one or all the skirmishes, is important in assessing the fate of the Iroquois at the end of the seventeenth century.

MIGRATION

Migratory movements indicate the resiliency of the Iroquois system. Other contemporary native groups in the region were less efficient and organized. For the Iroquois, the move to the north shore and return to the homeland involved the relocation of thousands. A move of similar magnitude occurred in the migration of Outouac (Ottawa), Sauteur and Mississauga into southern Ontario after removal of the Iroquois, but was a very different migration.

Immediately prior to French expansion into the Lake Ontario region in 1665, Iroquois settlement was confined to the homeland south of Lake Ontario and the distribution of villages closely resembled the pattern that prevailed during the first half of the seventeenth century[35] (Fig. 10.2). During the period 1647 to 1665, the Mohawk consistently occupied three major villages Tionontoguen, Ossernenon, and Andagoron clustered in the Mohawk Valley.[36] Although the village Gandaougue may have been occupied at this time,[37] details of its existence prior to the 1670s are sketchy. The Oneida and the Onondaga each occupied one major village. During the late 1650s the Jesuit mission to the Iroquois was located at Ganentaa, on the small lake north of the Onondaga "town" and on

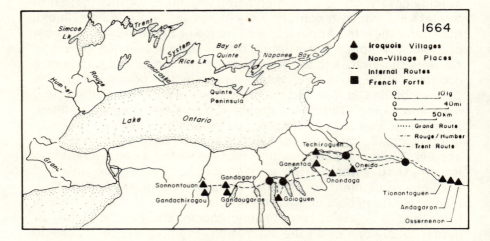

Figure 10.2 Changes in the Iroquois Settlement System, 1664.

the trail to Lake Oneida.[38] This trail from Onondaga led to
Techiroguen, the principal fishing village of the Iroquois.[39]
Goioguen, the main village of the Cayuga was located a few miles
west of Lake Cayuga.[40] At this time settlements did not exist at
Onontare and Thiohero.[41] Thiohero, however, was an important fork
in the trail network for the place is marked if not identified on the
detailed maps of the Iroquois country. The Seneca occupied the
two major villages of Sonnontouan and Gandagaro, immediately
west of the Finger Lakes area, and two lesser settlements,
Gandachiragou and Gandougarae, respectively associated with the
larger settlements. Although additional Iroquois villages are
alluded to in the documents,[42] names and locations are not
provided.

By 1670, six villages appeared on the north shore (Fig. 10.3).
Substantial cartographic and written evidence indicates relatively
sudden development of north shore settlements, except
Teyaiagon.[43] It was occupied three years later to complete the
village array on the north shore: Ganneious on Napanee Bay, an

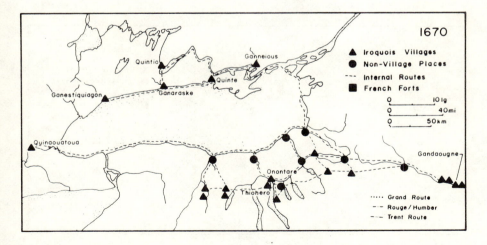

Figure 10.3 Changes in the Iroquois Settlement System, 1670.

arm of the Bay of Quinte; Quinte, near the isthmus of the Quinte peninsula; Ganaraske, at the mouth of the Ganaraska River; Quintio, on Rice Lake; Ganestiquiagon, near the mouth of the Rouge River; Teyaiagon, near the mouth of the Humber River; and Quinaouatoua, on the portage between the western end of the Lake and the Grand River (Fig. 10.4).

Whereas minor changes in Iroquois settlement south of the lake occurred by 1680, the major villages in each tribal area persisted (Fig. 10.5). On the north shore, with the defeat of the Andastes in 1675,[44] removed the reason for Iroquois, and in particular, Cayuga settlement. The Cayuga could return to their traditional homeland south of the lake now that the aggressive Andastes had been subdued. Sulpician correspondence traces the population decline of the eastern north shore villages due to migration, and indicates that by 1680 there were no more than seven or eight Cayugas left at Quinte.[45] Pritchard suggests that the Indians were returning to their homeland south of the lake.[46] This certainly seems a logical alternative for the Cayuga since the fur trade routes on the eastern end of the lake had declined in importance. To the south, their tribe was celebrating victory over the Andastes and planning war with the Illinois.[47] Before the end of the decade all of the villages were

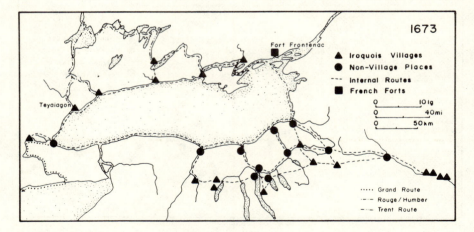

Figure 10.4 Changes in the Iroquois Settlement System, 1673.

Figure 10.5 Changes in the Iroquois Settlement System, 1680.

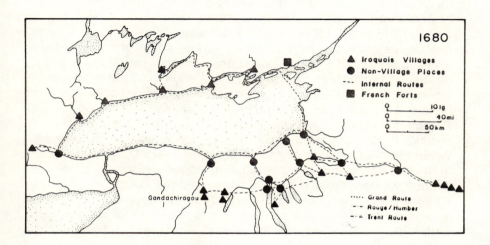

abandoned and the Iroquois moved back to their respective tribal territories and relocated in home villages.

Historical maps of the second half of the seventeenth century depict the Mississauga and particularly the Sauteur encroaching on the old Huron territory and the Lake Simcoe area. Their migration involved relocating entire bands and severing connections with previous homelands. For example, the Mississauga left their homeland of less than a century on northern Lake Huron and moved to village locations abandoned by the Iroquois on the north shore of Lake Ontario. Unlike the Iroquois who migrated cautiously to new lands, and sustained connections with the traditional homeland, the Mississauga, who originated in the Ohio valley, migrated to new lands often.[48] In turn, other Algonquian bands relocated in the lands vacated by the Mississauga.

SETTLEMENT SYSTEMS

Differences in migration also created differing settlement systems. Mississauga villages were clustered along trade routes at strategic access points to and from the lower Great Lakes and at locations where fish resources were plentiful.[49] Little is known of their settlements in the seventeenth century but fragments of information in the *Jesuit Relations,* combined with inferences from oral tradition related by George Copway[50] and Peter Jones,[51] outline a pattern of seasonal occupation focused on large villages during productive seasons and dispersed among small encampments at other times of the year. Locations which afforded access to multiple and ample food resources for bands of 200 or more people were chosen, and spatial organization appears to be resource based. As illustrated on historical maps and described by E.S. Rogers,[52] traditional villages were clustered along the north shore of Lake Huron, Georgian Bay and along the Trent-Severn waterway. When the Mississauga moved into the southern Ontario Peninsula in the wake of Iroquois migration, they continued to cluster villages in southwestern Ontario but also occupied the abandoned Iroquois villages on the north shore of Lake Ontario. These Iroquois village locations, like their sister settlements to the south of Lake Ontario, had highly organized spatial plans. Features of the Iroquois settlement system may be summarized:

(1) settlements on the north shore and in the homeland were distributed along east-west axes;
(2) distances between settlements on the north shore tended to be greater than distances between settlements to the south of Lake Ontario;
(3) there were more connections between places in the homeland system;
(4) the north shore villages were connected to the homeland settlements through fishing camps on the south shore;
(5) the distribution of north shore villages resembled more closely the distribution of south shore camps;
(6) the north shore villages occupied locations on routes leading north from the homeland rather than independent locations on the north shore of Lake Ontario.

In essence, the north shore system was less complex than the traditional system south of the lake and in fact resembled the distribution of access points on the south shore.

Routes leading north from Lake Ontario were employed by all the Iroquois tribes to gain access to the hunting and trading territories beyond the lower Great Lakes. Whereas the Seneca would approach the north shore from the western end or "fond du lac," other tribes chose the eastern route. Rarely did the Iroquois attempt to cross the lake in their canoes. Once on the north shore the interior and the northwest were accessible by three main routes: from Lake Ontario to the Grand River and on the the upper lakes, from either the Rouge or the Humber, across the moraine, into the Lake Simcoe drainage basin and on to Georgian Bay, and the traditional route to Georgian Bay via the Trent system of lakes, rivers and short portages. Additional portages from the north shore to Rice Lake and across the Prince Edward County isthmus complemented the Trent route. North shore villages occupied strategic positions on each of these routes; in all likelihood these were favored and convenient temporary campsites of previous years. Except for Quinaouatoua and Quintio, all the villages were located at points where the routes leading to and from the north had to join the Lake Ontario circumnavigation routes to the Iroquois homeland. Quinaouatoua occupied a commanding position on the Grand River portage and Quintio occupied a branching point on the Trent route. At no other points, and with no fewer villages, could the Iroquois as effectively facilitate and control the flow of furs from the northern hunting and trading territory to their homeland.

It appears that an Iroquois desire to align the flow of furs by established tribal hunting territories saw the corresponding system of villages formed by tribal affiliation. North shore settlements were not affiliated with one Iroquois tribe alone, nor were they villages of a distinct tribe. Rather they were communities affiliated and aligned with the traditional Iroquois tribes in the homeland. Captions on historical maps suggesting socio-political unity, and the many references to the "Nation" on the north shore are misleading.[53] Although no tribal affiliation is given for Quinaouatoua, ample documentary evidence substantiates that Teyaiagon and Ganneious were Oneida.[54] Robinson provides no evidence for his identification of Quintio as a Cayuga village, but the proximity of this shortlived settlement to Ganaraske strongly suggests the small village-large village or permanent village-temporary village pattern represented to the south,[55] and as such supports his claim that Quintio was Cayuga. Although the lack of Mohawk settlements on the north shore is attributed to the location of Mohawk hunting territories in northern New York,[56] no reason for the absence of Onondaga villages is given. The Cayuga, Oneida and Seneca were continually harassed by the Andastes during the 1660s and it was in response to this pressure that some Cayuga,[57] and probably some Seneca and Oneida as well, moved north of Lake Ontario. This initial advantage may have precluded any Onondaga establishment there for the other tribes already had the trade routes covered.

SUBSISTENCE AND TRADE

The conservative extension of the Iroquois settlement system is also reflected in the restrained departure from any subsistence, trade, or other activity found in the traditional villages south of the lake. Seneca colonies were located close to the Seneca homeland and on routes familiar to Seneca warriors and hunters. In fact, north shore Seneca, Cayuga and Oneida villages were located within the extended tribal lands which included hunting territory.[58] While settlements were located only within the tribal territory, boundaries did not restrict hunting. As in the area to the south of Lake Ontario, "permissive hunting"[59] prevailed and Iroquois hunters on the north shore and from the homeland could hunt in each other's territories. Consequently, the Mohawk and particularly the Onondaga could and did hunt to the north of Lake Ontario.[60]

North shore villages served functions not emphasized to the same degree south of the lake. One was a base for extensive winter hunting activities in the area north and west of Lake Ontario. Trouve describes the Sulpician attempts to follow the Indians on their hunts.[61] Apparently these hunts became increasingly important in the "Iroquois du Nord" seasonal round of activities after 1670, for the Sulpicians found it increasingly difficult to minister to their charges who spent the winter months away from the villages.[62] Hennepin adds that the Indians travelled as far as 200 leagues from their settlements in search of food and furs for the trade.[63] This seasonal occupance pattern represents an exaggerated form of that carried on by the Iroquois brethren to the south.[64] The Iroquois limited their traditional League village extension, and permanent villages were not established beyond the north shore.

These settlements formed bases for their own people and provided stopovers for Iroquois brethren on their way to and from the beaver hunt. Numerous accounts, including reports by Talon, Courcelles and Frontenac stress the extensive nature of Iroquois hunting activities on the north shore.[65] Both Fenelon and Hennepin were first-hand observers of the constant traffic along routes commanded by the "Iroquois du Nord" villages.[66] Here the south shore brethren could secure food and supplies, socialize and coordinate hunting activities. Perhaps they stored their own maize at these villages for use during the winter. Furs could also be temporarily stored prior to shipment south of the lake and into Albany.

The north shore villages, particularly Teyaiagon, also served as terminal points for Ottawa fur brigades on their way to trade with the English. This design was not fully realized before the establishment of Forts Frontenac and Denonville in 1700.[67] In the meantime, the villages were the scene of extensive trade between both the French and Dutch-English traders and the Iroquois. Much of the trade involved the exchange of fur for liquor and brought considerable violence. Belmont's *Histoire de l'eau de vie en Canada* records numerous incidents of maiming and death at Ganestiquiagon, Teyaiagon and Ganneious.[68]

Maize, the Iroquois staple, as well as pumpkins and squashes were stored in villages.[69] Food and other acquired items were distributed by the matriarchs in longhouses identical to those south of the lake (Fig. 10.6). Houses, village plan, foodways, hunting and trade all closely resembled patterns from the homeland.

Among the Mississauga, subsistence was based on hunting beaver, moose and deer as well as growing maize and squash, but the most important food source was fish.[70] Mississauga and Sauteur fishermen were highly adept at taking whitefish and sturgeon in large quantities near their lakeside villages and at waterfalls and rapids in the region. The Mississauga were not as dependent upon agriculture as were the Iroquois. Crops grown adjacent to the settlements were abandoned at times and did not

Eleuation des Cabannes Sauvages

Figure 10.6 "Eleuation des Cabannes Sauvages." Inset "Plan du Fort Frontenac ou Cataracouy." 1720 M.s map collection, France, Cartes Marines No. 108. *Maps in the Ayers Collection* (Newberry Library, Chicago), Item 150.   Courtesy of the Edward E. Ayer Collection, The Newberry Library, Chicago

always mature.[71] Extensive annual migrations to hunt and gather wild grains and berries meant fewer and less productive crop harvests and also insured that dependence on agriculture would not develop.

SOCIOPOLITICAL ORGANIZATION

Constant annual movement, accompanied by extensive migrations during the seventeenth century, prevented the stabilization of Mississauga and other Ojibwa societies.[72] Small bands, consisting of several hundred people, were headed by a chief installed by a special ceremony:[73]

> In one instance, the chief of the Amika died and his
> eldest son three years later intended to assume his
> father's title. He invited various bands to attend the
> games and other ceremonies that he wished to hold in
> his father's honor. At the same time, he planned to
> resuscitate his deceased father by taking his name.

New social units emerged as patrilineal and nonlocalized totemic associations (spatially extensive clan affiliations) due to band dispersal, reduction in numbers and intermingling. The system of identification with symbolic totems allowed people to maintain and recognize bonds with each other over large territories sparsely occupied by moving bands.

Sociopolitical change on this scale was not possible among the Iroquois unless the group virtually broke ties with the League and their brethren living in traditional villages. For example, a few Oneida from Ganneious moved to Fort Frontenac where the Recollet missionary program of acculturation had a limited effect on this Iroquois settlement.[74] Fig. 10.7 provides a view of Fort Frontenac and environs in 1682. The longhouses and their concentration in a village are evident although no palisade is apparent. Like the inhabitants of the homesteads and the mission, the Indians were under the protection of the fort.[75] However, their village is located adjacent to the spring (G), a traditional locational requirement, and their cultivated area does not exhibit the rectangular regularity of French fields. The occupants of this small Oneida settlement, although not mentioned in Duchesneau's Census of Christian Indians,[76] apparently lived in association with the French settlement like their Iroquois brethren near Montreal. The Christian Indians, acknowledged Iroquois and regularly journeyed to Albany to trade and were definitely not under French

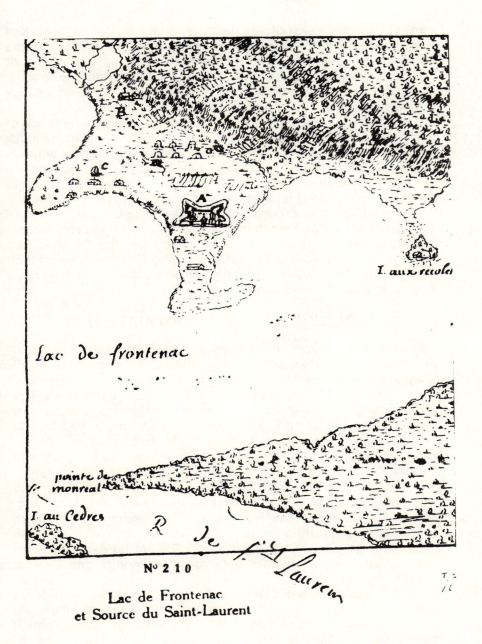

I. aux recolei

Lac de frontenac

pointe de
monreal

I. au Cedres

R de f. Laurent

Nº 210

Lac de Frontenac
et Source du Saint-Laurent

Figure 10.7 "Lac de Frontenac/et Source du Saint-Laurent." Minet,
1682. 1 mss. map. PAC, National Map Collection. H 3/902/1682.

control, but they were outside the traditional political framework of the League.[77] Their villages, spatially segregated from the League settlements, and politically autonomous, were an expression of League retrenchment. Fenton feels that local (village) autonomy and centralized League authority had been in a state of uneasy balance ever since the formation of the League.[78]

The strain on centralized League authority and the resurgence of village autonomy is also evident, but to a lesser degree, in the north shore village system. The north shore villages each sent their own representatives to meet with Count Frontenac in 1673 because the villages retained traditional tribal autonomy in the League. However, the League affiliation was acknowledged because the representatives were escorted by the chief of the League.[79] With the establishment of the French on Lake Ontario, the need for Iroquois solidarity became more marked. The Cayuga, though they had never borne arms against the French,[80] were settled within striking distance of Fort Frontenac and as such were the first to be wooed back to the south by tribe and League.

IROQUOIS RETREAT AS ADJUSTMENT

By 1688, the Iroquois settlement system again was restricted to the area south of Lake Ontario (Fig. 10.8) and the distribution of villages closely resembled that prior to settlement expansion. Major settlements in the respective tribal territories remained. The small Seneca villages of Gandachiragon and Gandougarae cannot be accounted for by 1688 and may have been destroyed by the French in the Denonville raid of 1687. The two principal villages either survived the attack or were subsequently rebuilt. No details of the fate of the small villages are recorded, and it is not certain if or where they existed. According to Heidenreich, in time of war, the inhabitants of small Huron villages moved to the well defended, larger settlements in the tribal area.[81] Apparently, the Seneca reacted to external threat in a similar fashion. The other Iroquois tribes were not directly affected by the Denonville campaign and small villages persisted in the Cayuga, Onondaga and Oneida territories.

For the Iroquois, few possibilities for change existed. In the move to the north shore, as in the homelands to the south, establishment of new settlements was controlled by social and technological restrictions, and limited by a finite resource base. Consequently, traditional settlement features, the longhouse and the village, were maintained. The distinctive distribution of settlements, while an

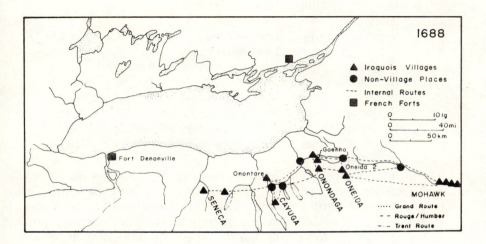

Figure 10.8 Changes in the Iroquois Settlement System, 1688.

innovation, can be traced back to the traditional pattern. Territorial constraints and the knowledge of previously occupied and strategic locations certainly played a major role in determining the distribution of the north shore villages. Settlement continuity existed in every sense whereas among the Mississauga adaptation was the rule and an extremely loose settlement and social structure allowed them to adjust while on the move. The Iroquois were limited and adjustment was possible only through retreat and consolidation.

Historical maps of the second half of the seventeenth century place the Mississauga and Sauteurs encroaching on the old Huron territory and the Lake Simcoe area. They were an invading group in the sense that they defeated the Iroquois in several skirmishes, but moreso because they filled the void on the north shore caused by Iroquois retrenchment. New evidence on Iroquois agriculture, especially the extreme devastation wrought by insects,[82] suggests that after almost twenty years of occupation it may have been necessary for the agriculturalists to abandon their settlements. This alternative to warfare was an impetus to migration and contracted territoriality. Meanwhile, a greater French control of the region added pressure for Iroquois consolidation. In any event, the

Iroquois left gracefully and transferred their abandoned habitations and lands on the north shore to the Mississauga in a treaty recorded by an English fur trader:[83]

> They say,
> We have come to acquaint you that we are settled on Ye North side of Cadarachqui Lake near Tchojachiage (Teyaiagon) where we plant a tree of peace and open a path for all people, quite to Corlaer's house (house of the English Governor) and desire to be united in Ye Covenant Chain, our hunting places to be one; and because the path of Corlaer's house may be open and clear, doe give a drest elke skin to cover Ye path to walke upon.

Viewed in the broader context of late seventeenth century native and ex-European relations, migrations and cultural changes, Iroquois settlement expansion and retrenchment is seen as a complex process. Examination of Iroquois interaction with other native groups, notable Algonquian speakers from the north and west, emphasizes the sustained importance of intertribal and native cross-cultural relations during the late seventeenth century. French pressure on the Iroquois was modified and sometimes neutralized by Iroquois arrangements with other native groups. Pressure from native enemies was diffused through systematic settlement expansion and retraction, and countered with settlement realignment in the cultural hearth and fortress south of Lake Ontario. The re-evaluation of the retrenchment proposed in this essay emphasizes that military campaigns against the Iroquois, by both French and Amerindian foes, do not alone account for the Iroquois return to their homeland. The heavy anchor of Iroquoian cultural tradition, the highly systematic nature of Iroquois settlement organization, and the possible depletion of north shore food and fur resources were factors in the return migration. Together they provide a more satisfactory understanding of Iroquois retrenchment than the simpler, causal explanation based on military conflict resolution.

NOTES

1. William J. Eccles, *The Canadian Frontier* (New York: Holt, Rinehart and Winston, 1969).

2. Leroy V. Eid, "The Ojibwa-Iroquois war: the war the Five Nations did not win," *Ethnohistory* 26 (Fall, 1979):297-324.

3. Bruce G. Trigger, *The Children of Aataentsic: A History of the Huron People to 1660.* 2 Volumes (Montreal: McGill-Queen's University Press, 1976).

4. Primarily the *Jesuit Relations.* R.G. Thwaites, ed., *The Jesuit Relations and Allied Documents* (hereafter JR) 73 Volumes (New York, 1957).

5. See for example George Copway, *The Traditional History and Characteristic Sketches of the Ojibway Nation* (Toronto: Coles, 1972) (Reprint).

6. Arthur Parker, "Analytical history of the Seneca Indians," *Researches and Transactions of the New York State Archaeological Association (Rochester, New York, 1926).*

7. Victor Konrad, "An Iroquois Frontier: the north shore of Lake Ontario during the late seventeenth century," *Journal of Historical Geography* 7 (1981):129-144.

8. Bruce G. Trigger and James F. Pendergast, "Saint Lawrence Iroquoians," In Bruce G. Trigger, ed., *Handbook of North American Indians, Northeast* (hereafter HNAI) Volume 15 (Washington, Smithsonian Institution, 1978), pp. 357-61; Trigger, *op. cit.* 2:725-82; Marion E. White, "Neutral and Wenro," *HNAI* 15:407-11; Marian E. White, "Erie," *HNAI* 15:412-17; Conrad E. Heidenreich, "Mapping the location of native groups, 1600-1760," *Mapping History* 2 (1981):6-13.

9. Trigger, *op. cit.* 2:588-600, 725-66, 751-840.

10. Konrad, *op. cit.* Table 1. See also C.E. Heidenreich, "Seventeenth-century maps of the Great Lakes: an overview and procedures for analysis," *Archivaria* 6 (1978):83-112.

11. See selected citations from *JR* listed later in this paper.

12. Particularly useful are maps drawn by Galinee, (Jolliet), Franquelin, Belmont, Bernou and Raffeix. Konrad, *op. cit.* Table 1.

13. The best source is C. Trouve, "Abrege de la Mission de Kente, pp. 119-28 of Dollier de Casson, *Histoire du Montreal, 1640-72* (Montreal, 1871), 1672.

14. Raffeix maps, particularly "Le Lac Ontario/avec les lieux circonvoisins . . .." Raffeix. 1688. 1 ms. map. France, BN, Geographie, Ge.D. 8043, pf. 40, No. 37, Bibliotheque du Roy; PAC, NMC, H3/902/1688.

15. J.S. Pritchard, ed., *Journey of my Lord Count Frontenac to Lake Ontario* (Kingston, Ontario, 1973) being a translation of Archives des Colonies, CHA, IV, 12-26, Voyage de M. le Comte de Frontenac au Lac Ontario en 1673.

16. This route change is recorded on the historical maps before 1680.

17. Pierre Margry, ed., *Decouvertes et establissements des francais dans l'ouest et dans le sud de l'Amerique septentrionale, 1614-1754: Memoires et documents in edits* (hereafter DEF) 1:500-1, 2:115 (Paris, 1879-88).

18. Conrad E. Heidenreich, "Mapping the Great Lakes/The period of exploration," *Cartographica* 17, 3 (1980):32-64.

19. Trouve, *op. cit.,* pp. 123-125.

20. *DEF* 2:14.

21. Richard A. Preston and L. Lamontagne, eds., *Royal Fort Frontenac* (Toronto, 1958), pp. 90-91.

22. Eid, *op. cit.,* pp. 302-5.

23. *DEF* 4:50-1; E.B. O'Callaghan, ed., *Documents relative to the colonial history of New York* (hereafter *NYCD)* 9 (Albany, 1858), pp. 228-32 (1684), 296-303, (1687) 319-22, 324-30.

24. J. Hampden Burnham, "The coming of the Mississagas," *Ontario Historical Society, Papers and Records* 6 (1904-05):7-10.

25. William N. Fenton, "Northern Iroquoian Culture Patterns," *HNAI* 15:296-321.

26. Pritchard, *op. cit.,* pp. 27-57.

27. Eid,*op. cit.,* pp. 302-6.

28. Heidenreich, "Mapping the location of native groups, 1600-1760."

29. George T. Hunt, *The Wars of the Iroquois, A Study in Intertribal Relations* (Madison: University of Wisconsin Press, 1940).

30. See for example J.F. Lafitau, *Customs of the American Indians Compared with the Customs of Primitive Times.* Edited by William N. Fenton and Elizabeth L. Moore in 2 Volumes (Toronto: Champlain Society, 1977), 2:98-172.

31. Keith Otterbein, "Why the Iroquois Won," *Ethnohistory* 11 (1964):56-63.

32. Eid,*op. cit.*

33. Lafitau,*op. cit.* 2:101.

34. Fenton,*op. cit.*

35. B.G. Trigger, "Settlement as an aspect of Iroquoian adaptation at the time of contact,"*American Anthropologist* 65 (1963):86-101.

36. *JR* 31:39, 45, 51, 83; 40:127, 135, 139, 145; 49:257-65; 51:295.

37. *JR* 51:187.

38. L. Campeau, *Gannentaha, Premiere mission Iroquoise (1653-1665)* (Montreal: Bellarmin, 1983).

39. *JR* 57:29.

40. *JR* 8:298; See also the J.S. Clark map in C. Hawley, *Early chapters of Cayuga history: Jesuit mission in Goi-o-gouen, 1656-1684. Also an account of the Sulpitian mission among the emigrant Cayugas about Quinte Bay in 1688* (Auburn, New York, 1879).

41. *JR* 49:257-65.

42. *JR* 43:263.

43. Reasons for Teyaiagon's absence are documented in Konrad, *op. cit.,* p. 133.

44. Hunt, *op. cit.,* p. 142.

45. Preston and Lamontagne,*op. cit.,* pp. 90-101.

46. J.S. Pritchard, "For the glory of God: the Quinte mission, 1668-80," *Ontario History* 65 (1973):105.

47. *JR* 49:245.

48. Burnham, *op. cit.,* p. 7-8.

49. E.S. Rogers, "Southeastern Ojibwa," *HNAI* 15:762-4.

50. Copway,*op. cit.*

51. Peter Jones,*History of the Ojebway Indians* (London: A.W. Bennett, 1861).

52. Rogers,*op. cit.,* pp. 760-1.

53. *JR* 52:47.

54. P.J. Robinson,*Toronto during the French regime* (Toronto, 1933), p. 24.

55. J. Tuck, "The Iroquois Confederacy,"*Scientific American,* 224 (1971):2, 40.

56. *NYCD* 9 (1671):80.

57. *JR* 52 147, 175; 47: 111; 51:527.

58. F.F.C. Wallace, "Political organization and land tenure among the northeastern Indians, 1600-1830," *Southwestern Journal of Anthropology* 13 (1957):312.

59. *Ibid.,* p. 316.

60. *NYCD* 3 (1686):417.

61. Trouve,*op. cit.,* pp. 123-7.

6.2 Louis Hennepin, *A new discovery of a vast country in America* (R.G. Thwaites, ed.) 2 (Chicago 1903), p. 116; Preston and Lamontagne,*op. cit.,* pp. 90-4.

63. Hennepin,*op. cit.* 1:19.

64. *JR* 44:117.

65. *NYCD* 9 (1670):65 *Ibid.*, (1671) 80; Pritchard, "Journey of Count Frontenac," *op. cit.*, pp. 41-7.

66. A. Yon, "Francois de Salignac-Fenelon, Sulpicien:son memoire sur le Canada, 1670,"*cahiers de dix,* 35 (1970):159-65; Hennepin, *op. cit.*, pp. 1 24.

67. *NYCD* 4:472, 694.

68. J.P. Donelly, ed., "The history of brandy in Canada," *Mid-America* 34 (1952):53.

69. Trouve, *op. cit.*, p. 122.

70. W. Vernon Kinietz, *Indians of the Western Great Lakes,* 1615-1760 (Ann Arbor: University of Michigan Press, 1965), pp. 322-5.

71. Rogers, *op. cit.*, p. 762.

72. *Ibid.*

73. *JR* 55:137; quoted in Rogers, *op. cit.*, p. 762.

74. Hennepin, *op. cit,* 1:54-5.

75. *Ibid.*, pp. 18, 19, 35.

76. *NYCD* 9 (1680):145.

77. A.W. Trelease, *Indian affairs in colonial New York: the seventeenth century* (Ithaca, New York, 1960), pp. 250-1; C.H. Torok, "The Tyendinaga Mohawks," *Ontario History* 57 (1965):67-77.

78. W.N. Fenton, "Locality as a basic factor in the development of Iroquois social structure," *Bureau of American Ethnology Bulletin* 149 (1951):52.

79. Pritchard, "Journey of Count Frontenac"*op. cit.*, pp. 57-9.

80. *JR* 51:255.

81. Conrad E. Heidenreich, *Huronia: a history and geography of the Huron Indians, 1600-50* (Toronto: McClelland and Stewart, 1973), pp. 133-4.

82. William Sarna, George R. Hamell and William L. Butts, "Northern Iroquoian horticulture and insect infestation: a cause for village removal," *Ethnohistory* 31 (1984):197-207.

83. *NYCD* 4:494,476.

Chapter 11
Women in Indian Removal: Stresses of Emigration

Joseph T. Manzo

Indian removal has been studied from a variety of themes including victimization, economics, people-place relations and culture change. This chapter, about women, isolates the various stresses on them during the process of being relocated during Indian removal. While scholars recognize the lack of primary material regarding women in removal, the re-awakening social consciousness of the last few decades, which pointed out that "a gender masculine or neutral" approach does not provide a complete perspective (coupled with an obligation to know as much about Indian removal as possible), justifies such an undertaking.[1] It should be noted that the available data do not, in all cases, directly provide documentation of women's roles or interaction in the removal process. However, the intent of this chapter encourages the extrapolation of the data from a masculine or neutral gender focus to a feminine focus.

This study takes examples from movements north and south of the Ohio River during Indian removal and presents the range of possible stresses experienced during forced migration.

BACKGROUND TO REMOVAL

The notion of Indian territory began with the British, was mentioned by Washington and Jefferson, was implemented through volunteerism by Monroe and became law under Jackson.[2] Suggested Indian locations were always on the fringe of settlement. By Jackson's time the area west of the state of Missouri and southwest of the Missouri River became more acceptable to those who both supported and opposed Indian rights. This acceptability was due to the generally held view that Euro-Americans would not want to settle in those areas. For those supporting Indian rights it became a place to preserve Indian culture away from the corrupting influence of whites.

Eastern Indians had a heritage of movement. James Clifton, whose intent is not a benign interpretation of movement, makes reference to such a heritage when describing the Potawatomi:[3]

> From the year they first entered the historical scene, down to 1833, there was no time in which some portion of the tribe, large or small, was not on the move somewhere else. Indeed for nearly two centuries migration had been a favored adaptive strategy, one used to cope with external stress.

And Elisha Chester, in his dealings with the Cherokee, wrote to his superior, "In my last [letter] I mentioned that there has been made suggestions by some of the Cherokee about removal to the pacific."[4] For Indians, moving per se was generally not a problem. However, like Anglos they were not interested in the particular areas set aside for them and cited concerns regarding the lack of timber and game, the insalubrious nature of the country, love of home, and social conditions as their justification.[5] Because of these objections, removal negotiations were not totally successful. It has been estimated that well over 12 percent of the eastern Indians involved never permanently relocated in the West; instead, they back migrated, moved to Canada or Mexico, or remained in the East.[6]

Finally, it should be noted that, for some Indians, removal was less traumatic in nature. The annals of the Shawnee Methodist Mission and Indian Manual Labor School recorded the following: "June 1, 1833, the Hog Creek band of Shawnees under the leadership of Joseph Parks, Interpreter, left Ohio for Kansas."[7] This entry is followed by one dated September 15, 1833: "The Hog Creek band of Shawnees reached the Kansas River."[8] The implication is they had little if any trouble along the way. A relatively smooth migration also occurred for a group of Potawatomi. Clifton writes of Potawatomi led by Caldwell and Padegokshek that left the Chicago area in early winter for the West: "Of the 712 persons . . . only one died in route. It was a particularly hardy group, or one well cared for."[9] Nonetheless, for most, removal was harsh and unjust in nature. Further understanding of the stresses involved in this process can be gained by focusing on generic aspects of the Cherokee migration. These aspects are the ambivalent attitudes expressed toward removal, the loss of personal property, mental stress, and the hardships of the forced emigration itself.

A CHEROKEE EXAMPLE

The Cherokee are an Iroquoian speaking tribe who occupied the southern Appalachians at the time of European contact.[10] Prospering in this region the Cherokee, along with the Seminole Creek, Chickasaw and Choctaw, became known collectively as the "Five Civilized Tribes."

By the time the Indian Removal Bill was signed, the Cherokee had adopted both good and bad from American society. For example, their government was modeled after the government of the United States and although there was personal ownership of land, there were slave holders as well. Thus for the Cherokee, acculturation/assimilation was not the overriding rationale for their removal as it was for some Indian groups. Increasing pressure for Cherokee removal is directly attributable to gold having been discovered on their land and the resultant conflict with the state of Georgia.

The Cherokee, as did other Indian groups, gained information about removal to the West from a variety of sources. As a result the Cherokee exhibited mixed feelings toward emigration and each other.[11]

Through bribery, misinformation, and personal interest individuals thought emigrating best for themselves and others and said so publicly. The majority, however, had positive attitudes toward home and negative attitudes toward the environment and social conditions in the West which would make them reluctant to leave their eastern homelands. Some, it turned out, did not leave at all.

Another generic aspect of Cherokee removal was the loss of personal property. Grant Foreman writes of intruders who were allowed "to come upon their land from all sides and ravage their property."[12] Mary Young adds that when troops forced the Cherokee to move in 1828 they left behind "wash pots, skillets, looms, rifles, saddles and fish hooks" among many other items of a personal nature.[13] Michael Doran has noted that "many mixed bloods converted their assets in the East into slave property at the time of removal" in order to ease the economic loss.[14] Of course, as for any household at any time, some property was, in terms of absolute and sentimental attachment, of more importance than others. For many Cherokee it was the family homestead. The story of Joseph Vann is illustrative. Vann had been accused of violating Georgia law by employing a white man on his farm. His home was seized in December of 1833 by both the state and a private individual. As a gunbattle ensued between those claiming possession of the property, Vann and his family fled their home seeking refuge in Tennessee.[15]

The Cherokee people had to endure mental stress as well. For example, they had difficulty accepting the voiding of earlier treaties which protected them and their homelands.[16] As well, they were anxious about their future in a western land where "all the inviting parts . . . are pre-occupied by various Indian nations" who would regard "us as intruders and look upon us with an evil eye."[17] This stress carried over from anticipation to departure as noted in the following passage:[18]

> The banks of the river were thronged with people . . . who . . . saw us off . . . the parting scene was more moving than I was prepared for . . . I saw many a manly cheek suffused with tears. Parents were turning with sick hearts from children who were about to seek other homes in a far off and strange land; brothers and sisters with heaving bosoms and brimful eyes were wringing each others hands for the last time. And often I observed . . . some young wife who was tearing herself from mother, father, kith and kin, to follow the fortunes of her husband.

The major portion of the Cherokee nation, approximately 15,000, still had not migrated by the time of departure stipulated by the treaty of New Echota. To secure their removal, the United States government appointed General Winfield Scott to enforce the removal policy. On May 10, 1838, General Scott warned the Cherokee people that every "man, woman, and child must be in motion towards the west."[19] To this end Cherokee were plucked from their fields and their dinner tables. They were driven to newly-erected stockades where they were held until it was time to move west.

The hardships endured by the Cherokee are well documented. Examples from the chapter in Cherokee history which Grant Foreman refers to as "The Trail of Tears" and Grace Woodward "The trail where they cried," tell the story of some of the worst hardships suffered by any of the Indian groups north or south.[20] The travelers had to contend with harsh weather, swamps, unsafe riverboats, insufficient food and shelter, illness, injury and death. The estimated loss is just over one third of the population secured by General Scott, or approximately 4,000 people.[21] While emigrants of both sexes were subjected to these hardships in one form or another, this chapter will focus on women. It will survey their degradation, frustration, and anomie in this experience. Also examined will be the impact of the lack of food, clothing and shelter, the circumstances of personal hygiene, births, deaths and injury.

EFFECTS ON ALL INDIANS

After James Monroe and Andrew Jackson began pressing the issue of Indian removal the vast majority of documented negotiations available for historical interpretation were between males. However, that women were involved is implicit. According to Jess McKee and Jon Schlenken, "When removal was completed it was estimated that 12,500 [Choctaw] had migrated, 2,500 had died, and 5,000 to 6,000 persons remained in Mississippi," they are writing about women too.[22] When Wyandot leader William Walker noted that upon their arrival at the junction of the Kansas and Missouri Rivers they felt "truly . . . like strangers in a strange land," he spoke for women as well as men and children.[23] Clifton writes of one of "the sorriest episodes in the whole history of the great disapora" referring to the removal of Menomini and his group, including women.[24] When an English teacher visiting Creek Indians described " . . . miserable wretches who had been dislodged from their ancient territory and were wandering about like bees whose hive had been destroyed," there was no need to differentiate on the basis of sex since all were in pitiful condition.[25] In the case of the Delaware, all felt the frustration and disorientation of each Indian agency passing "the Indian migrants along as speedily as possible, to avoid the numerous problems that had to be handled when Indians were delayed at any one point."[26] The letter from John Baldridge, John Ross and Joseph Vann to Lewis Cass which stated that "removal under existing circumstances beyond that father of Rivers would produce [fatal] consequences" spoke for all their Cherokee constituency.[27]

Also, situations noted during the removal process were in instances not unique to migration. Theda Perdue cited the journal of Daniel Butrick concerning Cherokee women and white soldiers which led to "poor native women . . . debauched through terror and seduction."[28] In the same vein but after relocation, William Smith, in a letter from Shawnee Village, Kansas, writes of "the practice of every vice" initiated by whites on Indians "that they may be the more easily victims, debauching their wives and daughters."[29] While caution is necessary when moralistic judgments are involved, these situations are seen as assaults on women through shame, guilt and physical abuse. The following sections focus on women just prior to removal and during the journey itself.

Degradation, Frustration and Anomie. As the negotiation process developed, families began to be traumatized by the impact of government policy. Perdue, writing of the degrading and frustrating affect of the removal policy on Cherokee women, states: "Missionaries reported that men, helpless to prevent seizure of their property and assaults on themselves and their families, vented their frustrations by beating their wives and children."[30] Elsewhere in the old Southwest, Choctaw "leaders with their bands were all captured before the summer was over. The men were placed in irons, and with their wailing women and children . . . were forcibly moved to the west."[31] North of the Ohio River life was also degraded by events that developed beyond the control of the Indians. John Beach wrote of the Sauk and Fox who refused to move and whose "women came with tears in their eyes pleading for food from the agent, while in the New York agency the news of removal left women weeping in their houses, [and] along the roads."[32]

For some, the reduction from a feeling of being in control according to one's customs and beliefs to a feeling of helplessness increased the Indians' exasperation. In the South in 1839, "General Taylor shipped 196 Indians [Seminole], consisting of warriors, women, children and negroes westward. The women were very reluctant to go and upbraided the men for cowardice."[33] C.A. Weslager wrote of a Delaware woman's anger as she prepared to move from Kansas to Oklahoma in 1967:[34]

> Nora Thompson Dean's paternal grandmother tried to sell some of their iron kettles before the family left Kansas since there was no room for the utensils in the overloaded wagon. The settlers refused to buy kettles expecting to have them without cost after the Indians departed. As a consequence her grandmother broke the kettles to pieces before they left their farms.

Sometimes extreme actions resulted because of the frustration. For example, William Hagan wrote that: "Morgan, a Fox, was frustrated by land negotiations . . . the headstrong Morgan . . . led a war party from the village and deliberately invited war by killing a Sioux woman and taking . . . another woman."[35]

Anomie represents another form of frustration as social disorientation leads to an individuals's personal state of unrest. For older Delaware "it was a frightening experience" as they "were wary about boarding the swaying boats to cross the great river."[36]

Imagine the feelings of the Brant family in the Seneca and Shawnee migration when Powlas Brant, the head of the household, left his family while on route," or when families were separated for their views on removal or forcibly separated by Anglos.[37] Other examples of anomie include the changing environments, language barriers and scheduled time frames which were unknown to American Indians prior to their implementation.[38]

Non-Removers. In political situations resulting in a refugee movement it might be expected that some individuals will steadfastly resist leaving their homeland. Seminole, Cherokee, Potawatomi, and Sauk and Fox stand as good examples of defiant behavior in the face of overwhelming pressure to remove. The vast majority of non-migrating women were fugitives from the law. Some, however, were granted land in the East as a result of treaties. In other cases, land was gained due to the mixed blood status of families (particularly in the husband's) with the United States government. The women of Choctaw leaders Greenwood LaFlore and Mushulatubbe were part of such a transaction as both men received four sections of land on the eastern tribal property.[39] In the Potawatomi Treaty of 1832, Josette Beaubien and the wife of Joseph LaFramboise were given land.[40] In other cases women were granted land on the basis of being the head of a household. A Choctaw woman, Delila, was awarded a quarter section of land on which to settle along with her "five fatherless children . . . also the same quantity to Peggy Trihon, another Indian woman residing out of the nation and her two fatherless children and to the widows of Pushilabla and Pucktshenubbe who were formerly distinguished chiefs of the nation."[41] In the Chicasaw Treaty of 1836 land was set aside for both male and female orphans.[42] Many examples of such land grants exist. Most land seems to have been quickly sold leaving the women and, in cases, their dependents landless. It should also be borne in mind that individuals may have had to accept American citizenship (renouncing their own heritage) or may in some fashion conspired with the enemy in order to receive such benefits. One may also construct a scenerio whereby on the trail those conspiring were accorded special privilege

Food, Clothing and Shelter. Food, clothing and shelter are obvious prerequisites to travel. There were many times when these commodities were in short supply. Thus, the hardship of travel was compounded by poor nutrition and exposure to the elements. Records are replete with accounts of food shortages and spoiled provisions.[43] In some cases, Indians rightfully expected the worse to happen. Lieutenant J.J. Albert, a topographic engineer, wrote to Lewis Cass on June 2, 1833, concerning the

Creeks: "In my opinion . . . they fear starvation on the route."[44] The Delaware arrived in Missouri where "resources were limited." There was not "the quantities of food necessary to provision them for continuation of their journey."[45] Certainly, reports of food-associated problems may be found in many accounts of Indian removal.

The lack of clothing was also a problem on those occasions when Indians were hurried into stockades or processions and erroneously told sufficient blankets and clothing would be available. Joseph M. Street wrote the following to Elbert Herring Prairie Du Chien on July 24, 1833: "It was the most shameful scene . . . ever witnessed. The poor creatures who pass here migrating are naked and some wounded."[46] From the area south of the Ohio River comes a report of Choctaw problems: "There is no question of the fact of those Indians being in suffering condition at the time the blankets were furnished them."[47] About an unidentified group of New York Indians in 1832, a letter from Green Bay read "Owing to the severity of the weather . . . many of the Indians who were bad off for clothing" were prevented from leaving.[48]

Shelter was also a problem in terms of the inadequate protection of brush lean-tos, caves and linen tents. In some cases there was none at all. Missiourians living on the route of Choctaw migration observed "there were aged persons and very young children in the company; many had nothing to shelter them from the storm by day or night."[49]

Environmental Hazards. Notwithstanding the social disruption there also existed environmental hazards to be faced. In some instances hazards were perceived as well as experienced. The Potawatomi, Ottawa, and Chippewa, for example, voiced their pre-removal environmental concern during treaty negotiations when they stated: "All is prairie [in the West], nothing else . . . could we take our women and children to such a country."[50] A spokesman for the Miami was "sorry the government was forced to adopt such strict measures for their removal," but the country intended for them was "a miserable barren section, without wood, without water, in fact in the open prairie where no one could exist."[51]

For some, the reality of migration may have been worse than anticipated. A conductor of the Shawnee and Wyandot noted, "The weather is against all, and some women have been taken sick in consequence."[52] For one Creek group "the weather was so intensely hot in the day time that contractors obliged the emigrants to travel at night. Their limited equipment of twenty wagons was croweded with old women . . . small children were carried on the backs of their mothers and sisters."[53] The Choctaw "had to travel through fifty miles of swamp . . . this too was to be done in the worst time of weather I have ever seen in any country a heavy sleet having broken and bowed down all the small and much of the larger timber and this was to be performed under the pressure of hunger, by old women . . . without any covering for their feet."[54] Willie Harjo, a Creek, recounted a swamp crossed by his father and that it had to be crossed "also [by] men, women, boys, girls old or young."[55]

Of course, environmental hazards went beyond hot weather and standing water: there was intense cold, rough walking, turbulent water and "swarms of biting flies" with which to contend.[56] While there is documentation of women riding in wagons or on ponies while others walked and of women being ferried while others waded, for most, the enviromental hazards during travel were overwhelming.

Personal Hygiene. No record was found describing the disruption of personal hygiene in terms of toiletry or menstruation. It may be be assumed that personal habits were disrupted and customs and rituals regarding such habits intruded upon and forcibly broken. The disregard of the usually private nature and the alteration of habits (as dictated by culture) or many such personal acts contributed to the women's alienation.

Death and Injury. Death away from home at the hands of an oppressor carries a connotation of meanness. For Indian women involved in removal death occurred on a variety of scales and in several ways. Angie Debo reported of the Creek: "The greatest single loss of life occurred when a large boat, the Monmouth, sank in the Mississippi and more than three hundred were drowned."[57] As devastating for those involved, but on a smaller scale, is Foreman's documentation of death in a Choctaw removal party. He writes: "While camped . . . a severe storm of rain and wind had set in and just after comfortable quarters had been secured, a large tree was blown down among the camps, and two women, mothers of large families were crushed to instant death."[58]

Heavy drinking by the Indians occurred and continued through the removal process. North of the Ohio River the Wyandots prepared to leave for the East. "Some of them proceeded to get intoxicated . . . prior to the final exodus from Ohio;" four deaths occurred that night, one of them a woman.[59]

Sickness also led to the death of many as resistance to illness decreased with hardships encountered and as once healthy minds slipped against the onslaught of anomie. Foreman writes: "On all the steamboats coming down the Mississippi river deaths occurred from the disease [cholera] . . . the freedom called here [Memphis] yesterday . . . onboard . . . a lady [was] said to be dying."[60] Clifton notes one Potawatomi removal where sickness, agedness and death went hand and hand. "On the 13th [September, 1838] two physicians reported 160 cases . . . of malarial fever . . . this day a woman more than a hundred years old . . . died."[61]

Injury occurred along the way as women were run over by wagons or fell off horses. Some received cuts and bruises, while others suffered broken bones or gunshot wounds. Many injuries were directly caused by Euro-Americans. However, injury was also inflicted by Indians on other Indians. The Creek, for example, in an effort to prevent Indians from preying on fellow Indians, passed a law calling for "the punishment of fifty lashes upon any person who shall be found guilty of theft. Two girls suffered the penalty . . . they were whipped before the whole camp."[62] With regard to violent injury, no mention of rape was noted. However, it would be naive to suppose there was no instance of forced sexual encounters between Anglo and Indian or Indian and Indian given the other events of violence that were reported such as strippings, whippings, and beatings.[63] Perhaps the difficulty lay in reporting such incidents under the system of Anglo authority existing at the time of Indian removal and the expected satisfaction an Indian would gain. For most, injury and death became a routine matter to be recorded in a journal report or letter. A fall from a tree, a snake bite, or as is recorded by the conductor of the Seneca and Shawnee on December 18, 1832, "one child died — belonging to the family of Tallman's widow," exemplify the routineness of death.[64]

It is important to note that death statistics should be approached cautiously. Indians generally verified headcount. However, conductors were paid per person, per day making it convenient, at times, for unscrupulous ones to add people fictitiously to their enrollment. Later, those nonexistent emigrants were recorded as dead.

Births. Indian populations began decreasing with increasing Anglo contact until the twentieth century. Certainly the mental and physical hardships of removal took their toll. Debo estimates over a forty percent drop in Creek population between 1832 and 1859.[65] Although faulty reporting occurred, when well known Sauk and Fox, Potawatomi, Cherokee and Seminole are included, the figure indeed grows larger. Yet, throughout the process of relocation and population loss, births occurred. Perdue writes of hardships and shame suffered by Cherokee women: "Many gave birth along side the trail, and the military escort was less than sympathetic ... troops frequently forced women in labor to continue until they collapsed and delivered in the company of soldiers. One man even stabbed an expectant mother with a bayonet. Many women did not survive such treatment."[66] The entry of the Seneca and Shawnee migration by Conductor Dunihue provides a matter-of-fact set of newborn recordings: "December 18, 1832, one birth on the route, in Baptiste family; one birth on the route in Setting Bear's family; one brith, while on the route, in the family of Peter Knox's son."[67] Although conditions were harsh, infants were undernourished and more likely to succumb, births symbolize hope and ongoingness in the face of desperate times.

SUMMARY AND CONCLUSION

Indian removal involved men, women and children. While all suffered, this paper focused on Indian women. From the available data we find that certain events such as injury, death, frustrations, anomie, shame, environmental hazards and inadequate food, clothing and shelter affected all, while birthing and degradation associated with family role distinctly affected women (Fig. 11.1).

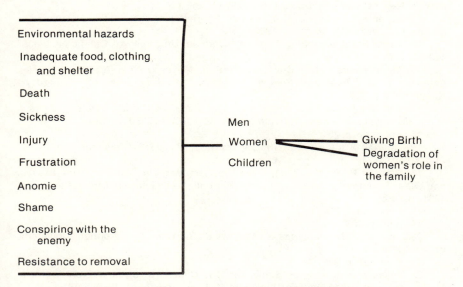

Figure 11.1. Factors affecting women in migration.

NOTES

1. James Clifton and Theda Perdue, personal correspondence, spring and summer 1985; Janice Monk, personal correspondence, March 1983. The classic explanation of the problems faced in studying Indian history comes from Stanley Pagellis, "The Problem of American Indian History," *Ethnohistory*, 4 (1957): 133-114.

2. Annie Heloise Able, "The History of Events Resulting in Indian Consolidation West of the Mississippi River," American Historical Association Annual Report, 1906, Vol. 1 (Washington, D.C.: Government Printing Office, 1908); Francis Paul Prucha, *American Indian Policy in the Formative Years* (Cambridge: Harvard University Press, 1962).

3. James A. Clifton, *The Prairie People: Continuity and Change in Pottawatomi Indian Culture 1665-1965* (Lawrence: Regents Press of Kansas, 1977), p. 279.

4. Correspondence dated July 10, 1932, Record Group M-234, Microfilm Roll 75 (Washington, D.C.: National Archives).

5. Joseph T. Manzo, "Emigrant Indian Objections to Kansas Residence," *Kansas History*, (1981): 246-254.

6. Ibid., p. 254.

7. Correspondence dated September 15, 1833, Annals of the Shawnee Methodist Mission and Indian Manual Labor School (Topeka, Kansas: Kansas State Historical Society, 1939).

8. Ibid.

9. Clifton, *The Prairie People*, p. 292.

10. Frederick W. Hodge, (ed.), *Handbook of American Indians North of Mexico* (New York: Pagent Books Inc., 1959), pp. 246-249.

11. Joseph T. Manzo, "The Indian Pre-Removal Information Network," *Journal of Cultural Geography*, 2 (1982): 72-84.

12. Grant Foreman, *Indian Removal* (Norman: University of Oklahoma Press, 1931), p. 238.

13. Mary Young, "The Cherokee Nation: Mirror of the Republic" in *The American Indian: Past and Present*, Roger Nichols (ed.) (New York: Alfred A. Knopf, 1986), p. 160.

14. Michael F. Doran, "Negro Slaves of the Five Civilized Tribes," *Annals of the Association of American Geographers*, 68 (1978): 335-350.

15. Foreman, p. 251.

16. Charles Kappler, (ed.), *Indian Treaties 1778-1883* (New York: Interland Publishing Co., 1973).

17. Francis P. Prucha, (ed.), *Cherokee Removal: The William Penn Essays and Other Writings by Jeremiah Evarts* (Knoxville: University of Tennessee Press, 1981), p. 260.

18. Foreman, p. 254.

19. Ibid., p. 286.

20. Ibid., p. 229, 294; Grace S. Woodward, *The Cherokee* (Norman: University of Oklahoma Press, 1979), pp. 192-219.

21. Foreman, p. 312.

22. Jesse McKee and Jon Schlenken, *The Chocktaw: Cultural Evolution of a Native American Tribe* (Jackson: University of Mississippi Press, 1980) p. 76.

23. Frederick Norwood, "Strangers in a Strange Land," *Methodist History,* 13 (1976): 45-60.

24. Clifton, *The Prairie People,* p. 297. The sorriest episode is recorded in "Wisconsin Death March," unpublished paper, James A. Clifton.

25. Angie Debo, *The Road to Disappearance: A History of the Creek Indians* (Norman: University of Oklahoma Press, 1979), p. 95.

26. C.A. Weslager, *The Delaware Indian Westward Migration* (Wallingford, PA: The Middle Atlantic Press, 1978), p. 210.

27. Correspondence dated January 28, 1833, Record Group M-234, Microfilm Roll 75 (Washington, D.C.: National Archives).

28. Theda Perdue, "Cherokee Women and the Trail of Tears," paper presented at the Western Historical Society (October 1984), p. 11.

29. Correspondence dated July 22, 1833, Indian Collection, Jackson County Historical Society (Independence, Missouri).

30. Perdue, p. 2.

31. Foreman, p. 101.

32. Donald Berthrong, "John Beach and the Removal of the Sauk and Fox from Iowa," *Iowa Journal of History,* 54 (1956): 331; Correspondence dated 1840, Record Group M-234, Microfilm Roll 75 (Washington, D.C.: National Archives).

33. Foreman, p. 370.

34. Weslager, p. 227.

35. William Hagan, *The Sac and Fox Indians* (Norman: University of Oklahoma Press, 1958), p. 117.

36. Weslager, p. 211.

37. Journal of Daniel Dunihue, December 18, 1832, Senate Document 512, 23rd Congress 1st Session, Vol. IV (New York: AMS Press, 1974).

38. Letters received at the Indian Agencies 1824-1881, Record Group 75, Records of the Bureau of Indian Affairs M-234; Russell Thornton, "Cherokee Population Loses During The Trail of Tears: A New Perspective and a New Estimate," *Ethnohistory,* 31 (1984): 290.

39. Senate Document 512, Vol. V.

40. Kappler, p. 313.

41. Ibid. p. 353.

42. Ibid., p. 381.

43. Senate Document 512, Vol IV, p. 423.

44. Ibid., p. 428.

45. Weslager, p. 210.

46. Senate Document 512, Vol. IV, p. 484.

47. Senate Document 512, Vol. I, p. 449.

48. Senate Document 512, Vol. III, p. 53.

49. Foreman, pp. 63-64.

50. Council held with the Potawatomi, Ottawa, and Chippewa at Council Bluffs, November 10, 1846, Record Group M-234, Microfilm Roll 75 (Washington, D.C.: National Archives).

51. Ibid., Microfilm Roll 416.

52. Ibid., Microfilm Roll 603.

53. Foreman, p. 185.

54. Foreman, p. 104.

55. Debo, p. 211.

56. Weslager, p. 211.

57. Debo, p. 102.

58. Foreman, p. 57.

59. Carl Klopperstein, "The Removal of the Wyandots from Ohio," *The Ohio Historical Quarterly,* 66 (1957): 134.

60. Foreman, p. 64.

61. Clifton, *The Prairie People,* p. 111.

62. Foreman, p. 156.

63. Ibid.; Angie Debo, *A History of the Indians of the United States* (Norman University of Oklahoma Press, 1977) p. 121.

64. Senate Document 512, Vol. IV, p. 77.

65. Debo, "The Road," p. 103.

66. Perdue, "Cherokee Women," p. 12.

67. Senate Document 512, Vol. IV, p. 77.

ACKNOWLEDGMENTS

A special thanks to Evelyn Morris for her research assistance in the early stages of this project. Also, to Theda Perdue, Clemson University, for her contribution on Cherokee Women. A thank you to James Clifton, Frankenthaler Professor of History, Wisconsin-Green Bay, for his comments on an early draft of the paper.

Chapter 12
Cultural Change and the Houma Indians: A Historical and Ecological Examination

Janel M. Curry-Roper

The study of cultural ecology emphasizes relationships between environment and human societies. The ecological approach attempts to separate cultural values and elements of social organization closely related to the environment from others.[1] Environmental features, such as climate, take on significance in terms of their functional importance rather than their inherent properties. Cultural traits viewed in this way become dependent variables; environment becomes the independent variable.[2] Steward summarized the approach succinctly; cultural ecology "introduces the local environment as the extra-cultural factor in the fruitless assumption that culture comes from culture."[3]

Some anthropologists have argued that the proposed relationship between the dependent variable, culture, and the independent variable, environment, is deterministic.[4] We must, in fact, reject the notion that cultural traits follow inevitably from particular environmental conditions, but this does not mean that we should reject the ecological perspective. Environment limits the choices open to a society, though it does not always decide them.[5]

This chapter explores the possibility that certain cultural changes within the Houma tribe of southern Louisiana came about through a history of environmental modification. Adaptation to a new environment was an internal social transformation that constituted a creative process brought about by the interaction of historic and ecological factors.[6] The value of this view lies in its contrast to the naive assumption that traditional societies suffer culture loss when their world is transformed around them. I argue that culture is not lost, but creatively transformed.

HISTORY OF THE HOUMA TRIBE

The Houma tribe traditionally shared many characteristics with other southeastern tribes, particularly the Choctaw. For example, both languages belonged to the Muskoghean language group.[7] Western explorers first mentioned the Houma in 1682, when LaSalle passed their village as he ascended the Mississippi River. Bienville, who succeeded LaSalle, actually visited the village later in the century and remarked that it was located about two and one half leagues (6-7 miles) inland opposite the mouth of the Red River. The village contained 350 warriors and the tribal hunting territory stretched as far south as a red post placed five leagues above Bayou Manchac. This place is the present day site of Baton Rouge, Louisiana. The Houma lived and hunted above the "baton rouge," and the Bayogoula tribe lived and hunted below.[8]

The area the Houma tribe inhabited was pine forest with hilly terrain. The village was located on the top of a "mountain," with a level central square that was the center of activity.[9] The tribe's subsistence activities were evenly divided between agriculture and hunting, typical of most of the southeastern tribes.[10] In 1706, the French heard that several tribes aligned with the English had joined to move against tribes allied with the French. In response, the Houma moved south into the lower Mississippi Valley hoping to secure French protection. This move, to the area opposite the present town of Donaldsonville, Louisiana, represented a very minor environmental change, but showed the Houma's willingness to adapt to external forces.[11]

In 1763, the Treaty of Paris transferred all French land west of the Mississippi River to Spain, and all land east of the river to the English. The Houma found themselves in English territory after almost a century of alignment with the French. The Houma people thus no longer felt comfortable and their uneasiness was compounded by an increasing scarcity of fish and game so the tribe moved once more, to the place that bears its name — Houma, Louisiana.[12] According to tribal oral tradition, the Spanish government gave the village an area between the Atchafalaya River and Barataria to the Houma (Fig. 12.1).[13]

After the Louisiana Purchase, the Houma were pushed into the coastal marsh south of Houma as white settlers took the agricultural land on the edge of the coastal marsh. As a result, the tribe's economy changed from agriculture to hunting and gathering. The central village gave way to several Houma communities across eighty miles of coastline. Social organization also changed when the last strong central leader died in 1885. By that time, the tribe had become well integrated into the hunting and gathering life of the marsh.[14] This transition from the stable agricultural economy of northern Louisiana to a migratory, decentralized life on the coastal fringe changed many aspects of Houma existence. Several areas of change most connected to the historic change in the Houma's environment are population, settlement patterns, socio-political organization, and economic patterns.

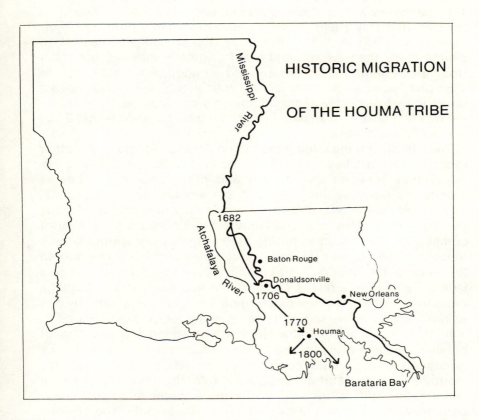

Figure 12.1. The Houma tribe migrated from the pine woods region on the Louisiana-Mississippi border to the coastal marsh between 1796 and 1800.

POPULATION

The population of the Houma tribe fluctuated within a specified range during their recorded agricultural era. The tribe's highest population was estimated at 1,000 people in 1650.[15] In 1811 Governor W.C.C. Claiborne stated that there were no more than eighty Houma left.[16] Around this time, the tribe moved into the coastal marsh. As they made adjustments to the new environment and its resources, they also experienced a population explosion. By the late nineteenth century, the Houma tribe had about 1200 members.[17] This demographic change was significant even if the 1811 estimate was low. The growth rate continued into the twentieth century, and Roy Nash of the Bureau of Indian Affairs put their number at 3,000 in 1931.[18] Presently, the United Houma Nation claims more than 8,700 members. I originally mapped the main Houma communities in 1978 and did an additional field check in 1986 and found a minimum of 605 households, with most having fewer than five people. This number did not include close urban centers and small Indian settlements, so from my knowledge, 8,700 is a realistic estimate.

The Houma are the largest tribe in Louisiana — most of the other tribes in the state have fewer than 500 members. The difference in population between the Houma and other Louisana tribes is significant because they share a certain amount of historical experience. Variations in resource availability may account for the demographic differences. The Houma experienced a great deal of competition for resources during their early history, particularly in frequent conflicts over territorial boundaries with the Bayogoula to the south of the Houma.[19] The Houma moved at least once due to a lack of resources. Francis Gallet, a Houma man, stated that the move to the area of present day Houma, Louisiana was partially due to diminished wildlife and white competition for food resources.[20]

In their early history, the Houma carried on the practice of burying alive any twins that were born, which can be interpreted as evidence that population controls existed within the society.[21] No mention of this tradition appears within the last 175 years in historical or cultural records, nor is there evidence of population controls within the twentieth century Houma society. The obvious explanation for the end of the practice of burying twins is the influence of the Catholic Church in the area. However, this church influence coincided, and perhaps interacted with the changed resource base of the tribe.

The marshlands into which the Houma moved afforded many resources. Wildlife such as deer were plentiful; fish and seafood were abundant year round; and important fur-bearing animals also inhabited the area. By 1850, a lack of competition for the land allowed the Houma to expand quickly across eighty miles of coastline and remain undisturbed on the rich land until well into the twentieth century.[22] The new environment supported a greater population with unlimited resources as long as the Houma had access to the land. This Houma experience illustrates the tendency for population among hunters and gatherers to increase to levels just below resource exhaustion.[23] Other tribes in the state did not experience this dramatic increase in resources and in fact had to continually deal with the problem of a diminishing land base due to European encroachment.[24] They also did not experience dramatic population growth. The Chitimachas are the second most populous tribe in Louisiana with only 520 members.[25]

SETTLEMENT PATTERNS

The Houma tribe was historically divided into two separate villages, Petit Houmas and Grand Houmas. These "towns" were organized around a central square with households scattered in clusters among the fields.[26] A 1722 description placed them about twenty-three leagues (60 miles) above New Orleans, with the Petit Houmas on the right as one ascended the Mississippi River and the Grand Village one half league above (1-2 miles). Eight French settlements were located between the two villages.[27] By 1733, the Petit village of the Houma had moved to the west bank of the Mississippi River.[28] Later, a 1766 Spanish census confirmed these locations.[29] When the tribe moved south to the area of present day Houma, Louisiana, in the latter part of the eighteenth century, they continued this tradition of dual settlements. Charles Billiot, a Houma man, called one of the villages *Chufuhouma*.[30] The name *Chufuhouma* is close to the word *Chukahouma* that means Red House village. Red and white were the traditional colors in the moiety cleavages typical of southeastern Indians.[31] Towns were divided into "red" towns and "white" towns among the Creeks, and the Houma villages were also evidently connected with social organization and kinship.[32]

When forced to move south from their villages, the Houma again formed two groups. One group settled on Pointe Barre on lower Bayou Terrebonne and the other group on land along Bayou Petit Caillou. The two settlements were separated by about four miles of marsh. The two villages gave way to a more decentralized settlement pattern as the Houma adjusted to a life of hunting and gathering. Land records of 1850 showed Houma families as far west as Bayou DuLarge and east to Bayou LaFourche. The most concentrated community remained around Pointe Barre however, where the last leader with centralized power lived until about 1885.[33] By 1907, when John R. Swanton of the Smithsonian Institute visited the Houma, they had developed a settlement pattern much more typical of a hunting and gathering economy where people were identified with places or territories rather than moities.[34] Frank Speck noted this settlement pattern in the 1940s when he saw "evidence of local band affinity and cooperation among the families who fish and trap the same bayous, and whose camps are located on its levees and hummocks, whose occupational movements follow the course of the same bayou from the Gulf to the borders of the cultivated land held by whites."[35] These groups that worked together were identified by the names of the bayous on which they lived. Swanton named eight such communities and they still exist today. The communities, from west to east, are Bayou DuLarge, then Dulac on Bayou Grand Caillou, Montegut on Bayou Terrebonne, Pointe Barre, Point au Chene, Isle de Jean Charles, Grand Bois, and Gold Meadow on lower Bayou LaFourche (Fig. 12.2).[36] Other smaller communities exist even farther east of Bayou LaFourche. Individuals have a wide range of choice in movement between areas and groups, consistent with that of other societies based on band structures.[37] Each individual Houma community is a linear settlement stretching along the bayou on the natural levee. Land is not sufficiently available elsewhere for houses and garden plots. Trailers and houses are in clusters of family groups, with matrilocality predominant, a vestige of the past. Traditional Houma society followed the Choctaw custom where the husband left his parents' household to reside with his wife in a house next to his parents-in-law.[38] Such a custom remains quite obvious in patriarchal French Louisiana.

SOCIO-POLITICAL ORGANIZATION

The Houma were traditionally a matrilineal people; one belonged to the mother's family or clan and power passed from a man to his sister's son or daughter. This transfer kept power within the clan since a man's own children belonged to his wife's clan and not his own. A mother's brother was in turn responsible for his nephews and nieces and marriage was forbidden within such a clan.[39] That the Houma had such a structure is evident from several aspects of

THE DISTRIBUTION OF HOUMA HOUSEHOLDS IN
TERREBONNE AND LAFOURCHE PARISHES

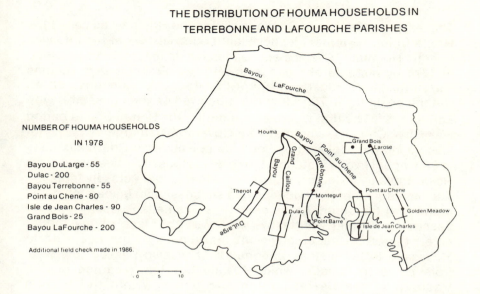

NUMBER OF HOUMA HOUSEHOLDS

IN 1978

Bayou DuLarge - 55
Dulac - 200
Bayou Terrebonne - 55
Point au Chene - 80
Isle de Jean Charles - 90
Grand Bois - 25
Bayou LaFourche - 200

Additional field check made in 1986.

Figure 12.2. Houma settlements today are spread over 80 miles of coastline. They go from as far west as Bayou DuLarge to the Mississippi River to the east, with the main concentrations in Terrebonne and LaFourche Parishes.

their life. First, their settlement patterns reflect such structures. Second, many cultural characteristic of the Houma show relationships characteristic to other southeastern tribes that were also matrilineal. Third, Houma descriptions of a past leader contain further evidence. They had difficulty in differentiating between the leader's father and the leader's mother's brother. In a matrilineal system, the mother's brother played a role to his nieces and nephews that is similar to that of the father at present.

Leadership succession of the matrilineal Houma can be traced from first contact with Western explorers. The first leader recorded was a woman who died about the year 1699. Father Gravier, a Catholic missionary, wrote of her in 1700:[40]

> The old man who keeps up the fire which he called to us louak or loughe (sacred fire), showed us the bones of the woman chief who died last year. This woman had rendered herself so important by the blows she had struck against the enemy, having led several war parties in person, that she was regarded as an amazon and as the mistress of the whole village.

The leader at the time of Gravier's visit to the Houma was called the Grand Chief.[41] The next leader identified in historical records was Poucha-Houmma.[42] Calabe succeeded him in leadership as verified in 1774 by his sale of Houma land to two Frenchmen.[43] Thomas Hutchins, a British geographer, wrote about the next chief, Natchiabe, in the 1770s when the tribe lived on the banks of Bayou LaFourche.[44] The first Houma chief during the United States period was Chac-Chouma, who met with Governor Claiborne in 1811. He was soon after replaced by Louis de la Houssaye Courteaux alias le Sauvage.[45] In one instance, Louis de la Houssaye is referred to as De la Houla by a Houma man, a name that is more closely Indian.[46] The best documented evidence of a succession in leadership came in the next transition. At the death of Louis de la Houssaye, power passed to Rosalie Courteaux, who was the niece of the former chief; therefore leadership went matrilineally from Louis de la Houssaye to his sister's daughter.[47] Land also passed this way, from Louis to Rosalie, while Rosalie Courteaux carried on the tradition of female leadership and power within the Houma society.[48]

The original Houma social structure, and its centralized power passed matrilineally, gradually shifted in the late nineteenth century as the tribe adapted its traditional agricultural economy to hunting and gathering.[49] The family hunting band became the basic social unit. Since the hunting band could only maintain a limited number of family units, the Houma tribe became decentralized and socio-political structures in turn changed to make the necessary adjustments. Frank Speck described the relationship between this new economic situation of the Houma and the resultant social structures when he stated that "the absence of definite clans, the family social group or band, and the lineal system of relationship seem to go together in the same stage of nomadic hunting culture.[50] The change from strong matrilineal relationships to loose kinship ties paralleled the movement toward identification with places, i.e. Dulac. Once again this was typical of hunters and gatherers.

With the change in social organization, leadership came to be held by individuals in each separate area or family. This change was consistent with Julian Steward's observations that with hunting and gathering people, "most common leader or so called 'chief' was the head of the family cluster, who was obeyed by common consent if he had qualities of leadership."[51] The membership to such local groups was based on kinship or friendship and the composition or leaders changed from year to year. This shuffling of people was necessary for the continual exploitation of the environment. The family or group leaders among the Houma mainly function as those who give advice, a function often combined with that of medical treatment. These responsibilities are the same as the matrilineal leaders, but take on a decentralized pattern due to the dispersal of the population.

On Isle de Jean Charles, visitors to the colony were taken to a man known as Chief Naquin,[52] a local leader related to all the families on the island. Similarly at Dulac, all adults remember and speak of Jean Baptiste Parfait, who was not formally chosen, but naturally emerged as a leader. Parfait had exactly the same responsibilities as were ascribed to Rosalie Courteaux, the last matrilineal leader. A consistency in the leadership pattern thus emerged but took two separate organizational forms. Both leaders were consulted when a couple planned to be married, and gave advice as "healers" before someone was taken to the doctor.

The Houma tribe's utilization of decentralized leadership has led most recently to a more formally structured tribal government. The present tribal council system lets traditional patterns determine the persons representing the tribe by creating community representation. Each Houma community thus keeps its identity.

The Houma still have representative elements from the period of strong matrilineage in spite of the more recent socio-political change in leadership. These remnant structures remain because they were not affected by the ecological changes the tribe experienced. Families remain strongly matrilocal and normally live with the wife's family or maintain closest ties to the wife's family. The inheritance of land and property remains egalitarian. Lastly, the Houma tradition of female leadership has been maintained; women still play active roles in the social and political life of their communities. Helen Gindrat's leadership as tribal chair in the late 1970s illustrated this continuance of a Houma tradition.

The Houma tribe clearly exemplify the transition of a matrilineal people to a group based on band organization. The force behind the transition was a changing resource base. They combined old elements of their past tradition that were not affected by environmental changes with structures that were relatively new to them. The tribe acquired the basic characteristics of band organization intrinsic to hunters and gatherers. Service described this "stage," and ultimately the new Houma structures, when he said that such societies had no specialization in economic life, and no separate political life outside of family heads. Furthermore, "the fact that the family and band are simultaneously the sole economic, political and religious organization greatly influences the character of these activities. The economy, polity, and ideology of the culture of bands is unprofessionalized and unformalized; in short, it is familistic only."[53]

ECONOMY

The Houma were traditionally an agricultural people and their ceremonies and technology were related to such subsistence activities. Forced into the marshlands by the advancing Europeans, they gave up their traditional way of life and solved the economic problems of their livelihood through a new pattern of existence. Speck found that:[54]

> The cultural pattern to which the Houma have been long habituated, and to which they have achieved a balanced economic and social adjustment, is a mode of life determined largely by conditions of the coastal fringe of marshes. The essential elements of the cultural life of a group of people thrust off into a peculiar economic set-up, thrust down by political and social conditions brought upon them by aggressive Europeans, have apparently been answered in the evolution of the Houma people and culture in the Bayou country.

The shift that began in the early eighteenth century included a change to nomadic hunting and gathering lives. The new reality was internally stable, evidence of native adaptation. As the Houma adjusted to their new environment, they combined subsistence methods from their earlier existence and new elements that allowed for greater exploitation of the coastal fringe.

The Houma acquired new technology, necessary to exploit the marsh, that showed ties to South American and Caribbean culture.[55] The Houma used tools well into this century, the origin of which has evoked great discussion. Baffling items such as solid wood blowguns and fine mesh cast nets, a type ascribed to the Caribbean area, have been added to the more traditional North American items of dugout canoes and mortars. The net was used to catch shrimp into the 1950s and was swung by both hands while a part of it was held by the teeth. The use of this item was directly related to marsh life and the Houma adaptation to the consumption of seafood. Such cast nets were not found elsewhere among the continental tribes of the United States.[56] Other articles found among the Houma tribe were typical of the southeast: dugout canoes crafted by burning out a cypress log, and mortars made with two pestles. Both of these items are still made by the Houma as well as blowguns made from the marsh elder *(Sambucas Canadensis,* or *S. intermedia).* A more unusual type of blowgun, made from cypress may represent another ecological adjustment to the area. The blowgun was made from two grooved pieces of split cypress pole that were fitted together, glued, and wrapped with cotton twine.[57] Both types of blowguns were used mainly for fowl, but the cypress blowgun was also used to hunt small game.

The Houma also adapted their housing technology when they moved to the marsh. In the early twentieth century the Houma lived in several types of dwellings, all of which were semi-permanent so as to allow a nomadic lifestyle. During the trapping season families lived on camp boats that could be easily moved. The only suitable places for more permanent dwellings were on the natural levees along the bayous. Here two styles of homes were built by the Houma, both adaptations to marsh life that used indigenous materials. The first house type had palmetto roofs, and walls of daub and wattle made of clay and Spanish moss. These homes were somewhat like traditional housing of the lower Mississippi and the southeast.[58] The second house style was called a shotgun home, denoted for its rectangular, narrow and long dimensions. They were made with palmetto thatched walls and a gabled roof.[59] This latter style shows West African influence that may have come to the Houma through the Caribbean. Shotgun houses can still be found in the Caribbean today. The form has continued to be used in Houma areas even though original materials have been replaced by those of more permanence. A cultural survey of southeastern Louisiana revealed that the shotgun style home diffused outward from the lower bayous and then moved into agricultural sections to the north.[60] This information supported the idea that the Houma were the original borrowers of this style of house. A non-European knot used in the construction of the original dwellings also supported Houma borrowing from nonwestern cultures in response to environment rather than assimilation. The Houma houses today, though made of wood, still have the low pitched roof with a ridge pole that runs from front to back, reminiscent of earlier models that utilized palmetto. Such construction, using the ridge pole, is of nonwestern origin. European models would have rafters.

The new technology acquired by the Houma allowed for a new seasonal movement pattern that supported a diversifed economy and utilized varying numbers of people at different times of the year. Until recently, the Houma seasonal patterns presented another interesting mixture of an economy of former times, corn agriculture, hunting, fishing, and the new activities of trapping, catching shrimp, and gathering oysters. Small family groups spent the winters in the vast marshes, trapping muskrat and nutria. They consistently went to the same place each year, sometimes as far away as fifty miles. A decline in these trapping patterns has come about within the last twenty-five years with the loss of land to private companies, competition with white people, and oil and gas development in marsh areas. Some families still go into the marsh to trap during the winter, but it no longer represents the overall pattern of the tribe. When the traditional marsh movement patterns were still in operation, the Houma all met along the sandbars of the coast in the spring at the end of the trapping season.[61] Here, as an entire tribe, they caught fish in a funnel trap, dried and smoked them. The fish, when dried, were called *taso,* and both *taso* and the trap were typical of Louisiana tribes.[62] After the *taso* making, Houma families returned to their more permanent settlement areas, and divided into the approximately eight communities already identified. For the remainder of spring and on into fall they gardened along the natural levees of the bayous. Corn remained an important staple until recently, and was supplemented by okra, sweet potatoes and other vegetables. Shrimp season coincided with this garden season and was important to the Houma diet. Shrimp also served as a source of cash for the Houma. Oysters and other seafood were available year-round.

In recent years, the Houma tribe's well diversified economy has experienced multiple pressures. The Indians have lost their lands; industrial canals have caused salt water to flow ever farther inland, resulting in the erosion of the land the Houma formerly occupied; the oil industry, while providing much needed jobs, has caused pollution to oyster beds and other wildlife; and there is the ever present encroachment of sports fishermen who exploit those resources needed for the livelihood of the Houma. These pressures have caused the majority of the Houma to depend more exclusively on the seafood industry for making a living rather than a variety of different seasonal occupations. Greater dependence has also led to a deterioration of subsistence living and more reliance on the white economic system. Since many of the Houma use smaller boats that are not suited for open water, employment is restricted to certain inland water seafood seasons. Jobs in the oil industry have also diminished with recent drops in oil prices.

With increasing population and decreasing resources, the Houma are forced to deal with many difficult issues, all of which seem beyond their control. The Houma had developed a stable marsh economy through native adaptation by 1943 when Frank Speck warned, "to advocate change in the economic life of the group would be experimental and risky.[63] But such change has been forced on the Houma tribe with ever increasing intensity so that presently they are once again faced with major economic adjustments.

CONCLUSION

For the Houma, the natural resources of the marsh environment and their culture are intertwined. One responds to the other in creative adaptations. The impact of environmental change is also evident in the mythological beliefs of the Houma. Recently, the Houma mythological creatures called "l'homme de bois," or woodsmen disappeared. These figures, according to Houma oral tradition, lived and ate in trees. I once asked a Houma woman about "l'homme de bois." Her response was there were no forests left (due to recent salt water intrusion caused by dredging of channels) so of course "l'homme de bois" were gone also. Resources change and so must reality, even on the mythological level.

Despite all the changes, the Houma have managed to maintain social integration. They have kept those elements of their past that made sense in their new environment and made adjustment in those areas that did not. This new culture is "internally satisfying and unifying enough to have preserved pride of tribal lineage and ideals, personal character as well as honor.[64] The fact that the Houma continue to maintain such social integration up to the present time perhaps says much about the strength and character of the people themselves.

NOTES

1. Robert M. Netting, *Cultural Ecology* (Menlo Park California: Cummings Publishing Company, 1977), p. 94.

2. Julian H. Steward, *Evolution and Ecology* (Urbana: University of Illinois Press, 1977), p. 115.

3. Julian H. Steward, *Theory of Culture Change* (Urbana: University of Illinois Press, 1955), p. 36.

4. Andrew P. Vayda and R.A Rappaport, "Ecology, Cultural and Noncultural," in *Introduction to Cultural Anthropology,* ed. J.A. Clifton (Boston: Houghton Mifflin, 1968), p. 486.

5. Eleanor Leacock, "The Montagnais-Naskapi Band," in *Band Societies,* ed. David Damas, National Museum of Canada Contributions to Anthropology, Bulletin 228 (Ottawa, 1969), p. 2.

6. Steward, *Theory of Culture Change,* p. 34.

7. John R. Swanton, *Indians of the Lower Mississippi Valley and Adjacent Coast of the Gulf of Mexico,* Bureau of American Ethnology Bulletin No. 43 (Washington, D.C.: Government Printing Office, 1909), p. 28.

8. Jan Curry, "A History of the Houma Indians and Their Story of Federal Nonrecognition," *American Indian Journal,* 5 (February 1979): 11.

9. Curry, p. 12.

10. Fred Eggan, *The American Indian* (Chicago: Aldine Publishing Company, 1966), p. 17.

11. Curry, p. 13.

12. Ibid., p. 14.

13. Ibid., p. 15.

14. Ibid., p. 18.

15. John R. Swanton, *The Indians of the Southeastern United States,* Bureau of American Ethnology Bulletin No. 137 (Washington, D.C.: Government Printing Office, 1946), p. 140.

16. Curry, p. 16.

17. Roger W. Shugg, *Origins of Class Struggle in Louisiana* (Baton Rouge: Louisiana State University Press, 1939) pp. 309-311.

18. National Archives, Record Group No. 75, Central Files, Bureau of Indian Affairs, 1907-1939, Washington, D.C.

19. Curry, p. 11.

20. Francis Gallet, 1978, Houma collection of oral histories, Northwestern State University, Special Collection, Louisiana Room, Eugene Watson Library, Natchitoches, Louisiana.

21. Greg Bowman to Janel M. Curry-Roper, 7 November 1979.

22. Curry, p. 18.

23. Netting, p. 19.

24. For a legal history of loss of land by a Louisiana tribe, see Donald Juneau, "The Judicial Extinguishment of the Tunica Tribe," (document written for a lawsuit on behalf of the Tunica, New Orleans, 1978).

25. Bruce Duthu and Hilde Ojibway, "Future Light or *Feu Follet?, Southern Exposure,* 13 (November 1985): 27.

26. Eggan, p. 17.

27. Newton D. Mereness, *Travels in the American Colonies* (New York: Antiquanan Press Ltd., 1916), p. 34, 42.

28. Baron DeCrenay, *Carte Departie de la Louisiana,* 1733, Louisiana State University Archives, Baton Rouge, Louisiana.

29. Jacqueline K. Voorhies, *Some Late Eighteenth-Century Louisianaians Census Records 1758-1796* (Lafayette: University of Southwestern Louisiana Press, 1973), p. 164.

30. National Archives

31. William H. Gilbert Jr., "Eastern Cherokee Social Organization," in *Social Anthropology of North American Tribes,* 2nd edition, ed. Fred Eggan (Chicago: University of Chicago Press, 1955), p. 337.

32. Eggan, p. 19.

33. Curry, p. 18.

34. Steward, *Evolution and Ecology,* p. 157.

35. Frank G. Speck, "A Social Reconnaissance of the Creole Houma Indian Trappers of the Louisiana Bayous," *America Indigena,* 3 (1943): 213.

36. Curry, p. 20.

37. Andrew P. Vayda and Bonnie J. McCay, "New Directions in Ecology and Ecological Anthropology," *Annual Review of Anthropology,* 4 (1975): 300-301.

38. Eggan, p. 18.

39. Ibid., p. 24, 27.

40. John Gilmary Shea, *Early Voyages Up and Down the Mississippy* (Albany: np, 1861), p. 144.

41. Ibid., p. 145.

42. LeBlanc de Villeneufve, *The Festival of the Young Corn or the Heroism of Poucha-Houmma,* ed. Mathe' Allain (Lafayette: University of Southwestern Louisiana Pres, 1964), p. 8.

43. United States Secretary of Treasury, *Houmas Claim* (Washington, D.C.: Government Printing Office, 1845), p. 32.

44. Thomas Hutchins, *An Historical Narrative and Topographical Description of Louisiana and West Florida* (Philadelphia: np, 1784), pp. 39-40.

45. Dunbar Rowland, ed., *Official Letterbooks of W.C.C. Claiborne 1801-1816* (Jackson, Mississippi: State Department of Archives and History, 1917), p. 274.

46. National Archives.

47. Marie Hilda Billiot and Marie Melodie Dupre, 1978, Houma collection of oral histories, Northwestern State University, Special Collection, Louisiana Room, Eugene Watson Library, Natchitoches, Louisiana.

48. Terrebonne Parish, Conveyence Records, Houma, Louisiana.

49. For an extensive description of the change of the Houma from matrilineal horicultural people to a bilineal hunting and gathering people, see Michael James Rees, "The Houma: A Story of Adaptation: Anthropological Report Written to Determine the Tribal Existence of the United Houma Nation within 25 C.F.R. 54 *et seq.* for the Period of 1803-1912, (manuscript submitted to the Bureau of Indian Affairs in 1985 as part of the Houma petition for tribal recognition).

50. Frank G. Speck, "The Family Hunting Band as the Basis of Algonkian Social Organization," *American Anthropologist,* 17 (1915): 304-305.

51. Steward, *Evolution and Ecology,* p. 378.

52. Harnett T. Kane, *The Bayous of Louisiana* (New York: William Morrow and Company, 1943), p. 118.

53. Quoted in Leacock, p. 3.

54. Speck, "A Social Reconnaissance," p. 140.

55. Ibid., p. 143.

56. Ibid., p. 143.

57. Raymond M. Harrington, "Among Louisiana Indians," *Southern Workman,* 37 (1908): 657-658.

58. John R. Swanton, *Source Material for the Social and Ceremonial Life of the Choctaw Indians,* Bureau of American Ethnology Bulletin No. 103 (Washington, D.C.: Government Printing Office, 1931), p. 39.

59. William Knipmeyer, "A Culturo-Geographic Analysis of the Bayou Settlements of Southeastern Louisiana," in *Cultural Survey of Louisiana* (Baton Rouge: Louisiana State University Press, 1941), p. K11.

61. "Warm Days in Marsh Recall Taso-Making of Indians," *Times-Picayune* (17 April 1938): 1, 3.

62. Fred B. Kniffen, "Historic Indian Tribes of Louisiana," *Louisiana Conservative Review,* 4 (1935): 7.

63. Speck, "A Social Reconnaissance," p. 142.

64. Ibid., p. 140.

Chapter 13
Cultural Fusion in
Native-American Architecture:
The Navajo Hogan

Stephen C. Jett

Cultural diffusion and the conjoining of cultural streams have characterized history and prehistory from their inception. The tendency of cultural recombination and cross-fertilization to accelerate over time with the evolution of increasingly efficient transport and ever-expanding trade has been particularly manifest since the "Age of Discovery," often attaining astonishing speeds in contemporary times.

Within North America, relations among Indian groups were well established long before the time of Columbus. Long-distance trade networks existed, resulting, for example, in Yellowstone obsidian from Wyoming reaching Ohio Indians, and macaw feathers and even live macaws from southern Mexico being traded into the American Southwest. With trade, often went ideas; along with the macaws and copper belts from Mexico came a host of cultural baggage, including the kachina cult, that transformed Pueblo religion. Trade and interinfluence also occurred between Puebloans and the Plains tribes, Pimans, Pais, and others.

Major migrations also occurred, both in prehistoric and historic times. Among the historically best known are those of Prairie and Rocky Mountain tribes into the bison-rich plains after the Spanish introduction and subsequent spread of the horse, and the U.S. government's forced removal of the Cherokee and other groups from the Southeast into Oklahoma. Of specific interest in this chapter is the movement, in late pre-contact times, of Athapaskan-speakers from present-day western Canada southward into New Mexico and Arizona, where they were to become the Apache and the Navajo.

These kinds of migrations resulted in the transplantation of entire cultures from one region to another, cultures which then interacted with the local societies. But the cultures of the immigrants often ended up more altered in the exchange than did the peoples already occupying the areas into which the intruders penetrated; this was certainly true for the Navajo, who adopted many Southwestern traits.

Of course, a different kind of migration, one involving conquest and colonization, even more profoundly influenced Indian groups. In the Southwest, first the Spanish and then the Anglo-Americans both intentionally and inadvertently wrought changes which have transformed many aspects of native culture.

For a variety of reasons, there is a great deal of variation from group to group in the degree to which foreign traits are accepted. Some societies resist all change; they are the ones most likely to be ultimately overwhelmed, demoralized, and culturally destroyed. Others have been far more adaptable. The Navajo are often cited as having been particularly successful in the adoption, albeit selective, and "nativization" of exotic traits. After arriving in New Mexico some centuries ago, the Navajo acquired farming, weaving, and complex ceremonialism from their Puebloan neighbors; new crops, animal husbandry and metal-working from Hispanos; and costume, modern transport, political and economic institutions, and other traits from Anglo-Americans. The classic statement of this adoptive characteristic of Navajo culture is by Evon Vogt, who termed the Navajo "incorporative." By this he meant that "elements from other cultures are incorporated into Navajo culture in such a way that the structural framework of the institutional core is maintained, and the borrowed elements are fitted into place and elaborated in terms of the pre-existing patterns."[1] Vogt's "institutional core" included the Navajo language, certain religious/ philosophical concepts, and various crafts; but most core traits were related to social structure and to allied settlement patterns. Whether or not one sees Navajo culture change in exactly the same terms as did Vogt, the Navajo — and, specifically, Navajo architecture — provide a particularly apt example of how cultural diffusion can result not only in adoption but also in reinterpretation and further evolution of cultural traits.

The Athapaskan-speaking pre-Navajo migrated to the Southwest perhaps 700 years ago, from western Canada, where they had been hunters, fishers, and gatherers.[2] They brought with them Northern Hunter patterns of settlement, including dispersal, mobility, and certain socioterritorial groups.[3] Once in the Southwest (or, possibly, en route), these newcomers adopted farming and certain other practices, including a taboo against fishing, from their Indian neighbors; in the process, they became what may be termed "proto-Navajo."

The Athapaskans also brought with them from the North a conical, probably pole-and-brush-covered dwelling supported by a tripod frame; in slightly modified form, this structure survives as a rare Navajo summer shelter.

Vogt considered the Navajo hogan — the historic "traditional" Navajo permanent dwelling — to be one of the "institutional-core" elements. In an important sense, he was correct. Until quite recently, the vast majority of Navajos lived in hogans: normally circular or polygonal one-room habitations that contrast strikingly with the multi-room, multi-story pueblos[4] and rectalinear houses of the Navajo's Pueblo Indian and Euroamerican neighbors. And yet, the various hogan forms of today all differ significantly from the tipiform pole-and-brush shelters of the Navajo's Northern Athapaskan ancestors and some of their Western Apache relatives. How, then, did the Navajo come to possess habitations which are neither "original Athapaskan" or "adopted Southwestern"?

Obviously, material culture change has taken place over time. Fortunately, history, archeology, and comparative ethnology permit a reconstruction of these changes to a degree probably unequaled for any other tribal people.[5] And what we discover is a combination of external influences and internal evolution that has broader implications for theories of culture change. Of the two sources of change — invention and diffusion — the latter appears to have played the greater role in this case. And yet, derivative though the various hogan forms are in many ways, they are still uniquely Navajo and not to be mistaken for any other Native American form.

CONICAL FORKED-POLE AND LEAN-TO HOGANS

The building of conical pole-and-brush shelters based on tripod foundations was brought to the Southwest by the migrating pre-Navajo. Single and double brush-covered lean-tos were also probably among the original dwelling types used by these incoming Athapaskans.

All evidence indicates that the most prevalent early Navajo dwelling type was the conical forked-pole hogan, a type still built in very small numbers.[6] This form employs:)1 a tripod frame, the forked ends of whose poles interlock; 2) a large number of poles leaned onto this framework; 3) chinking of sticks, juniper bark, brush, or other vegetal material; 4) a covering of earth. An extended entryway is commonly present, and the floor is frequently excavated. The conical form, the tripod frame, and the pole-and-bark or -brush covering are all clearly continuations of the Northern Athapaskan building tradition. The use of interlocked forked pole ends rather than simple lashing of unforked poles, also seems to be of northern origin, occurring among the linguistically related Beaver Athapaskans of Canada[7] and among the White Mountain Apache.[8]

Most Northern Athapaskans using conical dwellings covered them only with bark, brush, or hides held in place by leaned-on poles.[9] And although two Athapaskan groups of British Columbia sometimes covered their conical habitations with sods,[10] Navajo use of earth covering seems more likely to have originated in the Southwest; neither the Navajo's linguistically closest northern relatives nor non-Navajo Southern Athapaskans covered their dwellings with earth, and construction with close-set poles plus vegetal matter plus earth is identical to that of Puebloan roofs,[11] except that hogan sides are inclined, not horizontal. The Zuni Puebloan word for "hogan" means "brush or leaf shelter," implying that the Navajo dwellings earliest observed by Zunis lacked the earth cover.

Most of the earliest known archeological hogans are in the Dinetah, where a major influx of Puebloan refugees from Spanish reprisals took place about A.D. 1700, and firm dates for hogans commence at about that time (the adoption of earth covering and the stronger, more numerous leaners to support it would have led to better archeological preservation.) This influx of Rio Grande-area Puebloans was crucial in the emergence of fully Navajo culture. Among the novelties probably introduced to these Athapaskans at this time were Spanish-derived sheep, and blanket-weaving — destined to become economic mainstays — pottery making, complex ceremonialism, and certain building techniques. Among the latter was the earth-covered roof described above, that seems highly likely to have inspired the earth covering of the Athapaskan-style conical dwelling form.[12]

The origins of two other features of the conical hogan are more problematical. Western Apaches[13] and some Northern Athapaskans employed extended entryways, but those northerners linguistically closest to the Navajo and those whose predominant dwelling was the conical hut apparently did not. Thus, this feature may be a local innovation (or, at least, elaboration) intended to exclude wind and to keep precipitation out of hogans with excavated floors. It also provided a vertical entry from which a hide or fabric door could be hung, and may also have had a defensive function.

Some Western Apache wikiups have excavated floors as do Navajos hogans,[14] but conical Northern Athapaskan dwellings apparently did not. Thus, Navajo excavation of floors presumably began in the Southwest. In that region, prehistoric pithouses had existed but were probably extinct by the time of proto-Navajo arrival. Therefore, this practice may be a local re-invention, intended to increase dwelling headroom in a land where long, straight timbers were seldom available, and to provide the earth for covering the exterior. However, floor excavation may also represent a link between the religious role of the hogan and that of the semi-subterranean kivas (ceremonial chambers) of the refugees' home pueblos. The earthern shelf left between the excavation and the wall base would then be analogous to the kiva's peripheral masonry bench.

Earth covered, single or double lean-to hogans, with one or two uprights, are now extinct. Like conical hogans, they probably represented basically northern forms whose brush covering was replaced, in the Southwest, by a Puebloan-style juniper-bark-and-earth cover. (Earth-covered roofs have, of course, insulation qualities superior to those of brush — one factor which may have encouraged their adoption.) This form was probably never common, and likely ordinarily served more as a temporary, summer dwelling than true, year-round hogan.[15]

David M. Brugge, in an essay on probable sources of the features of the conical forked-pole hogan, wrote, "This mixture of [Athapaskan and Puebloan] traits in a single complex, many showing considerable alteration in the process, cannot be characterized as an example of incorporation. A fusion of two cultural traditions is certainly the only way to describe the result."[16]

But whether one prefers to consider the conical forked-pole and lean-to hogans as examples of incorporations or of fusion, it is almost certainly the case that even these, the most "Athapaskan" of Navajo dwelling forms, have been substantially modified by influences from a very different foreign building tradition. The changes thus wrought may have helped generate what appear to have been innovations: the excavated floor and the extended entryway.

VERTICAL-POST HOGANS

Because of its spaciousness, another early hogan type, the leaning-log hogan,[17] seemingly served primarily as a ceremonial structure, until becoming secularized toward the end of the nineteenth century.

From the earliest example recorded (ca. 1697-1770) until the present century, most leaning-log hogans were subrectangular and were based on four vertical posts connected by stringers, against which leaned earth-covered poles; the structure — which, in effect, was four single lean-tos facing a central square — was spanned by a flat, earth-covered roof. This form has no exact counterpart in the North. Although it could have been invented by the Navajo as an extension of the lean-to concept, it seems far more likely that the primary inspiration was the Puebloan summer shade (ramada), a common field structure. The only difference between the leaning-log hogan and the most similar ramadas is that the latter's sides lack an earthen covering. The addition of earth to the walls in a fashion identical to the procedure with conical hogans would be a small step. Here, then, we seem to have a Pueloan form, the summer shade, "Navajoized" into a ceremonial structure by the application of a Puebloan house-roofing technique not only to the roof but to the sides as well. Further "Navajoization" occurred in this century, as the dwelling function eclipsed the ceremonial role: the subrectangular plan was increasingly replaced by a circular plan, in conformity with the conical-hogan tradition, by adding additional vertical posts with stringers. The wide availability of steel axes beginning about 1890 contributed to the rising popularity of this type, which required large numbers of logs. The combining of all of these ideas and procedures seems to be another case of fusion.

Additional evolution of the form occurred, this time due to Hispano and Anglo influences, producing a variant known as the palisaded hogan, a type emerging about the beginning of the twentieth century. The wall logs of this form are set vertically into a circular trench instead of being leaned against stringers. The origin of this hogan-building procedure seems to be the *jacales* or *palisados* — vertical-log houses — introduced to northern New Mexico from Mexico during the Spanish era. Significant Navajo use of the technique seems first to have been associated with the simplified Euroamerican-style houses they began to erect in small numbers during the 1880s, apparently after having observed the method applied in the construction of Ft. Wingate, a New Mexico military post dealing with the Navajo.[18] Palisade fencing, also an introduction from Mexico, began to be commonly used for corrals as well. It was perhaps inevitable, then, that the technique next be applied to the already similar leaning-log hogan, yielding the palisaded hogan. The vertical walls of this form had an advantage in connection with the adoption of European-style furniture. Although the Navajo apparently failed to adopt the Hispano morticing of the pales to a head plate,[19] the emergence of the palisaded hogan seems nevertheless to represent further cultural fusion, with a third stream of tradition, the Mexicanized Hispano, contributing to the Athapaskan and Puebloan.

STACKED-LOG HOGANS

By the end of the first third of the eighteenth century, a type of hogan appeared which had no precedent in Athapaskan construction. This was the corbeled-log hogan, a hemispherical structure built of successive tiers of horizontal logs, the logs of each tier being slightly shorter than those of the previous tier and being laid across the angles formed by the logs of the previous tier. The structure was chinked, and covered with earth.[20]

Almost identical structures had existed in and near Dinetah between A.D. 1 and 400;[21] but that was long prior to a Navajo presence. Nevertheless, there is good, though not unequivocal, basis for belief that this highly unusual building technique is a Peubloan legacy among the Navajo. This method of construction persisted until about A.D. 1300 among Mesa Verdean Puebloans of southwestern Colorado, for roofing kivas. Even though there is presently no evidence of later Puebloan use, some use *may* have continued sparingly over the centuries, providing a model for the eighteenth-century Navajo.

Because of the time gap involved, Brugge (personal communication) is inclined to the opinion that rather than being of puebloan derivation, this form evolved independently among the Navajo through attempts to roof, with short branches, circular piled-bough windbreaks, a common and widespread type of temporary shelter. Theoretically, this evolution would seem simple enough; yet the nearly total absence of the corbeled-log dome at any time anywhere in the world other than the Southwest[22] raises serious doubts. Provisionally, I prefer to see this as another case of synthesis — the Navajo idea of a circular, single-room dwelling combining with a Puebloan and pre-Puebloan construction technique. For roofs, the corbeled-log method was increasingly applied to vertical-post and stone-masonry hogans, which previously had employed Pueblo-style horizontal-beam roofs.

A second, later, stacked-log hogan type, involving a related but distinct construction technique, is the cribbed-log hogan, which seems first to have appeared about 1840.[23] Brugge considered this type to exemplify fusion; it indeed appears to represent a case of syncretism between the corbeled-log hogan —itself probably a cultural hybrid — and the European log-cabin-building tradition. In corbeling, logs are even-tiered, the log ends abutting at the midpoints of the logs of the previous tier. In cribbing, logs are alternate-tiered, the ends of the logs of one wall overlapping the ends of the logs of adjacent walls. Whereas corbeled-log hogans approach circularity in plan, cribbed-log hogans are polygonal. A complete gradation between corbelel — and cribbed — log hogans exists, and it is possible that the early evolution of the latter from the former was completely spontaneous. However, a tradition of rectangular cribbed-log buildings had existed among northern New Mexico Hispanos since at least the mid-eighteenth century,[24] apparently introduced from an area in Mexico settled by Silesians.[25] Thus, the emergence of the first cribbed-log hogans, apparently about 1840, reflects Hispano influence. This could have resulted from the fact that numbers of Hispanos kept Navajo slaves, especially after 1821; some slaves escaped, and brought back knowledge of Hispano ways.

Haile categorized cribbed-log hogans as primarily ceremonial in function, due to commodiousness;[26] they remained very rare almost until the turn of the century, when — apparently for the first time — the logs came to be notched and sometimes hewn, coincident with the wide availability of steel axes. The vertical, usually saddle-notched, mud-chinked log walls of the contemporary cribbed-log hogan seem to derive largely from the Euroamerican cribbed-log *house* tradition promoted among Navajo leaders by administrators at the Ft. Defiance, Arizona, Agency, beginning about 1881.[27] Thus, the wedding of the circular plan of a hogan type probably already largely of Puebloan derivation to a European technique designed for rectangular houses, yielded a compromise in the form of the polygonal cribbed-log hogan, usually provided with a domical corbeled-log roof. This form has, over the last three-quarters of a century, become the most popular hogan type, particularly in timbered areas. The popularity, as residences, of the relatively spacious vertical-post and cribbed-log hogans is probably connected with the adoption of stoves, which are more heat-efficient than were the open fires used previously.

One further late and uncommon variant horizontal-log hogan is the abutting-log hogan, a polygonal form in which logs are even-tiered, their ends abutting and nailed to a vertical post at each corner.[28] This form was presumably inspired by a similar Euroamerican log-cabin-building method, but the idea of vertical corner posts was already present among the Navajo in connection with leaning-log hogans.

PLANK HOGAN

The final evolution of wooden hogans was the probably post-1930 development of the plank hogan, particularly in the region surrounding the Tribal sawmill near Ft. Defiance. Undoubtedly, increased Navajo familarity with Anglo-American building materials and techniques — and even school carpentry training and construction-work employment — paved the way for the emergence of the various kinds of plank hogans. The usual technique was similar to that of the abutting-log hogan, using sawn or unsawn corner posts connected by nailed-on horizontal planks. A roll-roofing-covered pyramidal plank roof was typical. In this hogan type, contemporary commercial building materials had completely supplanted traditional ones. Modern Anglo-American frame house construction has been the primary inspiration for these hogans, which commonly carry a veneer of tarpaper, chickenwire lath, and cement stucco.[29] All that is left of the old Athapaskan dwelling is a concession to the circular plan to the extent of the hogans being polygonal instead of rectangular. And yet, this is perceived as being sufficiently true to native tradition as to make a plank hogan fully acceptable for Navajo ceremonies whereas a house, of whatever materials, is not.[30]

MASONRY HOGANS

Refugee Puebloans settling among the Navajo in the 1690s began building small stone-and-mud masonry pʻeblos (pueblitos). Navajos may have participated in some of this construction, and circular masonry structures fairly called stone hogans had appeared by the early eighteenth century (or possibly during the latter seventeenth century, according to Schaafsma's findings).[31] Although the chronology is not clear, basically rectangular masonry houses with rounded corners from this general time period may represent a transitional stage between rectangular puebloid structures and circular hogans. At any rate, the construction of vertical-walled, usually corbeled-log-roofed stone-masonry hogans has persisted in some areas, particularly where timber is absent, into modern times.[32] Here, again, fusion occurred: alien building materials and techniques previously used primarily for rectangular structures replaced traditional Athapaskan materials and techniques, leaving only the circular plan — itself sometimes altered to a polygon. And yet, there is no question that the stone hogan is a Navajo, and only a Navajo, dwelling type.

Cinder-block, adobe-brick, and poured-concrete hogans have also been recorded, but are so uncommon that they will not receive further attention here except by my again noting the cultural hybridization involved.

CONCLUSIONS

The conjunction of elements from at least four major cultural traditions created a set of unique dwelling types unequivocally and exclusively identifiable with one of those cultural traditions. If the first migrating pre--Navajo to reach New Mexico some centuries ago were able to see today's range of hogan types, he would probably not recognize any of them — with the possible exception of the nearly obsolete conical forked-pole hogan — as having any relation to Athapaskan housing. And yet, every Navajo today would unhesitatingly class every one of these structures as a hogan and therefore, by definition, Navajo. Certainly, as according to Brugge, cultural fusion has taken place time and again with respect to individual hogan forms. And yet, as Vogt contended, the more or less circular, single-room hogan has, as a general dwelling type, persisted — at least, until recently — as a core characteristic of Navajo culture.

We are confronted with the question as to exactly what comprises the essence, *sina qua non* of "hogan-ness." It is *not* overall form or facade or roof type: a hogan may be, among other possibilities, a cone, a truncated pyramid with rounded corners, a hemisphere, a cylinder, a hemisphere-on-cylinder, or a hemisphere- or pyramid-on-polygonal-solid. It is not materials: the primary construction material can be logs, planks, stones, adobe, or concrete. It is not construction technique: covering leaning logs, leaning logs on post-and-lintel, palisaded logs, corbeled and cribbed logs, abutting logs, masonry, or poured concrete can be used. Certainly function as a dwelling is basic — "hogan" means "home place" or "dwelling space" — but there are many possible alternative kinds of dwellings, and hogans may also simultaneously or successively be used for ceremonies, meetings, storage, sheltering animals, or as workshops.

Probably the essential condition of "hogan-ness" is the structure's being uniquely Navajo.[33] Most hogan types are essentially unique. That some similar forms were produced in ancient times and in other places is not known to most Navajos, and is of little relevance. With the exception of the tiny and highly Navajoized San Juan band of Southern Paiutes and the partial exception of the small, isolated Havasupai tribe,[34] the hogan has not been significantly adopted by non-Navajos.

But what physical characteristics define a hogan? A single room is one requirement; interiors of hogans are never physically subdivided. Yet, single-room rectangular cabins are not considered hogans. The plan of a structure *does* appear central to its hogan-ness, but within quite flexible limits. If the plan is basically rectangular, any corners must be rounded, not square. In the case of polygonal hogans, a minimum of five sides is required, so that all corner angles will exceed ninety degrees. But the main point of having some plan which is at least a small step away from a square in the direction of a circle is a centrality of focus for the dwelling interior and a concentric and radial conceptual sectoring of the interior space. This focus, slightly entryward of center, is the hearth on the dirt floor — or, today, the woodburning stove. It is around this source of warmth and site of cooking that hogan life revolves. The hearth is also the ceremonial center of the structure. Any stove is removed, and the hearth reestablished, during most ceremonies. A square house, too, may have a central hearth or stove, although it is often in a corner; but a house lacks any concession to the feeling that the dwelling walls should equally face or surround the fire (the perfect enclosure, like the perimeter of the world, is a circle[35]). In ritual, there is a prescribed, clockwise (sunwise), circuit around the hearth area, beginning and ending at the eastward-oriented entry. In Blessingway, the basic Navajo ceremonial, songs name and bless the various interior parts of the hogan. Also characteristic of the hogan, but not the house, is the smokehole, a usually square opening directly above the hearth; even when a stove and stovepipe obviate the need for a smokehole, the latter is ordinarily retained *in a hogan.* The smokehole is required for certain ritual acts.[36]

Clearly, the hogan is closely associated with Navajo religion. First Man and Woman erected a conical hogan (and a corbeled-log hogan, some say) at the Place of Emergence from the underworld, in which to plan the ordering of the earth and the heavens. Navajo myths describe and involve hogans. These are normally conical forked-pole dwellings, and although the myths prescribe rituals which involve alluding to or blessing various parts of the hogan, including the tripod and entry poles, the characteristic pragmatism of the Navajo which led to use of other, more spacious, hogan types for ceremonies also permitted the framework poles to be substituted for by stringers or walls in the same relative positions.[37]

Brugge noted that refugee pueblitos lacked kivas, the circular, subterranean ceremonial chambers characteristic of the refugees' pueblos-of-origin. He wrote.[38]

> The only round structures are hogans and these are sometimes, where pueblitos did have plazas, within the plaza areas. Hogans seem to have become the ceremonial structures of the mixed Navojo-[Pueblo] refugee population even before the refugees were beginning to be absorbed into the general [Athapaskan] population. Of particular interest in this regard are the few archeological hogans that have [air] deflectors [in front of the hearth, as in kivas]. . .hogans. . .quickly became ceremonial structures. . .a fusion of the kiva and home. . .I think this is why the hogan and Navajo religion remain so closely associated in Navajo thinking today.

The traditional functional and ritual subdivision of the hogan interior into concentric and radiating sectors[39] — apparently at least in part a northern legacy — no doubt also provided a strong impetus in the retention of at least some concession to the ideal of the circular plan. In reality, few of the features and procedures mentioned above could not be applied to the one-room square house. Yet the latter is perceived as essentially foreign and therefore unsuitable for Navajo religion, which is non-universalizing and relevant only to the Navajo. As long as a dwelling (or ceremonial structure) is Navajo-built, one-roomed, has a plan that at least makes a gesture toward circularity, and possesses a smokehole, it can be considered fully a hogan; it ought, too, to have its doorway oriented toward the dawn.[40]

The last quarter century has seen increasing acculturation and accelerating trend for Navajos to build and live in frame houses instead of hogans.[41] Although the hogan has been described as a symbol of Navajo ethnic identity,[42] the Navajo's sense of identity seems sufficiently strong that the majority are now prepared to yield to the forces attracting them to houses (e.g., "modernity," suitability for furniture, provision of private rooms). It seems, then, that the hogan *as a principal dwelling* is no longer a core element of Navajo culture. Yet, it still is required by Navajo religion, which retains enormous strength, and hogans continue to be maintained or built for ceremonies even by house-dwelling Navajos, who still think of the hogan as being in some sense "home." And as long as Navajo religion — truly a part of the cultural core — endures, so too should the Navajo hogan.

NOTES

1. Evon Z. Vogt, "Navaho," in *Perspectives in American Indian Culture Change,* ed. Edward H. Spicer (Chicago: The University of Chicago Press), pp. 307, 326-328.

2. David M. Brugge, "Navajo Prehistory and History to 1850," in *Handbook of North American Indians* 10, *Southwest,* ed. Alfonso Ortiz (Washington: Smithsonian Institution 1983), pp. 489-490.

3. Stephen C. Jett, "The Origins of Navajo Settlement Patterns," *Annals of the Association of American Geographers* 68 (September 1978): 351-362.

4. Victor Mindeleff, "A Study of Peublo Architecture: Tusayan and Cibola, *Bueau of American Ethnology, Annual Report* 8 (1891): 3-228.

5. For full documentation, see Stephen C. Jett and Virginia E. Spencer, *Navajo Architecture: Forms, History, Distributions* (Tucson: The University of Arizona Press, 1981). On the temporal sequence of hogan forms in specific areas, see: Miranda Warburton, "Culture Change and the Navajo Hogan," Ph.D. dissertation, Washington State University, Pullman, 1985, published in xerography by University Microfilms, Ann Arbor, 8610389; and Charles D. James III and Alexander J. Lindsay, Jr., "Ethnoarchaeological Research at Canyon del Muerto, Arizona: A Navajo Example,"*Ethnohistory* 20 (Fall 1975): 361-374.

6. Cosmos Mindeleff, "Navaho Houses," *Bureau of American Ethnology, Annual Report* 17 (1898): 475-517; Berard Haile, "Why the Navajo Hogan?" *Primitive Man* 15 (July and October 1942): 39-56, (Leopold) (Ostermann), "Navajo Houses," *The Franciscan Missions of the Southwest* 5 (1917): 20-22. I observed a newly built example in the Tall Mountain, Arizona area, in 1985.

7. Pliny Earl Goddard, *The Beaver Indians,* American Museum of Natural History, Anthropological Papers 10, No. 4 (1916): 210.

8. Margaret W.M. Schaeffer, "The Construction of a Wikiup on the Fort Apache Indian Reservation,"*The Kiva* 24 (December 1958): 14, 17.

9. Harold E. Driver and William C. Massey, *Comparative Studies of North American Indians,* Transactions of the American Philosophical Society 47, Pt. 2 (1957): 299, 303-306.

10. John J. Honigmann, *The Kaska Indians: An Ethnographic Reconstruction,* Yale University Publications in Anthropology 51 (1954): 59, 62.

11. V. Mindeleff, pp. 149-151.

12. Brugge, pp. 490-494.

13. E.W. Gifford, *Culture Element Distributions: XII, Apache-Pueblo,* Anthropological Records 4, No. 1 (1940): 109-110.

14. Gifford, p. 110.

15. Clyde Kluckhohn, W.W. Hill, and Lucy Wales Kluckhorn, *Navaho Material Culture* (Cambridge: The Belknap Press of Harvard University Press, 1971), p. 152.

16. David M. Brugge, "Pueblo Influence on Navajo Archietecture," *El Palacio* 75 (Autumn 1968): 19-20.

17. C. Mindeleff; Albert A. Ward, "Investigation of Two Hogans at Toonerville, Arizona,"*Plateau* 40 (Spring 1968): 136-142.

18. R.W. Shufeldt, "The Evolution of House-Building among the Navajo Indians,"*United States National Museum, Proceedings* 15 (1892).

19. See Charles Gritzner, "Construction Materials in Folk Housing Tradition: Considerations Governing Their Selection in New Mexico," *Pioneer America* 6 (January 1974): 25-39.

20. Dale Coolidge and Mary Coolidge, *The Navajo Indians* (Boston: Houghton-Mifflin Company), p. 81; John M. Corbett, "Navajo House Types," *El Palacio* 47 (May 1940): 105.

21. Frank W. Eddy, *Prehistory in the Navajo Reservoir District, Northeastern New Mexico,* Museum of New Mexico Papers in Anthropology 15, No. 1 (1966).

22. Exceptions: the ancient Bell Beaker people of the Netherlands, and contemporary Turks of the Erzurum area, Turkey.

23. Kluckhohn, Hill, and Kluckhohn, pp. 146-147.

24. Charles Gritzner, "Log Housing in New Mexico," *Pioneer America* 3 (July 1971): 54-62; "Hispano Gristmills in New Mexico," *Annals of the Association of American Geographers* 64 (December 1974): 518.

25. John J. Winberry, "The Log House in Mexico," *Annals of the Assocation of American Geographers* 64 (March 1974): 54-69.

26. Haile, pp. 55-55; see also, Coolidge and Coolidge, p. 82; Edwin M. Wilmsen, "The House of the Navajo,"*Landscape* 10 (Fall 1960): 18.

27. Jet and Spencer, p. 107.

28. Gordon B. Page, "Navajo House Types," *Museum* (of Northern Arizona) *Notes* 9 (March 1937): 48, Plates V, VI.

29. Marc Adelard Tremblay, John Collier, Jr., and Tom T. Sasaki, "Navaho Housing in Transition," *America Indigena* 14 (July 1954): 187-219; Virginia E. Spencer and Stephen C. Jett, "Navajo Dwellings of Rural Black Creek Valley, Arizona-New Mexico," Plateau 43 (Spring 1971): 166, 167, 169, 170.

30. Haile, p. 56; Charlotte Johnson Frisbie, "The Navajo House Blessing Ceremonial,"*El Palacio* 75 (Autumn 1968): 34.

31. Curtis F. Schaafsma, *The Cerrito Site (AR-4), a Pierda Lumbre Settlement at Aibiquiu Reservoir* (Santa Fe: School of American Research, 1979).

32. Corbett, p. 105; Kluckhohn, Hill, and Kluckhohn, pp. 152-153.

33. Haile, p. 40.

34. Leslie Spier,*Havasupai Ethnography,* American Museum of Natural History Anthropological Papers 29, No. 3 (1928): 178.

35. Rik Pinxten, Ingrid van Dooren, and Frank Harvey, *The Anthropology of Space: Explorations into the Natural Philosophy and Semantics of the Navajo* (Philadelphia: University of Pennsylvania Press, 1983) pp. 10-11.

36. Haile, pp. 46, 51-52.

37. Haile, pp. 53-55.

38. David M. Brugge, personal communication, 1979.

39. C. Mindeleff, Pl. 90; Haile, pp. 49-51; Jett and Spencer, pp. 22-23. See also, Susan Kent, *Analyzing Activity Areas: An Ethnoarchaeological Study of the Use of Space* (Albuquerque: University of New Mexico Press, 1984).

40. See, for example, Amos Rapoport, "The Pueblo and the Hogan," in *Shelter and Society,* ed. Paul Oliver (New York: Frederick A. Praeger, 1969), pp. 77-78; Warburton, pp. 150, 156.

41. Tremblay, Collier, and Sasaki; Spencer and Jett.

42. N. Ross Crumrine, *The House Cross of the Mayo Indians of Sonora, Mexico: A Symbol of Ethnic Identity,* University of Arizona Anthropological Papers 8 (1964).

Part Five
Population Studies

Chapter 14
The Urban American Indian

Terrel Rhodes

Of the various ethnic and racial groups within the United States, none has received more attention throughout our history, has provoked more fascinated interest, or suffered more severe deprivation than the Native American. From childhood games of cowboys and Indians to U.S. history school books, from television and movie westerns to the Bureau of Indian Affairs takeover, water rights disputes, Wounded Knee and the Passamaquoddy land claims in Maine, we have never been far from an account of the American Indian experience in this country.

Because the Indian peoples were here before the white man, there developed a special relationship between the Indian tribes and the white central government. Unlike most Americans, Native Americans are not only citizens of the United States, their state and city, but are also usually members of tribal organizations or groups even though a majority of American Indians now live in urban areas, not on reservations. In an organizational chart, tribal groups may rank on a par with states in that tribal lands held in trust by the federal government, but owned by Indian tribes, are administered directly by the federal government rather than by or through the states. Tribal reservations, or trust lands, are not creatures of the state governments as are local government jurisdictions. Although some state laws extend to reservation trust lands, in most states, states cannot tax trust properties or income derived from them, and there are limits on the applicability of state civil and criminal codes in cases that involve only Indians. Of particular importance here is the status and experience of Indians who now live in urban areas.

The evolution of federal Indian policy contains an inherent dichotomy revolving around the social, political, and legal status of Native Americans. Due to the conflicting, and often contradictory, principles underlying the governmental policies that have emerged thus far, structures and procedures have evolved that create a distinct dilemma for many contemporary Indians: shall I, as an Indian, remain in rather abject poverty on a reservation and continue to qualify for federal Indian programs and maintain my "Indian" way of life, or shall I move off-reservation to improve my economic prospects, but lose most federal services specifically provided for Indians, and perhaps much of my way of life as an Indian?[1] It is not so much that cultural conflict and identity are the issues, although to an extent they are; but rather, that Indians did not choose to become American citizens voluntarily and often they do not freely choose to leave the reservation for urban areas. Individual freedom of choice has traditionally been a key principle of American democratic theory.[2]

Congress is the federal entity that appropriates money for Indians, creates Indian programs, and enacts the basic law that governs Indians. Historically, the Bureau of Indian Affairs (BIA) has been the federal administrative agency that has implemented congressional actions on reservations and represented Indian interests in Congress. The BIA has acted as a broker, attempting to obtain programs and money for itself and its Indian clients, while at the same time administering and implementing congressional policy on Indian reservations.

As federal policy has shifted its goals and objectives over the years, one theme has been fairly constant: a desire to assimilate Indians into the dominant white culture. Even if assimilation had not been a policy objective of the federal government, the forces of our modern technological society would most likely have been sufficient to continue the assimilation of non-Indian cultural values and patterns into Indian cultures. Federal Indian policy was in the past, and to a degree still is, encouraging assimilation into the dominant culture. Under the Dawes Severalty Act (General Allotment Act of 1887),[3] as tribes became "civilized," their tribal lands, or reservation lands, were allotted among the individuals enrolled in the tribe, thus providing families and individuals with homesteads similar to those owned by whites.

From 1879 to 1934 Congress and the federal bureaucracy attempted to break up the reservation system and to end tribal governments as political bodies possessing various inherent powers. Individualization of property previously owned tribally, education, and extension of state and local laws over individual and tribal Indians were seen as the best ways to end the need for reservations and thus open former reservation land and its resourcs to whites.

The desire of Congress to be out of the "Indian business," to terminate federal trust responsibility, culminated in 1953 with House Concurrent Resolution 108 (PL 83-280).[4] The act extended civil and criminal jurisdiction over Indian tribes in certain states and created a permanent procedure whereby other states could, in the future, do likewise, thus undermining the powers of tribal governments to govern themselves and restricting their ability to utilize tribal resources as they wished. Although the federal trust responsibility was not automatically terminated, such was the goal of the legislation. Building on the rather explicit policy formalized in the Dawes Act designed to break-up reservations, the federal government pursued policies to reduce the on-reservation population.

World War II was the major stimulus for the first large-scale population movements from reservations to urban areas. During this period 23,000 Indian men, approximately 32 percent of all able-bodied male Indians between the ages of eighteen and fifty years, served in the armed forces. In addition, 800 Indian women served in the military. Approximately another 46,000 Indian men and women, equally distributed between agriculture and industry, left the reservations in 1943 to obtain wartime employment. In 1944, another 44,000 left reservations.[5]

After the war, most Indian workers in defense-related industries were laid off and subsequently returned to the reservation. The high incidence of unemployment on reservations created by the influx and the lack of employment opportunities on the reservations began to attract attention. In 1948, in response to the problem of widespread unemployment and poverty on reservations, the Bureau of Indian Affairs established a program of job placement services for the Navajo. With the added impetus of Congressional support for termination of federal responsibility for Indian affairs during the late 1940s and early 1950s, the Bureau of Indian Affairs launched its first full-scale relocation program for Indians who desired permanent employment away from the reservation.

In 1952, 442 applicants participated in the relocation program, or 868 if dependents were included. By the peak year of 1957, 2,882 (5,728 with dependents) individuals were involved. The number of participants fluctuated between 1,600 (3,400 with dependents) and 2,600 (5,600 with dependents) with an approximate average of 1,800 (4,000 with dependents) per year.[6] In most recent years, the emphasis on relocating Indians in cities has been replaced with a greater emphasis on increased funding for local job training and placement, and on creation of reservation employment possibilities and job skills.

Has this federal policy of relocating Indians to urban areas resulted in a significant impact? It is difficult to say whether Indians would have left reservations in the numbers they have during the last decades if there had not been federal programs and money available. It is true, however, that twice as many Indians have migrated to cities without federal assistance than with it. The primary reason for migrating has uniformly been the lack of economic opportunity on reservations and the existence of economic opportunity in urban areas. In this respect federal employment and relocation programs have provided an alternative to reservation poverty.

Over the past forty years the increase in the American Indian population has been dramatic, especially the urbanization of Indian peoples (Table 14.1). Since most of the Indian population was

Table 14.1

American Indians in the United States

Year	Total Population	Urban (Percent)	Rural
1940	333,969	8	92
1950	343,410	16	84
1960	523,591	28	72
1970	763,594	45	55
1980	1,418,195	70	30

relocated to areas west of the Mississippi River, the largest concentrations of urban Indians are also found in cities west of the Mississippi, i.e., Los Angeles (48,000), Minneapolis (16,000), Tulsa (13,700), Oklahoma City (10,400), Anchorage (8,900), Albuquerque (7,300), Seattle (6,300), and San Diego (5,100). Substantial Indian communities are found also in New York City (13,800) and Chicago (6,100).

Much like the population of the United States as a whole, the Indian population has shifted from a predominantly rural residential pattern to a predominantly urban one. The percentages are somewhat misleading, though, in that the Bureau of the Census defines any place of 2,500 or more population to be an urban place. Wide variation exists among these towns and cities and the urban experience that results for their residents. Best estimates are that approximately three-quarters of the urban Indian residents are a permanent part of the community where they reside.[7] The remaining twenty-five percent appear to constitute a mobile sub-group that moves among cities and between city and reservation in search of employment and better economic opportunities.

Many who go to the city in search of a job and a better life soon leave again, having become discouraged and disillusioned by the high costs of urban living and problems of finding and maintaining employment. Those who find work and who remain in the city do better than their non-urban counterparts on socio-economic measures, but not as well as the majority white population.

Table 14.2 presents median income figures for urban and non-urban Indians. Income has increased for Indian men and women regardless of where they live, but urban Indians far exceed non-urban Indians in average income. These figures suggest that migration to urban areas does result in better economic well-being than remaining on or near reservations.

Table 14.2

Per Capita Median Income for Native Americans

Median Income years old	1970[1]		1980	
	Urban	Non-urban	Urban	Non-urban
Male 16+	$4,200	$1,675	$9,320	$6,660
Female 16+	999	360	4,744	3,609

1. Median for 1970 was approximated from existing data on income distribution.

A comparison of average personal income figures is somewhat limited. the problem with this simple mode of comparison is that the figures only include those who received some income during the preceding years, therefore excluding a large part of the population, e.g., only 64 percent of the female white population reported some income in 1970.[8] Furthermore, there is no distinction concerning the types of income, e.g., part-time, full-time, part-year, only Social Security, AFDC, etc., or what the participation rates of women and minorities are over time compared to majority males, since the rates differ substantially.

A comparison between urban and non-urban Indian populations is also not very revealing of the socio-economic condition of Indians vis-a-vis the majority white population. Urban Indians may be doing better than non-urban Indians, but how do they compare with white urban residents who set the standard by which other groups measure their relative status?

The median household per capita income measure avoids the exclusion of individuals without income and individuals who live alone and are not members of families but do constitute households. In addition, income gets divided from whatever source among those within the household, thus presenting a clearer idea of the real distribution of income within a population group. The median insures that half the group has less, avoiding the possibility of the mean masking a rather skewed distribution. Table 14.3 presents the ratios that result when the median household per capita income for Native Americans is divided by the median household per capita income for the majority population. Median household

Table 14.3

Native American Median Household
Per Capita Income Compared to Majority Income

	Raw Measure			Social Indicator Value (Ratio of Raw Measure to Majority Male)		
	1970[a]	1976[a]	1980[a]	1970[a]	1976[a]	1980[a]
For All Households						
Native Americans	$1,122	$2,453	$4,631	.43	.57	.58
Majority	2,601	4,333	7,929	1.00	1.00	1.00
SMSA	N.A.	3,279	5,480	N.A.	.76	.69
Non-SMSA	N.A.	1,916	3,665	N.A.	.44	.46
For Female-Headed Households						
Native American	$ 711	$1,310	$2,191	.27	.30	.28
Majority	1,658	2,563	4,248	.64	.59	.54

Source: [a] Adapted from *Social Indicators of Equality for Minorities and Women: A Report,* United States Commission on Civil Rights, August, 1978, p. 50, Table 4.2.

per capita income is not presented separately for men and women because of the impossibility of determining decision making and production/consumption patterns in male-female households.

Households headed by Indians in 1980 had a median household income only 58 percent of the majority headed households' median income. Substantial improvement has occurred for Indians in absolute dollars relative to the majority, but the inequality of income is still great. For households headed by Indian women, median income has worsened in relation to the majority, with a median household income of slightly more than one-fourth of the median income of majority-headed households. Native Americans living in Standard Metropolitian Statistical Areas (SMSA's) do better than Indian households in general, but the gap appears to be closing slowly. Indians in SMSA's show a declining houshold per capita income of just over two-thirds of the majority household income; while non-SMSA Indians, although they have increased their per capita income, are not marginally improved over 1976 levels when compared to the majority population.

Another indicator of economic well-being is a poverty indicator that compares the percentage of Indian families and unrelated individuals who are below the poverty line with the proportion of majority families and unrelated individuals who are. The ratios in Table 14.4 indicate that although the proportion of Indian men and women officially living in poverty declined from 1970 to 1980, the likelihood of Indian women living in poverty has increased. Indian families and unrelated individuals are two and one half times as likely to be living in poverty than majority-headed families. In this instance, female-headed *majority* families and unrelated individuals do better than Indians in general and Indian female-headed families and unrelated individuals in particular. If you are Indian and female, heading a household, you are almost five times more likely than majority families and unrelated individuals to be living in poverty. In fact, Indian female-headed families and families in SMSAs are more likely to be in poverty in 1980 than they were ten years earlier.

Even with federal efforts to provide job training programs with money earmarked especially for Indians, i.e. the Comprehensive Employment and Training Program (CETA) and most recently the Jobs Training Partnership Act (JTPA), poverty continues to be a severe problem for Native Americans even with the earnings benefits that appear to be resulting from JTPA programs. In a study of Indian JTPA programs, Indian population was poorer than the majority population generally within the service delivery area in which the programs were located. Whereas 67 percent of the program areas studied had overall poverty rates below the national average of 12.4 percent, 97 percent of the areas had Indian poverty rates that exceeded the national average. Poverty rates

Table 14.4

Poverty Index

Families and Unrelated individuals	Ratios (Native American Majority Male)			Percentage Below Poverty Line		
	1970	1976	1980	1970	1976	1980
Native American	36	26	29	2.77	2.89	2.64
Majority	13	9	11	1.00	1.00	1.00
SMSA-Native American	26.7	21.5	28	2.05	2.39	2.55
Female-Headed Families and Female Unrelated Individuals						
Native American	54	49	53	4.15	5.44	4.82
Majority	28	22	16	2.15	2.44	1.46
SMSA-Native American	47	51.1	58	3.62	5.68	5.27

Source: Adapted from *Social Indicators of Equality for Minorities and Women,* U.S. Commission on Civil Rights, August, 1978, p. 62, Table 4.6, and the 1980 U.S. Census.

were higher in rural areas (35.8 percent) than in urban areas (26.4 percent); again suggesting that urban Indians are economically better advantaged.[9]

Having the necessary education, training, and skills is fundamental to obtaining and keeping a job; therefore, whether Indians are being equipped with the necessary skills, i.e., are they becoming more employable, is crucial to an evaluation of their position in metropolitan areas. Indians living in urban areas in 1970 had many more years of education on the whole than rural residents, including almost twice the proportion of high school graduates. By 1980, their educational levels had improved substantially nationwide. The proportion at all levels of education improved significantly, but the change among non-SMSA Indians was more dramatic than among urban Indians. Remaining in an educational institution for longer periods of time was becoming an accepted, widespread phenomenon among American Indians.

The simple proportion of individuals completing a particular number of years of schooling is not adequate as a measure of how well individuals or groups are doing compared to the majority population. Table 14.5 presents figures on delayed education, i.e., the percentage of 15-, 16-, and 17-year olds who are two or more years behind the modal grade for their age. In addition to the social stigma that may accompany the child who is considerably older than his grade cohorts, or who has been held back, is the cumulative problem of reaching a point when a student can legally leave school but still be lacking the necessary skills and credentials for moving into the job market. Later entry into the job market makes it more difficult to compete with one's age group for promotions, raises, etc. As the data in Table 14.5 indicate, there was an increase in the proportion of Indian males who were two or more years behind in school, but a decrease among Indian females. For both groups the likelihood of being behind in school followed the same pattern, improvement among Indian women and a worsening among Indian men.

Table 14.5

Delayed Education For 15 · 16 · 17 Year Old

Native Americans

	Percentage 2+ Years Behind in School				
	U.S. 1970	U.S. 1976	SMSA 1976	U.S. 1980	SMSA 1980
Males					
Native American	35	32	14.7	44	43
Majority	12	10	--	10	--
Females					
Native American	23	26	37.2	16	15
Majority	6	7	--	5	--

* From *Social Indicators of Equality for Minorities and Women,* U.S. Commission on Civil Rights, August 1978, p. 6, Table 2.1.

Native Americans in SMSA's in 1976 appeared to be considerably different than the average Native American in the nation as a whole. Indian men in SMSA's were half as likely as the average Indian male to be two or more years behind in school at these ages, while Native American women were almost half again as likely to be two or more years behind. By 1980 the likelihood of being educationally delayed among SMSA Indians closely approximated the national Indian pattern, although living in urban areas marginally improved educational progress. Native American women, and women in general, are much less likely to be educationally delayed than men. Being educationally delayed increases the likelihood of dropping out of school before graduation which makes it even more difficult to obtain many types of jobs that require high school diplomas.[10]

The years of schooling and the rate of progress are descriptive of the quantity of education received, but more important is what happens to Native Americans who attain the educational levels of the majority, attain those levels at the appropriate modal times, and move into the job market. Do they attain similar jobs, make similar amounts of money, or enjoy similar levels of prestige? These questions are of greater impact as Native Americans move closer to the levels enjoyed by majority males.

Using the Department of Labor's *Occupational Outlook Handbook,* occupations can be divided into those requiring a high school diploma and those requiring at least some college. The U.S. Commission on Civil Rights developed an indicator that revealed those individuals who were overqualified in terms of education for the jobs they were occupying .

Native American men and women high school graduates were as likely in 1980 to be in a job that required less than the educational credentials they possessed as in 1970. In 1980, Native American male high school graduates were 52 percent more likely to be in a job that did not require a high school diploma than were majority males. Native American male college graduates were more likely to be overqualified for their jobs in 1980 than in 1970, while Native American women college graduates approximated the majority population. The encouraging aspect of these data is that as the amount of education and training increases, the degree of over-qualification decreases for Indian women. The distressing aspect is that for Indian men the reverse is true. The job market appears not to be qualitatively expanding as quickly as the pool of workers.

Given the economic and educational status of urban Native

Americans, how do they actually feel about life in cities? The National Opinion Research Center (NORC) surveys provide indications that a proportion of Native Americans are persistent urban dwellers. The 1974, 1975, and 1976 NORC survey samples were combined to obtain a large enough sample of Native Americans to allow for some generalization to be made. The 1980 and 1982 NORC survey results were combined to form a second group for purposes of comparison. There is little difference between SMSA and non-SMSA Native American respondents concerning levels of satisfaction with their basic living environment except in the most recent sample with regard to satisfaction with where the respondent lived. Native Americans in SMSA's appear to be substantially less satisifed with city life than in the mid-seventies. Non-SMSA Indians have actually increased their levels of satisfaction with where they live. Clearly family and friendships provide the consistently highest levels of satisfaction; although job satisfaction has increased as a source of satisfaction, and among non-SMSA Indians, rivals family and friends as a source of satisfaction.

An additional indication of the existence of an Indian community in metropolitcan areas relates to a series of questions asked about the frequency of social interaction with several social networks. The assumption underlying the questions was that the higher the frequency of social contact with friends and relatives, the more stable the community would be; and that the more ties there were that hold the community together, the greater the sense of identity with the community would be. The difficulty was that there was no indication of where relatives lived, or what constituted a neighborhood. This was not, however, a major problem since the responses did not seem to reflect a significant variable response pattern. Consistently, relatives were the chief contact points in social networks for Native Americans. Indians who lived in non-SMSA areas, however, were consistently more likely to never socialize with friends, relatives, or go to a bar than were SMSA residents. SMSA Native Americans were much more likely to frequent a bar than non-SMSA Indians. Non-SMSA Indians may simply not have had bars nearby to patronize, but may have indulged in drinking as a social activity outside of a formal establishment. Non-SMSA Indians were less likely to drink than SMSA Indians, but appeared to be much more likely to drink to excess. These responses support the idea that drinking among non-SMSA Indians was more likely to occur outside of a bar or a tavern and perhaps in a less social situation which might encourage more consumption. Combining these responses with those on going to a bar (Table 14.6), we can conclude that alcohol consumption was much more prevalent among SMSA Indians; while among those non-SMSA Indians who drank, excessive drinking was a serious problem.

Table 14.6

Incidence of Drinking Among Native Americans

(NORC 1980/82)

		SMSA	Non-SMSA
Ever drink alcoholic beverages	Yes	76%	50%
	No	24%	50%
Ever drink too much	Yes	26.3%	45.5%
	No	73.7%	54.5%

The picture that emerges is one of a rather satisfied, relatively established, socially active Indian community in metropolitan centers across the country. The pattern is not uniform, nor clearly established, but the bulk of the available evidence supports the contention that healthy Indian communities are present in metropolitan areas.

At a national level, the prevailing ideology in the early 1980s for addressing the needs of low income groups and to generally stimulate the economy was one of "trickle-down"; remove restrictions on economic activity, encourage those with capital to invest and expand that capital, and the resultant expanded economy would benefit everyone including the most disadvantaged. The results of this approach are not totally clear, but there is not much evidence to support the theory in practice. Indeed, the bulk of the evidence on the status of lower income people is that their socio-economic position is worse since 1980. The cutbacks in federal support for economic development compound the situation. H. W. Arndt wrote that: "No reputable development economist ever, explicitly, entertained any such theory ... 'trickle-down' is a myth which should be exposed and laid to rest."[11] In his examination of the historical basis for the "trickle-down" theory, Arndt argues that the leveling forces that created a more equitable distribution of economic benefits were not primarily market forces. Rather, political struggle and political change preceded most movements toward more even distribution, and not without often prolonged periods of serious friction and tensions.[12] Our evidence suggests that some degree of political struggle is occurring but that the movement is more in the direction of a more uneven distribution of economic benefits.

In the late 1970s efforts at economic development on reservations, and the attendant creation of jobs, created a reverse migration pattern between 1978 and 1980. On some reservations over 50 percent of the job openings were filled by urban Indians coming home, while Indian employment opportunities in nearby urban centers were going unfilled.[13] This phenomenon supported the earlier finding that a substantial proportion of urban Native Americans would return to the reservation — to home — if employment opportunities existed there. It was suggested, with substantial justification, that the Indian controlled reservation programs and the Indian operated urban centers, even if they had not achieved very efficient or successful records, were building a pool of skilled people as future resources and they contributed a considerable psychological boost to the Indian community as it struggled to improve its socio-economic status.[14]

This study has relied on very limited data to describe the impact of major federal policies and programs on urban Native Americans. The 1970 Census of Population, the 1976 Survey of Income and Education, and the 1980 Census of Population are the most recent nationwide surveys that have a large enough sample of American Indians to enable generalizations to be made about their social and economic status nationwide. For the most part, the Census and the SIE data are comparable, but the manner in which the data, especially the Census data, are presented restricts many possible comparisons.[15]

For Indians in general, and urban Indians in particular, there is a clear need for increased efforts to improve their socio-economic position. More money will help; however, it will not be sufficient. The emergence of new programs, e.g. job training programs, has been a boon for Indians; not solely because of the additional money, but also because of the additional options and the additional opportunity for Indians to gain skills and training. The programs have also helped create and facilitate a strong pattern of migration between reservations and urban centers. As the American Indian Policy Review Commission found:[16]

This decision that Indians should be moved great distances for the sake of work was modified by Indian attitudes. The migration patterns evolved in Indians themselves have tended to take them no further from the reservation than is necessary to obtain basic work and housing. Urban concentrations of Indians . . . are part of a migration pattern that includes the reservation, so that there is a balance struck between on- and off-reservation life. Several studies have examined this arrangement and have concluded that the ability to maintain close contact with the reservation while earning a living beyond its boundaries reflects an important development, because to some extent, it combines the social and economic facets that have been split apart by the migration to distant cities.

The urban Indians are learning: They are supporting the creation of urban Indian centers; they are establishing their rights to federal services; they are creating urban Indian communities with close ties to the reservation; and they are increasingly using the pluralist system to their own advantage without having to abandon their traditional culture. And although there are some disadvantages to these new patterns, there is also more hope and more freedom. The nomadic migration patterns of the past are re-appearing, but but Indians no longer follow the buffalo, the beaver, or the good earth; they follow the paved highways.

NOTES

1. Elaine Neils, *Reservation to City: Indian Migration and Federal Relocation* (Chicago: University of Chicago, Department of Geography, Research Paper No. 131, 1971), p. 2.

2. Russel L. Barsh, "The Nature and Spirit of North American Political Systems," *American Indian Quarterly, 10 (1986): 181.*

3. Act of February 8, 1887, chap. 119, 24 stat. 389.

4. 67 Stat. 132 (1953).

5. Alan L. Sorkin, *American Indians and Federal Aid* (Washington, D.C.: The Brookings Institution, 1971), pp. 104-105.

6. *Ibid.,* p. 106.

7. One of the biggest problems in addressing issues of Indian urbanization is the difficulty in obtaining accurate reporting of the number of Indians who reside in a given location, how long they have been there and other relevant information. In an effort to improve the accuracy of the data on Indians, the Bureau of the Census moved to self-identification for the decennial census; but even with this change in reporting technique, the 1980 Census was criticized for undercounting Indians.

8. *Characteristics of the Population, Part 1, United States Summary,* U.S. Department of Commerce, Bureau of the Census, 1970 Census Population, Section 2, Table 245.

9. Polaris Research and Development, *The Indian and Native American Employment and Training Program: Operations Under the Job Training Partnership Act,* San Francisco, CA (January 1985), pp. 3-24, 3-25.

10. U.S. Commission on Civil Rights, *Social Indicators of Equality for Minorities and Women,* August 1978, p. 7.

11. H.W. Arndt, "The 'Trickle-Down' Myth," *Economic Development and Cultural Change,* 32 (October 1983): 1.

12. Ibid. p. 8.

13. Interview with Dean Brasgalla, Department of Labor liaison officer with Bureau of Indian Affairs, Red Lake Indian Reservation, July, 1978, and Interview with Mr. Norm DeWeaver, Center for Community Change, Washington, D.C., July, 1979 and August, 1985.

14. Alan L. Sorkin, *The Urban American Indian* (Lexington, MA: D.C. Heath and Company, 1978), p. 110.

15. See Paul T. Manka, Customer Services Branch, Data User Services Division, Bureau of the Census, *Micro Data File User's Guide* (Washington, D.C.: Government Printing Office, 1978).

16. AIPRC, *Report on Urban and Rural Non-Reservation Indians, op cit.,* p. 34.

Chapter 15
Early Twentieth Century
Hopi Population
Elliot McIntire

Except where a great deal of acculturation had already occurred, it has been very difficult to examine the demographic characteristics of any American Indian society in detail. Early ethnographic studies were primarily concerned with material and non-material culture of the pre-contact period and paid little attention to demographic features. In part, this was due to the virtual impossibility of obtaining accurate information about a period often several decades in the past, and in part because the importance of such data was not realized until comparatively recently. In recent years there has been a rapid increase in the number of studies which examine past demographic features. Most of this research has dealt with groups in western Europe and the United States, since records which reveal demographic data are most readily available for these areas. Few if any of these studies have dealt with American Indians.

Manuscript census materials for 1900 and 1910 now make it possible to carry out detailed studies of that period concerning the few tribes which were still largely unacculturated. Most of these were located in the Southwest, primarily New Mexico and Arizona. Almost uniquely among Indians in the United States, the puebloan peoples of the Southwest were able to retain at least some of their traditional lands, and to maintain much of their traditional lifeways into the twentieth century. Of these groups the Hopi of northern Arizona were probably the least acculturated at the beginning of the twentieth century, because of their isolation.

During the late nineteenth century, the Hopi, like most American Indian tribes, steadily declined in population. It was widely assumed by both the general public and by government agencies that Indian societies would disappear within a few decades at most. As the populations died off and social systems broke down, the few remaining individuals would be assimilated into the dominant culture of the United States.

Such a view, of course, turned out to be erroneous. Around the beginning of the twentieth century many tribes began to increase in population, some at a very rapid rate. The exact time of this reversal in population trends varied from tribe to tribe, and the details are often sketchy, largely because it is very difficult to obtain detailed demographic information that would enable study of the events of this critical period.

Although the Hopi are one of the most studied groups in this country, (a recent bibliography of Hopi studies contains nearly 3000 entries),[1] only a handful of these studies deal with the demographic characteristics of the tribe. Those which do exist are often excellent, but examine only one, or occasionally two or three villages, and are confined to a single time period, usually in the 1920s or 1930s, utilizing data obtained during a single summer field season.[2] As such they can provide useful insights into Hopi social organization or kinship systems, but tell us little about longitudinal changes in Hopi demography.

The recent release of the manuscript censuses for 1900 and 1910,[3] and the manuscript materials in J.W. Fewkes field notes, preserved in the Smithsonian's National Anthropological Archives, now make it possible to examine the demographic characteristics of the Hopi for this time period, particularly those living on First Mesa.[4] The Fewkes field notes include sketch maps of the three First Mesa villages, and detailed maps of First Mesa for a slightly earlier date exist in the Mindeleff brothers' studies of puebloan architecture.[5]

The manuscript census materials provide masses of data previously unavailable for any Indian tribe. First, they attempt to enumerate the entire population, rather than simply one or two villages. Second, they include a large amount of information on each individual, and third, because they were taken at regular intervals, they enable us to trace changes through time, both village by village and for the population as a whole. Such analysis could be extended to the level of family units, but this is beyond the scope of this study. It is my intention to examine the size of the Hopi population in total and village by village from the late 1890s to the early 1910s, and to focus particularly on the three villages of the First Mesa Hano, Sichimovi, and Walpi, for which preliminary work for 1900 has already been done.[6] Although the data are more plentiful for the three First Mesa villages, evidence suggests that most of the generalizations made apply to the other Hopi villages as well.

By 1900 the Hopi had only just begun to be strongly influenced by American society, while virtually every other tribe had already suffered serious dislocation as a result of American expansion. For many this meant physical removal from their traditional homelands. At the very least it meant a radical restructuring of tribal society, and in many cases a nearly complete breakdown of traditional systems. This was not true for the Hopi, however.

Because they inhabited an area that was not conducive to American-style agriculture, and because no significant mineral resources had been found near them, the Hopi were able to remain in their original homeland. Some of the villages have been continuously occupied on or near their current locations for nearly a thousand years. Because of this isolation, there had been very little disruption of traditional social systems by 1900. By the 1890s, a few Hopi children had begun to attend school at nearby Keams Canyon, and a handful had been sent to boarding schools in Phoenix, Chilico, Oklahoma, and Riverside, California. However, as late as the 1890s it was impossible to find any adult English — speaking Hopi, even on First Mesa, which was the closest to the school and agency, and was slightly more acculturated than the other Hopi villages.

Missionary activity, which undermined the social structure of many tribes, was notably unsuccessful among the Hopi. Unlike their cultural counterparts in New Mexico, the Rio Grande Pueblos, the Hopi villages were not greatly influenced by Christian mission efforts during the Spanish colonial period. No permanent missions among the Hopi were reestablished after the Pueblo Revolt of 1680. Even after Arizona become American territory little effort was made to missionize the Hopi. It was several years before missionaries arrived to establish the first school for the Hopi, with little success. In addition to the Presbyterians, who were involved with the school at Keams Canyon, which was operated only intermittently until 1887, Baptist and Mennonite missions were established by the 1890s at Second and Third Mesas, respectively. Mormon settlers in the area made repeated attempts to spread their faith among the Hopi. All such efforts met with little success. Well into the twentieth century only a very small minority of the Hopi had become Christian, and, it could be argued, this is true to the present time.

It was 1869 before an Indian Agent for the Hopi was appointed, and no agent lived near the Hopi until 1874. Even then the agency was established at Keams Canyon, nearly fifteen miles from the nearest village, and the post was often vacant. Only in the closing years of the nineteenth century was there regular contact between the Hopi and the U.S. government through the Office of Indian Affairs.[7]

As a result of their isolation, the Hopi who were enumerated by the 1900 and 1910 census takers reflected to a very large degree the lifestyle, economy, ceremonial and kinship systems, house types, clothing, and language of their ancestors. Few other tribes were so unaffected by American society in 1900 as the Hopi. As famed photographer Edward Curtis observed:[8]

> There is a subtle charm about the Hopi and their high-perched homes that have made (my) work particularly delightful. This was especially so in earlier years (1900-1910) when their manner of life indicated comparatively slight contact with civilization. Certainly no other place in the United States afforded a like opportunity to observe native Americans living much as they did when the Spanish explorers first visited the desert land of our Southwest.

Therefore, the data provided by the census give us a unique glimpse into an essentially "aboriginal" society. Earlier censuses do not provide comparable information for other tribes because it was not until the late nineteenth century that detailed demographic information was collected by the U.S. Census. For instance, in 1850 for the first time the names and ages of minor children were recorded on the Schedule of Population: Indians, unless taxed were generally not enumerated at all. Some census material on Indians was collected in 1880 (although not in the Arizona Territory), and only in 1890 were "Indians not Taxed" systematically enumerated. Unfortunately, the manuscript materials from that census were nearly all lost in a fire in the 1920s. Of those censuses which might be useful in a study of American Indian groups, only the 1900 and 1910 materials have been released, and by 1900 most tribes had been greatly changed by culture contact.

HOPI CENSUS MATERIALS

In 1900 the census takers collected a variety of information about each individual on special schedules for Indians. While the format in 1910 was slightly different, the information collected was essentially the same. The census taker visited each household, and for each inhabitant listed name, age, and relationship to the head of household. Data were collected regarding occupation, education, type of house, proportion of non-Indian blood, and the state of birth and tribal affiliation for each individual and their parents. These last several items were recorded on special census forms for Indians.

In the case of the Hopi, much of this information is of limited value. For example, since the Hopi had been quite isolated there was very little intermarriage, and virtually every individual is listed as being full-blooded, with both parents Hopi, born in the Arizona Territory; However, a few individuals do not fit this pattern. A few marriages with Navajos or with other Pueblos, such as Zuni, are recorded, and at least one woman on First Mesa is listed as an Oklahoma Indian. This anomaly is explained by the notation that the husband, a Hopi, had gone to school at Chilico Indian School in Oklahoma, and presumably met his wife there. One can only wonder at the impact of such a marriage on a family in a matrilineal, matrilocal, traditional society.

The question of the age of respondents is of course a crucial one for any detailed demographic study. An uncritical examination of the returns for 1900 for the Hopi could easily lead the researcher to faulty conclusions about the precision of the data included. Exact birth dates (month and year) are given for each individual. However, it should be obvious that no records for these dates exist, and the Hopi themselves were little concerned about such concepts. Clearly the birth years listed were simply the enumerators' best guess as to the age of the individual, perhaps assisted by questioning about such things as the earliest major event remembered by the individual. Month of birth was probably even more the result of the enumerator's perceived need to fill out the form completely. Indeed, analysis of the months listed shows a decided preference for some months, while others are generally neglected.[9]

The 1910 manuscript census included a modified schedule for the enumeration of Indians, very similar to the 1900 schedule. However, in 1910 the difficulties of determining the age and date of birth were explicitly recognized, and some additional questions regarding marital status were included, such as number of times married, if marriage was polygamous, and if so, whether the wives were sisters. Some additional information about education was also included.

The shortcoming of estimating the age of individuals was minimized in the case of younger nuclear families, where the relative age of children and their approximate chronological age could be estimated by inspection. The age of parents, and especially of older members of the household, however, continued to be quite imprecise.

The problem of listing month and year of birth for Indian respondents was eliminated by the formulation of the enumeration forms for 1910, which only called for the individuals' age at their last birthday. This was only a partial solution. The listing of year of birth was still deceptively precise. However, by 1910 another trend was at work, which partially offsets this problem. For younger individuals, who could be expected to have attended school at some period of their life, school records would give a more exact indication of age, at least to years, and many Hopis less than, say, twenty years of age in 1910, would have some fairly accurate knowledge of their own age. Even so, there is considerable lack of precision, well illustrated by the case of Albert Yava, whose autobiography gives his date of birth as 1888, while the 1900 and 1910 censuses give 1892.[10] Estimates of the age of the well known potter Nampeyo, born sometime during the 1880s, vary by as much as seven years.

Some indication of the approximate nature of age estimates can be gathered by comparing the age of siblings or parents and children living in different households. This cannot be done on the basis of the census material alone, since inter-household familial relationships can only be determined by kinship data provided by Fewkes family/clan lists. Comparison of these two sources indicates that the age of individuals can not be used except as very rough approximations.

Another, and perhaps even more frustrating aspect of the census materials is the difficulty of tracing individuals from one census to the next. In both 1900 and 1910 the majority of individuals were simply listed by the enumerator's transcription of the Hopi name. Since Hopi contains a number of sounds and sound clusters which are uncommon in English, this often resulted in widely differing transcriptions. This makes it difficult to compare documents, because each recorder used highly idiosyncratic transcription systems, which have little resemblance to each other.[11] Examples of the variety of transcriptions are given in Table 15.1.

In some cases the difficulty is increased by the occasional use of English names for some individuals. When Hopi children went to school they were often simply assigned "English" names. Sometimes these names were retained, and can be identified with specific individuals, but in other cases the name was used only in school, and was quickly abandoned when school was done. Since the enumerators were often familiar with these names[12] they were

Table 15.1

Examples of Transcriptions of Names

Stephen (1890-93)	Fewkes (1900)	Abbott (1900)	Thayer (1910)	Lowie (1915)
	Koiyabi	Cooybai	Quoyabi	Qoyavi
	Talawinu	Talawena	Talawina	Silas
	Tcosro	Chuzro	Emma Chooro	Emma
	Tuwanainimu	Tawanginema	Tiwangainima	Towanainomo
	Tae	Tieh	Taih	Tai
	Cikuli	Seculah	Siklu	Ciaqale
	Tcuahoya	Tanuhuyu		David Chaohoya
	Ee	Ewetsauwa	Aechanwa	
Navayoiyava	Yeba	Yeabah	Albert Yava	
	Koyowaiamu	Harry	Harry Kianwaima	

It is clear that many individuals were recorded by several different visitors, but the names given are so divergent that identification as the same person is impossible.

entered in the census materials, but, unless there is other information, it is often impossible to equate these "names" with the Hopi names found in other records. Again, Albert Yava provides a case in point. At birth he was named Nuvayoiyava, but when he went to school this was shortened to Yava, and he was arbitrarily given the name "Albert." At his initiation into the One Horn Society, he received the name Eutawisa. However, Albert Yava persisted in common useage.[13] There are also such cases as 'Tom Sawyer,' listed in the 1900 census as a Paiute 'slave,' and who is found in no later records. Since there is no kin linkage for him, it is impossible to determine anything more about him.

FAMILY STRUCTURE AND MARITAL STATUS

Examination of the census data also reveals some interesting aspects of the question of marriage and divorce among the Hopi, although it is perhaps more accurate to say that it is government policy and white attitudes toward the Indians which are laid bare.

Early government policy toward many western tribes, and certainly toward the Hopi, was for many years strongly influenced by religious groups. Most early contacts between the U.S. government and the Hopi were through the Presbyterian Church which, for many years, provided not only missionaries to the Hopi, but organized and operated the schools at First Mesa and Keams Canyon, and not infrequently nominated the Indian Agent as well. This arrangement often created difficulties.[14]

Even when agents were not selected by the churches, they tended to reflect late nineteenth century morality, and were not generally sympathetic to the culture of the Indians and their desire to maintain traditional behaviors and social customs. Although a few agents recognized the conflicts this created, their general attitude was to try to turn their wards into carbon copies of the standard Americans of the day. This almost always entailed suppression of the native languages, prohibition of religious practices, and restructuring of social and familial units. This is in contrast to the attitude of anthropologists and other scholars, who were interested in studying these societies before they disappeared, and in some cases even made some efforts to help preserve elements of native cultures.[15] The conflict between the expectations and values of the Anglo population (Agents, missionaries, school personnel, etc.) and those of the Hopi shows up most clearly in the census materials in the data on marriage.

The data are clearly biased by the assumptions and attitudes of the enumerators regarding family structure, marriage, divorce, and tribal affiliation. Some of this is due to the enumerators' ignorance of, or refusal to recognize, Hopi family structure. In each case, the older adult male in each household is listed as "Head of Household," and all other residents are listed with their relationship to him. This can create some odd situations, since, in Hopi society, houses are owned by the matrilineal clan, and the "Head of Household" is the senior woman in the family group, which often consisted of her daughters and their husbands and children. The sons-in-law had no important role in that household, but returned to their mothers' home for clan social and religious activities.

Another example also illustrates the enumerators' confusion about the Hopi. In 1900 all residents of First Mesa (with a handful of exceptions noted above), are listed as Hopi, even though it was widely recognized by scholars and presumably by the Agency staff (census takers were often Agency employees) that the residents of one of the three villages on First Mesa, Hano, were in fact not Hopi at all, but rather Tewa speaking Indians, who had moved to the Hopi area from the Rio Grande Valley only a few centuries ago.

In defense of the census takers, however, it must be noted that the village of Hano represents a very complex social and demographic situation. Like the Hopi, the Tewa were (and are) matrilocal, and many of the women of Hano had taken Hopi husbands, mostly from the other two First Mesa villages. Although the language of the home continued to be Tewa, and clan and tribal affiliation, being matrilineal, remained Tewa, the census takers, operating with their own cultural filter, listed the adult male in each family unit as "Head of Household." In many cases this was a Hopi man. Although this cultural perception results in a number of very peculiar listings in the manuscript census, knowledge of the culture makes it possible to note, and correct for it.

Similarly, enumerator Sarah Abbott did not record a single divorced person in 1900, although examination of years of marriage and age of children makes it quite clear that divorce and remarriage was fairly common.[16] Anthropological data also indicate that divorce was fairly common, and quite easy in traditional Hopi society. Mischa Titiev's data for Third Mesa (collected in the 1930s), indicated that at least one-third of all adults had been married more than once, and in one case, eight times.[17]

Clearly Miss Abbott simply was not willing to recognize the existence of divorce, and did not record its occurrence. Unmarried adults were invariably recorded as "widowed," although the Hopi attitude toward divorce had been known for many years. A letter from the Hopi Agent in 1882 to Dr. Yarrow of the Bureau of American Ethnology notes that "Their notion of the marital relations between husband and wife are not as good as they should be, as they are often broken up, frequently from merely the incompatibility of tempers, the only cause of separation."[18]

Interestingly, the manuscript census for 1910 provides far more information in this regard, although the enumerator for the Hopi was a missionary, who, one might assume, would have strong negative feelings about divorce. In the column indicating Marital Status enumerator Thayer marked each individual as either "S" (single), "M" (married), "Wd" (widowed), or "D" (divorced). In addition, he included numerical subscripts to indicate the number of each if more than one. While the instructions to enumerators only call for this in the case of marriages, Thayer extended the practice to Widowed and Divorced as well. It is interesting to note that the instructions to enumerators for the Indian schedule in 1880 had included the statement, "Marriage and Divorce will be entered in accordance with Indian customs and not the laws of civilization.''[19] This statement was dropped from later census schedules.

It was very rare, based on these census records, to find an adult Hopi who had never been married. In fact, many late teens had already begun their married lives. Table 15.2. indicates the relative proportions of married, widowed, divorced and single adults in 1910. An analysis of the subscripts indicates that approximately twenty percent had been married more than once, although this need not involve divorce, since adult mortality rates were fairly high. The number who had been married more than twice was less than five percent, and a few individuals were recorded as having gone through several marriages. Only about nine percent of the adult population was listed as divorced at the time of the census, while about thirteen percent were listed as widowed, and six percent as single. The enumerators in 1910 clearly made an effort to accurately record the marital history of those enumerated, which enables us to form a much more accurate picture of the society at the turn of the century.

POPULATION CHANGE 1900-1910

It has generally been assumed, based on the available population figures, that the Hopi population, after a period of decline throughout the nineteenth century, stabilized at just under 2000 at the beginning of the twentieth century, and then began a gradual

Table 15.2

Married/Widowed/Divorced 1910

	Married	Divorced	Widowed	Single (20 or older)	Total Population
Hano	71	5	13	7	189
Sichomovi	89	6	18	5	224
Walpi	77	8	15	8	199
Shipaulovi	47	12	6	4	120
Shongopovi	105	12	13	3	352
Mishongnovi	83	21	21	11	288
Bacobi	45	2	6	4	120
Oraibi	146	17	26	13	418

Data from U.S. Manuscript Census, 1910.

increase sometime between 1910 and 1920. Indeed, there is nothing in the population figures which have been available that would contradict this assessment. In fact, the only reason to suspect any problem with the census figures has been the recognition that some of the Hopi, strongly opposed to white intrusions in their society, avoided enumeration by the census, just as this faction refused to send their children to the schools being opened by the U.S. government. However, most researchers have assumed that the unenumerated fraction gradually declined through time, and therefore would, if anything, contribute to an apparent population increase.

The manuscript cenus for 1900 and 1910 cast a different light on this issue, however. Analysis of the data by village and by age group within each village shows that there was a substantial increase in population totals for each of the villages on First and Second Mesas, due to a large number of children born during the decade. Parenthetically, one might note that there was a substantial number of young children enumerated in the 1900 census as well, but in the absence of data for 1890 it is impossible to determine whether population totals started to increase before 1900 or not. Such an increase, at least for First Mesa, seems unlikely, however, since there are indications of substantial mortality due to a smallpox epidemic in the late 1890s. Table 15.3 shows the population change by village between 1900 and 1910. Note that, if only First and Second Mesa are considered, total population increased by only 17 percent during the decade, with village increases ranging from 9 percent (Walpi) to 27 percent (Mishongnovi). Actual increases may not have been so dramatic, however, since some 125 Hopi children were enumerated at Keams Canyon School in 1900 but were included with their home villages in 1910. Virtually all of these children were probably from First and Second Mesa. Nevertheless, even if *all* of these children are included with First and Second Mesa for 1900, there is still an increase in total population of nearly 4 percent.

When the population for Third Mesa is considered, the picture becomes more obscure. For a number of reasons discussed below, Third Mesa must be viewed as a single unit when comparing populations. In 1900 its population is given as 767, while the 1910 population is only 702. There is no evidence of serious epidemics or other factors that would account for such a dramatic decrease in population. There was, however considerable social turmoil which resulted in the establishment of several new villages. Close examination of the data makes it clear that one of these new

Table 15.3

Hopi Census, 1900 & 1910

Village	1900	1910	Change	Percentage
First Mesa	**520**	**606**	**+ 86**	**+ 14**
Walpi	178	195	+ 17	+ 9
Sichomovi	174	224	+ 50	+ 29
Hano	168	187	+ 19	+ 11
Second Mesa	**534**	**628**	**+ 94**	**+ 17**
Shipaulovi	109	120	+ 11	+ 10
Shongopovi	208	232	+ 24	+ 12
Mishongnovi	217	276	+ 59	+ 27
Third Mesa	**767**	**702**	**−65**	**−8**
Oraibi/New Oraibi	767	403	−364	−47
Bakobi	--	120		
Moenkopi	--	179		
Keams Canyon				
School	125	--		
Total	**1957**	**1936**	**−21**	**−1**

Data from U.S. Manuscript Censuses for 1900 and 1910

villages was not included in the totals for 1910. As far as I know, this omission has never been noted by earlier studies of the Hopi. Since we know from other sources that this village, Hotevila, was of substantial size, it is clear that even on Third Mesa population had increased during the decade, although the size of that increase is unknown. An attempt to estimate the size of Hotevila is included below.

For the moment, however, if one assumes that the population increase for Third Mesa was approximately the same as that of the other two mesas (between ten and fifteen percent), then the 1910 population would have been about 840-880, or a total for all Hopi of approximately 2030-2070, rather than the 1936 given by the census totals. Even if one assumes a much lower increase of only about five percent, there would still be a noticeable increase in the population of Third Mesa. However, examination of the probable age structure of Hotevila (see below) indicates that the figure of percent is likely to be much closer to the actual figure.

THIRD MESA POPULATION CHANGE

It may seem paradoxical that examination of the 1910 manuscript census leaves us with less certain knowledge about the size of the population on Third Mesa than we had before, but such is the case.

Until the release of the manuscript materials, it was assumed that each of the censuses had enumerated essentially all of the resident population, although it was probable that some of the "hostiles" had not been counted. Therfore, the nearly identical figures for total population in 1900 and 1910 was thought to represent a low point in the growth curve, with population increase coming only after 1910. Close examination of the manuscript materials shows that this was not the case.

Village by village comparison shows that each of the villages on both First and Second Mesa had increased substantially between the two censuses, while the total for Third Mesa dropped sharply. But when the figures for Third Mesa are examined, the reason for this becomes clear. The population which had clustered in a single village in 1900 (Oraibi, with its subsidiary New Oraibi) was divided into five units by 1910 (Oraibi, New Oraibi, Moencopi, Bacobi, and Hotevila) and one of the villages Hotevila, was not enumerated!

This should not be at all surprising, given the history of this group *vis a vis* the American authorities. There is a long series of entries by the agents for the Hopi during the late nineteenth century to the effect that "the Hopi on Third Mesa still refuse to be enumerated." It was, in fact, the faction most opposed to cooperation with the U.S. Government who were responsible for the move to establish the new village of Hotevila in 1906. It is therefore not unexpected that the residents of that village would decline to be counted by the 1910 census. (One can only speculate as to how many of them may have also avoided enumeration in 1900.)

In 1900 virtually all of the population of Third Mesa was resident in Oraibi, although a significant fraction maintained homes at least seasonally in the valley below the mesa, in the area which became known as New Oraibi, and some also spent at least part of the year near their fields at Moencopi, some forty miles west of Oraibi. Two individuals entered returns for the village of Oraibi in 1900, Anna Ritter and Herman Kaupmeier. Examination of the lists makes it clear that Ritter, who enumerated 559 individuals, was in Oraibi itself, while Kaupmeier, enumerating 208 Hopis, plus a few Anglos and several Navajo families, was in New Oraibi and nearby areas.

By 1910 internal dissension and the declining threat to outlying locations due to pacification of the Navajo and Utes had led to major changes. Most important was a split within Oraibi between progressive and conservative factions (usually labeled "friendlies" and "hostiles" by Anglos), with the conservative faction withdrawing and founding a new village, Hotevila, some miles north of Oraibi. A subsequent split within this group led to establishment of yet another village, Bacobi, between Oraibi and Hotevila.

So by 1910 the situation on Third Mesa was much more complex than it had been in 1900. In addition to the establishment of the two new villages of Hotevila and Bacobi to the north of Oraibi, many of the Oraibi residents who had previously spent the growing season in Moencopi had taken up permanent residence there, which made Moencopi socially and politically an additional Third Mesa village, although located physically some distance away. The 1910 census, however reflects only some of these changes. Enumeration schedules are included for Oraibi (418) (although there is no separate enumeration for New Oraibi), Bacobi (120), and "Hopi Indian Village" (179) on the Coconino County roll, which can only be Moencopi, although it is not listed by name. There is no listing for Hotevila in the 1910 census.

Population totals for the Hopi for 1910 are therefore clearly incomplete, lacking data for one of the new villages. Comparisons of the population totals for 1900 and 1910 are, as a result, quite misleading. Although they would seem to indicate that the total population of the Hopi was essentially static during the decade, with a sharp drop on Third Mesa, it now becomes clear that, in fact, there had been a substantial increase in total population. Just how large this increase was is difficult to estimate. The attempt below at making a reasonable estimate of this number is admittedly subject to criticism, and is based on several assumptions, not all of which may be justified. Nonetheless, it represents a substantial advance on what was previously known.

It is my belief that the population of the new village of Hotevila in 1910 was approximately 450. This is based on the following assumptions, in decreasing order of certainty. First, there were no serious demographic disasters effecting the mesa during the decade. No epidemics are known for this period, for example, although smallpox resulted in many deaths on First and Second Mesas during the previous decade, and influenza seriously effected all mesas in 1917-18. Second, that there was little net migration of Third Mesa residents during the decade. It is known that there was occasional intermarriage between the mesas, but Fewkes clan data for First Mesa in 1900 indicate that this involved only a handful of individuals, and this is probably true of Third Mesa as well, and other evidence shows almost no Hopi living off the reservation as late as the 1930s. Third, and perhaps least defensible, I assume that the censuses for 1900 and 1910 were both essentially complete and accurate (except for not enumerating Hotevila in 1910). Independent listing in Fewkes materials indicate that the totals for First Mesa were quite accurate. We must assume equal accuracy for other villages.

Given these assumptions we can compare the total population for Third Mesa from the 1900 census by age group with the total enumerated population by age group for 1910. If both are fairly accurate, and allowing for some mortality, especially in the older population, there should be a noticeable, and otherwise unexplained, drop in population for each cohort. This "missing" population should represent the proportion of the population which had moved to Hotevila. While age designations are not completely accurate, comparison of the total populations of First and Second Mesas in 1900 and 1910 indicate that, overall, they were fairly close.

In fact, comparing cohorts for Third Mesa does reveal a substantial drop in most, although not all, age groups. Totalling these differences, while allowing for some mortality, gives a "missing" population of about 250. In order to estimate the number of children born between 1900 and 1910 the number of women between fifteen and thirty-five in the "missing" population was totalled, and proportions identical to those for women in the same age groups on First and Second Mesa and the rest of Third Mesa were applied. If we assume that the fertility rate for women in Hotevila was about the same as for the rest of the Hopi population, then the number of children born to them during the decade would have been about 200, giving a total population for Hotevila of 450.

This total seems quite reasonable, and is supported by some other approaches to this problem. For instance, First Mesa population increased by some 14 percent during the decade, while Second Mesa increased by 17 percent, while using the census figures. Third Mesa population *declined* by some 8 percent. Since there is no known reason for such a decline, it must represent the uncounted population of Hotevila. It should be emphasized at this point that the fact that Hotevila was not enumerated in 1910 has not been previously known, and the population drop was therefore quite inexplicable. If, on the other hand, we assume that Hotevila had a population of about 450 in 1910, then the total population of Third Mesa, rather than decreasing, *increased* substantially during the decade. The estimate of 450 for Hotevila may be a bit high, but a population of at least 400 for the village seems justified, and may have been somewhat higher.

POLACCA

Although not as obscure as the situation at Hotevila, the growth of the First Mesa village of Polacca also creates a number of difficulties. Since this new settlement was not a 'traditional' village, scholars took little notice of it, and since many of its residents also maintained mesa-top houses, which they regarded as their 'true' residences, the census also failed to distinguish this new village.

Although there are occasional references to the development of the settlement that later became known as Polacca in the valley below First Mesa beginning in the late 1880s, there are no indications of its size. In part, this is due to the nature of this settlement. For many years, these valley houses represented second homes for families who considered their place of residence to be one of the mesa-top villages. These homes were frequently occupied only seasonally, and even after families took up year round residence they still considered their "official" residence to be on the mesa. All religious ceremonies were held on the mesa, for example. Polacca never developed a ceremonial cycle of its own. Since membership and participation in these ceremonies was vital to the life of the Hopi, individuals would maintain their links to the mesa-top, even though they might never actually live there.

At the time of the 1900 census, it is likely that virtually all residence in Polacca was seasonal, although a few families may have been in year round residence. Since the enumerator did not identify First Mesa residents' location by village, the location of individual families must be interpolated from Fewkes' sketch maps and kinship lists. Since Fewkes was not interested in Polacca, he gave no indication of residence there, and the population of Polacca can only be interpreted from a careful study of the census roles, largely by tracing the path of the enumerator through the villages. When this is done one finds a series of census entries listing people known from Fewkes data to live in each of the three villages, in apparent random sequence, as if the enumerator was jumping from village to village. These clearly must represent families living in the valley (Polacca). Given the limitations of interpreting this information, I am reluctant to make very definite statements about the population of Polacca in 1900. In an earlier study I indicated that it seemed that at least seven to ten families, totalling forty to fifty individuals were living in Polacca, and that the total might be as much as twenty-four households with up to 125 individuals.[20] (There is some evidence that up to eight families had built at least seasonal homes on the valley floor by 1890, and the agent at the time thought an additional forty (individuals?) could be induced to move down from the mesa if they were given some assistance).[21]

The data for 1910 are a bit more precise, in that three villages of enumeration are indicated for First Mesa. Although only Tewa (Hano), Sichimovi, and Walpi are listed, some of the sheets are headed "Sichimovi and Scattered," which must indicate, based on plotting the path of the enumerator, those houses in Polacca. (The most accessible trail from Polacca to the mesa-top leads to Sichimovi.) These figures indicate that in 1910 some fifteen households were located in the valley, with a total of eighty-five persons. If we accept the more conservative estimate for 1900, we can estimate that the population of Polacca roughly doubled during the decade. We should note that a similar trend also occured on the other mesas, particularly at Third Mesa, but the lack of specific information on the location of families, partially due to the non-enumeration of families which moved to Hotevila, make it difficult to assess the importance of valley floor settlement at Second or Third Mesa in 1910.

CONCLUSIONS

Because of the availability of the manuscript censuses for 1900 and 1910 it is now possible to make much more precise statements about the size of the Hopi population at the turn of the century. Far from the stagnant situation described in early studies, it is now clear that there were substantial changes taking place during this period, both in the size of the total population, and also in the location of those individuals, with several new villages appearing, while older villages, with the exception of Oraibi, increased in size. Table 15.4 thus represents the first accurate assessment of the Hopi population at the turn of the century, as well as an indication of the approximate sizes of two villages for which no data have previously been available.

It has always been very difficult to make precise statements about the demographic characteristics of groups for which detailed census materials are not available, and American Indian societies are no exception to this statement. Because most tribes were

Table 15.4

Estimated Hopi Population 1900-1910

Village	1900	1910
Hano	158	182
Sichomovi	149	154
Walpi	168	185
Polacca	45	85
First Mesa	**520**	**606**
Shipaulovi	109	120
Shongopovi	208	232
Mishongnovi	217	276
Second Mesa	**534**	**628**
Oraibi	667	253
New Oraibi	100	150
Bacobi	—	120
Hotevila	—	450
Moenkopi	—	179
Third Mesa	**767**	**1160**
Keams Canyon School	125	
Total	**1946**	**2346**

Data from U.S. Manuscript Censuses, 1900 and 1910, and other sources described in the text.

greatly acculturated before the U.S. Census began to collect detailed information on them, and we lack other sources, such as parish records, which have allowed the reconstruction of a number of communities in western Europe for which there are no census materials, we have been forced to speculate, and to deal in sweeping generalities whenever demographic statements are made. The material examined here enables us, for the first time, to take a careful look at the population change of an essentially unacculturated American Indian society. As with any such study, the questions raised are often thornier than those answered. For instance, it would be useful to know how many Third Mesa residents were not enumerated in 1900. How much change had there been between 1890 and 1900? Had population already started to increase by that time? Do the difficulties encountered in the use of this census material negate the conclusions reached?

Many of these questions can only be answered by further work, if at all. This study has examined only the Hopi, but it seems clear that similar efforts could be made with the handful of other tribes which were still largely unacculturated at the beginning of this century, most notably the puebloan peoples of New Mexico, for which, like the Hopi, there are abundant enthnographic data, but little demographic information. Much could also be done with the Navajo, or the Papago in southern Arizona. Those familiar with other parts of the country may find other groups which could be studied profitably in this way.

Although such questions are intriguing, at least some conclusions can be drawn from this study. First, the Hopi population had begun to increase *before* 1910, contrary to previous assumptions; second, the new village of Hotevila was *not* enumerated by the 1910 census, but probably had a population of about 450 in 1910; and third, the new villages at the foot of the mesas were already of considerable importance by 1910. Fourth, this study points out that the manuscript censuses, although presenting a number of problems, can be extremely useful in the study of at least some American Indian societies.

NOTES

1. W. David Laird, *Hopi Bibliography* (Tucson, Arizona: University of Arizona Press, 1977).

2. See, for example, Frederick R. Eggan, "The Kinship System and Social Organization of the Western Pueblos with Special Reference to the Hopi Indians." Ph.D. Dissertation, Univ. of Chicago (1933); J. Walter Fewkes, "The Kinship of the Tusayan Villagers," *American Anthropologist,* 7 (1894); 394-417; J. Walter Fewkes, "Archeological Expedition to Arizona in 1895," *Seventeenth Annual Report of the Bureau of American Ethnology,* Part 2 (Washington, D.C., Government Printing Office, pp. 519-742, 1898); Walter Hough, *The Hopi Indians* (Cedar Rapids, Iowa: The Torch Press, 1915); Alfred L. Kroeber, "Zuni Kin and Clan," *Anthropological Papers of the American Museum of Natural History.* Vol 28, Part 2 (1917): 37-205; Robert H. Lowie, "Hopi Kinship," *Anthropological Papers of the American Museum of Natural History,* Vol. 30, Part VII (1929): 368-379; and Robert H. Lowie, "Notes on Hopi Clans," *Anthropological Papers of the American Museum of Natural History,* Vol. 30, Part VI (1929): 307-317.

3. Manuscript census materials are kept confidential for a period of 72 years after the census. Thus, the 1910 manuscript material was released in 1982.

4. U.S. Department of Commerce, Bureau of the Census, *Arizona. 1900.* National Archives Microfilm Publications, T623, Roll Number 46 (n.d.); U.S. Department of Commerce, Bureau of the Census, *Arizona, 1910.* National Archives Microfilm Publications, T624, Roll Numbers 39 and 41 (n.d.); J. Walter Fewkes, Field Notebooks, on file in the National Anthropological Archives, Washington, D.C. File No. 4408, Items 4 (letters), 31 and 33 (Field Notes) (1899-1900); J. Walter Fewkes, "Tusayan Migration Traditions," *Nineteenth Annual Report, Bureau of American Enthnology,* Washington, D.C., Government Printing Office (1900) 573-634.

5. Elliot G. McIntire, "First Mesa Hopi in 1900: A Demographic Reconstruction," *Journal of Cultural Geography,* 2 (1982):58-71; Cosmos Mindeleff, "Localization of Tusayan Clans," *Nineteenth Annual Report of the Bureau of American Ethnology.* Washington, D.C., Government Printing Office (1900) 635-653; Victor Mindeleff, "A Study of Puebloan Architecture," *Eighth Annual Report, Bureau of American Ethnology,* Washington, D.C.; Government Printing Office (1891) 3-228.

6. McIntire, 1982.

7. Elliot G. McIntire, "Without Reservation: the Hopi Indian Agency to 1883," Unpublished manuscript (1979).

8. Edward S. Curtis, *The North American Indian; Being a Series of Volumes Picturing and Describing the Indians of the United States, The Dominion of Canada, and Alaska* (Cambridge, MA.: Harvard University Press, Vol. 29, 1922), p. xi.

9. Sarah Abbott, who enumerated First Mesa in 1900, favored birth months of March, April, May, and November, but rarely listed birthdates in June or July. One suspects that, since the census was being taken in June and on into July, birthdates in these months would have complicated her "calculation" of years of age, hence their avoidance.

10. Albert Yava, *Big Fallowing Snow: A Tewa-Hopi Indian's Life and Times and the History and Traditions of His People* (Edited and Annotated by Harold Courlander) (New York: Crown Publishers, Inc., 1978).

11. In the case of some individuals on First Mesa we have transcriptions of their names by five or more people: notably Alexander M. Stephen, *Hopi Journal* (Edited by Elsie Clews Parsons) (New York: Columbia University Press, 2 volumes, 1936) (data collected in the early 1890s); Fewkes (field notes, and 1900) (data from the late 1890s); Sarah Abbott (census enumerator in 1900); Rev. Lee Thayer (census enumerator in 1910); Robert Lowie (1929) (data from 1915); and Edward Curtis (1922) (data from 1900-1920).

12. Sarah Abbott (1900) was a field matron at the school in Keams Canyon, while the Rev. Lee Thayer (1910) was a missionary to the Hopi.

13. Yava, p. 3.

14. For an examination of the relationship between the Presbyterians, the Indian Bureau, and the Hopi, see Stephen C. McCluskey, "Evangelists, Educators, Ethnographers, and the Establishment of the Hoip Reservation," *The Journal of Arizona History* (Winter 1980): 363-390.

15. The conflict between anthropologists and Indian agents is well known. One need only examine the case of Frank Cushing at Zuni, or the less well documented case of Jeremiah Sullivan and the Hopi to see how this conflict interfered with both the government agents and the work of the anthropologists. The role of the Bureau of American Ethnology in this situation is quite interesting. Under the direction of John Wesley Powell, ethnologists were sent out to record the remaining Indian societies of the west, and many clearly came to admire the people they studied. Cushing was made a member of a secret society at Zuni, and Sullivan lived essentially as a tribal member at First Mesa for several years. Indian agents, of

course, felt that such behavior by scientists undermined their efforts to "civilize" the Indians, and ethnologists were sometimes threatened with expulsion from the reservations. There is a letter in the files of the Bueau of American Ethnology from Alexander Stephen, then living at First Mesa, reporting on the vailed threats of Agent Collins to have him removed from the reservation, and requesting that BAE director Fewkes have the Secretary of the Interior specifically endorse Stephen's presence.

16. McIntire (1982) p. 63.

17. Mischa Titiev,*Old Oraibi: A Study of the Hopi Indians of Third Mesa* (Papers of the Peabody Museum of American Archeology and Ethnology, Harvard University, Vol. 22, 1944) pp. 39-43.

18. John H. Sullivan, "The Moquis Indians," *The America Antiquarian and Oriental Journal* 6 (1884): 101-103.

19. U.S. Department of Commerce, Bureau of the Census, *Twenty Censuses: Population and Housing Questions 1790-1980.* Washington, D.C.: Government Printing Office (1979) p. 25.

20. McIntire (1982) p. 67.

21. Yava, p. 164.

Chapter 16

The Lumbees: Population Growth of a Non-Reservation Indian Tribe

Thomas E. Ross

Scholars are uncertain about how many Indians lived in what is now the United States when the first Europeans of record arrived. Almost 400 years later, in 1860, the U.S. Census counted only 44,021 American Indians in the United States. From that apparent low point, the Indian population began a phenomenal climb, particularly since the mid-twentieth century. An Indian population of about 340,000 in 1950 more than doubled, reaching about 770,000 by 1970. The increase after 1960 amounted to an annual increase of about 4.25 percent, a figure higher than that of any country on earth in the early 1970s.[1] By 1980, the Indian population was almost double that of 1970 and, for the first time since the Bureau began enumerating Indians in 1860, surpassed one million. While not all of the more than 200 tribes/bands/nations in the United States shared in this growth, some tribes surpassed the national average. One such tribe is the Lumbee, a group of nonreservation Indians living in Robeson County, North Carolina (Fig. 16.1).

More than 35,000 Indians, most of whom identify with the Lumbee tribe, live in Robeson County. At least 15,000 additional Lumbees live in surrounding counties and in urban areas such as Baltimore, Charlotte, and Greensboro. The Lumbee people make up the second largest Indian group in the United States, surpassed only by the Navajo, which number 105,000.[2]

As with other Indian groups, the Lumbee population appears to have been growing at a rapid rate over the past 100 years. According to the 1890 census, there were only 174 Indians in Robeson County in 1890.[3] But sociologist Roland Harper believed that the census contained enumeration problems which undercounted the Indians and supported his argument by citing the state school report for 1889-90, which showed 649 boys and 593

Figure 16.1. Robeson County in North Carolina.

girls between the ages of six and twenty-one in the Indian population of the county.[4] By 1900, the number of Indians listed in the census had increased to 3,877[5] and the 1940 census showed that more than 16,000 Indians lived in the county.[6] Thus the twentieth century has been a period of rapid increase for the Lumbee. This chapter examines the population trends and factors behind the apparent Lumbee population explosion. It is my hypothesis that the increase in Indians in Robeson County is not due solely to a higher birth rate than non-Indians, but includes, among other things, the willingness of more inhabitants of the county to identify themselves as Indian.

THE PEOPLE

The uniqueness of the Lumbees and the mystery of their origin calls for a brief history of their evolution as an Indian tribe. Unlike most other Indian groups, the Lumbee have been referred to by several names, none of which are completely satisfactory to the total population.[7] The Lumbee also differ from most other Indians in that although the Congress of the United States recognizes the Lumbees as Indians, the tribal members are not entitled to Bureau of Indian Affairs benefits. The Lumbees do not live on reservation lands or do they have a formal tribal government or tribal council.

The first European settlers of record arrived in Robeson County in the early 1730s and oral tradition indicates that they reportedly discovered "a tribe of Indians speaking broken English, tilling the soil in a rude manner, and practicing in rather imperfect ways some of the arts practiced by the civilized people of Europe."[8] According to Hamilton McMillan they "call themselves 'Melungeans.' "[9] McMillan argued that these Indians were descendants of Sir Walter Raleigh's ill-fated "Lost Colony" of 1587. He wrote that it seems certain the English settlers left Croatan Island voluntarily and that:[10]

> the finding of crosses and letters carved in the bark of trees in the region . . . known as Secotan, corroborates the statement of White . . . that on his departure for England they were preparing to remove 'fifty miles into the main.' If the colonists went to Croatan, and from that point removed fifty miles into the mainland, they must have located in . . . the region of Secotan, . . . and in the very region where Rev. Morgan Jones found the Doegs or 'White Indians' in 1660.

McMillan also used the diffusion of the scuppernong grape (a hybrid which can only be propogated from cuttings) from the northeastern part of North Carolina into Robeson County and evidence that Lumbee ancestors served in the Revolutionary War as further support for the Lumbee-Lost Colony connection. Another argument involved the language of the late nineteenth century Lumbees. According to McMillan, "the language of these people is old English and similar to that used in the time of Chaucer. Among the numerous uneducated class *hit* is used for it, *hwing* for wing, *aks* for ask, *housen* for house, *hosen* for hose, *lovend* for loving, *mension* for measurement, and *mon* for man."[11] It should be pointed out, however, that similar pronunciation exists in other places, for example in the more isolated parts of Appalachia and among some of the inhabitants of Jamaica. He also wrote that "In an old medical work, brought to North Carolina by some immigrants over two hundred years ago, are found many curious remedies for treatment of diseases prevalent among the English in the seventeenth century. It is significant that many of these quaint remedies are in common use among the Indians . . . today."[12] In addition, he claimed that the "only name given by these people to their Indian ancestors is Cherokee, and there is communication between persons of this tribe and the Cherokees in Indian Territory." He continues by writing that "they are very proud of their English origin, but complain very bitterly of their treatment by the whites in 1835 in depriving them of the elective franchise and classifying them as 'free persons of color.' "[13] McMillan contended that the group "now numbering about thirty-five hundred, was at one time more numerous than at present. In the northern part of Robeson County . . . are found thousands of 'camp fires,' arranged in straight lines and crossing each other at right angles. These camping places show a numerous population in former times."[14] He cited other evidence, including remnants of stone buildings, crossways on swamps, iron tomahawks and wrought iron rods which he thought must have been brought in by non-Indians (Lost Colony settlers) since the Indians did not possess the technology to make these items.[15]

McMillan was not the only nineteenth century writer to be convinced that the Robeson Indians were descended from a coalescence of the Hatteras (Croatan) Indians and Raleigh's colonists. Stephen Weeks also thought that the Indians' peculiar English dialect and their family names supported the Lost Colony theory.[16] He emphasized that the 1587 colony had 95 different surnames and that of these, 41, or derivatives of them, existed in the names of Robeson Indians. Among the names he cited were Cooper, Sampson, Howe, Gramme (now Graham), Chevin (now Chavis), and Brooks.[17]

More than 60 years after McMillan's testimony, Adolph Dial and David Eliades also advocated that Lumbee roots extend back to the Lost Colony.[18] While acknowledging the paucity of evidence for determining with certainty the origin(s) of the Lumbees, they wrote:[19]

> Clinging fiercely to their Indian origins, the Lumbees nonetheless have no remnants of their Indian language which might provide clues to their relationship with other Native Americans. Only traditions and folktales remain as evidence, tales which link this unique group with the lost survivors of the Roanoke Colony as well as with the Eastern band of the Sioux Indians, the . . . Cherokee, and the Tuscarora Indians. Each tradition has its supporters; each has its detractors.

Most notable of the detractors was John Swanton of the Smithsonian Institution, who strongly opposed the argument that there was any connection between the Robeson County Indians and the Lost Colony.[20] He claimed to have examined the problem in great detail and referred to a report by Special Indian Agent O. M. McPherson to the Secretary of Interior in 1914. According to Swanton, McPherson:[21]

> interviewed an old ... Indian ... who claimed to be almost 80. This old man informed him that 'he was told by Aaron Revels, then 100 years old ... that these Indians came from Roanoke in Virginia. That after remaining in Robeson County for some time they went to the mountains with the other Cherokees, but a number returned ... where they mixed with the other tribes and probably with several of the whites.

Swanton took issue with the general interpretation of this statement argued that it had been misunderstood "on account of an obsession that the Robeson County Indians were Cherokee and confusion between Roanoke River and the City of Roanoke. When we understand the facts regarding Cherokee history, these statements begin to have meaning and the story is consistent." According to Swanton:[23]

> Previous to 1700 they had settled on the Dan River near the southern line of Virginia ... the Dan and Staunton unite to form the Roanoke. They moved south about 1710 ... and established themselves on the Upper Pedee near the present settlements of the 'Croatans,' some Occaneechi, Saponi, and Tutelo who had been living near the junction of the two rivers, perhaps accompanying them. Later we know that some Cheraw moved to the Catawba country and this accounts for the tradition that 'they went to the mountains with the other Cherokee.' The return of part of them at a later date is not recorded in any history of the section ... but is highly probable.

Swanton summarized his report by writing:[24]

> Confusion of these Indians with the Cherokee was probably due in part to the fact that the Cherokee have been their nearest neighbors of consequence for a long period and in part because of the resemblance between the names Cheraw and Cherokee.
> Evidence that these people were connected with the Croatan is still less valid. Croatan was the name of an island and an Algonquian Indian town just north of Hatteras, to which the survivors of the Raleigh colony are supposed to have gone ... But, assuming that the colonists did remove to Croatan there is not a bit of

reason to suppose that either way they or the Croatan
Indians ever went farther inland . . .

. . . .

. . . . The evidence . . . seems to indicate
that the Indians of Robeson County who have been
called Croatan and Cherokee are descended mainly
from certain Siouan tribes of which the most
prominent were the Cheraw and Keyauwee, but they
probably included as well remnants of the Eno, and
Shakori, and very likely some of the coastal groups
such as the Waccamaw and Cape Fears.

Other theories of Lumbee origin can be found in scholarly
journals,[25] most of which are not accepted as valid by the Lumbees.
But whatever their origin, the Lumbees are now recognized locally
and nationally as Indians and have, at least according to United
States census data, been multiplying rapidly.

POPULATION TRENDS

The confusion surrounding the Lumbee band dates far back
into American history and may well be partially the fault of
terminology used by the Bureau of the Census, particularly
with the category "free colored," which until 1860 included Indians
and other non-whites as well as freed blacks. In the 1790 census
no Indians were listed for Robeson County, but there were 277
persons of "free color," about five percent of the total population.
By 1860 the number of free colored had grown to 1462, almost
ten percent of the county's population. Undoubtedly these figures
included free blacks, but Robeson county's "free colored"
population had been about three times the state average as
far back as the first census.[26] There is no reason to believe that
Robeson County had more free blacks than other coastal plain
counties with similar economies, so one could infer that the above
average proportion of free coloreds could be accounted for by a
substantial Indian population. Harper found that "in 1860
the colored population, both free and slave, of each county was
divided into black and mulatto, and that only . . . 0.2 percent of the
free colored in Robeson County were blacks, as compared with 25.8
percent in the whole state,"[27] indicating a substantial free mulatto
or Indian population. No Indians were listed for Robeson County
in the 1860 census, in fact no Indians were listed in Robeson
County census returns until 1890 (Table 16.1).

Table 16.1

Indians In Robeson County and the U.S. Census

Year of Census	Number of Indians Listed
1870	0
1880	0
1890	174
1900	3,877
1910	5,895
1920	8,917
1930	12,404
1940	16,629
1970	26,486
1980	35,528

Source: Prepared by the author from Bureau of the Census publications.

The twentieth century has seen a dramatic increase in Indian population in Robeson County. As shown in Table 16.1, about 3,900 Indians were enumerated in 1900, but 80 years later more than nine times that number (35,525) were listed. When the estimated 15,000 Lumbees living outside Robeson County are included, the rate of increase is even more spectacular. By comparison, the white population just barely managed to double during the same period (from 19,577 to 39,788), while blacks increased by about 50 percent, growing from 16,917 to 25,216. Thus the Indian population increase outstripped by about 2,000 the combined increase of blacks and whites. The expansion of the Indian population may also be viewed by looking at the proportion of Indians in the total county population. In 1900 only 9.6 percent of Robeson County's population was reported to be Indian. That proportion had almost doubled by 1930, having risen to 18.9 percent. Fifty years later the proportion of Indians in the county had nearly doubled again, to 35.3 percent of the total population. How can such increases among the Indian group be explained?

Birth Rates and Death Rates

A significant factor in the Indian population explosion is a high birth rate. In 1980, 22.2 percent of the Indian population was under ten years of age, compared to 14 percent for county whites and 20.3 percent for county blacks (Table 16.2). Statewide, 14.4 percent of the population was under ten years of age. The figures for Indians indicate a high probability that they have a substantially higher birth and lower death rate than the state average and the other racial groups in Robeson County. In 1985, as shown in Table 16.3, Indians do in fact have a higher birth rate than blacks or whites. The Indian rate is almost twice that of whites and slightly higher than that of blacks. The Indian death rate is considerably lower than that of whites and blacks, in part a reflection of the generally younger Indian population. However, as the Indians become more financially secure their birth rate will most likely tumble. The Lumbees may now be entering a demographic transition period and will begin deliberately to limit their birth rates. However, if present trends in birth and death rates continue, the Indians will be the majority (more than 50 percent) ethnic group in tri-racial Robeson County by the end of this century.

Table 16.2

Population by Race and Age, Robeson County, North Carolina: 1980

Age (Years)	White	Black	Indian
Under 5	2620	2531	3840
5-14	6006	5609	7996
15-59	24791	13959	20641
60-64	1878	1046	998
65 plus	4868	2455	2032

Source: Compiled by author from *U.S. Census of Population and Housing, 1980,* Summary Tape File 3A (50).

Racial Self-Identification

Another explanatory factor that must be seriously considered in assessing the Indian population increase is the greater willingness of people to be counted as Indians. Hence a considerable proportion of the increase could be attributed to a shift in racial self-identification. Also important are Census Bureau changes incorporated into the census of 1960 and the

Table 16.3

Birth and Death and Population Rates in
Robeson County, North Carolina: 1985

	(Percent)	
	Birth Rate	Death Rate
White	10.4	10.0
Black	19.0	11.2
Indian	20.4	6.0
Other	0.5	0.0

Source: Compiled from data provided by Velvet Hardin, Lumber River Council of Governments.

censuses which followed. The most important change was that residents would determine "their own racial category, rather than having it recorded by an enumerator. One result was an increase of 48 percent increase in the [national] Indian population."[28] Thus people previously counted as non-Indian could now choose to be counted as Indian if they wished. Net overcounts in some age categories, such as the estimated net overcount of teenage Indians in the 1970 census, suggests a shifting racial self-identification phenomenon on a national level during the 1960s.[29] The increased Indian ethnic consciousness of the period was most likely accompanied by changes in racial self-identification. The result is that offspring of racially mixed marriages in which one parent was Indian tend to identify themselves as Indian.[30] This is characteristic of the children of racially mixed marriages among the Lumbee.

The past two decades have witnessed a decline in discrimination against Indians in Robeson County. This has led to increased respectability as Indians have taken positions of responsibility, both in the Indian community and in the community at large. The willingness of the majority ethnic group to accept Indians in leadership positions has probably been partly responsible for individuals who earlier have been identified as non-Indian to assert their Indian identity. Robeson County, like much of the rest of the country, has experienced a decrease in prejudice among the different racial groups and this may encourage previously hesitant individuals to assert their "Indianness," especially if the individual can reap economic and political rewards regardless of racial identification. Thus, although at this time it cannot be quantified, we may assume that many Indians who previously had been categorized as white or black may now insist upon claiming their Indian heritage, and in Robeson County this has been partly responsible for a rapidly growing Lumbee population.

Furthermore, as illiteracy among the Indians decreases they will be more likely to complete census forms themselves and therefore will be able to claim Indian status without being observed by a non-Indian census taker. Illiteracy has most certainly been involved in past underenumerations of Indian population. As the Indian population becomes better educated, it learns that cooperating with the Bureau of the Census is politically and economically harmless. Therefore, more previously unlisted individuals and families will participate in the enumeration process, which in turn will be reflected in larger Indian population figures.

Migration

Both in and out migration of the Lumbee population must also be considered. Lumbee historian Adolph Dial wrote that "almost all Lumbees call Robeson County home and expect to return to it someday."[31] Thus it is reasonable to expect that many Indians are returning home, especially as more economic opportunities become available in their home region, Indian family income, while not as high as that of whites, is considerably higher than black family income (Table 16.4). It is shown that Indian households comprise a higher percent of the total number of households in the county (32.3) than blacks which make up 22.3 percent. Thus if all races were equally represented in household income categories one would expect the percentage of whites, blacks and Indians within each category to be the same as each group's percentage of the total households in the county. For example, the $5000-$7499 income category would be comprised of 45.4 percent of white households, 22.3 percent of blacks and 32.3 percent of Indians. But it is evident that such is not the case — in the categories exceeding $10,000 the blacks are underrepresented and in those above $20,000 the Indians are underrepresented. The poverty status of the three major ethnic groups (Table 16.5) reflects household income and suggests that Indians are in better financial condition than blacks but are not nearly as well-off as whites. Perhaps the more favorable economic situations for Indians, as compared to blacks, are responsible for slowing Indian out-migration and increasing the Indian return to the Robeson County region.

Table 16.4

Family Houshold Income, by Race, in Robeson County, North Carolina: 1979

(expressed as percentage of total number of households within each category)

	White	Black	Indian
Total County Households	45.4	22.3	32.3
Income in dollars			
0-5000	24.5	39.2	36.3
5000-7499	34.2	29.9	35.9
7500-9999	35.0	24.5	40.5
10,000-14,999	43.5	22.2	34.3
15,000-19,999	48.0	19.0	33.0
20,000-24,999	60.8	13.8	25.4
25,000-34,999	65.4	11.7	23.0
35,000-49,999	72.6	5.9	21.5
50,000 or more	80.1	5.0	14.9
Median Income	$20,150	$11,345	$14,134

Source: Compiled by the author from *Census of Population and Housing 1980,* Summary Tape File 3A (50).

Table 16.5

Poverty Status in 1979: Robeson County, North Carolina

	Above	Below	Percent Below
Total	75065	24859	24.9
White	34604	4653	11.9
Black	15186	9973	39.6
Indian	25068	10119	28.8

Source: Compiled by the author from *Census of Population and Housing 1980, Summary Tape File 3A (50).*

CONCLUSIONS

It has been established that the Lumbee population growth rate exceeds that of non-Indian population in Robeson County. Several factors must be considered to explain this rapid expansion of the population, but the most significant are high birth and declining mortality rates, and the fact that more county residents are identifying themselves as Indians because of a resurgence of ethnic pride. Increased economic opportunity is another factor as is the decline in discrimination against Lumbees. But the rapidly expanding Lumbee population base has negative as well as postive implications for the Indians in Robeson County. For example, by the end of this century Indians could be the majority ethnic group, and in the early part of the twenty-first century could politically control the county. Just as important, though, is the fact that the younger Indian population will be faced with difficult decisions, especially if the economic climate of the county does not substantially improve to absorb the growing number of Indians in the labor force. Will the Indians leave the region or will they opt to "stay home" and accept low-paying jobs? If they stay, and remain relatively economically deprived, Indian population growth rates will most likely continue their rapid ascent well into the twenty-first century, with perhaps catastrophic results, in terms of economic progress.[32] Although a rapidly expanding population would enable the Lumbees to gain political control of Robeson County, they could lose their position as one of the most affluent Indian groups in the United States if economic development in the county does not keep up with the rate of their population increase. Thus rapid population expansion, without comparable levels of economic growth within the region, could slow or even reverse the economic progress the Lumbees have made in the twentieth century.

NOTES

1. Jeffrey S. Passel, "Provisional Evaluation of the 1970 Census Count of American Indians," *Demography* 13 (1976): 407.

2. U.S., Department of Commerce, Bureau of the Census, *United States Census of Population: 1980,* supplementary report, *American Indian Areas and Alaska Native Villages: 1980.*

3. During this period many Lumbees were labeled mulattoes. Furthermore, until the 1950s racial designation was usually made by the physician present at a child's birth.

4. Roland M. Harper, "A Statistical Study of the Croatans," *Rural Sociology* 2 (December 1937): 445.

5. U.S., Department of Commerce, Bureau of the Census, *Twelfth Census of the United States: 1900,* vol. 1, *Population,* part 1.

6. U.S., Department of Commerce, Bureau of the Census, *Sixteenth Census of the United States: 1940,* vol. 2, *Characteristics of the Population,* part 5, New York-Oregon.

7. In the first original recognition by North Carolina these people were designated 'Croatan Indians.' The state in 1911 changed the name to 'Indians of Robeson County,' and in 1913 to 'Cherokee Indians of Robeson County.' Finally they were named 'Lumbee Indians' in 1956.

8. U.S., Congress, House, "Hearings Before the Committee on Indian Affairs on S.3258," 1913.

9. Hamilton McMillan, *Sir Walter Raleigh's Lost Colony* (Raleigh: Edwards and Broughton Company, 1888), p. 25.

10. Ibid., p. 43.

11. Ibid., p. 44.

12. Ibid.

13. Ibid.

14. Ibid., p. 43.

15. Ibid.

16. Stephen B. Weeks, "Raleigh's Settlement on Roanoke Island," *The Magazine of American History* 25 (1891): 117-139.

17. Ibid., p. 138.

18. Adolph Dial and David Eliades, *The Only Land I Know: A History of the Lumbee Indians* (San Francisco: The Indian Historian Press, 1975).

19. Ibid., p. 1.

20. John R. Swanton, "Probable Identity of the 'Crotan' Indians," Smithsonian Institute, United States Department of the Interior, Office of Indian Affairs, 1933.

21. Ibid., p. 3.

22. Ibid., pp. 3-4.

23. Ibid., p. 4.

24. Ibid., p. 5.

25. Calvin L. Beale, "American Triracial Isolates," *Eugenics Quarterly* 4 (December 1957): 187-196; and Edward T. Price, "A Geographic Analysis of White-Negro-Indian Racial Mixtures in Eastern United States," *Annals of the Association of American Geographers* 43 (1953): 138-155.

26. Harper, p. 447.

27. Ibid.

28. Laurence S. Rosen and Kurt Gorwitz, "New Attention to American Indians," *American Demographics,* April 1980, p. 21.

29. Passel, p. 407.

30. Ibid., p. 404.

31. Adolph L. Dial, "The Lumbee Indians: Still a Lost Colony?," *New World Outlook* 32 (May 1972): 22.

32. Based on the assumption that lower income groups generally tend to have higher birth rates than the more affluent groups within a society.

Conclusions

Chapter 17
American Indian
Problems and Prospects
Thomas E. Ross

In the preceding chapters selected problems associated with American Indians, with particular emphasis upon cultural geography,[1] have been analyzed. Although all Indian problems and all aspects of cultural geography are not included here, the book provides a representative cross-section of Indian problems and Indian groups in the United States, and to a lesser extent, Canada. Questions are raised as to the future of the American Indian and in many cases the authors offer suggestions to improve the lot of the Indian. Another important contribution is that several misconceptions about Indians are exposed and more correct alternatives are provided.

The cultural and economic conditions of the diverse pre-Columbian Indian population in what is now the United States and Canada will never be fully and accurately learned. Numerous accounts of Indian cultures indicate, however, that great cultural changes were incurred by Indians as large numbers of Europeans advanced into their domain. Most of those changes were, as far as the Indians were concerned, negative and made life more complex while lessening the odds of survival.

PROBLEMS

The availability and control of substantial tracts of land is a necessary prerequisite for economic development in any society. The Indians had access to the entire continent of North America before the white man arrived and through hunting and fishing used much of it for food production. From the European point of view, the Indians had not fully developed the land. Thus a cultural clash, in terms of landuse and land control, developed

early on in the contact period between whites and Indians as
the whites attempted to take "unused" land for their own uses.

Many of the problems faced by Indians today are rooted in
past government actions, such as trade restrictions, forced removal
to reservations and the subsequent allotment of reservation land,
assimilation policies, termination laws[2] and self-determination
policies.[3] Other problems stem from non-Indians' perception of
Indians as being less "civilized" and less capable of operating
within a highly technological culture. But the overriding and
ubiquitous problem is the transfer of massive acreages of land from
the Indian to white culture.

Why was the white man so callous in taking Indian land? David
Eliades points out in Chapter 3 that Europeans held the Indian
cultures in low regard and that whites and Indians differed as to
what both considered to be "empty land." Thus lands that appeared
empty or unused to the whites, at least early in the contact
period, were in many cases being fully utilized by the Indians,
yet they were confiscated by the whites. Later the Europeans
would claim that they alone were capable of using the land to
its maximum potential and that the Indian, because of an
inferior culture, was wasting much of the land resource. Claudia
Notzke, Ronald Janke and Richard Weil all point out that many of
the problems experienced by Indians result from the loss of their
lands to the whites. Notzke claims that the Indians cultural-
economic survival depends upon a substantial landbase. Janke
agrees but notes that although the Indians lost tremendous
amounts of land in Wisconsin, Montana and elsewhere, perhaps
the greatest problem is associated with fragmented reservations.
For example, as shown by Weil, Indian reservation governments
find that police, fire, medical and social services are difficult
to provide in areas of intermingled white and Indian landholdings.
Janke claims that such fragmentation makes it impossible for
Indians to possess landholdings large enough to carry on profitable
forestry, grazing and farming activities. Another complication
resulting from fragmentation is that non-Indians rent or lease much
of the Indian land in Wisconsin and Montana. Although the Indian
retains legal title to the rented or leased land, the reality is that
even more land is effectively removed from Indian use, therefore
adding to the economic misery of the Indians.

The availability and control of substantial tracts of land is a
necessary prerequisite for economic development in any society.
The Indians had access to the entire continent before the white
man arrived and used land as it met their needs. Whether it was

fully utilized from the perspective of the Europeans is immaterial. We must keep in mind that different cultures have different ideas about what is valuable and what constitutes effective use of resources.

An effective degree of sovereignty and tribal government is another problem faced by many Indian groups. Those groups without capable tribal leadership usually experience severe economic problems. Jesse McKee's study of the Mississippi Choctaw, however, show that federal assistance, without paternalism, *and* effective tribal leadership can lead to an economically successful experience. Thus, when given the opportunity Indians can be as successful as other ethnic groups in the United States.

Other problems present among the Indians are those of cultural identity. Most population movements in which two or more cultures make contact result in cultural modification as old ideas and traits are discarded and others are introduced. In many instances these cultural changes are accompanied by a blending or fusion of cultural characteristics as well as changes in the demography of the societies involved. The contact of two cultures in which one is much more dominant generally results in the cultural traits of the weaker culture being modified or lost. If the weaker culture experiences a decline in population, which is usually the case, these cultural changes may be more pronounced.

Several contributors examine various elements of migration and cultural change. Victor Konrad analyzes Iroquois migration in the seventeenth century and concludes that their return to the "homeland" was not the result of military setbacks, as previously believed, but was due to a planned and systematic attempt to return to an area where the social and economic needs of the population could be more effectively realized. He argues that expanded trade areas, lack of adequate agricultural production, and political realignment, not military defeat, made resettlement necessary. Contact and competition with other societies, Indian and white, were very much a part of the Iroquois decision to return to the land they had earlier left. In another study, Janel Curry-Roper points out that contact created both cultural and ecological changes and in her study of the Houma points out that it is necessary for the weaker group (Houma, or Indians) to strive to maintain those parts of their culture that are feasible in a new environment but that they must accept change when necessary to ensure their survival. Regardless of the specific groups involved, we see that the weaker group must make changes, and that in most cases these changes are at the expense of their culture and could very well be the initial stages in assimilation, or at best, acculturation.[4]

In summary, most of the problems are, in one way or another economic. The complexity and harshness of the problems are rooted in the loss of lands, but although land, or the lack of it, is the cause of the problems, no single, simple, feasible solution has been proposed to resolve the problems. But efforts are being made by federal, state and tribal governments to attack the problems, with the realization that it will be many years before the Indians can practice their cultural values without suffering economic hardship.

PROSPECTS

President Ronald Reagan has established an Indian policy in which self-determination is central. Goals have been set that enable the Indian tribes to become more effective governing agencies. Indian self-government generally, unless specifically limited by treaty or act of Congress, includes the following:[5]

> 1) The right to a form of government of their own choosing,
> 2) The right to determine membership requirements,
> 3) The right to regulate domestic relations of the membership,
> 4) The right to determine how municipal legislation is enacted,
> 5) The right to administer justice, and
> 6) The right to levy taxes and regulate how land is used within the tribe's territorial jurisdiction.[5]

The success of his policy depends upon the ability of the smaller tribes to develop basic managerial and administrative skills. Reagan's policy also "recommends actions to clarify the legal privileges of the tribal governments and give them the tax status of states and other local governments"[6] and strongly supports and emphasizes the development of Indian reservation economies to ensure the success of self-government. To enhance its success the president has promised that the federal government will assist in developing managerial capability on the reservation as well as attracting private capital.

Just what does the future hold for the Indian? Assistant Secretary of Indian Affairs Kenneth L. Smith, a Wasco Indian says: [7]

> I believe in the strengths of Indian people which have enabled them to endure times of adversity and oppression unparalleled in history. I believe Indian people have the will and ability to self-govern and exercise wisely their sovereign powers. I believe the fulfillment of the hopes and aspirations of Indian people and their tribal governments must come from within — from their own will and determination. I believe Indian people and their tribal governments — not the federal government — have the prime responsibility for improvement of their social and economic growth and development.

The prospects for Indian survival may very well be greater than at any time since the initial contact with Europeans. Indian population is rapidly expanding (birth rates are high, mortality rates are declining, and a resurgent pride in being Indian is leading more people to identify themselves as Indians) and thus creating more awareness of the Indian and Indian problems among the general public. This should generate more public support for solving some of the problems faced by Indians.

But the most important factor working for the Indians is that the federal government has decided to abandon its paternalistic policy and to support Indian self-government. This policy permits Indian tribes, not bureaucrats from another culture, to manage their own resources and affairs. This is especially important for the reservation Indians.

To be effective in economic development, though, the tribal government must be stable and enjoy the support of the entire tribe. A tribal government that is not challenged by internal factions is one of the important elements in creating a climate for economic development in which private investors can be persuaded to locate on the reservation. This is particularly vital for those reservations without an abundance of natural resources. McKee's chapter on the Choctaw in Mississippi illustrates this well. The Choctaw do not have mineral, timber, or tourist oriented attractions but have succeeded in bringing industry to their reservation because of creative, intelligent and industrious tribal leaders.[8] This tribe of about 5,000 members has over the past few years created approximately 1,000 jobs by attracting the private sector to their lands. Other successful examples of economic development occurring as a result of effective self-government include the Blackfeet Indian Tribe in Montana (oil and gas), Gila River Indian Community (irrigated farmland, rubber from guayule, and industrial parks), Comanche Tribe of Oklahoma (oil) and the Passamaquoddy Tribe of Maine (blueberry farm).[9] According to the U.S. Census, Indian-owned businesses increased by more than 300 percent between 1972 and 1977. It is estimated that since then the increase has risen by another 200 percent. There were 1,819 Indian firms in 1972 with gross receipts of almost 50 million dollars. By 1977 there were 4,263 businesses with gross receipts of more than 326 million dollars. In 1984 the Minority Business Development Agency forecasted about 8,000 Indian firms with net receipts of about 500 million dollars. These figures do not include all of the Indian arts and crafts cottage industry.[10]

The contributors to this volume have analyzed many of the problems experienced by the American Indians and have offered suggestions for improvement. But we must keep in mind that no quick and easy solution exists, but it is heartening to know that if a group as disadvantaged, in terms of natural resources, as the Mississippi Choctaws can succeed, then there is great hope for most other Indians. The means for change and survival for the Indian, then, rests within the Indian community itself. All that is required is fair treatment from the majority population.

NOTES

1. Three of the contributors are not geographers, but have worked closely with geographers or have an academic background in geography.

2. The object of these laws was to cut the special federal relationship of Indian tribes with the United States and to treat Indians the same as other citizens.

3. Present (1987) policy aims to remove the federal government from its governing role in favor of stronger tribal governments.

4. Acculturation can be defined as the change that occurs in the weaker culture when contact is made with a more advanced culture whereas assimilation results in the complete disappearance of the weaker culture.

5. Adapted from U.S., Department of Interior, Bureau of Indian Affairs *American Indians*, by Vince Lovett and Larry Rummel (Washington, D.C.: Government Printing Office, 1984), p. 24.

6. Ibid., p. 4.

7. Ibid., p. 31.

8. Ibid., p. 37.

9. These and many other examples are discussed by Lovett and Rummel.

10. Lovett and Rummel, p. 39.

Appendix A

AMERICAN INDIAN POPULATION LIVING ON AND OFF RESERVATIONS BY STATES: 1980

States	Total	On Reservation	On tribal trust lands	Off Reservation
California	198,275	9,265	77	188,933
Oklahoma	169,292	4,749		164,543
Arizona	152,498	113,763	465	38,270
New Mexico	107,388	61,876	21,556	23,906
North Carolina	64,535	4,844		59,692
Washington	58,186	16,440	310	41,436
South Dakota	44,948	28,468	4,657	11,283
Texas	39,740	859		38,881
Michigan	39,734	1,607	183	37,944
New York	38,967	6,734		32,233
Montana	37,598	24,043	1	13,554
Minnesota	34,831	9,901	218	24,712
Wisconsin	29,320	9,361	79	19,880
Oregon	26,591	3,072	12	23,507
Alaska	21,869	942		20,927
North Dakota	20,120	11,287	1,753	7,080
Utah	19,158	6,868	17	12,273
Florida	19,134	1,303		17,831
Colorado	17,734	1,966		15,768
Illinois	15,846			15,846
Kansas	15,256	715		14,541
Nevada	13,306	4,400	339	8,567
Missouri	12,129			12,129
Ohio	11,985			11,985
Louisiana	11,969	210	185	11,574
Idaho	10,418	4,771	3	5,644
Arkansas	9,364			9,364
Virginia	9,211	118		9,093
Pennsylvania	9,179			9,179
Nebraska	9,145	2,846		6,299
New Jersey	8,176			8,176
Maryland	7,823			7,823
Indiana	7,682			7,682
Alabama	7,502			7,502
Massachusetts	7,483	1		7,482
Georgia	7,442	30		7,412
Wyoming	7,057	4,159		2,898

Mississippi	6,131	2,756	410	2,965
South Carolina	5,665	728		4,937
Iowa	5,369	492		4,877
Tennessee	5,013			5,013
Connecticut	4,431	27		4,404
Maine	4,057	1,235		2,822
Kentucky	3,518			3,518
Rhode Island	2,872			2,872
Hawaii	2,655			2,655
West Virginia	1,555			1,555
Delaware	1,307			1,307
New Hampshire	1,297			1,297
Washington, D.C.	996			996
Vermont	968			968

Source: Adapted from *American Indian Areas and Alaska Native Villages: 1980.* 1980 Census of Population, Supplementary Report PC80-S1-13. August 1984. U.S. Department of Commerce, Bureau of the Census, Page 14 .

About The Contributors

Patricia C. Albers is a member of the anthropology faculty at the University of Utah. She received her Ph.D. in anthropology from the University of Wisconsin-Madison in 1974. She is co-editor of *The Hidden Half: Studies of Plains Indian Women* and is currently working on a book dealing with the popular photographic images of American Indians. Other recent publications have appeared in *Plains, Anthropologist, Critique in Anthropology, Review of Radical Economy, Minnesota History,* and the *Journal of Ethnic Studies.*

Donald J. Ballas is a professor of geography at Indiana University of Pennsylvania (IUP). He received his B.S. from Clarion State College, M.A. from the University of Pittsburgh, and the Ph.D. from the University of Nebraska. Specializing in historical and cultural geography, he has authored more than thirty articles in a variety of geographical journals, including the *Journal of Geography, Geographical Survey and Journal of Cultural Geography.*

Janel M. Curry-Roper is an assistant professor of geography at Central College, Pella, Iowa. She did her undergraduate work at Bethel College in St. Paul, Minnesota and received her doctorate from the University of Minnesota. She has written several articles and co-authored a book on the Houma tribe based on research done while she lived in Louisiana and worked for the Mennonite Central Committee in conjunction with the United Houma Nation. Her research interests include resource policy and land ownership change.

David K. Eliades is a professor of history and American Indian studies at Pembroke State University, where he has taught since 1967. He earned his B.A. degree in history and journalism from the University of North Carolina at Chapel Hill, his M.A. in history from East Carolina University, and his Ph.D. in history from the University of South Carolina. He has co-authored *The Only Land I Know: A History of the Lumbee Indians* (The Indian Historian Press, 1975) and *Pembroke State University: A Centennial History.* He is currently at work on a history of the Yemassee War.

Ronald A. Janke is an historical geographer specializing in American Indians. He completed his undergraduate education at Marquette University, his master's degree from the University of Wisconsin-Milwaukee and received his doctorate from the University of Minnesota. Presently an associate professor of geography at Valparaiso University, he also taught at the University Wisconsin-Stevens Point and Macalester College. He has authored numerous journal articles, book chapters, and books dealing with economic conditions inside United States Indian reservations.

Stephen C. Jett is professor of geography at the University of California, Davis, where he has taught since 1964, following a year's teaching at Ohio State. He received his A.B. in geology from Princeton and a Ph.D. in geography from Johns Hopkins. His research is focused upon the prehistory, history, material culture, and cultural geography of the Navajo and other indigenous groups of the southwestern part of the United States, as well as upon the question of pre-Columbian influences between Old and New worlds. Dr. Jett is the author of scores of scholarly books and articles, including the award-winning *Navajo Wildlands* (Sierra Club) and *Navajo Architecture* (Arizona).

Jeanne Kay is associate professor of geography at the University of Utah in Salt Lake City. She received her B.A. from Mount Holyoke College, and her M.S. and Ph.D. from the University of Wisconsin-Madison. Her work on the historical geography of North American Indians and the fur trade has appeared in conference proceedings, book chapters, and journal articles, including the *Annals of the Association of American Geographers, Ethnohistory, Environmental Review,* and *Wisconsin Magazine of History.*

Victor Konrad is an associate professor of anthropology at the University of Maine at Orono. A native of Germany, Dr. Konrad was educated in geography at York (B.A., M.A.) and McMaster (Ph.D.) Universities in Canada. His research interests range from Native North American historical geography to material cultural transfer and the philosophy of historic preservation. He has published more than thirty articles, book chapters and edited volumes in these fields and the geography of Canada and Canadian-American relations. He is an editor of *The American Review of Canadian Studies* and director of the Canadian-American Center at the University of Maine.

G. Malcolm Lewis is a senior lecturer in geography at the University of Sheffield, England. Educated at the University of Sheffield (MSc) and the University of Wisconsin, he has a long-standing interest in cultural differences in the cognition and representation of earth space and environment. In recent years this has led to a research interest in the maps and mapping activities of pre-literate peoples in general and North American Indians and Inuits in particular. He has published extensively in geography journals and has contributed several chapters to books dealing with Indians.

Joseph T. Manzo is an associate professor of geography at Concord College (West Virginia). He holds a bachelor's degree from Southwest Missouri State University and the M.A. and Ph.D. from the University of Kansas. His research interests include ethnic geography and geographic aspects of popular culture. He has published several articles in professional journals.

Elliot McIntire is professor of geography at California State University, Northridge, in Los Angeles. After an undergraduate education at the University of California, Riverside, he received a masters degree from the Johns Hopkins University and a doctorate in geography from the University of Oregon. His dissertation dealt with the settlement and land use patterns of the Hopi Indians, and he has continued to study the Indians populations of the American southwest.

Jesse O. McKee is professor and chairman of the Department of Geography and Area Development at the University of Southern Mississippi. He received his undergraduate degree from Clarion University (Pennsylvania) and his Ph.D. from Michigan State University. Some of his recent works include *The Choctaw: Culture Evolution of a Native American Tribe* (co-author) (University Press of Mississippi, 1980) and *Ethnicity in Contemporary America* (editor), (Kendall/Hunt Publishing Company, 1985). Research emphasis areas include cultural/historical geography and population.

Tyrel G. Moore is a lecturer in the Department of Geography and Earth Sciences at the University of North Carolina at Charlotte. He received the B.S. degree in geography and history from Western Kentucky University and the M.S. and Ph.D. degrees in geography from the University of Tennessee, Knoxville. His research interests include cultural geography, regional economic development and the historical geography of the Appalachian South.

Claudia Notzke is a geographer at the University of Lethbridge (Alberta). She received her education at the University of Dusseldorf, University of Cologne, both in the Federal Republic of Germany, and at Rhodes University in the Republic of South Africa. She completed her Ph.D. at the University of Calgary. Her research interests include the "Fourth World," i.e. problems encountered by indigenous peoples worldwide, and the geography of Africa south of the Sahara. Her research on Indian reserves in Canada and the United States was preceded by work on the South African "Homelands."

Terrel L. Rhodes is associate professor of political science specializing in public administration at the University of North Carolina at Charlotte. Educated at Indiana University and the University of North Carolina at Chapel Hill (Ph.D.), his research interests include employment assistance programs and urban Indians, emergency response planning at nuclear power plants and administrative ethics.

Thomas E. Ross is professor of geography and chairman of the Department of Geology and Geography at Pembroke State University (North Carolina). He graduated from Marshall University (B.A. and M.S.) and the University of Tennessee, Knoxville (Ph.D.). Ross has published in diverse professional journals and his research ranges from studies of alternatives to chemical insecticides to geopolitical essays. His latest book, *Buffer States in World Politics* was published by Westview in 1986. Present research includes plans for a book on Indian economic development.

Richard Weil is a geographer specializing in population movements and with a particular interest in American Indians. Born in New York City, he received his Ph.D. from Rutgers University. Having worked both as a planner for the South Dakota government and as an assistant professor at Bemidji State University, he now lives in Bloomington, Minnesota. The author of *A Bibliography of American Indian Land Claims* (Vance, 1987), he has written articles on such diverse topics as the geography of international adoptions and the end of silver coinage.

INDEX

Aleuts. 25
Algonquin groups. 191-192
Alloted lands, inside
reservations. . . . . 134 (table)
American federal Indian policy,
evolution of. 259-261
American Indian Areas, definition
of. 6
American Indian Reservations,
     definition of. 6
     early concept of. 213
American Indian territorial systems,
discussion of. 47-49, 52-57
American Indians,
     alcohol consumption. 270
     economic progress, 317-318
     in the United States. 262
     (table)
     Policy of self-government. . . 316
     prospects for cultural
     survival. 317
     urbanization of. 259-273
Amerindian Culture areas. 18-20
Apache. 23, 135-136
Area Redevelopment Act of 1961. . 10
Arizona Indian Reservations,
1985. . . . . 137 (map)
     land ownership. . . . . . . 138 (map)
Arizona Navajo Reservation,
economic conditions. . . . 7-8, 135-139
. . . . 145-146
Assiniboin. 128
     joint utilization of land
     with Chippewa. 54
     socio-political structure, 51-56
     territory shared with
     Cree. 56, 67, 69-70
     trade with Cree. 73
     See Also Pre-reservation
     Indian Lands

Athapaskan. 17, 71, 243-245
     architectural styles. 243-245
Band type society. 51
Biogeographic regions of central
North America. 93-102
Blackfoot. 128
     reservation, loss of
     lands. 130-131
     socio-political structure. 51
     See Also Pre-reservation
     Indian Lands
Bureau of Indian Affairs. 174
     administrative power. 260
     unemployment programs. . . . 261
Canadian Government,
     Indian policy. 107-110
     conflicting land use. 111-112
     philosophy of Indian
     reserves. 107
Canadian Indians,
     Alberta land claims. 108-110
     survival related to land
     base. 124-125
     See Also Stoney, Peigan
Cayuga, territory occupied by
Iroquois,. 191-193
Census of 1824, Wisconsin
Indians. 62
Cherokee,
     acculturation and assimilation
     American society. 215
     allotment with Crow
     Reservation. 131
     present conditions. 10, 20
     removal of 1828. 215
     removal of 1838. 215-217
     removal to Oklahoma. 20
     reservations. 28
     stress of removal. 216
     stress of removal on

women............217-218, 223
Trail of Tears..............216
Cheyenne.......................128
Chicasaw, Treaty of 1836.......219
Chippewa...................128-129
   aversion to west in
   removal....................220
   joint utilization of land with
   Assiniboin...................54
   joint utilization of land with
   Cree......................54,69
   law enforcement
   problems..............157-158
   Red Lake Reserve, history of
   development...........154-157
   service delivery
problems.................157-158
   trade and hunting with
   Dakotas.....................56
   warfare with Dakotas........56
   Wisconsin reservations. 140-141
   See Also Pre-reservation Indian
   Lands
Choctaw..........................10
   change in employment
   patterns....................185
   (table)
   communities.........175 (map)
   conditions during
   removal...............220-221
   demographic characteristics
  181-184
   economic programs..........
   ....179-181, 184-186
   educational attainment
   ....183 (table)
   government................174
   historical development.. 173-174
   land granted to individuals
   through treaty..............219
   population changes.. 182 (table)
   removal...........174, 217-218
   vocational training
   programs...............176-177
   women in removal.........218
Comanche, band type
society...........................51
Comprehensive Employment and
Trainng Program.................265
Comprehensive Jobs Training
Partnership Act.................265

Cree, 129-131
   joint utilization of land with
   Chippewa................54-69
   socio-political structure...51, 56
   territorial sharing with
   Assiniboin.........56, 67, 69-70
   trade with Assiniboin........73
   See Also Pre-reservation
   Indian lands
Creek,
   conditions during
   removal...........218, 220-222
   population decline during
   removal....................222
Crow.......................127-129
   reservation, loss of
   lands..................129-130
   socio-political structure......51
   See Also Pre-reservation
   Indian lands
Cultural ecology............4-6, 227
Culture areas, American
Indian.....................19 (map)
Dakota,
   socio-political structure......51
   See Also Pre-reservation Indian
   lands
Dawes Act...21, 27, 131, 144-145, 260
Delaware
   stress in removal...217-218, 220
   treaty of 1778..............149
Delimitation of Amerindian
regions..........................18
Drinking (alcohol) among Native
Americans 1980-1982.....270 (table)
Education, delayed for 15-17 year old
Native Americans.........267 (table)
English,
   alliance with Indians......40-41
   theological attitudes toward
   Indians...................41-42
   view of Indians as
   inferior...................38-40
Eskimos.........................25
Euro-American attitudes
toward land.......................4
European attitudes toward
   Indian sovereignty........34-35
   Indians' cultural inferiority...34
   Indians....................33
   proper use of land...........34

European impact, on Indian
demography.................35-36
European-American landuse.....4-5
Flathead........................128
    reservation, loss of lands....131
Fort Laramie Treaty of 1851......131
Fort Peck Reservation, loss
of lands......................130-131
French, alliance with Indians......37
General Allotment Act of 1887. *See*
Dawes Act
Great Lakes Indians, territorial
sharing of lands...............58-67
Gros Ventre.................128-129
Historic Areas of Oklahoma,
definition of........................6
Hogans,
    evolution and form......245-252
    log construction........247-250
    plank and masonry
    construction.. 251-152
    reglious association..253-254
Hopi Indians,
    Arizona reservation. 136
    demographic change early
    twentieth century.......284-285
    demographic examination based
    on manuscript census...278-281
    demographic research......276
    married, widowed, divorced,
    1910.................286 (table)
    retention of culture.....277-278
    social structure.........282-284
    transcription of
    names...............281 (table)

Houma Indians,
    architecture............236-237
    cultural change.............227
    economic base. 228, 230-231, 236
   238-239
    fishing nets............236-237
    linkages with South American
    and Caribbean
    cultures................236-237
    matrilineal social
    structure...............232-236
    migration,
    1796-1800.............229 (map)
    population 1650-1986.......231
    relations with French and
    Spanish................228, 230

settlements..........223 (map)
    traditional lands........228-231
Hudson's Bay Company,
    exploration of tundra-forest
    potential.................95-98
    reliance on Indian maps...98-99
Hulapais....................136-137
Huron,
    territory....................192
    trade routes...............192
Income,
    Native American per capita
    household, compared to
    majority.............264 (table)
    Native American per capita
    median..............263 (table)
Indian,
    attitude toward nature.......3-5
    attitudes toward land
    ownership....................4
    aversion to individual land
    ownership....................4
    economic conditions.......7-10
    landholdings, comparison in
    United States 1887 and
    1934.......................27
    maps, accuracy of
    forest-grassland transition
    zones.......................99
        as predecessors of European
        maps...............100, 102
        compilation and content
       93-94
        Forest-Grassland, Boundary,
        North America......101 (map)
        utilization by Hudson's Bay
        Company..............98-99
        "Woods Edge" in America,
        ....97 (map)
    Old fields 4
    Population distribution 1980
    6-7
    Population total percentages. 6
    Reserves, Canada,
        defined by Indian Act. 120-121
        land tenure..........119-124
        Morley...................107
        Peigan..............119-123
        philosophy of government107
        Rabbit Lake.............107
        southern Alberta.........107

Indian Removal Bill of
1830............................ 26
Indian Reorganization Act
of 1934.................. 28, 131, 174
Iroquois,
    agricultural system..... 203-204
    early distribution......... 191 ff
    extention into territory of
        Cayuga.............. 191-193
        Oneida.............. 191-193
        Seneca.............. 191-193
    house type, 203 (illustration)
    political organization... 204-206
    reasons for territorial
    contraction............. 206-208
    relations with French....... 191
    settlement related to
    fur trade................ 202-203
    settlement systems, changes in,
    .... 207 (map)
        1664.............. 196 (map)
        1670.............. 197 (map)
        1673.............. 198 (map)
        1680.............. 199 (map)
        1688.............. 207 (map)
    seventeenth century migrations
    and settlements........ 196-200
    territorial expansion. ... 193-195
    trade routes............ 200-201
    war with Ojibwa........ 200-201

Jicariila Apache.................. 10
    economic conditions......... 10
Jurisdiction of Indian lands.. 150-151
Kootenai. *See* Kootenay.
Kootenay........................ 128
Land Bridge Theory............... 16
Land claims, complexities of shared
territory....................... 80-82
Land ownership,
    Indian aversion to
    individual...................... 4
    inside Montana
    reservations................. 132
    (table)
    types by tribe and by
    individuals........... 133 (table)
Land use,
    contrasts between European
    and Indian view............. 5-6
Legislation, Area

Redevelopment Act of
1961........................ 10
Comprehensive Employment
and Training Program....... 265
Comprehensive Jobs Training
and Partnership Act........ 265
Dawes Act............... 21, 27
    impact on Indian
    land losses........... 144-145
    intent of land
    ownership............... 260
Fort Laramie Treaty
of 1851..................... 131
General Allotment Act of 1887,
See Dawes Act.
Indian Removal Bill of
1830........................ 26
Indian Reorganization Act of
1934................ 28, 131, 174
Natural Resources Act of 1930
(Canada)................... 111
Public Works and Economic
Development Act of 1965..... 11
Reorganization Act of 1934. *See*
Indian Reorganization of 1934.
Self-Determiniation Act of
1975....................... 178
Termination Act of 1953..... 176
"termination and relocation
acts"..................... 28-29
Treaty of Hopewell (1768).... 173
Treaty Seven, provisions for
reserves................ 113-119
Wheeler-Howard Act of 1934.
See Indian Reorganization Act
of 1934.
Loss of lands,
Indians............. 129-131, 144-145
Lumbee,
    confusion with
    Cherokees.............. 300-302
    fertility rates........... 303-304
    historic use of Old English
    speech..................... 299
    income and poverty........ 307
    increased representation in
    census................. 304-306
    "Lost Colony" connection
    299-302
    migration patterns......... 306
    population change

1860-1980......297-298, 302-303
relation to Siouian tribes.... 302
self-identity............304-306
theories of origin.......298-302
urban distribution..........297
Manuscript census as data source
for Indian studies...............275
Melungean.....................299
Menominee.....................139
Migrations........199, 204, 215, 229,
...............243-244, 261-263, 306
Mississauga,
migrations............199-204
reliance on fishing..........203
traditional lands............199
villages....................199
Mohave.......................137
Montana Indian
Reservations, 1985........129 (map)
landownership........132 (map)
white ownership and
leasing.................133-135
Natchez Indians, early
distribution..................18
Nation-State Model of Tribal
Territory...................48 (map)
Natural Resources Act of 1930...111
Navajo Indians...........23, 135-136
adoption of culture traits
from other cultures........244
cultural background....244-245
hogans. *See* Hogans.
Northwest Coast Indians.........24
wood-working skills.......24-25
Ojibway Indians,
band type society............51
war with Iroquois, 1912......195
See Also Pre-reservation
Indian lands
Oneidas....................141-142
territory occupied by
Iroquois................191-193
Osage reservation.................27
Ottawa Indians,
aversion to west in
removal....................220
Paiute.........................136
Papago.........................137
Peigan Indians,
land claims................114-119
Pima...........................135

Plains Indians, territorial sharing of
lands.........................67-74
fur trade and social
networks..................76-77
historical background.....20-21
intermarriage and interfamilial
relations................1, 64-67
kinship linkages..........78-80
kinship relations in settling
land claims..............82-83
territorial sharing of
lands.....................67-74
Population,
American Indian, Eskimo and
Aleut, 1980, 8 (map) 9 (graph)
American Indians, distribution
1980 and 1970, 7 (table)
American Indians, Eastern
States, Colonial times.........5
North American total,
Colonial times................5
Potawatomi.................139-140
aversion to west in
removal....................220
history of movement.......214
removal and malaria.......222
removal from Chicago
area......................214
Treaty of 1832..............219
Poverty, among American
Indians................265-266
Poverty Index............266 (table)
Pre-Columbian Indians,
trade relations.............243
Pre-reservation Indian lands,
south-central Canda and
midwestern U.S.............48
Pueblo culture and tribes.........21
Public Works and Economic
Development Act of 1965..........11
Reorganization Act of 1934
See Indian Reorganization
Act of 1934.
Reservation Indians, total
population...................7
Reservation lands, quality and
use of lands.............144-146
Reservations,
Arizona, compared to Wisconsin
and Montana...........145-146
Blackfoot..................128

Cheyenne River. 132
Crow. 128
Flathead. 128
Fort Belknap. 128
Fort Peck. 192
land tenure. 127
law enforcement. 152-153
Minnesota, Red
Lake. 149, 154-157
South Dakota, Rosebud . . . .
. . . . 149, 160-164
spatial fragmentation of,
. . . . 149, 168-169
Robeson County, North
Carolina. . . . . 298 (map)
Birth, death, and population
rates, 1985. . . . . 307 (table)
income, family household by
race 1979. . . . . 307 (table)
Indians and United States
Census. . . . . 303 (table)
population by race and age
1980. . . . . 304 (table)
poverty status 1979. . . 307 (table)
Rosebud Reservation, diminishment
of. . . . . 164 (map)
Self-Determination Act of 1975. . . 178
Seminole,
economic conditions. 10
present conditions. 10
Seneca territory. 191-193
occupied by Iroquois. . . . 191-193
Shawnee, removal from
Ohio. 214, 219
Sioux,
Fort Totten Reservation,
present conditions. 10
Nation, breakup. . . . . . . 161 (map)
Reservation. 21
Rosebud Reservation,
history of
development. 160-162
law enforcement
problems. 162-163
service delivery
problems. 162-164
Sisseton Reservation,
cessations. . . . . 165 (map)
history of
development. 164-166

law enforcement
problems. 167-168
service delivery
problems. 166-168
Socio-political structures of
pre-reservation Indian
groups. 50-53
Southern Alberta,
Indian Reserves. . . . . . . 109 (map)
Stoney Land. . . . . 115 (map)
Peigan Reserve, disputed
areas. . . . . 118 (map)
Spanish view, of Indians'
inferiority. 36-37
Stoney Indians. 107-108
Kootenay band, economic
impact of land claims, 111
land use controversy,
110-112
traditional land use,
. . . . 110
land claims. 114
Wesley Band, controversy in
establishment of
reserves. 110-113
Stoney Land. 115
Termination Act of 1953. 176
Territorial sharing of lands,
Great Lakes Indians. 58-67
Plains Indians. 67-74
Trade relations, among
pre-Columbian Indians. 243
Trail of Tears. 216
Treaty of Hopewell (1768). 173
Treaty of 1832. 219
Treaty of 1836. 219
Treaty of Paris. 228
Treaty Seven, provisions for
reserves. 113-119
Tribal territory,
nation-state model. 48
overlapping range,
northern Great Plains. 68
Tribal trust lands,
definition of. 6
governing policy. 259
Tribe, definition of. 49-50
Urban American Indians,
concentrations. 262
educational characteristics,
. . . . 266-268

income characteristics,
.... 263-268
migration from reservations,
.... 261-263
satisfaction with urban
life..................... 269-270
socio-economic status,
.... 270-272
Wheeler-Howard Act of 1934. *See*
Indian Reorganization Act of 1934.

Wisconsin Indians..................
   Census of 1824.............. 62
   reservations............... 140
     land owership........... 143
Women, effects on migration,
   .... 223 (illustration)
Wyandot, stress in removal...... 221
Yuncan......................... 135